Bertrand's Brother

Bertrand's Brother

The Marriages, Morals and Misdemeanours
of Frank, 2nd Earl Russell

Ruth Derham

AMBERLEY

To Ian, who understands.

First published 2021

Amberley Publishing
The Hill, Stroud
Gloucestershire, GL5 4EP

www.amberley-books.com

British Library Cataloguing in Publication Data.
A catalogue record for this book is available from the British Library.

ISBN 978 1 3981 0283 5 (hardback)
ISBN 978 1 3981 0284 2 (ebook)

Typeset in 10pt on 12pt Sabon.
Typesetting by SJmagic Design Services, India.
Printed in the UK.

Contents

Preface

Thursday, July 18, 1901

SOCIETY SCANDAL

TRIAL OF EARL RUSSELL

Magnificent Mediaeval Pageant in
The House of Lords

Nine-thirty in the morning and already the sun beat down on early arrivals congregating outside the Victoria Tower: a small group of pressmen and several well-dressed ladies, all eager to enter the House. Anticipation had been rising alongside the barometer ever since Earl Russell's arrest some four weeks previously and his subsequent appearance before the Bow Street magistrate. The papers (wrongly assuming his lordship had some say in the matter) had begun by speculating as to whether he would exercise the privilege of rank and demand a trial by his peers, before hastily turning their attention to the whys and wherefores, to reminiscences of the last time the Lords exercised their judicial powers in this manner with the trial of Lord Cardigan some sixty years previously, and, of course, to the identity of the mysterious lady whose attraction Lord Russell had found himself apparently powerless to resist.

Forgotten, for a short while, were the dissenters who deplored such flamboyant, medieval pageantry at the dawn of the modern age, as presently the doors opened and 'ticket holders only' were ushered into the Royal Gallery, the largest of all the stately chambers in the new Palace of Westminster. The magnificent gilt-panelled chamber had been designed to reflect Britain's military might. Light streamed through its shield-emblazoned stained-glass windows, drawing an awe-inspired eye up towards an elaborate ceiling – Maclise's vast depictions of *The Death of Nelson at Trafalgar* and *The Meeting of Wellington and Blücher at Waterloo* adding a sombre tone to the opulent décor. Ordinarily, the voluminous chamber stood empty awaiting the reigning monarch's procession towards the state opening of Parliament, save for the sentinel warrior kings and queens of old on plinths around its walls whose protection of our shores had earned them their exalted positions. But this day being decidedly extraordinary, the statues of those most gilded of past monarchs looked down upon a scene utterly transformed by the labours of the gentlemen of the Office of Works.

At the north end, a richly carpeted crimson-coloured dais had been erected and a large golden throne set upon it, complete with crimson canopy and framed by the arched door leading to the Prince's Chamber. Its purpose? To support the fiction that all state trials take place before the king himself. In front of it was the large oak seat of the true judge – Lord Halsbury, the Lord Chancellor, appointed lord high steward for the occasion in the king's absence – who, from this vantage point, would soon look down on a woolsack, also of crimson cloth and similar to that in the Lords Chamber itself, where would sit the ten judges of the law courts, summoned to advise him. Beyond the woolsack, tables for the various officials and clerks filled the space between judges and counsel, whose benches formed two lines in front of a single plain oak chair positioned in opposition to the throne, waiting for the accused. Along either side of the gallery rose four tiers of crimson-covered seats reserved for 200 peers. On either side of the throne, as the clock ticked round towards the hour, eighty other such seats began to fill with the peers' eldest sons and eighty more with peeresses, who, in their finery, added a touch of glamour to the occasion, as might be found at an exclusive society function. Such splendour, quite worthy of the coronation of king and emperor, was, perhaps for the last time, to be employed to settle the marital affairs of a wayward peer of the realm.

Over the course of the next half-hour, at the south end of the chamber and separated from the court by a bar spanning its full width, the area allocated to MPs and other dignitaries also filled. Twenty or so pressmen occupied their time scribbling down the names of the most noteworthy attendants. They registered the Speaker, the American Ambassador and his wife, the Duke of Teck and Lord Grey, who, like Lord Peel, had come in mufti, declining to take his place as judge of his fellow peer. Between the MPs and seats opposite, allocated simply to 'strangers', the witnesses sat pensively waiting: Revd Henry Compton Dickins, who ten years previously had officiated at the marriage of Earl Russell to Miss Mabel Edith Scott; William Brown, Assistant King's Proctor, whose task it had been to enquire into the legality of his current marriage; and Benjamin Franklin Curler, attorney-at-law, judge of the Second Judicial District Court of Nevada and star witness, delivered across land and sea at great expense by the prosecution.

Finally, at 10.45, a rustling of robes at the south entrance announced the arrival of the Attorney General, the Solicitor General and supporting counsel for the prosecution. They were followed by Messrs Robson, Avory and Matthews for the defence. A sombre silence fell as they passed through the bar and took up their seats. Then, from behind the throne, the peers were marshalled into the Royal Gallery by Norroy King-of-Arms from the main chamber, where, prayers having been said and the roll called, the Lord Chancellor had instructed their lordships to do their duty.

Such a grand procession it was, as 200 peers of the realm, resplendent in their parliamentary robes of scarlet, slashed with bands of white ermine and gold lace, and all wearing their three-cornered black hats, slowly made their way two-by-two into the hall, stepping out from behind the throne as from a magisterial arc of a former age. Before them came the black-gowned grey-wigged judges to the woolsack, then the scarlet-robed barons with their two white bands as befitted their rank, to fill the seats to the left of the throne, followed by the bishops of Winchester and Ripon. Then came the peers of higher degree in ever-increasing bands of ermine to take up their seats on the right: viscounts, earls, marquesses and dukes, followed by the Lord Privy Seal, the Archbishop of York (in the absence of the Archbishop of Canterbury), and the House officials: the Sergeant-at-Arms, the Purse Bearer, Garter King-of-Arms and the Gentleman Usher of the Black Rod, carrying, as tradition demanded, the king's white staff. Last of all, Lord Halsbury, to lead the proceedings.

Halsbury made three reverences towards the throne, then turned to face the court. With all due pomp and ceremony, as if performing a well-rehearsed play, the officials of Crown and Parliament stepped forward in turn. The Clerk of the Crown in Chancery, head of the Crown Office, approached the dais, made three reverences, and presented Halsbury with the king's commission, received it back again, made three more reverences and returned to his seat.

'Oyez, oyez, oyez!' called the Sergeant-at-Arms. 'Our Sovereign Lord the King strictly charges and commands all manner of persons to keep silence upon pain of imprisonment.'

Halsbury then asked that all peers stand and uncover while the commission was read by the clerk; the Sergeant-at-Arms closed the reading with the requisite, 'God save the King!' This being their cue, Norroy and Black Rod advanced, made their reverences, and handed the white staff – the symbol of the lord high steward's authority – to Halsbury, who, having publicly received it, promptly handed it back to Black Rod for the duration. The writ of *certiorari* giving the House jurisdiction over the case was then read, followed by the Central Criminal Court's return, before the clerk was invited to read the indictment: that the Right Honourable John Francis Stanley, Earl Russell, having been married to Mabel Edith Scott on 6 February 1890, and she still living, had, on 15 April 1900 at the Riverside Hotel at Reno in the County of Washoe in the State of Nevada in the United States of America, feloniously and unlawfully married and taken to wife one Mollie Cooke, otherwise known as Mollie Somerville.

It was hardly surprising that some who knew and recognised Mrs Somerville at this pronouncement risked a surreptitious glance towards the proud figure sitting serenely just beyond the bar, unostentatiously dressed in grey muslin with large white hat. It was even less so that many, on hearing the proclamation that the prisoner be brought forward and a second 'Oyez, oyez, oyez!' boom forth, chanced a more determined glance in his direction. Earl Russell – Frank to his friends – emerged through the Norman Porch. In sharp contrast to the medieval garb of his peers, he cut a fine figure in his thoroughly modern light-grey frock coat, his characteristic red neck-tie an expression of his political leaning more than a bent towards high fashion. A tall and imposing figure, of genial expression yet with hard, steel-blue eyes partially obscured behind small, equally hard steel-rimmed spectacles, he appeared, both literally and metaphorically, the coolest man in the room as he walked determinedly and reverentially towards the bar.

'John Francis Stanley, Earl Russell,' continued the Sergeant-at-Arms, 'come forth and save you and your bail, or else you forfeit your recognizance.'

Pausing at the bar to make his own reverences, Frank stood with head bent until Halsbury spoke his name: 'Lord Russell, you are indicted for the crime of bigamy, committed at the time and place and under the circumstances disclosed in the indictment which has been read.'

For good measure, the Clerk of Parliaments stepped forward and read the indictment again. As the solemn voice of the clerk droned on, who among those present could guess what went on behind the calm exterior of the solitary figure at the bar? Perhaps Frank was wondering how, as the son of a viscount and grandson of a former prime minister, with all the advantages of his upbringing and a Winchester and Oxford education behind him, he could have come to this. Perhaps, though appearing calm, he was in fact railing against the fates that saw him born into one of the most illustrious of aristocratic families, with all the state and press attention that afforded. Or perhaps he wryly considered his position compared with that of his forebear, Lord William Russell, third son of the Duke of Bedford, tried and hanged for his part in the attempted assassination of Charles II two centuries previously.

As he looked around the chamber, picking out familiar faces, perhaps Frank's eyes fell on Nelson or Wellington, forever captured in the pivotal moments of their respective lives, just as *he* no doubt soon would be in the illustrated London papers, and as heroically in his own way. Not a bigamist in any disreputable sense, but a moral man in his thirty-fifth year, fighting single-handedly the injustices of the law; a misunderstood victim of the age in which he lived. Perhaps he reflected on his misfortune at having been caught by the duplicitous Mabel Edith, or, through the corner of his eye, considered Mollie – a vastly superior specimen of womankind, class notwithstanding – for whom he had risked a term of imprisonment that could span mere days or long years, depending on the verdict of the rapidly overheating, fusty old relics of the Victorian age seated before him. Or perhaps, sure of himself and not easily prone to disquiet, none of these thoughts entered his head and with a cool rationality he transcended both the irony and injustice of his situation as the voice of the clerk cut through the silent anticipation of the court, and he cleared his throat in readiness to reply.

'How say you, my Lord, are you guilty of the felony with which you are charged, or not guilty?'

List of Illustrations

Russell Family Tree

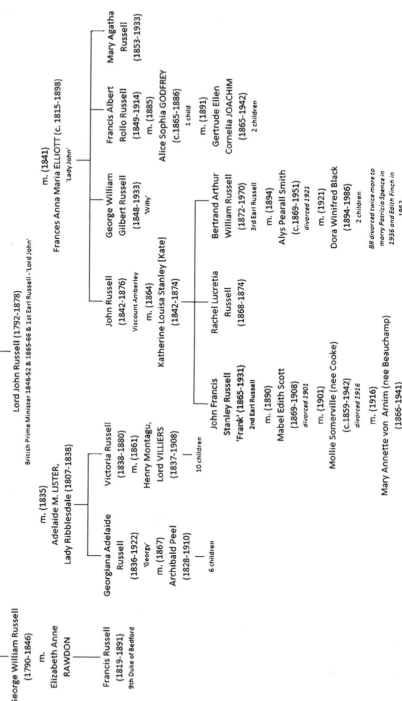

John Russell (1766-1839)
6th Duke of Bedford
m.
Georgiana Elizabeth BYNG (c.1768-1801)

Lord John Russell (1792-1878)
British Prime Minister 1846-52 & 1865-66 & 1st Earl Russell - 'Lord John'

m. (1841)
Frances Anna Maria ELLIOTT (c. 1815-1898)
'Lady John'

Francis Russell (1788-1861)
7th Duke of Bedford
m.
Anna Maria STANHOPE

George William Russell (1790-1846)
m.
Elizabeth Anne RAWDON

Adelaide M. LISTER, Lady Ribblesdale (1807-1838)
m. (1835)

William Russell (1809-1872)
8th Duke of Bedford

Francis Russell (1819-1891)
9th Duke of Bedford

Georgiana Adelaide Russell (1836-1922)
'Georgy'
m. (1867)
Archibald Peel (1828-1910)
|
6 children

Victoria Russell (1838-1880)
m. (1861)
Henry Montagu, Lord VILLIERS (1837-1908)
|
10 children

John Russell (1842-1876)
Viscount Amberley
m. (1864)
Katherine Louisa Stanley [Kate] (1842-1874)

John Francis Stanley Russell 'Frank' (1865-1931)
2nd Earl Russell
m. (1890)
Mabel Edith Scott (1869-1908)
divorced 1901
m. (1901)
Mollie Somerville (nee Cooke) (c.1859-1942)
divorced 1916
m. (1916)
Mary Annette von Arnim (nee Beauchamp) (1866-1941)

Rachel Lucretia Russell (1868-1874)

Bertrand Arthur William Russell (1872-1970)
3rd Earl Russell
m. (1894)
Alys Pearall Smith (c.1869-1951)
divorced 1921
m. (1921)
Dora Winifred Black (1894-1986)
2 children
BR divorced twice more to marry Patricia Spence in 1936 and Edith Finch in 1952

George William Gilbert Russell (1848-1933)
'Willy'

Francis Albert Rollo Russell (1849-1914)
m. (1885)
Alice Sophia GODFREY (c.1865-1886)
1 child
m. (1891)
Gertrude Ellen Cornelia JOACHIM (1865-1942)
2 children

Mary Agatha Russell (1853-1933)

Stanley of Alderley Family Tree

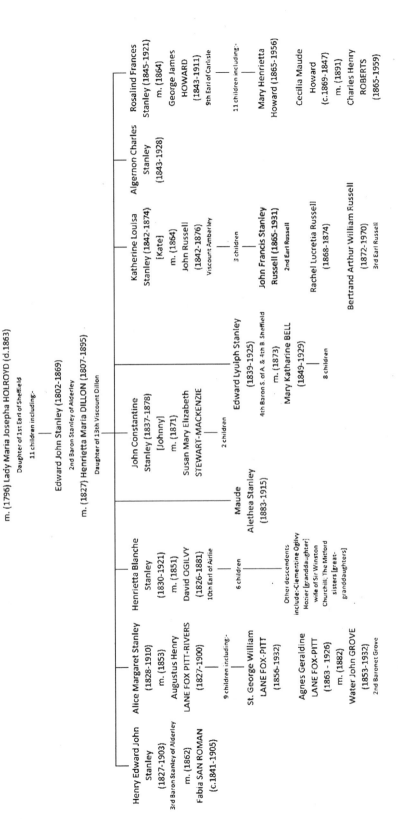

John Thomas Stanley (1766-1850)
1st Baron Stanley of Alderley
m. (1796) Lady Maria Josepha HOLROYD (d.1863)
Daughter of 1st Earl of Sheffield
11 children including:-

Edward John Stanley (1802-1869)
2nd Baron Stanley of Alderley
m. (1827) Henrietta Maria DILLON (1807-1895)
Daughter of 13th Viscount Dillon

Henry Edward John Stanley (1827-1903)
3rd Baron Stanley of Alderley
m. (1862)
Fabia SAN ROMAN (c.1841-1905)

Alice Margaret Stanley (1828-1910)
m. (1853)
Augustus Henry LANE FOX PITT-RIVERS (1827-1900)

9 children including:-

St. George William LANE FOX-PITT (1856-1932)

Agnes Geraldine LANE FOX-PITT (1863 - 1926)
m. (1882)
Water John GROVE (1853-1932)
2nd Baronet Grove

Henrietta Blanche Stanley (1830-1921)
m. (1851)
David OGILVY (1826-1881)
10th Earl of Airlie

6 children

Other descendents include:-Clementine Ogilvy Hozier [granddaughter] wife of Sir Winston Churchill; The Mitford sisters [great-granddaughters]

John Constantine Stanley (1837-1878)
[Johnny]
m. (1871)
Susan Mary Elizabeth STEWART-MACKENZIE

2 children

Maude Alethea Stanley (1883-1915)

Edward Lyulph Stanley (1839-1925)
4th Baron S. of A. & 4th B. Sheffield
m. (1873)
Mary Katharine BELL (1849-1929)

8 children

Katherine Louisa Stanley (1842-1874)
[Kate]
m. (1864)
John Russell (1842-1876)
Viscount Amberley

3 children

John Francis Stanley Russell (1865-1931)
2nd Earl Russell

Rachel Lucretia Russell (1868-1874)

Bertrand Arthur William Russell (1872-1970)
3rd Earl Russell

Algernon Charles Stanley (1843-1928)

Rosalind Frances Stanley (1845-1921)
m. (1864)
George James HOWARD (1843-1911)
9th Earl of Carlisle

11 children including:-

Mary Henrietta Howard (1865-1956)

Cecilia Maude Howard (c.1869-1847)
m. (1891)
Charles Henry ROBERTS (1865-1959)

Introduction

Nearly a thousand years ago, a Chinese writer observed, 'People who do not get into scrapes are a great deal less interesting than those who do.'[1] It's an observation that resonates with me and probably explains why I chose to write about Frank instead of one of the many more illustrious Russells. There have been Russells influential at Court – John Russell, 1st Earl of Bedford, for example, who was ennobled by Henry VII and became equerry to and personal friend of Henry VIII – and Russells who made their mark architecturally – the 4th Earl, Francis, who undertook London's first urban planning scheme in Covent Garden with Inigo Jones, and the 5th Duke, another Francis, who developed vast swathes of Bloomsbury and St Giles to create streets and squares still familiar today. In Marchmont Street just off Russell Square, one can enjoy a pint in the Lord John Russell pub, named for Frank's grandfather, former British prime minister and architect of the 1832 Great Reform Act. In every reputable bookshop are multiple texts by or about Frank's younger brother, the celebrated philosopher and mathematician Bertrand Russell. Yet, to me, Frank, who by his own admission was not a worldly success, is more interesting – largely because of his scrapes.

In part, it's the nature of those scrapes. By the time Frank found himself midway through his life being tried for bigamy in the House of Lords, he had already been involved in a ten-year *cause célèbre* instigated by his first wife; her shocking accusations of homosexual behaviour had been reported worldwide alongside the infamous misdemeanours of Oscar Wilde. Frank's reaction to those scrapes also intrigued me. His seriousness over his imbroglios adds to them an unintentional element of humour, while the courage it took to face down his accusers is sobering. Male same-sex relationships were reviled by the Victorians and sodomy was then punishable by up to ten years' penal servitude. Popular reaction to Frank's scrapes adds still another level of interest, revealing much about society's organisation, values, preoccupations and hypocrisy.

As a whole, for its high drama, Frank's story could have jumped from the pages of a late Victorian novel, its object lesson the cultural tensions and moral prejudices of the age.

Yet Frank was not your average rogue. Every one of his actions he viewed as morally defensible. Some of this had to do with his upbringing, which was highly unorthodox. In a society far more rigidly hierarchical than today's, the advantages of being born into nobility came at a price. They were dependent on a code of conduct that demonstrated good character. A good character had two principal components: 'the habit of self-command which defined the rule of the will over one's own desires, and being known for such a faculty amongst one's friends and associates'.[2] At its foundation was a moral code laid down by the Established Church, accepted by the majority of society unquestioningly and upheld by, among other things, the self-imposed censorship of the press. Yet within this narrow framework, there were a minority of more radically minded families who, away from the glare of society, encouraged free-thinking with regard to religion, morality and social politics. Frank was born into such a family – at least on his mother's side – where around the dinner table the unquestionable was discussed openly and without censure. His story, along with that of brother Bertrand, begs the question, what was it like to be brought up with this as your norm – at odds with convention, accepting narrow restrictions uncomfortably and sometimes not at all? And what would the consequences be if, like Frank, your temperament was rebellious and your values self-determined and uncompromising? Conflict, it would seem, and scrapes.

Doubtless, Frank would think me discourteous in introducing him to a new audience as 'Bertrand's brother'. I am conscious, too, of its irony given that a hundred years ago Frank's standing was such that Bertrand was introduced in the popular press as his. But Frank is so little known today, and given so little credit for the manner in which he championed radical policies and turned negative divorce court experiences into positive action for reform, that it seemed necessary to contextualise him for a modern reader. The brothers' relationship was complicated by their differing personalities and by circumstance, with Frank often dismissed as Bertrand's 'unfortunate' brother. It has been his fate either to be overlooked – quite a feat for such a larger-than-life character – or to be portrayed very one-dimensionally. My own introduction to him was in his cruel lampooning by his third wife, Elizabeth von Arnim, in her horribly revealing semi-autobiographical novel *Vera* (1921), written in the wake of their disastrous marriage. Negative perceptions were further bolstered by Elizabeth's subsequent comic autobiography *All the Dogs of My Life* (1936) and her daughter's posthumous *Elizabeth of the German Garden* (1958). It seemed to me a bitter irony that Frank's reputation, so vociferously defended against the onslaught of his first wife, should rest for posterity on the wit of his third, who came to regard him as 'evil'.

One might have imagined Frank would set the record straight in his 1923 autobiography *My Life and Adventures*. Completely candid in some respects, it details events others might have sought to downplay for reputation's sake, demonstrating the extent to which Frank played by his own rules. A friend from his university days said it 'reveals his character admirably, because unconsciously: – self-centred, overbearing, impulsive, well meaning, headstrong'.[3] But *Life* (to give it an accessible shorthand) also conceals much. Though it was written in the wake of *Vera*, in its pages Elizabeth is completely ignored. It is also oddly one-sided. Critics have described it as 'self-serving', particularly in reference to Frank's first marriage and early misdemeanours.[4] Accordingly, the only person to attempt to give a full and honest account of Frank (himself included) was his good friend, the cosmopolitan philosopher George Santayana, who dedicated two chapters of his memoirs, *Persons and Places* (1944–53), to describing Frank's character, their adventures together and his own understanding of the events Frank sought so desperately to rewrite or conceal.

Santayana wrote as he lived – in detached observation. As such, *Persons* is a valuable source, particularly since the 1986 critical edition put back some content curtailed by its original publisher's fear of litigation. Santayana's usual objectivity, however, was sometimes skewed by his feelings for Frank, which were strong and latterly complicated by disagreement. Additionally, though Santayana was in Frank's confidence, it was impossible for him, from his residence at Harvard University, to have been cognisant of all events as they unravelled so many hundreds of miles away. Much of what he described was from letters Frank had written him and memories of his annual summer excursions to England, which he himself described as more accurate in essence than fact.[5]

The purpose of this first full biography of Frank, then, is to revisit his story objectively, using a wide range of archival material, to reveal the extent to which his self-determined morals, as much as his misdemeanours and marriages, informed and shaped his life; to fill in gaps, correct errors (intentional or otherwise) and offer a sympathetic account of the man as he was known publicly and privately. Frank was fascinating, though not always likeable. He was a radical in an era of social and political change; an aristocrat at a time when their influence was waning but their misdemeanours still made good press. He provoked strong reactions: he was hated and loved, respected and ridiculed. In a story populated by better-known personalities – George Bernard Shaw, H. G. Wells, Oscar Wilde – he holds his own. Everything being a matter of perspective, this is mine.

1

Origins and Inheritance

At 6.45 a.m. on Saturday 12 August 1865 – nearly seven years before Bertrand and exactly nine months and four days after his parents' marriage – Frank Russell burst into the world. Throughout his life, he liked to boast of the timing, taking some perverse thrill perhaps in being 'just legal'. He did *not* boast that it placed his conception at Woburn Abbey, the palatial family seat of the Bedford Russells, loaned to his father – Johnny, Viscount Amberley[1] – by the 8th duke for his honeymoon. Frank cared not a jot that his father's marriage to Katherine Louisa Stanley (Kate), fourth daughter of Edward, 2nd Baron Stanley of Alderley, had united two ancient and powerful families, nor that he was the product of it – though the fact would always show. Bertrand's future wife, Dora, would say that one only had to see the two brothers together 'to recognise in both the characteristics, good and bad, of a long line of ancestors deemed superior to ordinary men, born to attain distinction and rule'.[2] Appropriate, then, that Frank's birthplace should be his mother's family home, the magnificent Alderley Park in Cheshire, where his arrival had been eagerly anticipated, though his eventual coming was quite a shock. For in his birthing, as in everything else throughout his life, Frank took the law into his own hands, refusing to wait for the doctor's arrival and barely giving his mother time to draw breath. The whole labour lasted little more than an hour and left Kate pained and fatigued but proud to have produced a son and heir, healthy and strong. He had 'such fists and long feet and so full beautiful hair', according to Kate's sister Maude, 'but what chiefly strikes one is his manly appearance'.[3] He was 'so thoroughly a boy' and (it would appear) had such a set of lungs – and used them to make his sudden presence felt. With the drawing of his first breath, Frank's cries reverberated around the corridors of Alderley and continued to do so, night and day, for nigh on six weeks.

Why did the infant holler so? Did the weight of family expectation hang so heavily over his crib? Frank was, after all, the eldest son of an eldest son. To him would fall the responsibility of upholding the family name and, by the rule of primogeniture, the family's fortunes. Historian David Cannadine described 'family' as 'the most fundamental unit of upper-class existence'. It included 'the sense of interconnection between the generations dead, living and yet unborn'.[4] As such, it was expected to be the eldest son's *raison d'être*. His name quite literally became his identity through the custom of grandees signing themselves by title alone: their superiority, power, duty and responsibilities all encompassed in the signing of that one word. *Russell*. It was an inheritance Frank would always lament. Did, then, the infant sense his grandfather's hope that his arrival might have signalled the coming of another British prime minister? It is tempting to think so, but actually it was nothing so perspicacious. Frank was simply hungry and demonstrating that, far from being a true Russell, he was in fact a 'regular Stanley'.[5]

He howled with the temper of a Stanley. He refused his mother's breast with the rebelliousness of a Stanley. He retained his obstinacy through a long line of wet-nurses with the tenacity of a Stanley and in so doing demonstrated another Stanley quality: pernicketiness. One by one the mothers of the surrounding villages failed the famous Stanley scrutiny. It was not until the arrival of the sixth, the recently married Lizzy Williams, that Kate was satisfied and Frank satiated. In a few short weeks Frank had revealed the *modus operandi* he would employ for the rest of his rebellious life.

What a predicament then (for the Russells *and* for Frank) that it should fall to him to uphold the Russell name. True, both the Stanleys and Russells were overtly political, staunchly Whig families, but there the similarities ended. In appearance, temperament and outlook they differed and both had misgivings about the other. Frank voiced some in describing his inherited Russell qualities:

> ... bad eyes, some sense of art, a certain capacity for speech and writing coupled with a certain inherent ineffectiveness and hesitation which prevent my being good at games, taking any interest in competition, and blustering my way through life with the superb assurance and self-satisfaction of the true Stanley.[6]

Bertrand, by contrast, was considered predominantly a Russell, though he was a little more circumspect in his family alignment. Where Frank 'loved the Stanleys and hated the Russells' and Bertrand initially 'loved the Russells and feared the Stanleys', he later concluded:

> I owe to the Russells shyness, sensitiveness, and metaphysics; to the Stanleys vigour, good health, and good spirits. On the whole, the latter seems a better inheritance...[7]

Shyness was the predominant Russell characteristic and in Frank's grandfather, Lord John, was mixed with a certain remoteness. Throughout his career, he was criticised for appearing aloof and failing to curry favour with the increasingly influential press. Though a committed reformer (it was said that by the time he left office in 1852 the only institution left unchanged was the army), he could hardly be called radical. He did not have the character of Palmerston or Gladstone to pull off grand political gestures. Today, he is better remembered as an architect of the 1832 Great Reform Act than for anything achieved during his premiership and was ascribed the nickname 'Finality Jack' for his resistance to further electoral reform. He was supported ('unfortunately', Bertrand suggested) throughout his life and the majority of his political career by second wife Fanny – Lady Frances Anna Maria Elliot, daughter of the 2nd Earl of Minto, subsequently known to her contemporaries as 'Lady John'. Tragedy had made their family rather a mishmash: Lord John's first wife, Lady Adelaide Lister, had died in childbirth with the second of their two daughters less than four years into their marriage. Fanny was considered an ideal replacement. Reared in rural Scotland, staunchly religious and with a strong sense of obligation and responsibility, she had a true Whiggish belief in the value and necessity of public service. She was twenty-three years younger than Lord John but had, in 1841, aged only twenty-five, stoically and wholeheartedly taken on not only the role of politician's wife to a man fast becoming an elder statesman of his country but also his two children by Lady Adelaide *and* the four from Lady Adelaide's former marriage to the deceased Lord Ribblesdale.[8] Over the next twelve years, Fanny would add another four of her own: Frank's father, Johnny; two other sons, Willy and Rollo; and a daughter named Agatha.

Lady John's letters suggest that while the role of mother and stepmother came easily, the role of politician's wife did not:

> ... how completely worn out both mind and body often feel at the end of a common day ... London, hateful London, alone is at fault. Anywhere else my duties and occupations would be light...

She despised the political scene, and felt its criticisms alike: 'I am reckoned cold, dull, and unworthy of such a husband; and it is quite right, for I never appear anything else.' The conflict between her 'passion for quiet, leisure, and the country' over the 'countless miseries of office' became critical in 1845 when Queen Victoria summoned Lord John and asked him to form a government. On 8 December, she wrote to her husband that, though 'the words go to my very heart of hearts', she thought he should accept and become 'head of the most moral and religious government the country has ever had'. On the same day, to her sister, she wrote, 'It is all loss, all sacrifice – every favourite plan upset – London, London, London, and London in its worse shape.'[9] Wittingly or otherwise, her reaction influenced Lord John and he turned the offer down.

In fairness to Lady John, she had been unwell the previous year and continued to have poor health, suffering several miscarriages throughout the 1840s. But this single event is illustrative of the restraining influence she was deemed to have. She would be blamed for Lord John's dithering and vacillations throughout his career. He eventually became PM in 1846, and in 1847 Victoria gave them Pembroke Lodge in Richmond Park as their London residence to enable them to live a quieter 'country' life in the city. Here, Lady John also succeeded in creating an atmosphere Frank would shudder to recall:

> At every point it recoiled as the young ladies with the vapours who swooned in Victorian novels used to do from the touch of real life and anything so vulgar as facts. Religion might occasionally be spoken of with bated breath and in a hushed curate sort of voice, but sex, birth, swearing, trade, money, passion, were subjects I never heard mentioned.[10]

Pembroke Lodge was known to the family as 'PL', and the shorthand was extended by Frank and Bertrand to signify the house, its residents and atmosphere, which was so vastly different from that of the Stanleys' London residence, 40 Dover Street. The Stanleys were a much more dynamic, outspoken, free-thinking and lively family. Nancy Mitford – herself a Stanley – described them collectively thus:

> Their common characteristics were a sort of downright rudeness, a passion for quarrelling, great indifference to public opinion, an unrivalled skill in finding and pointing out the weak points in other people's armour, thick legs and eyebrows, lively minds and a great literary sense.[11]

It was this passion for quarrelling that Bertrand feared, never knowing when during their disputatious Sunday luncheons the whole pack would turn on him. Frank relished them, though even he would find himself 'rather bewildered and struck dumb' after the 'solemn mausoleum-like quality of P.L.'[12]

Lord Stanley was a friend and staunch supporter of Lord John's nemesis, Palmerston, and served in all his cabinets. His Westminster nickname was 'Sir Benjamin Backbite' for his capacity to be malicious. At the time of Frank's birth, Stanley was Postmaster General. A domineering and independent man, he was beloved by his family and few close friends, but was otherwise unpopular and, despite his wife's protestations regarding his alleged romantic interest in Palmerston's stepdaughter Lady Jocelyn, never gave up his habit of touring unencumbered by the family for two months every summer, having spent much of the year in London while his wife presided over the family seat in Cheshire or retreated to her favourite holiday destination of Carlsbad. This is not to suggest that Lady Stanley did not exert any influence over her husband; indeed, quite the opposite. When in December 1851 Lord John removed Palmerston from the Foreign Office, replacing him with Lord Granville, thereby making Stanley's position as undersecretary in the office untenable, it was Lady Stanley who directed his next course of action:

> It is evident Lord John never liked you & the offer he made you [of going to America to settle boundary differences] is tantamount to an affront …

I thought for a moment you were going to shew some spirit, & now you are drooping again & will just stay under Granville long enough for everybody to insult you ... Do come away, it is much more dignified...[13]

Stanley did as his wife advised. Like Lady John, she often directed her husband's political career. Lord Palmerston once introduced her to a foreign visitor as 'our Chief of General Staff'.[14]

Henrietta Maria, Lady Stanley of Alderley was by birth a Dillon. Of Irish descent, she lived most of her young life abroad. Until her husband's death in 1869, she chiefly supported him and raised their nine children. Afterwards, she channelled her determined energy into the advancement of women's education. She was a founder of Girton College, Cambridge, and Queen's College, London, and was a strong and compelling force in her family and beyond. Her children's interests were wide and varied. Collectively, they combined an aristocratic instinct with what another Stanley descendant, Lady Agnes Grove, described as 'the critical faculty developed by intelligence and culture'.[15] Maude, for example, followed her mother's interest in women's advancement by establishing a working girls' club in London, while Lyulph invested his energy into politics and the London School Board. Kate became outspoken on women's rights and went on to support her husband in the campaign for birth control. Rosalind became a protagonist for the temperance movement. But their main divergence as a family was religious, and their various positions were said to be taken simply to annoy each other. The eldest son, Henry, became a Mohammedan, while Algernon converted to Catholicism and rose through the Church to become Domestic Prelate to Pope Leo XIII. For such a family, who also boasted an agnostic and Anglicans (both high and low), it can be imagined that their dinner table debates were quite something. It may well have also been a factor in the Russells' reluctance that their son should too hastily attach himself to Kate Stanley, for such was the case.

Johnny Russell – Viscount Amberley – was a serious young man, shy like his father but also morose with morbid sensibilities. Most likely, he was introduced to Kate by his half-sister Georgy, who was already intimate with the Stanleys. On 25 June 1863, he danced with Kate at Lady Westminster's Ball and thereafter they met and conversed often. By the time he found himself mid-October carving his name into a tree on her family's estate, it is clear that she was similarly well on the way to carving her own name deeply into his heart. Kate was high-spirited and had professed herself bored by the usual suitors who wooed her at balls, preferring the society of Lyulph's intellectual friends. She saw herself partnered with someone who could respect her intelligence as much as her gaiety and wit; someone who would discuss topical issues with her, guide and educate her yet allow her to form her own opinions. Amberley fitted the bill. In turn, he found her 'wonderfully intellectual'. They spoke on a wide range of subjects and, to his delight, 'somehow agreed remarkably well'. That summer they played croquet together at PL and picnicked in Epping Forest, after which Kate presented Amberley with a photograph of herself inscribed 'Kate Stanley, the unconventional'. In December, for his twenty-first birthday, she gifted him a scroll she had fashioned listing all his favourite great men (and a few of her own). It was more to his liking than his mother's gift – a 'paper of admonition' highlighting his 'faults of manner and conduct', his dogmatism and tendency to be 'occasionally morose about trifles'. To this last he conceded, but confided to his journal a longing for 'one friend to whom I could confide the plan of my life'; someone who would understand that his moroseness was often the result of 'petty interruptions caused by visits to country houses' and the inconvenience of having to conform to others' expectations. He felt his 'lonely and unsocial temperament' and his growing sense that the whole of dogmatic Christianity was built on false foundations alienated him from his family.[16] Increasingly he looked to Kate to fill the void. If only he could believe she would accept him.

The thought did not go unnoticed. In February 1864, Lady John spoke to Amberley about the prudence of not getting involved. He was young and could not be trusted to judge for himself. It was too late. By early March, Amberley and Kate had confessed their mutual feelings and rumours of a secret engagement spread. The horrified Russells responded by insisting that Amberley go away for six months to test the strength of their affection, with no commitment on either side and no blame should either have a change of heart. Amberley was unhappily dispatched to Paris, from where he learned that Kate's nineteen-year-old younger sister, Rosalind, had become engaged to George Howard, future Earl of Carlisle. For six agonising months, no contact was permitted between the lovers – though both confided in Georgy (who was sworn to secrecy) and Amberley wrote several times to Lady Stanley for reassurance. Needless to say, as soon as his exile was over, he returned to Alderley and claimed his waiting bride. Within two months they were married.

The story is poignant and revealing. It demonstrates the disapproving and controlling mindset of the Russells which would ultimately be deplored by both their grandsons: by Frank, in his resenting the constant questioning 'which always implied that I had probably been doing something I shouldn't',[17] and by Bertrand in finding himself in a remarkably similar situation when in 1894 he wished to marry the much-disapproved-of Quaker Alys Pearsall Smith, and was similarly banished. It demonstrates the strength of the Amberleys' affection, which would shape Frank's early life, and offers some character similarities between Frank and his father that he only ever attributed to his 'Stanley blood'. None of this would have been quite so significant if Frank's parents had been long-lived. But their early deaths, and the title from which Frank could not escape, were destined to have dire and lasting consequences and set the scene for much that would follow.

2

A Limb of Satan

Frank's early childhood was spent at Rodborough Manor, overlooking the Stroud Valley in Gloucestershire. The property, purchased by Lord John in 1855, was situated in the parish of Amberley, from which came his lesser title. It was 'green and cheerful and varied and pretty outside, snug and respectable inside' and always intended as a country estate he could leave to his children.[1] It became the Amberleys' residence for the next five years. In her journal for March 1865, Kate recorded her gratitude for their peace and happiness there 'far from the turmoil of life'.[2] The couple had just returned from Leeds, where Amberley was fighting his first election campaign and where Kate, then pregnant with Frank, attended raucous meetings she had promised the Russells she wouldn't, having already upset them by skating in the park at Alderley while in the same 'delicate' condition. Amberley performed well, but failed to take the seat. 'We neither of us minded very much,' recalled Kate, despite her obvious thrill at the excitement of it all.[3] The following year, Amberley would win in Nottingham, and enter Parliament as a member of his father's government.

Meanwhile, Kate set about organising the family home. It was not all plain sailing. Though she relished the beauty of her new surroundings – the large estate, with woods and long walks across the surrounding common and to the nearby village of Woodchester – her early letters to Maude were full of concerns about the many difficulties of motherhood and housekeeping. First it was the servants: how much and with what should she feed them? How she should control them? And what *was* the name of the book on domestic economy that mama gave to Rosalind?[4] Maude was sworn to secrecy not to let anyone know Kate's private doubts as she struggled to find her feet as mistress of the house. The only member of staff she found wholly dependable was Lizzie Williams, the wet-nurse who had accompanied them from Alderley. After revealing to Kate that Frank's nurse would 'stuff the sponge in his little mouth' when she washed him and 'push her finger (beast!) in his dear little throat' and leave him to scream for hours, she became Kate's closest, most confidential and indispensable servant.[5]

Of less concern was the question of how to raise Frank. Kate and Amberley had discussed this at length while Kate was pregnant, and the suggestion that they would not blindly follow convention was immediately illustrated by their choice of Harriet Grote as Frank's godmother. Harriet was the wife of classical historian and radical politician George Grote and author in her own right of serval works including *Philosophical Radicals of 1832* (1866), in which she openly criticised Lord John for his limited commitment to reform. The Amberleys were also friendly with philosopher John Stuart Mill and his stepdaughter Helen Taylor, and had discussed parenting with them. Kate was impressed by Mill's assertion that he owed his success to his home education and by Helen's account of her own upbringing:

> She was allowed to read every book she wished ... She was never taught to believe anything but to judge for herself ... Her mother used to say all that should be done was to awake the moral nature & leave the intellect & mind quite free.[6]

The Amberleys embraced this approach with Frank, alongside that of philosopher, biologist and anthropologist Herbert Spencer, who had much to say on the rearing of children in accordance with the self-regulating laws of nature. They also took advice from educationalist W. F. Collier, who, in 1869, wrote to Kate that children must be treated 'with candour and sincerity, with gentleness and amiability' and talked to 'as rational beings & equals according to their capacity'.[7] Frank later described how this was put into practice:

> ... never, absolutely never, was 'do this to please your mother' or 'father orders it' offered as a sufficient motive for any action on my part ... it was always reasoned.[8]

For a mid-Victorian aristocratic family, this was modern and highly unorthodox. Almost as soon as Frank found his feet and voice, he set about demonstrating its results. Early indications were positive. At the end of 1867, the Amberleys toured the US, leaving the two-year-old Frank at PL. Lord John reported affectionately,

> [Franky] is amused & amusing, not at all spoilt & stronger than he was – he learns any word, & any name at once, he does not like to cry Viva Garibaldi, which I taught him, but he does it very well.[9]

Rather more sentimentally, Lady John wrote a poem for Frank during this stay in which she described him as 'my darling and my joy', so strongly did he remind her of the infant Amberley.[10] On their return, Kate observed with satisfaction that Frank was developing into a confident and self-assured little man:

> He comes in every morning when they are all at breakfast and when the newspapers come he goes up to Lord Russell and says 'What's the news' which his Grandpapa always tells him and he then goes back to his Granny and repeats it to her as if it was his own with emphasis.[11]

But the fine line between self-assuredness and mischievousness was soon crossed. At a tea party three months before his third birthday, a 'very wild and excited' Frank rather inappropriately relieved himself in the bushes in front of his guests. When his nurse admonished, 'Everyone is shocked, all the little children are shocked,' he rejoined, 'Even the dogs are shocked!' His proud mother noted, 'He is much more independent than most of his age and observes a great deal more.'[12] She delighted in every display of Frank's precocity, embracing Collier's belief that the only agreeable behaviour is that which is spontaneous and natural. These qualities, she understood, must not be suppressed. Only very rarely do her journals and letters suggest that, to her, Frank was in any way a handful. Much later, Bertrand would say that there always existed something of an understanding between them that Frank never achieved with anyone else.

1868 saw the arrival of the Amberleys' second child, Rachel Lucretia,[13] and Amberley's attempt for a South Devon seat in the general election – both bruising experiences in their different ways. Rachel was premature, one of twins, the other stillborn. Once again Kate suffered during childbirth, straining the ligaments between her lower back and pelvis, which pained her for the next six months. And South Devon was a dirty and vicious fight, not helped by Amberley voicing opinions that were 'perhaps rather too advanced' for a traditional Tory stronghold.[14] The South Devon Liberals had been determined to have Amberley, convinced he would return a large majority – Lord John having held the seat himself at the start of his political career – but in the midst of the campaign, Amberley made a speech at a closed meeting of the Dialectical Society which affronted medical men by daring to suggest that population growth could be controlled without celibacy or emigration through birth control. An indignant article appeared in the *Medical Times*: Amberley was asking them to become 'accomplices in unnatural crimes' by encouraging women 'to enjoy the privileges of selfish lust, and to evade the duties of matrimony'.[15] It was picked up by the wider press and Amberley was accused of encouraging the 'pure wives and mothers of England' in 'infernal practices'.[16] Misunderstandings increased when the Bishop of Liverpool declared from his pulpit that Amberley advocated infanticide! Amberley accused the Tories of muck-spreading and lost the seat. His committee turned on him, writing to the *Times* that he had failed 'as nearly all the young candidates have failed who have attempted to stand on their principles alone ... expecting to take the world by storm'.[17] Lord John's suggestion that if he was not too tired he could campaign again in a year or so fell on deaf ears. Amberley's health was seriously depleted by a liver infection. Though a year later the Newcastle by-election was briefly discussed, he would never fight another seat again.

Not unsurprisingly, 1869 was a quiet year. The Amberleys retreated to Rodborough where Amberley embarked on his monumental *The Analysis of Religious Belief* (1876), posthumously published by Lady John. The year was also marked by the death of Kate's father and the passing of the family title to older brother Henry, who took the opportunity to announce that he had been secretly married to a Spanish Catholic named Fabia San Roman for seven years.[18] It also saw the birth of a third daughter to Lizzie Williams, whose husband, Isaac, had by then also joined the family as gardener. Frank remembered their eldest two daughters – Catherine (called Kate, for her mistress) and Ellen – as childhood playmates. The whole family would have a significant role to play in events that shaped Frank's young adult life.

Then, towards the end of 1869, Lord John announced his intention of selling Rodborough, and the Amberleys began the search that would lead them to Trelleck in Monmouthshire, where they purchased a ten-bedroom property called 'Ravenscroft' in 40 acres for £5,000. By the end of July 1870 they had moved in.

Frank remembered nothing of Rodborough but, with what he later described as early evidence of his engineer's mind, was able to recall every detail of the house and grounds at Ravenscroft, where he lived from age five to ten. It was a remote property, high on the hills between Tintern and Trelleck and bordered at the back by the Duke of Beaufort's woods. At the front, a large meadow ran down to the road; beyond were fields surrounded by larch and beech plantations and a public footpath that ran from the village to Cleddon Falls. Views across the Wye Valley were poor and the landscape too tame for Kate's tastes, but the dressed-stone house, with large bay windows, imposing veranda, stone-flagged kitchen, ample stables and coach house, was ideal for improvement. Frank remembered 'helping' with the construction of a small square garden where fuchsias were planted and a circular rockery that took a year to complete.

Here the Amberleys continued their withdrawn lifestyle. Few visitors came, but among those who did was Thomas Sanderson, an old Cambridge friend of Amberley's who had likewise been a frequent visitor at Rodborough and who relished the 'depths of human sympathy' he found there.[19] Frank remembered 'Sandybobs' as a 'cheery, active, gambolling friend of my young days' very much devoted to – if not in love with – his mother.[20]

Here also, Kate continued her policy with the children. Frank and Rachel were given complete freedom to explore. Frank remembered driving Rachel about 'in a little goat carriage in which we went sailing gaily about the country roads quite unchaperoned and quite unprotected'.[21] He also remembered being encouraged to run around barefoot and ride his pony bareback, engendering in him a physical dexterity that enabled him to 'walk along the edges and ledges of roofs, and up inclined poles, like a cat'.[22] A useful skill to have when, a few years later, a tutor was employed who did not share Kate's aversion to corporal punishment and Frank found himself spending an increasing amount of time hiding on Ravenscroft's roof.

Increased freedom naturally led to increased mischievousness. The young Frank stole apples from the nearby farmer, jam from the larder and secretly sipped from his father's medicine bottle. His grandmamma, Lady Stanley, thought him 'an unwashed, ill-bred, impertinent little child dressed in rags'. He was told that he had 'a very naughty and passionate temper', but by the time he sat down to write *Life* didn't remember it. In any case, he had an excuse: 'I had some kind of brain illness as a result of which the doctor gave orders that I was not to be overworked, and not to be contradicted.'[23]

This was a most curious episode. After their removal to Ravenscroft, Kate had stepped up her tutelage of Frank, encouraging him to read whatever he chose, and began a long search for a German governess 'brought up in the Kinder Garten way'.[24] Conceived by German educationalist Friedrich Froebel, the Kindergarten system advocated children learning through play and interaction with their elders and their natural environment – its name signifying both a garden *for* children and a garden *of* children. As such, it was analogous with the teachings of Collier and Spencer. Its philosophy was based on the premise that all men were intrinsically good and capable with self-determination of overcoming any evil impulse on their own. A child so guided – never thrust back, misunderstood, or misled, never crushed nor misdirected by traditional forms of discipline which suppressed and distorted their intrinsic nature – would always turn out well. Negative qualities, such as 'self-will, defiance, laziness of body and mind, greediness, vanity, and conceit, self-assertion and masterfulness' only developed in those who had been *wrongly* directed.[25] As Kate had followed their example to the letter, she determined there must be something wrong with Frank. He was prone to outbursts of anger and excitement if not given what he wanted immediately and complained of headaches and aversion to bright light. He was duly taken to a London physician who diagnosed 'an attack of brain' from overwork. Frank, it would appear, had overstimulated himself and was ordered to have no lessons for two to three years – and, as Frank said, no contradiction.

What power this gave the six-year-old. His wilfulness increased; his behaviour worsened. After a visit to Alderley in the spring, Lady Stanley wrote,

> [I] pointed out he was to be kind to Rachel but he has been beating her again & says he does it at home but I did not follow up the inference that you approved of it.[26]

Whether Kate did or not, her policy remained unchanged. At age six, Frank still slept in her room and breakfasted with her before being sent outside for the best part of the morning with Rachel 'alone & unwatched'. They dined and spent the early evening with their parents before retiring at 7 p.m. Their only obligation was to undertake certain chores:

> They make their own beds fold up their own things at night & on coming home & I like & care for them to learn to be *useful & independent* as much as anything else – *Work* of all sorts is to be taught them as necessary & desirable...[27]

Then, in August 1872, Amberley took Frank on what became a disastrous trip north – to Rosalind and George Howard at Naworth and then on to Yarrow to visit his old friends, the Frasers.[28] From the first, Amberley seemed at a loss to know what to do with Frank, who was 'frequently troublesome'. Frank's 'total indifference to the convenience or wishes of other people' made him 'an annoying child to have'. Amberley was saddened by his 'intense selfishness' and 'vindictive spirit' whenever he was crossed, and alarmed by the way he addressed his orders to his father in 'the most peremptory tone & is furious if they are not at once obliged'. 'It is very tiresome,' he wrote to Kate. 'You have no idea how dispirited I feel about it.'[29]

The trip had been Amberley's idea. Kate had advised against it and predicted the outcome. 'I doubt the Yarrow air & excitement of a new place & new people will be good for him,' she had written. 'When in the house with children & without me he gets so wild & ungovernable.'[30] The experience made Amberley question their approach. He wrote to Kate that Frank needed 'strict discipline' and suggested public school might be the answer. He ceased to believe it possible to manage Frank with love: 'He loves you more than anyone & yet you know how angry he is when you oppose him.'[31] He asked Kate to think about it, but she continued to sympathise with Frank, which irritated Amberley: 'I think *I* was more to be pitied than "poor Frank" who was only unhappy during his angry state, but was perfectly happy directly after it, slept sound & suffered neither in body or mind, whereas I suffered in both & slept ill...'[32] Lord John comforted Amberley with the thought that his Whig hero, Charles James Fox, had also been mischievous, but as a sensible child had cured himself of it. But in Amberley's view, 'a good boxing of the ears' was called for; and Frank's improved behaviour after an exasperated Mrs Fraser took him in hand, reducing him to penitence by refusing to speak to him after he threw a bottle of medicine at the cook and slapping the back of his hand after he had thrown a stone at her, only strengthened his opinion.

In spring 1873, Frank was sent to PL alone, and while there, Lady John believed she had found a way of managing him:

> ... nagging & unnecessary 'do this' & 'do that' & 'don't do that,' or even a loud or angry voice towards him, are destruction to his temper, & only tend to harden him – still worse is a pitched battle between him & the Authority, whoever that may be... He is quite clever enough to feel when love to him is guiding those about him, & good enough, dear darling, & will give love in return – But he is variable no doubt – & great consistency & "even-handed Justice" are all the more necessary for him.[33]

Though her policy did not always guarantee success, the letter shows significant understanding. The qualities Lady John describes – good and bad – would accompany Frank through life and her approach remained the only one even remotely successful. Still, over the years Frank would try and test her love and patience. Though it is perhaps an exaggeration to say that the Russells regarded Frank *'from the first* as a limb of Satan'[34] – an alarming-sounding but common expression in Victorian times – it is clear that as time went on it became harder for them to think well of his behaviour.

Into this increasingly unhappy situation, Bertrand was born on 18 May 1872, providing a welcome addition to the family. Then, in summer 1873, came the divisive Douglas Alexander Spalding, introduced into the family by Mill as a tutor for Frank. Spalding was of humble origins and had worked to finance his education at Aberdeen University, where he read literature and philosophy. His main interests, however, were scientific, and while at Ravenscroft he undertook many experiments which later appeared in *Macmillan's Magazine* and *Nature*. Frank remembered assisting him in cutting the hearts out of freshly killed salmon to see how long they would continue to beat, decapitating wasps to see if they would continue to clean where their head had once been, and separating newly hatched chicks from their mothers to see how quickly they would begin to peck if left alone. To Sanderson's disgust, chickens were allowed to roam the drawing room. But it was not Spalding's experiments that led to a general hatred of him by others close to the Amberleys, nor his occasional beating of Frank. Rather, it was the 'sinister' nature of his influence.

It is not entirely clear whether Spalding's dubious reputation was deserved or what exactly this influence was – Frank was vague about it and the Russells later destroyed everything concerning him. Perhaps as a youth Frank had not been fully cognisant of its exact nature. The most he would say was that he found it intriguing that Spalding, being a consumptive, breathed through a little wooden tube and that in general he didn't like him. Much later (after Frank's death), Bertrand revealed that Spalding had had an affair with Kate with Amberley's full knowledge and approbation. Evidently, in December 1873, when Frank and Spalding accompanied the Amberleys on a trip to Italy, Spalding had declared his love for Kate. The three of them had discussed the matter and in a curious piece of logic agreed that, while it was unwise for Spalding to have children of his own on account of his tuberculosis, it did not follow that he should be condemned to a life of celibacy and that Kate would become his lover.[35] Whether Frank had any inkling of this arrangement as to increase his dislike of Spalding is unknown. How Bertrand came to the conclusion that Kate derived no pleasure from it is also unknown. But the rumour of it would ultimately save Frank and Bertrand from his clutches. For quite apart from Spalding's growing influence, an evil dispensation of quite another kind accompanied the family home from the Continent.

On their return journey in May 1874, Frank complained of a sore throat and inability to swallow. On reaching London, he was diagnosed with diphtheria, put under the care of renowned English physician Elizabeth Garrett Anderson and nursed by his mother and Maude. He improved, and the family, having stayed away as long as was necessary to be safe, travelled home to Ravenscroft. Initially, all seemed well. But as time went on, reports from Ravenscroft made for increasingly tragic reading. On 21 June, Lady Stanley received a letter from Kate in which she heard that their precautions had been insufficient and that Rachel had caught the disease. Four days later, she heard that Kate too was suffering, having contracted the illness from nursing Rachel. On the 28th, the attending physician wrote to say that Kate had died; and on 3 July, Amberley's cup of misery overflowed as he watched Rachel fade away too. He wrote to his mother,

> I have lost forever the sweet caressing ways and the affectionate heart that might if anything could have been some consolation. And now I feel that the desolation is indeed complete... Of all the children she was the dearest to me, and so my two greatest treasures in this world are gone almost at one blow. It is cruel, unspeakably cruel![36]

Lady John tried to rally her son with thoughts of Frank and Bertrand 'who look to you for all the tenderness of father and mother combined in order to be as happy as children ought to be', but his grief was all-consuming.[37] Spalding took over control of the house, and Amberley busied himself with the completion of his book before falling ill with bronchitis. On 9 January 1876, less than two years after the death of his beloved wife and daughter, with Lizzie Williams at his bedside, he kissed his two sons, bid them goodbye forever and breathed his last.

Frank did not recall his feelings. He took himself off to the frozen water holes in the peat bog outside their plantation and went sliding on the ice. 'I knew I had lost my father,' he wrote. 'I suppose in some way it meant the break up of the home I had known, but that really had come to an end with the death of my mother and the subsequent eighteen months had only been a sort of dreamlike waiting.'[38] Waking from that dream would become something of a nightmare for all.

Within days, Thomas Sanderson and Maude arrived at Ravenscroft and the outrages of Amberley's will were revealed. The executers and trustees of his estate were not members of his own family, as convention would dictate, but friends: Thomas James Sanderson and Douglas Alexander Spalding. Further, his two surviving children were left to the sole guardianship of Spalding, who was likewise given 'sole control of their education and religious training'. He was to continue as their tutor and be retained for the sum of £300 p.a. until Bertrand turned twenty-one. If he died before then, he had the power to appoint a replacement guardian and tutor of his choosing.

How must the Russells have perceived this? As the result of pressure applied by Spalding on the grief-stricken Amberley, or as an act of Amberley's own madness or defiance? It is unclear whether they knew any details of the will beforehand (it having been witnessed by Maude and one Mary Davis of the Post Office in Trelleck), but by their actions it can be assumed that their approval was never sought nor granted. While Maude stayed on to clear the house and Sanderson removed the children to London, Lord John took legal advice. Under threat of action, Spalding and Sanderson quickly renounced probate. Lady John, her brother George Elliott and her son Rollo were appointed guardians, and the boys returned to Pembroke Lodge.[39]

'It was fortunate for me that I escaped the tutelage of Sanderson,' said Frank, possibly under the misapprehension that Sanderson had been given the same level of control over his education as Spalding, but 'less fortunate that my other grandmother, Lady Stanley of Alderley, was not also appointed a guardian'. There is no evidence she ever contemplated the idea. Had she, Frank felt, he would have had the chance of 'a happier boyhood, and a better upbringing';[40] or at least one more in keeping with and understanding of his nature. As it was, the next few years would be filled with bitter conflict from which none would emerge unscathed.

3

Natural Freedom and Frankness

Pembroke Lodge began as a humble molecatcher's cottage, became a gamekeeper's lodge and is now a large, rambling villa open for tea in the park or for hire as an exclusive wedding venue. From the gardens, visitors can watch planes take off from Heathrow over the distant iconic profile of Windsor Castle; from the drive, Canary Wharf and the City of London form an instantly recognisable skyline. During the Russells' occupation, a stream of notable guests passed through their doors: the Queen and Prince Consort; political grandees such as Palmerston and Gladstone; several of Lady John's literary idols, including Thackeray, Dickens, and Browning; and the Russells' good friends, Lord and Lady Tennyson. None of this meant much to the ten-year-old Frank, who, quite apart from the loss of his parents, was preoccupied with the sudden change in his situation. Though he had spent a great deal of time at 'PL' while his parents were alive and therefore knew his guardians well, the reality of living with them permanently was still something of a shock.

Lord John was now in his eighties, a vague figure of a frail and fading old man confined to his bath chair. Lady John was sixty and presided over the house. Her life had been repeatedly touched by grief – not just from the loss of Amberley, Kate and Rachel, but also by the death of her own beloved sister, Lady Dunfermline, in April 1874 – and her outlook darkened the already doleful atmosphere.

The Russell household had never been a lively one. Soon after she had married into the family, Kate had described it as 'stuffy'. She felt oppressed by the atmosphere of 'never finding fault but openly being vexed'.[1] Frank likewise described its pervasive attitude as one 'of halting, of diffidence, of doubts, fears and hesitations, reticences and suppressions, and of a sort of mournful Christian humility'.[2] In addition to Lord and Lady John, its surviving members included their two youngest children, Rollo, twenty-six, and Agatha, twenty-three. Their other son, Willy, had been declared insane and moved to a private asylum in Chiswick.

Willy's is a desperately tragic tale. As a lieutenant in the 9th Lancers, he was teased by his fellow officers for being taciturn, awkward and chaste. In May 1874, their bullying culminated in him fleeing his regiment after a bear – kept as a regimental mascot – was set upon him, supposedly in sport. He was found wandering in a village in Cheshire 'stupid, slovenly, and apparently unconscious' and was taken to a local workhouse where he lashed out, cutting the throat of one man and stabbing another. He was committed to Manor House Asylum, where he remained for the rest of his life in a semi-stable but weakened condition. In his deluded state, he refused to recognise Lady John and believed that Lord John was an imposter. From this point on, his name was never spoken at PL. Bertrand was completely unaware of his existence until the fact of his condition was used by Lady John as ammunition against his choice of bride some twenty years later. There is no evidence that Frank had any further contact with him. Willy died aged eighty-four, having been confined for nearly fifty-nine years and was buried not in the family vault at Chenies but in the Paines Lane Cemetery in Pinner, near Harrow.[3]

Of the remaining PL Russells, Frank considered Agatha the most alive. She was involved with the running of a school provided by Lord John for the children of Petersham, was available for the occasional game of tennis and took it upon herself teach Frank to play the piano – an occupation for which he had no aptitude or enthusiasm. Frank thought she had more common-sense than his grandmother but was otherwise quite characterless, adapting herself 'quite completely to the colour of her environment'.[4] Though for a long time Frank was unaware of it, Agatha had, to a lesser degree, also been touched by insanity. In 1884, her engagement to a curate would be broken off after she became convinced he was a murderer and tried to have him arrested. The loss became a permanent affliction. In years to come, her interference during the failure and fall-out of Frank's first marriage would become a huge source of irritation and frustration to him.

Frank's greatest contempt, however, was reserved for Rollo; not least because of the manner in which, after Lord John's death, he was esteemed and deferred to by Lady John and Agatha. Thankfully for Rollo, he was long dead before Frank publicly recorded his opinion of him, but he could have been in no doubt as to its flavour:

My Uncle Rollo possessed the outward figure of a man, but was a perfect production of the sheltered life, the extreme instance of what a man can become when he spends his whole life surrounded by adoring females ... In speech he was halting, inconclusive and nervous: in appearance small and shy. It will have been gathered that I did not admire him...[5]

Bertrand had very different memories of Rollo: he found him droll and appreciated their scientific conversations. The only thing Frank recorded in Rollo's favour was enjoying canvassing with him for Herbert Gladstone during the 1880 election. The fact that in 1876, Rollo had taken time out to instruct Frank in the science of frictional electricity (based on John Tyndall's series of lectures at the Royal Institution) and had facilitated the setting up of a laboratory at PL, in which Frank could undertake further explorations into voltaic electricity and telegraphy, all became inconsequential as their relationship deteriorated. Full of exasperation, Frank deeply resented the authority Rollo had over him as one of his guardians.

Chief among his guardians, however, and architect of his time at PL was Lady John. As adults, her grandsons would say that she was widely read but 'unworldly'; that she viewed everything through a mist of Victorian sentiment; that she was austere and, though tolerant of the opinions of others, was more so from habit, duty, and politeness than conviction that their viewpoints were in fact tolerable. Frank in particular had mixed feelings about her. On the one hand he described her as 'one of the best women who ever lived' – witty, amusing, kind, dutiful – devoted, even – but on the other, her diffidence, sentimentality and the restrictions she placed on him would make it difficult for him to really respect her. Determined to counter the laxity of Ravenscroft, she employed a strict moral code in Frank and Bertrand's upbringing, shaped by deeply held religious convictions. Suddenly, Frank was expected to dress smartly, to not go about barefoot or beyond the grounds into the park 'for fear I should get run over or lost'. Nearby towns were out-of-bounds for the 'possibility of scarlet fever or of my meeting someone who was not nice'. For the first time, there were forbidden books (though the upper shelves of the schoolroom were still full of forgotten texts ripe for plundering). Church was another new experience and Frank was made to attend morning prayers and received regular lectures of morals, ethics and conduct 'with which I did not agree'. Answers to his searching questions were refused. Very quickly, his grandparents' home became a prison.

Frank sought solitude on the PL roofs and perfected the art of 'climbing trees and remaining aloft' to evade the constant barrage of convention.[6] He chafed against the restrictions and resented the suspicious questioning with its constant inference that he must be up to no good. The pace and colour of his new life was the antithesis of ebullient youth. The manner in which everything was done – the chaperoned walks around the park with his tutor; the painfully slow carriage rides with Rollo where the horses were restrained to walking pace for fear of rabbit holes; the twice weekly 'At Homes' when Frank was expected to present himself with hair nicely brushed, hands washed and clothes tidy – were all infuriating. To the young Frank, it was as if this was all done simply to enrage him. While Bertrand, being that much younger and more adaptable to his new environment, was cherished and loved (albeit sentimentally), Frank, resentful and rebellious, was frowned upon:

> The most frequent and maddening P.L. expression was that it was 'so sad'. My father's later life was 'so sad': any attempt to draw the immaculate Bertie into mischief of the most innocent kind was 'so sad': my unkind and wicked want of affection was 'so sad': the way in which I failed to appreciate the love that surrounded me was 'so sad'. I had a permanent

feeling I was looked upon as a brand to be plucked from the burning, and nobody likes to be treated permanently as a brand.[7]

But Frank's reputation within the family was not without foundation, and he certainly took it upon himself to live up to it. Examples of his behaviour have been recorded by visitors to the house. Childhood friend Annabel Grant-Duff 'had an immense secret admiration for him' but was sorry to find Frank 'sympathized with my brother's point of view about little girls and used to tie me up to trees by my hair'.[8] At the same time, distant cousins Diana and Flora Russell remembered Frank as 'very violent': 'A nurse-maid once came into a room to find that Frank, having lost his temper with Flora, had chased her round the room and was apparently trying to throw her on the fire.'[9] The worse Frank's behaviour became, the more he was censured by the family, and soon this extended into his being kept apart from Bertrand to ensure that his wickedness did not rub off. By the summer of 1877, the situation had become critical and Frank decided to do something about it.

In July, the family had moved temporarily to Broadstairs, Kent for the good of Lord John's health. They took the Archbishop of Canterbury's rather magnificent 'Stone House', a nineteenth-century property overlooking the sea. Bertrand remembered their time there as 'delightful'; Frank did not. He decided to run away. Armed with a traditional Dick Whittington-style bundle and £3 taken from his grandmother's purse, he snuck out at night and made for the railway station where he was instantly recognised by a policeman and promptly returned to the house. The butler locked him in the pantry while he went to rouse the family, but, before he could return, Frank was off again, slipping out through the window and this time heading off cross-country. He spent most of the night in an obliging haystack before continuing the 4 miles to Margate station, where once again he was picked up by a policeman and returned in time for morning prayers and a stern lecture from his grandmother. His response to her reprimand provides an early example of his strength of conviction in his right-mindedness. He told his grandmother 'quite frankly and firmly' the reason for his running away. He defended himself against her accusation of theft by pointing out that it was 'obviously a case of necessity' and refused 'absolutely and entirely' to promise never to run away again, only conceding that he would 'give notice' before making any further attempt.[10]

The whole episode Frank described as 'one of the wisest and happiest actions of my life'. By taking matters into his own hands, he managed to avoid the fate that awaited Bertrand. He had clearly become uncontrollable, and the prospect that he would remain at PL and under the influence of the Russells until it was time for him to enter university was no longer viable. There was only one solution.

Soon after their return to PL, the twelve-year-old Frank was dispatched to Cheam preparatory school, then a pious Anglican school under the headmastership of Revd Robert Tabor. No record survives of Frank's time there beyond his own published reminiscences, in which he recalled his surprise and indignation at suddenly finding himself addressed as Viscount Amberley. In addition, he recalled his apparently much easier adaptation to the daily routine of school than that of PL, some brief details of the friends and masters he met there, a few anecdotes concerning lessons and outings, but more than anything, the bitterness of his Sundays, characterised by Bible study and letters home. Week after week Frank refused to write to Lady John (despite the punishment of being deprived his much-loved puddings) from the 'instinctive feeling that I could not say the kind of things she would like me to say'.[11] Frank hated insincerity and would rather have appeared rude and unfeeling than be coerced into doing something against his will. As such, correspondence with his grandmother would always be difficult. In his early twenties, he reportedly threw many of her letters into the fire unopened.

It was while at Cheam that, three months before his thirteenth birthday, Frank learnt of the death of his grandfather and his ascension to the title Earl Russell. Queen Victoria extended her sympathies to Lady John with the hope that her grandsons would 'grow up to be all that you could wish'.[12] With Frank, this did not look likely. As time went on and Frank moved from Cheam to Winchester College and then on to Oxford, his lack of respect for the Russells and dissociation from them would only grow. His surviving diaries reveal its extent: 'Unsympathetic embodiments of self-satisfied propriety as my uncle & aunt are, how can I care to live with them?' he wrote in spring 1884 on his return to PL from Oxford.[13] Increasingly, he chose to spend his vacations at Lady Stanley's Dover Street residence, having always believed that while it was in her power to do so, Lady John put obstacles in the way of him accepting his maternal grandmother's invitations. The residual effect was an overwhelming and deep-seated bitterness:

> The sad thing about it was that I was pining for love, understanding and companionship, and bubbling over with the exciting confidences of youth; and as often choked off by the hostile and suspicious way in which they were received ... The iron entered into my soul, and I never entirely recovered my natural freedom and frankness.[14]

The fact and tone of this comment, the failings that Frank heaped on the shoulders of the Russells and his blaming them for injustice in their treatment of him, reveal more of Frank's character than anything he could have said of himself. It is a theme that will be revisited in different circumstances and with different people throughout his life. Santayana concluded that the comments were 'a mixture of liberal cant and psychic inversion', a conscious hypocrisy to excuse himself from blame and say to the world, 'You see, I was provoked to be a rebel.'[15] Others took a more sympathetic view. George Bernard Shaw applauded Frank's 'laudably unapologetic *Apologia*' and wrote to him saying that he had had the same free sort of upbringing as Frank's at Ravenscroft and could not think of anything 'more damnable' than being thrust into the PL environment after having 'acquired an adult freethinking habit of mind and character'. He went on: 'You say you have a bad temper; but the fact that you neither burnt the lodge nor murdered Uncle Rollo is your eternal testimonial to the contrary. No doubt Winchester saved Rollo and his shrine.'[16]

There is truth in both perspectives. Frank had already proved himself quite capable of rebellion before either of his parents died, but at the same time, being plunged into so rigid an environment, so much the antithesis of the one he had known and loved, was never going to end well. Orphaned and with no respect for his elders, there would be no check on his ego. Winchester would indeed for a short time become his salvation – and, for the rest of his life, his spiritual home – but would ultimately fail to temper his arrogance and prevent the collision course on which he had already embarked.

4

Manners Makyth Man

In stark contrast to the bleak picture Frank painted of Pembroke Lodge, to Winchester he professed 'a love for every stone, a reverence for its tradition, a feeling of building into one's self as a κτῆμα ἐς ἀέι Meads, School, Hills, and the whole school life'.[1] The Greek translates as *a possession for all time*,[2] and the four chapters of Frank's memoirs dedicated to it Bernard Shaw hailed as 'the only really descriptive description of one of the great boy farms I have ever read'.[3] Yet they speak of more than just nostalgia. They reveal the extent to which Winchester excited within the youthful Frank a 'passionate devotion of service as of Dante for Beatrice, as of Sir Galahad for the Holy Grail, as of an Englishman for his fair England, with a sense of peace, of security beyond expression, of a spiritual home and membership of a great family stretching back five centuries'.[4] In Santayana's view, Winchester was 'the only place he loved and the only place where he was loved'.[5] It certainly worked its magic on him. Here, the insolent child became a moral man.

Established in the fourteenth century by William of Wykeham, with a senior foundation (New College) at Oxford, the school's original purpose was to educate seventy *college men* or scholars in readiness to dedicate themselves to God and public service. Its stone and flint buildings, concealed behind the fortress-like Outer Gate and arranged in a medieval quadrangle around the central Chamber Court, were more austere and intimate than later, grander colleges, such as Eton. Collectively, along with the Chapel that dominated the cobbled courtyard, the cloister-enclosed Chantry and the playing field at the rear (known as *Meads*), they reflected Wykeham's intention as much as did the motto he gave his school: *Manners Makyth Man*. Though by the time Frank arrived the school had been significantly expanded, opening its doors to so many fee-paying sons of the nobility (known as *commoners*) that they outnumbered college men five to one, in essence it remained unchanged. It was where intellectual boys went to assume the *manners* – the character set upon a man by his education – that would shape their lives, enabling them to take up places at Oxford, or the military academies at Woolwich and Sandhurst, to become articled lawyers, MPs or servants of Empire, or to enter the Church. On the whole, then, *Wykehamists* were not the sons of the idle rich.

As such, Frank's enrolment can be viewed as in accordance with Kate Amberley's ambition that he should be *useful*. But given Frank's lack of respect for authority, that alone would not explain his submission to Winchester. Add to it the fact that Winchester meted out the 'even-handed justice' Lady John had identified as essential with Frank, grounded in an unsentimental love of a deeply Christian, High-Church flavour, and it becomes easier to understand how Frank devoted himself to it and became so pious there as to be almost unrecognisable as the 'unwashed, ill-bred, impertinent little child' he had previously been – even going so far as to elect to be confirmed by the Bishop of Winchester in November 1880.

The headmaster when he went up was Dr George Ridding, who held the post from 1867 to 1884. He had been a college man himself and a graduate of Balliol, before returning to Winchester and marrying Mary Louisa, the second daughter of his predecessor, Revd George Moberly. His abrupt manner made many boys terrified of him, but Frank never was. To him, Ridding possessed 'qualities necessary to make a great schoolmaster: justice, firmness, humour, and the blind eye'.[6] Frank's housemaster was Frederick Morshead, who oversaw E-house from 1868 to 1905. Frank ascribed him similar qualities: he was 'reasonably stern, absolutely just, perfectly honest, and beneath the surface the kindest of men'.[7] The master Frank least admired – John Trant Bramston – was prone to favouritism: 'rather a fatal defect'. On one occasion when Frank was given lines for forgetting his book while another boy was merely told not to do it again, Bramston's injudiciousness provoked a PL-style rebellion: 'Injustice has always moved me profoundly, and I used passionate and indefensible language for which I refused to express regret.'[8]

All the masters had nicknames ascribed by the boys. Ridding was *Doctor* and Morshead, *Fred*; but Bramston was known as *Root* – as in 'the root of all evil' – so clearly not generally admired; unlike the second master, *Dick* – or, to give him his proper title, Revd George Richardson. Owing to his position, Dick was also housemaster to the college men and lived in Chamber Court with his wife, Sarah – *Mrs Dick* – the first of the second master's wives to move within the school walls. With the possible exception of Revd Henry Compton Dickins – *the Daker* – who was an ex-master of Winchester and in Frank's time the vicar of St John's, no one was more highly regarded by Frank than this couple. Dick was a large, good-humoured man and Mrs Dick made it her habit to mother the college men and any of the commoners who appeared in need of affection. Perhaps it was Frank's orphan status that made her look out for him. Once or twice every term, he was invited into their home with two or three others for Sunday luncheon and even more frequently for afternoon tea. His assertion that 'the friendship of these two kind and warm-hearted people was a great consolation to me for many years' is not an exaggeration, particularly when applied to Mrs Dick.[9] They corresponded throughout her lifetime and Frank paid her regular visits, taking close friends and love interests to Winchester for her approval. In due course she would publicly defend his honour; and when Santayana said that Winchester was the only place where Frank was loved, it was principally with her in mind. Described as possessing a 'kindly and unconventional spirit', she prized 'affectionateness to ... anyone needing sympathy and assistance' and truth and sincerity above all else. Like Frank, she cared little for what others thought of her opinions, which were 'forcible, sometimes not a little alarming' but 'never narrow minded'. When she died in 1909, she left Frank bereft. She wished her epitaph to be 'She hath done what she could'.[10] Without a doubt, she did for Frank, becoming the first of several mother figures he sought throughout his life.

The structure and hierarchy within the school and its organisation was logical to Frank. The warden was responsible for business and the prefects for discipline, leaving the masters free to teach without the additional burden of having to police the boys. Then as now, all boys boarded and central to its smooth running was the prefect system and the *fagging* of juniors – the system by which junior boys were ordered to do chores for seniors and were punished for not doing them. By modern standards it seems somewhat barbaric, but historically was vociferously defended by the school and its scholars alike. Robert Blachford Mansfield, who in the 1860s wrote a charming little book about his time at Winchester, and who admitted to having been 'always a fag, never having sufficiently advanced in the school to taste the sweets of power', still considered 'mitigated fagging a valuable institution'.[11] Frank described aspects of the system in his time:

> The powers of a Prefect over everyone below Sixth Book were practically unlimited; if he called 'here' everyone who heard it had to run to him and the last arrival got the job: he would check talking in chapel: he would keep order in toy-time: he would prevent disorder or bullying in the House; he had control over games, which were to some extent compulsory: and he could give practically any order he thought fit. His sanction was the power to inflict a tunding, and from his decision there was no appeal except direct to the Headmaster.[12]

Two things stand out from Frank's description: the language or *notions* unique to Winchester, and the sweeping powers of the prefects, instantly apparent whether the terminology is understood or not.

Notions described both words and customs peculiar to the school, and every new scholar was given two weeks to learn them before being examined.[13] So extensively were these terms used that it would be impossible for a boy to get along without them. Some described the organisation of the school. The three school terms, for example, were the *short-half* (autumn), *common-time* (Easter) and *cloister-time* (summer);[14] the first and second years in school were referred to as *junior* and *middle part*; thereafter scholars ascended to the *fifth* and *sixth books*. Other notions appear to have come into popular parlance as slang terms, as derivations from Latin or French, or have their origins in literature. In some cases, they denoted both word and custom. *Socius*, for example, which originated from the school rule *sociati omnes incedunto* (all must walk with a companion), was used as both verb and noun.[15] Any account of a boy's time at Winchester would be festooned with these notions, and Frank's – and therefore, ours – is no exception.

Which brings us back to the power of the prefect as epitomised by *tunding*. A tunding was a beating perpetrated by a prefect using a ground ash, 4 or 5 feet long, which was brought down on the rounded back of the offender as he stood in front of his assembled house, collar turned up, arms folded and head bent. It was a punishment applied to a junior for not adhering to the discipline of the school or his house. As a system one would imagine it would be open to abuse, but both Frank and Mansfield said not (despite the fact that Frank went up to Winchester just seven years after the great 'Tunding Row' and Mansfield had been a college man under the 'old regime' that did not restrict the number of strokes[16]). Frank stated that he only witnessed one in his whole time at Winchester (the offenders having been caught smoking) and heard of only one more (of two boys who were discovered to have surreptitiously attended the strictly out-of-bounds Stockbridge Races), and that he never received one himself (but only because he appealed against it) or had to give one (only because the victim appealed). Mansfield declared the system fair because transparent; the prefects were strengthened in their character for being trusted and therefore more likely to prevent older and larger juniors from bullying their companions, which was more common. Because of this, he said, prefects were looked up to and respected. Perhaps that is why, in his memoirs written some forty years later, Frank recalled all his house prefects by name.

Of punishments handed down by masters, lines were by far the most popular. The headmaster could also issue a *bibling*, or flogging; Frank said he only ever received one – for talking in class – but it did amuse him to recall some years later, when he had taken up his seat in the Lords and Ridding had been made a bishop, that he sat there on equal terms with the man who had once flogged him.

Of course, sometimes the boys took matters into their own hands. They lived day-to-day in very close quarters. Morning chapel, meals, school (which ran from 9 a.m. to noon and from 3 p.m. to 6 p.m.) and evening study, or *toy-time*, were all communal affairs. Toy-time took place in *Hall*,[17] a long, open room where juniors would sit at a double row of desks back-to-back down the middle, with the seniors in open cubicles positioned along the outer walls. These were called *toys* for the shelves which opened out to form each cubicle that held the boys' books and paraphernalia. Study was undertaken in silence under prefect supervision. The openness of Hall and likewise of each *gallery* or dorm, where beds were arranged as in old-style hospital wards, meant that the boys had no seclusion or privacy. One would imagine that this would have taken some getting used to, but to Frank its logic was self-evident:

> For my own part I think this an excellent training as it teaches people to concentrate quite regardless of what might be going on around them, and also to carry on all the ordinary operations of life without undue self-consciousness in the presence of their fellows.[18]

It did not, however, prevent tensions being released in the time-honoured way, as one entry in the fourteen-year-old Frank's diary reveals:

> Between 9–10 [p.m.] while we were up at House I had a mill with Willoughby; sat on him for about half-an-hour altogether & socked him completely, tho' he did scratch my hand most vilely ... it has been coming for some days & it was better for the storm to burst at once & to have it over.[19]

This communal living set Winchester apart from its great rival, Eton, the school famously started by Henry VI borrowing Winchester's headmaster, its statutes, and some of its scholars. It created a strong sense of community, which, alongside its other traditions, excluded outsiders. This sense of belonging Frank had not experienced since the death of his mother. Neither since his Ravenscroft days had he tasted freedom like that which was built into the boys' routines. On Tuesdays and Thursdays there were half-holidays, or *half-rems* (or *remedies*), which gave the boys complete liberty to explore without supervision anywhere to the west of the school, but not within the city itself. Frank made maximum use of it, going frequently to bathing places, boating on the river, or climbing *Hills* where the boys roamed freely. On Sunday afternoons, between three chapel services, he and others would take long walks as far afield as Twyford or Otterbourne, some 5 miles away, or cycle the 12 miles to Southampton. Additional *leave-out* required special permission and usually came at the invitation of family, on Sundays or Saints' Days, when there was no school.

Leave-out was not always a good thing, especially when Lady John used it to impose upon Frank's liberty. On one occasion he lamented, 'I am going to Granny at 7 Chesham Place to-morrow tho' it is not a fortnight since the half began'; and on another, 'Got a letter from Warburton's advising, perhaps I might say commanding, that I should go there every other Sunday.'[20] Mrs Isabel Warburton was the daughter of Lord John's first wife and therefore an approved 'sort-of aunt' with 'the P.L. touch'. Her husband had been canon of All Soul's, Oxford, but had retired to Winchester, and, due to proximity, had been asked to keep an eye on

Frank. Anything Frank tried to do without express permission – a trip to London, for example, in February 1881 with his Stanley uncle, Lord Airlie, to the Peer's Gallery in the House of Commons – resulted in a *jawing*, or lecture, from either the Warburtons or Lady John, which Frank continued to deeply resent.

He did, however, appreciate the intellectual freedom encouraged at Winchester and, outside timetabled classes, found he excelled at debating. Given his background it is perhaps unsurprising that the Debating Society should be his club of choice. Here he cut his teeth in the art of speech making; though as a Liberal in a sea of Tories, he was often on the losing side. His temperament allowed him to enjoy it nonetheless. In his maiden speech in February 1882 he launched straight into his outspoken, controversial career by commenting not so much on the topic of the debate but on the other debaters, pointing out the absurdity of their arguments and their prejudiced minds. In his second, he found himself for once with the majority when arguing against a motion condemning the construction of a Channel Tunnel. Economic considerations were more important than the slim possibility that the French might use the tunnel to invade and capture Dover, he argued; and fears about the lack of air inside such a tunnel were not insurmountable. But his two most notable contributions – and, in the circumstances, most ironic – were his arguments in favour of maintaining the judicial capacity of the House of Lords and his opposing of the motion 'That the freedom of the Press is now abused and should be curtailed'. Who would be the judge in such matters? he asked: 'Scandal is best suppressed by contempt, and free thought [encouraged] by free discussion. The liberty of the press is a very real advantage, and worth all the struggles made for it.'[21] It was a position he found difficult to maintain when in due course it was his own misdemeanours that made headlines. Much later, he would write, 'It was my misfortune and not my fault that practically the whole of my life has been chronicled in detail in the daily Press, [giving] a curiously distorted view of one's character and tastes.'[22]

The greatest joy, however, for Frank at Winchester – and perhaps the greatest stress – was the opportunity for friendship. He was not by any means a universally popular boy. He had been rather isolated at PL and one can imagine that his strong-mindedness and occasional outbursts of temper (which even Winchester could not cure) made him difficult to get along with. His diary is as festooned with accounts of scrapes with boys as it is with notions. Take the occasion, for example, when he went skating on the ice at Fisher's Pond in January 1880:

On the ice after I had been with Bilbro for some little time the little fool asked Mole to knock my hat off. When I of course resisted the rest of the Moabites came to help him ... The only way I could make him let go was to let out at his nose which I caused to bleed & him to lobster. But then the beastly Moabites made it too hot for me so that I had to leave...[23]

Yet friendship became his major preoccupation, and there developed a series of intimate friendships with a handful of boys – the most symbolic being with a young man called John Sanders Watney, who was six months younger than Frank and of the famous Watney Brewery family. He was not in Frank's house and only briefly in the same division. They shared few interests and hence their friendship is something of a mystery. Watney was a sportsman, excelling at football and often picked for *fifteens*; Frank was not. His own football career was short-lived and rather inglorious, resulting in only one review: 'In the hot Russell worked well, but was a good deal on the ground.'[24] Yet in 1880, their friendship rapidly developed; though to a large extent it was a one-sided affair, with Frank doing all the chasing. In his private diary, Frank recorded the strength of his feelings for Watney, which clearly drew attention and comment. On 4 February, he wrote,

> Socius Watney up from Chapel as usual. I wish Elliott & such-like brutes would not sport beastly notions about us & say that I get up early to go down to him. I don't like it myself & if he hears any he'll be infra-dig to me...[25]

It appears that Watney was quite often *infra-dig*, or scornful, of Frank's attentions, perhaps as a result of the *brocking* (teasing or badgering) of other boys. Whatever the cause, Frank always felt uncertain about him: Watney gave him 'small return' for his devotion. His diary became an obsessive record of the days Frank managed to *socius* Watney and the days he didn't. Soon, 'socius Watney up from chapel *es postulante*' became 'S.W.U.C.E.P.', which in turn became '*spruce*' – a Winchester notion synonymous with going on a spree and indicative, therefore, of the pleasure Frank got from Watney's company. On 12 March, Frank recorded triumphantly, 'I have now spruced for a fortnight continuously without one omission'; and on 18 April, 'Oh! it is joyful; joyful! to be next *him* in chapel.' But by mid-May, things had taken a turn for the worse and a non-compliant Watney – who now became 'Podgy' or 'Fat-One' in the diary – increasingly snubbed Frank. The rejection made Frank cruel – he confessed it amused him when Watney received the same treatment from another boy – but it also made him more determined. He pushed towards greater intimacy by calling him 'Sanders' and watching to see if he would object. He took every encouragement as an expression of affection, being 'frantically quilled' at the slightest suggestion of jealousy on Watney's part.[26] But when Watney refused to sit with him at the summer concert, a 'fearfully riled' Frank 'cursed him like anything'. It marked the beginning of the end. When they returned to school after the long vacation, Watney avoided Frank completely. On 13 October, his final comment on Watney read, 'Alas! alas! for Sanders.' It would appear they had no more contact. Watney would achieve that much-admired status of captain of a *fifteens* team in 1884. He would follow Frank to Oxford in 1885, but by that time events had taken over and Frank was no longer there. After Oxford,

Watney joined the family brewery as a wine merchant. He died of TB, unmarried, in 1896, aged only twenty-nine. Through sheer force of will, Frank had attempted to make him his own particular and exclusive friend and failed. It did not matter. An entry in his diary on the day preceding his last lamentation marked the arrival of another who would have far greater significance:

> ... Either Carey or Johnson will get books as matters stand now – I hope Johnson tho' he is a new man.[27]

5

A Spiritual Rebel

I saw one day in my div. a small pale faced College man with an oval face
and rather dark hair. It was an arresting picture; he looked like some young
saint in a stained glass window.[1]

It is tempting to ascribe a certain amount of artistic licence to this, Frank's
sentimental description of his first sighting of the late nineteenth-century
British poet Lionel Pigot Johnson as he was at Winchester, but Johnson was
a curiosity apt to provoke such reflections. Reminiscences of Johnson tend
to agree: he was the 'fairy changeling' at odds with the world; 'a diminutive,
ethereal creature, with a pallid beautiful face, an omnivorous reader, quite
remote from the ordinary interests of the school and indeed contemptuous
of them, but passionately enamoured of the beauties of Winchester'.[2] The
most common adjective applied to Johnson was 'aloof'. How then did he
become the chosen friend of the rash, emotionally volatile and demanding
Frank? Quite aside from the fact that college men and commoners were
largely separated by the structuring of the school, Frank and Lionel appear
on the surface to have had little in common. But Frank was prone to making
unconventional choices and when decided upon a course would pursue it
obstinately. So, just as he had with Watney, after several sightings of Johnson
in the school library, Frank became enamoured with him and made up his
mind they would be friends. His first attempts at conversation were rebuffed:

[Johnson] was obviously clever, but he showed little sign of any interest
in the human beings around him. He neither smiled nor gossiped ... but
after several further meetings in Moberley [sic] Library he condescended
to thaw a little, finding I suppose that I have some interests beyond cricket
and football.[3]

This series of encounters marked the start of a curious and fateful friendship
that led Frank to describe Johnson as the greatest influence of his life,

crediting him with his intellectual and emotional development. With this in mind, it is necessary to understand a little more of who – and what – Lionel Johnson was.

Lionel was born on 15 March 1867 into a Windsor-based family with a great military tradition: his father was a captain in the 90th Light Infantry and six paternal uncles achieved ranks of colonel or above. Lionel himself was exempt from such a career in part due to his stature: his height peaked at 5 feet 3 inches and from boyhood he was considered 'pale, slight, and weakly'.[4] His physical appearance belied his age. Santayana, who first met him in summer 1887, was told that Lionel was then sixteen – 'and I readily believed the report' – though actually Lionel was twenty, 'only a year and a half younger than Russell and three years younger than I'.[5]

Johnson went up to Winchester in autumn 1880 and immediately made his mark – not by sporting prowess or popularity (neither were qualities he possessed) but by working his way up the school lists which ranked the boys by academic achievement rather than age. Having been fifth on the election roll for college when he went up, he did indeed 'get books' in October 1880 as Frank hoped, meaning he was moved up to the next division in January 1881. Following which, the avid and 'omnivorous reader' set himself the task of reading every book in the school library and continued his early achievements with a succession of prizes, the editorship of the student magazine, the *Wykehamist*, and two of the five college prefect positions.

By contrast, Frank's academic career was not stellar. He struggled with classics, repeatedly ranking low in his class in 1880, but did make it (to his own surprise) as high as fourth on one occasion in the final term. In the mid-year exams, he came a disappointing fiftieth in French, twenty-eighth in science, and fourteenth overall in his division. A couple of times he *croppled*, or came last, in morning lines and French. When he *jockeyed up* a few places in history towards the end of the year, he recorded it as 'a most surprising fact', though not enough to prevent Uncle Rollo employing a tutor for the long vacation. Frank's senior years were better. By the time he left, he had made it to the senior division of fifth book, with only two classes above him.

Early in 1883, he and Lionel became friends. Lionel visited him at PL in May. They occasionally met at Mrs Dick's and walked together round Meads, but they did not really know each other until Frank went up to Oxford and they began to correspond. Possibly, they were drawn together through loneliness. Both had been thus described: Lionel by Frank, and Frank by Watney's younger brother, who was also up. Lionel further described himself as shy to the point of being unable to utter a word in company. Both sought escape in books and Lionel recommended many to Frank, who was awed by Lionel's erudition. Friendship with Johnson, however, wasn't easy:

... he appeared to be unimpressionable, unemotional, undemonstrative – in a word, he walked through life aloof like some ascetic saint.

My own temperament was the exact converse, and I recognize that I was often chilled by this aloofness, although I believe, so far as his nature permitted it, he was fond of me and valued my friendship.[6]

It was a friendship that was destined to be severely challenged on several notable occasions, first of all when Frank left Winchester. All boys had to leave at eighteen, so it was inevitable, given their respective ages, that Frank would go first. But as his birthday was in August, it was reasonable to assume that Frank would stay for cloister-time 1883 and then go straight to Oxford after the long vacation. In that last term, Frank expected to make sixth book, with the chance of becoming 'that most enviable of mortals', a commoner prefect. But Lady John and Rollo had already decided to remove him at Easter and place him with a private tutor in Limpsfield, Surrey for the summer term. The practice – to bring boys up to the required standard for Oxford – wasn't uncommon, but Frank took it personally. He recorded in his diary that his mind was 'racked' and his feelings 'harassed' by the decision. He wrote 'some very bitter and forcible letters' to Rollo and appealed to Fred and Ridding to overturn it. They tried, but failed. In yet another example of the lack of sympathy between Frank and his guardians, they appeared not to consider the strength of Frank's attachment to Winchester, while Frank assumed that the move was made purposely to spite him: 'Of course, P.L. decided against it ... If I was doing well at school, and if I actually had the audacity to be happy there, that showed that the public system had finally corrupted me, and the sooner I was removed from its baneful influence the better.'[7]

Frank's 'corruption' appears to have been nothing worse than the acquiring of rather 'lazy habits', which he readily admitted, but his reaction to Limpsfield did nothing to improve relations with the Russells. Frank found the tutor, Mr Bell, 'vulgar and mean in spirit', and his wife in possession of 'the same detestable middle-class gentility'.[8] The manners of the other students were distasteful to him and offended his moral sensibilities. The only thing that got him through it, he said, were letters from his Winchester friends.

The summer which followed was better. Released from his Limpsfield torment, Frank was back at PL, but as an eighteen-year-old was harder to restrain, and when not studying in preparation for Oxford, playing lawn tennis with Bertrand or introducing him to the delights of Euclid (Frank's one contribution to his brother's career), chose instead to spend most of his time on two vastly diverse occupations: telegraphy and Theosophy.

Frank had by this time set up a complete telegraphic system at PL and spent much of the summer extending, developing and fine-tuning it. He also took it upon himself to teach Bertrand's governess, Miss Bühler, how to use it. With the help of Phillips – a navy pensioner then employed as watchman in the park, who lived with his family in rooms above PL's stables – he set up a sounder in the stables and connected it to another in

Miss Bühler's room, through which they succeeded in transmitting long conversations. So proud was he of his achievements that he invited a local post office clerk to come and approve it. Under his Grandmamma Stanley's advice, he also took out lifelong membership of the Royal Institute to further his growing scientific interest.

His interest in Theosophy was sparked by another Stanley: his eccentric first cousin St George Lane Fox-Pitt. During his adolescence, Frank was in contact with many of his Stanley cousins and was particularly fond of the Howards – Aunt Rosalind's children, whom he would visit at their seats near Carlisle (Naworth Castle) and York (Castle Howard) – and the Fox-Pitts – the children of his mother's eldest sister, Alice, and her husband, the ethnologist and archaeologist Augustus Henry Lane Fox Pitt-Rivers. Frank recalled taking German lessons with cousin Agnes, who was so similar in temperament that they often argued, resulting on one particularly memorable occasion in a mutual hair-pulling. Agnes gave as good as she got.

By contrast, St George had a quixotic and generous nature along with the Stanley independent spirit. Nine years Frank's senior and seven years older than Agnes, his generosity was demonstrated by the manner in which he at one time or another took both of them under his wing. Later in life, he would write on education and free will and stand for election as a Liberal MP, cutting a striking figure with his full-length black bushy beard, but his early career was as an electrical engineer and inventor of some repute. In 1878, he presented a paper to the Society of Arts in which he described his system of automatic gas lighting using electricity which was then being applied to street lamps in the Pall Mall district; three years later, he presented another to the Society of Telegraph Engineers predicting the use of electricity for domestic heating and lighting. He was also responsible for inventing the Lane-Fox Carbon Filament Lamp in competition with Edison and Swan's light bulb, resulting in a series of financially crippling lawsuits over perceived breach of patents. He didn't win, but, true to his spirit, interpreted his failure as a necessary lesson: that one must overcome mundane desires and seek something far greater and nobler than fame and fortune.

St George's scientific credentials could only have encouraged Frank to take seriously his involvement with the Society for Psychical Research (SPR) and his interest in Theosophy and Buddhism. Frank admired St George enormously and was, as an eighteen-year-old, hugely influenced by him. The SPR's remit was the scientific investigation of psychic phenomena such as thought-transference, mediumship and apparitions. Theosophy blended spiritualism with eastern religions and scientific rhetoric. Buddhism in particular was allied to scientific thought and claimed a recognition of the doctrine of evolution some two millennia before Darwin. Empire had brought Victorians into contact with eastern philosophies, and a growing number of radical thinkers saw in them answers to their dissatisfaction with protestant Christianity. St George was one such thinker and lent Frank several key texts of the day, which he devoured. He read Alfred Percy Sinnett's *The Occult World* in one sitting and wrote in his diary that it is 'strange to say I half believe it'. He followed it with the supernatural novel *A Strange Story* by Edward Bulwer-Lytton, which he read in under a week. The monumental 1,400-page *Isis Unveiled*, by Theosophical Society co-founder Madam Blavatsky, he read in September and re-read in November. He wrote long letters to St George on the subject and received in return reports and pamphlets from the SPR. Together, they went to a séance and in August travelled north to visit the Howards at Naworth. On their return, Frank recorded having a long talk with Aunt Agatha on astral subjects, but found her 'perverse', content with her own 'unreasoning disbelief' and surprised at his 'now firm belief in thought reading'. A few days later, his own copy of *Occult World* arrived, along with Sinnett's follow-up, the newly published *Esoteric Buddhism*, which Frank recorded as being 'of the deepest interest', but found its meaning 'very hard to grasp'. He fell in line with St George's views 'about the absurdity of the general anthropomorphic conception of God' and mirrored his strict vegetarian diet with a 'semi-vegetarian' diet of meat only once a day![9]

Then, on 4 October 1883, he visited Lionel in Winchester and conveyed to him all his new learning. They ran about on Hills, 'got blown by the glorious fresh wind, talked about Buddhism & other such like things and enjoyed ourselves quite immensely'. Within two days, Frank had fully annotated *Esoteric Buddhism* and sent it to Lionel along with a six-page letter, sure he would be delighted with it. He then spent an apprehensive few days waiting for a reply, walking and thinking, not about his imminent removal to Oxford but on much loftier matters; revolving 'new ideas of the universe' in his mind and feeling oppressed by the magnitude and difficulty of their conception.[10]

Lionel's response signalled the start of a correspondence one side of which Frank published anonymously as *Some Winchester Letters of Lionel Johnson* some thirty-six years later.[11] Its publication was intended to demonstrate the awe and respect Frank felt for Lionel, who, he said, was 'apt to suggest an Epicurean God rather than a human being'. Subsequently, it has been criticised for showing 'poor transcription and extensive bowdlerization on Russell's Part'.[12] This criticism is something of an exaggeration, except as concerns Frank's personal affairs which crop up throughout the correspondence and are often as a direct result of it. Reading one side of a correspondence is often misleading, and though none of Frank's return letters survive, cross-referencing Lionel's with Frank's diary gives a clearer picture of both the nature of their friendship and events leading up to its first challenge. Rather ominously, it began with a word of caution:

> The same post that brought me your welcome letter brought me another from a clerical friend of mine, a young man of ultra High Church views; ... he referred to a strange movement in connection with Buddhism, which

was so fascinating in its assumption of high spiritual tone that he was certain it would ensnare me to my perdition. I am meditating a fitting reply to this excellent young man.[13]

Neither Frank nor Lionel was apt to accept the judgment of others; in fact, quite the opposite. A few years later, looking out across the rooftops from his New College rooms, Johnson would tell Santayana, 'Everything above that [sky]line is right, everything below it is wrong.' Lionel may well have been being deliberately provocative (as was his wont), but Santayana took it to mean 'that everything within him was right, and everything outside wrong'; Lionel would preach this message to Frank with disastrous results when inflated by Frank's ego.[14] But for the time being it was Frank preaching to Lionel, though not initially very successfully. After reading the first section of Frank's offering, Lionel wrote that though he sensed 'the power and nobility in the Buddhist system', it 'revolts me'. It rested too much on science. Religion should be accessible to the masses. 'Let the East keep its lofty ideals and the West a simpler Christianity,' he concluded. 'I would rather be a Roman Catholic.'[15]

Frank was deeply distressed. He had set his heart on converting Lionel, believing it was vital for his friend's salvation that he take up the system. Letters flew between the pair and within days Frank was relieved to hear that, despite his continued reservations about its practicability, Lionel had found something in it to satisfy his soul:

> I have hardly been just towards Buddhism! the chapter on Nirvana is too transcendentally grand not to be a real true ideal. But is it all practical? I mean, could the present world go on if Buddhism and the struggles it entails were prevailing ideas?[16]

They then spent a satisfying couple of months discussing differing views of religion: 'two of England's rising generation in search of a creed'. They read widely, and in a succession of letters passing between Oxford and Winchester discussed the respective opinions espoused in books that Lionel recommended: Edwin Arnold's *Light of Asia*, for example, and Matthew Arnold's *Literature and Dogma*. Frank was also drawn into conversations with his new Oxford friends about his Buddhist beliefs, which were reinforced by a visit in November from St George, who Frank introduced around and took to breakfast with the master, Benjamin Jowett. That Jowett afterwards asked St George to return to continue their religious discussion privately, and that St George reported he had made Jowett 'very uneasy' with his views, enabled Frank to bathe in the reflected glory of the 'great impression' his cousin had made.[17] Meanwhile, in Winchester, Lionel was finding confirmation of Buddhist ideals in Plato and including his findings in his school work. In an essay for Doctor Ridding, he 'dragged in a tolerably clear statement of Buddhism, expressing my personal views on the subject: I expect to be sat upon accordingly.'[18]

It was perhaps not a wise thing to do. Frank and Lionel's unorthodox discussions were starting to draw attention in a manner that only the overconfidence of youth stopped them finding alarming. On 13 November, Lionel wrote to Frank that Mrs Dick had been 'pouring out her motherly fears for you to me' saying Frank appeared melancholy. Lionel enlightened her on their religious discussions, 'speaking of it lightly as your latest fancy: she entreats me to discourage you: I said I would do my best'. Lionel also began skipping chapel, drawing from the headmaster the sarcastic enquiry as to whether he thought Nirvana akin to lying in bed. If so, it was 'as lucid as most people's, but that that was not saying much'.[19]

At the end of November, the two friends discussed whether Frank could further the cause at Oxford by forming a society under the auspices of the Theosophical Society. It was a short-lived ambition, quickly nipped in the bud by a visit Frank paid to Winchester at the beginning of December. He dined with the Richardsons and 'got a jaw from Dick afterwards for proselytizing Johnson & wasting his time'. The following week, he received a letter from Lady John saying 'she had heard things about me she could not refute' and summoning him to PL. 'This is the beginning of the storm,' he wrote. He returned to PL on 18 December and had a long talk with his grandmother:

She pointed out to me the dangers of conceit & the need which I deeply feel of the spiritual and holy life as the very first step: I was seized with bitter remorse & deep penitence which I have not yet (Dec. 22) quite recovered from, & in my anguish I wrote a long letter to Johnson asking for comfort and encouragement.[20]

He needed it. Frank had just learnt that St George was setting off on a pilgrimage to India. The separation couldn't have come at a worse time. He got the desired letter from Lionel, who 'advised the creation of fresh memories to bury the past: & acts of spiritual intention or achievement to be set as an atonement', but no response to a further suggestion that they meet in London. He wrote again, fearing Lionel might be unwell, and got the reply he dreaded. George Richardson had spoken to Dr Ridding, Ridding had written to Lionel's father, and Captain Johnson, 'regarding my influence as most baneful to [Lionel's] welfare as a Christian', demanded 'an entire cessation of our intimacy and correspondence'.[21] Lionel sent one last letter assuring Frank that the ban would not break their friendship even though he had no choice but to submit to his father's 'good intentions' – 'so farewell till – Nirvana, as far as I can see!'[22] Frank summed up his year in a statement combining remorse, self-pity and defiance:

This loss, the loss of St. George, Limpsfield, leaving Winchester ... with above all an abiding remorse for the bitter irrevocable past, have all combined to sadden me much this year. The very expression of my face has changed with the kind of settled sorrow that sits ever at my heart … But I have a confident hope in the future & a strength & a reliance within me which nothing can shatter.[23]

In truth he had learnt very little. Beneath his misery, his rebellious nature was alive and well. His sense of injustice would return and his friend's parents be dismissed as 'very narrow-minded and prejudiced Anglicans'.[24] There were diversions aplenty at Oxford and the friendship of many open-minded men to be had. Though Winchester had his loyalty, Oxford would provide him with 'the happiest days of my whole life',[25] until an altogether more sinister accusation would bring his time there to a sudden and abrupt end.

6

The White Flower of a Blameless Life

At the end of September 1883, Frank had found himself at Oxford sitting his *smalls*: a series of Latin and Greek papers, some arithmetic and algebra, and an oral exam, or *viva*, which he took on 5 October. After construing his requisite six lines from Homer's *Iliad*, he was told his work was satisfactory and was free to return to Haslemere in Surrey, where, that summer, the Russells had taken a house. The following week, he was back for a second round of exams: more Latin prose, papers on Cicero and Demosthenes; Homer and Virgil vivas; and a divinity viva led by the master, Benjamin Jowett, himself. Then there was the all-important allocation of rooms. Frank's were in the front quad and 'adequately furnished'. His quarterly allowance was £100 and a trip to London with Aunt Maude saw £15 of it go on the obvious student essentials: 'Tablecloths, pillowcases, sheets, dusters, tea-cloths, napkins, spoons, forks, knives, cigars, etc.', to which his aunt added a rather ancient and beautiful Crown Derby tea set. On 12 October, Frank heard that Jowett had expressed himself pleased with his papers, and four days later returned to Oxford for the matriculation ceremony. Jowett 'pronounced some mysterious Latin formula over us', Frank signed his name in the college books, or *matricula*, was presented with a certificate and statute book, and officially became a member of Balliol, one of Oxford's oldest colleges.[1] His chosen subject: *Literae Humaniores* (literally, more humane letters), otherwise known as *Greats* and subsequently *classics*. 'I trust that I always observed the Statues,' Frank later quipped about the seriousness of the undertaking. 'At any rate I can say with a clear conscience that I never played marbles on the steps of the Senate House.'[2]

For the most part, the atmosphere and reputation of Balliol in the 1880s was of Jowett's making. The son of a furrier, Benjamin Jowett was brought up a Methodist in a family that advocated religious tolerance. His father, though concerned for his advancement, was remote and unflattering, believing that praise led to arrogance. As a consequence, Jowett's natural shyness and sensitivity was compounded by a lifelong social awkwardness and a quiet but deep-seated ambition. After securing a Balliol degree in 1839, he became a Fellow and tutor of *Greats*. He was a senior dean by 1845, and by 1855 he was Regius Professor of Greek, largely responsible for changes in both the curriculum and teaching methods employed within the school. Balliol became revered for its intimate, Socratic tutorials – a powerful blend of pastoral supervision and intellectual stimulation – and through his pupils Jowett became hugely influential. 'Jowett worship' became a real phenomenon. By degrees, he turned his natural reticence into an asset, always seeming to be deep in thought and remaining calm in the face of opposition to his sweeping reforms. His broach-church views and shift of emphasis from Latin to Greek – to address fears of modern thinkers like Matthew Arnold that England was falling behind culturally just as she was leaping ahead in industry – led to accusations of heresy from the High Church establishment but did not prevent him becoming Master in 1870, just as the publication of his monumental translation of the whole of Plato's *Dialogues* cemented his renown as a leading Greek scholar. By the time Frank went up in 1883, Jowett's quip to Florence Nightingale – that he should 'like to govern the world through my pupils' – was scarcely a joke.[3] A degree in *Greats* from Balliol was regarded as the ultimate accolade. Balliol men consequently considered themselves superior. 'But how could we help it?' wrote Frank's university friend Edgar Jepson, when our 'contemporaries and immediate predecessors at Balliol were the chief rulers of the Empire for half a century'.[4]

As a confirmed bachelor and keen letter writer, whose sole focus was Balliol's advancement and who accepted the many proffered invitations from noble families that his position afforded, Jowett extended his influence beyond the college walls. Among his intimates were members of Frank's family, the Stanleys. Having won the admiration of Frank's uncle Lyulph, whom he tutored in the 1850s, he secured an introduction to Alderley and thereafter the lifelong friendship of Lady Stanley and Frank's aunts Blanche, Lady Airlie and Rosalind, Lady Howard. Others, were less impressed. After receiving Jowett at Rodborough, Frank's mother had written in her diary that Jowett was too prudent. Thomas Sanderson agreed: 'I do not like Jowett the more I see of him … [He] harps eternally on the compromise one is compelled to make between Truth absolute and Truth expedient.' He advised the Amberleys to 'let him go'. Another distant Stanley relation warned Frank before his matriculation to 'beware of Jowett; he will turn you out a polished infidel'.[5] By the 1880s, Jowett's duties as master and vice-chancellor denied him daily contact with students. The net result was that Frank never looked up to him as he had Dr Ridding or felt for him the devotion he'd felt for his housemaster, Fred. This lack of sympathy, Frank later concluded, had serious consequences.

For the time being, Frank found the Oxford atmosphere and society stimulating. He welcomed the 'untrammelled and unfettered discussions on everything in heaven and earth'. His interest in his studies increased and he 'worked like a tiger', favouring the writings of Lucretius and Aeschylus alongside the poetry of Browning that Lionel insisted he read.[6] His efforts were acknowledged by Jowett at the 'handshaking' at the end of his first year. It wasn't enough to stop Rollo proposing a tutor again for the long vacation – a proposal Frank refused to even consider – but it was an improvement.

Socially, too, Frank fully immersed himself in Oxford life, joining numerous clubs and societies – Balliol's Debating Society, the Brackenbury, the Russell and Palmerston Clubs and the Oxford Union. He was present at the re-run of the famous shall we/shan't we debate as to whether Oscar Wilde's *Poems* was suitable material for the Union library,[7] and at William Morris's controversial socialist call-to-arms at the Russell Club, introduced by John Ruskin and disguised under the title *Art Under Plutocracy*. The university authorities were horrified that students cheered and applauded as Morris tasked the working man with taking on his rich oppressor 'until absolute equality is attained'.[8] Frank declared himself 'interested' but 'didn't feel that I quite agreed with it all';[9] Morris was dismissed as Utopian – enthusiastic but impractical.

The picture Frank painted of his time at Oxford for public consumption was one of the highest moral standing: 'My most intimate friends were all as studious, as virtuous and as eager as I was.'[10] In the light of events that would follow, this sounds like an overstatement to exaggerate his innocence, but for the most part the image is not contradicted by his early Oxford diary. He recorded social engagements with visiting dignitaries afforded by his ancestry – an invitation from the Warden of Keble to meet Gladstone, for example, and his attendance at Jowett's dinner for future Prime Minister Lord Rosebery. There were frequent dinner invitations from George Brodrick, Warden of Merton College, whom Frank described as a very good friend. Otherwise, the diary comprises an endless list of Oxford men with whom he associated. He appeared to choose friends of similar moral rather than social standing and was put off by groups of undergraduates he considered 'fast sets'. After the austerity of PL, he was shocked to find 'such a number of iniquities perpetrated at once' by some Oxford undergraduates who drank 'enormous quantities of wine' at dinner, followed by coffee and snuff.[11] Even within his own crowd there were habits he found alarming:

Nov 28th: Went to Spender's till 12 & then Hawkins and Winkworth came to my room & drank whisky till 1, Maurice and I looking on in horror.[12]

The whisky drinkers were older men in their final year. Spender and Hawkins made regular appearances in Frank's rooms or Frank in theirs (Hawkins most often accompanied by his whisky bottle) and Frank was proud of entertaining 'such distinguished guests', whatever their habits. After Oxford, John Alfred Spender became editor of the *Westminster Gazette* and Hawkins dropped his surname and as Anthony Hope wrote *The Prisoner of Zenda* and many other adventure novels. Maurice Llewellyn Davies, by contrast, was a particular friend in Frank's own year whose father was vicar of Kirkby Lonsdale and a Fellow of Trinity College, Cambridge. Maurice was one of six extremely gifted brothers, all of whom Frank would come to know and admire; as he would their 'pretty & very sensible' sister, Margaret.[13] Frank had taken particular steps to cultivate Maurice's acquaintance, finding him 'clever, well read, of attractive manners' with 'extensive acquaintance among distinguished people'.[14] He was moral but fun-loving, and within a very short time Frank had loosened up somewhat too – at least enough to enjoy the occasional 'ragging' and odd glass of whisky. Frank was also a keen smoker, at a time when it was considered neither anti-social nor a health hazard. He had started on cigarettes at Winchester (much to his guardians' disgust), had a brief flirtation with the rather more exotic hubble-bubble, or hookah, at Oxford, but held a lifelong commitment to his pipe and the occasional cigar.

Other than this, Frank appears to have had few vices. He didn't get up to the sort of antics described by another friend, Edgar Jepson, in his memoirs, like breaking out of Balliol after hours to visit men in other colleges or ladies in the city. In fact, apart from enjoying the conversation of Miss Edith Brodrick, the warden's daughter, and infrequent contact with his cousin Cecilia Howard (with whom he 'fell in love' each time they met[15]), Frank seems to have had little interest in women at this time. His circle of male friends, however, quickly expanded. Jepson was a curious addition: Santayana said he spent more time cultivating his thick carpet of blond hair than his brain. But Maurice's old school friends from Marlborough College were more understandable – the future Liberal writer and theorist Leonard Trelawny Hobhouse, who had been sent to Corpus because his father 'distrusted the Balliol atmosphere',[16] and Charles Henry 'Long' Roberts MP, who eventually had the pleasure of marrying Cecilia. Maurice also introduced Frank to Charles Edward Sayle from New College, who had come up from Rugby and became librarian at Cambridge. Then there were two men from Christ's Hospital, P. U. Henn of Worcester College and Osman Edwards of Merton, who in turn introduced Frank to two friends then at Cambridge: Henry Currie Marillier of Peterhouse and Herbert Ainslie Roberts of Caius. Old school ties led to many excursions between the Oxbridge colleges such that Frank soon felt equally at home in both. Indeed, the bonds made with some endured the longest (though were not without their hazards): Harry Marillier, who later managed Morris & Co., would be best man at Frank's first wedding but side with his wife over their separation; and Roberts' association with Frank would almost ruin him.

The first sign, however, that Frank's Oxford career was anything other than immaculate was arguably his friendship with the wonderfully eccentric, highly intelligent and quick-witted Ion Thynne, whose rebelliousness and madcap antics were universally praised, and who was later described by Oscar Wilde as 'exquisitely corrupt'.[17] Baptised John Alexander Roger Thynne, Ion's father was the second son of the Marquess of Bath. Ion had been a prize-winner at Eton but was known as something of a rogue (or as writer Sir Henry Newbolt put it, 'an ugly loose lipped shambling boy' who 'took up the worst vices' and was 'sacked from Eton'[18]). At Oxford, he was reportedly more interested in reading lesser-known erotic Latin writers than his set texts and for starting several societies (which Frank joined) with ridiculous rules and peculiar names: the Cosmopolitan Unsectarian Purity Society (C.U.P.S!), the Dolores (a reading society named for Swinburne's poem) and the Unconventionals. Meetings were held in Ion's rooms with him presiding, sitting cross-legged on the floor under a large Japanese umbrella. He loved to drink and according to both Frank and Jepson was 'dangerous in his cups', being prone to strike perfect strangers with his cane for imagined impertinences. But his biggest downfall was women. According to Jepson, he was not a romantic but a 'pagan lover', who frequently promised marriage to his various paramours without thought of or reference to his family before disappearing off with her for so long as the infatuation lasted.[19] His antics drew the attention of the dons and he was sent down in 1886 for having lived outside college for two terms without permission, though whether as the result of women, alcohol or a combination thereof is unclear.[20] Both Frank and Jepson recorded his dismissal as a great loss.

But Frank's most perilous association was not with Ion. Since Winchester, his Achilles' heel had been his need for an intimate male friend, and, banned from corresponding with Lionel, the object of his affection at Oxford quickly became Charles Sayle. Initial impressions were not great. Frank recorded that Sayle was 'a ridiculous creature of 19 who looks about 14, with a piping treble voice'. He was effeminate, 'about 5 ft. high, of fat & ruddy countenance'.[21] In youthfulness, his resemblance to Lionel Johnson was uncanny and caused him similar difficulties: he still looked nineteen when he was thirty. But, unlike Johnson, Sayle was warm-hearted and Frank quickly charmed. Within a couple of weeks, after two hours spent walking and talking together on matters 'personal & philosophic', Frank recorded that Sayle was 'most kind-hearted & very nice to talk to. His father just dead was a Cambridge professor: I was glad to talk to him tho I don't know that I felt much merrier afterwards.'[22]

What possessed Sayle to tell Frank his deceased father had been a Cambridge professor when he was actually a draper in the city is not known. Perhaps he thought Frank would look down on him for it. Had he known Frank better, he wouldn't have worried. Frank's lack of merriment was due to the situation with Lionel, which was just drawing attention at Winchester, and nothing to do with any deficiency in Sayle. In fact, for the rest of that term and on their return to Oxford after Christmas, Frank was increasingly in Sayle's company. By the end of January, Frank wrote in his diary that Sayle was 'the most loveable & warm hearted of men'.[23] Like Lionel, Charley (as he quickly became) was poetic and had started the literary paper *The Leaflet* at Rugby with his school friend Jack Badley. At Rugby also, Sayle later confessed, he 'woke up' to his own 'true nature' in the letters of an older boy which he 'lived in', week by week for two years until he went up to Oxford.[24]

Charley and Frank talked about all manner of things: 'ourselves, our schools, our philosophies'. Their conversations quickly became confidential: 'we talked long & deeply & really,' Frank wrote in February. Their friendship, he felt, 'would prove a firm true & lasting one'. Like

Frank, Charley had suffered loneliness and grief. The death of his brother in 1878 had been particularly hard. Yet he was inspiring: 'it is marvellous how that man spreads abroad the milk of human kindness,' Frank observed, and took him further into his confidence by showing him his letters from Lionel and St George.[25] Presumably, Charley's reaction was favourable, for within weeks Frank had hit upon a solution to his problem with Lionel that would allow him to maintain contact without technically breaking the ban on their communication: he had Charley write in his place, establishing a strange three-way communication that made up a substantial part of *Winchester Letters*.

At first this seemed the perfect solution, but Lionel's letters to Charley sometimes made difficult reading for Frank. When Lionel wrote about his wretchedness at the 'state of separation and isolation that is forced upon me' and asked Sayle to give Frank his love and tell him 'that I am never forgetful of his having been the chosen minister to me of the truth, that I am really with him in spirit', Frank was unable to contain himself.[26] Despite having never told Lady John of the ban, he wrote asking her to plead his case with Lionel's father. Lady John's answer was not favourable: 'why had I not told them who knew & understood me best (God! how ironical the words sound): & why had I been so conceited as to go about corrupting youth with my opinions! Oh, well, I ought to have known it would be so.' In less than a week, Frank had written to Lionel anyway, a letter he would send 'in spite of any opposition for I think he *ought* to have an answer, and that the need is stronger than any other objections to the contrary'. He also convinced Charley to write to Lionel's father. The reply was 'kind but hopeless'. So, Frank instructed Charley to arrange with Lionel that they should visit him in Winchester, which they did in April 1884. To Frank's delight, Charley was 'struck with him just as I hoped & has acknowledged to me how high, exulted, pure & holy [Johnson's] noble spirit is: he tells me that he feels as I do, ready to fall down & worship him, & as if it was presumptuous to know him at all'.[27]

After four months of enforced separation, this meeting should have left a satisfied afterglow. But for reasons known only to himself, Frank chose this moment to offer Charley a few home truths on what he saw as his key character flaw: Charley had 'the kindness of hearts that makes one rejoice in his presence' but was arrogant, lacking in 'what Christian theologians call Repentance and abasement of himself to himself'. This is an extraordinary statement from one who was so often blind to his own conceit and gives a real insight into how pious Frank had become. Having observed the failing, Frank felt it his duty to point it out for Charley's own improvement, but his intervention was clumsy and Charley devastated. Two pages of self-flagellation follow in Frank's diary: 'If you had your due you would be beaten with knotted handkerchiefs & cut by all your friends for the many wounds your damnably cruel words are ever inflicting on the sensitive soul of one who so marvellously overflows with universal kindness & love.' He begged Charley's forgiveness, only to declare it too superficial to touch the depths of his self-pity when it was readily given.

Charley's was 'a careless of view of sin'. Lionel would understand – 'he has learnt Repentance & known self-torture'.[28]

Or had he? The very next day, the foundations of Frank's world shook as rumour reached him of some 'immoral' behaviour on Johnson's part, of sufficient gravity that there were calls for him to leave Winchester. Frank could not believe the 'terrible charges' – 'I reverence & trust too deeply, but like all the powers of hell, they seize me in their hideous grasp.' Not knowing specifics and powerless to approach Lionel directly, what could he do but accept Charley's forgiveness and dispatch him to write immediately on his behalf? The reply, when it came, was less than satisfactory. It was not wise to commit to paper anything that might be incriminating and Lionel skirted the facts, possibly assuming that Frank already knew them or would at least be able to follow his reasoning. From the next entry in Frank's diary, it appears neither were the case: '[Lionel] acknowledges what the world would call sin, I know not exactly what he means, he defends it by saying it is not sin to him, he does not know what sin is.'[29]

The facts, which to this day remain somewhat obscure, have been pieced together by Johnson scholars to produce a range of scenarios based on different interpretations of the letter he sent Sayle in response to Frank's turmoil. The most extreme reading is that Lionel was involved in sexual activity with other college men, leading to the largely unsubstantiated conclusion that 'in his last two years in College Johnson was one of the leaders of a homosexual circle'.[30] The most open interpretation, and probably most reflective of Johnson's personality, spirituality, ethics and aestheticism, is that Lionel was beginning to appreciate sensuousness as a distinct quality. He had been reading *The Imitation of Christ* – a pious work which offered advice on how to live a Christian life, encompassing such suggestions as 'Whatever a man cannot amend either in himself or in others he ought to bear patiently, until God orders things otherwise'[31] – and was now applying that advice to the judgment of his fellow college men. 'After reading *Thomas à Kempis* I can listen with no disgust to sensual conversation: I can return freely to walk over the downs,' he wrote; it was not that he shared their passion, but that it did not touch him. In an extraordinary statement of moral tolerance for its time and in one so young he said further that no one could excite his loathing or indignation: 'As I love the simple nobility of the literature, the beautiful world of nature, so I can take pleasure in the thoughts and minds of other natures.' He concluded that it was not for him – even as a prefect – to determine what punishment (if any) should be handed down to those who chose to express themselves in sensual or sexual behaviour, but God's. He appreciated that this view brought him 'very near to infringement of the world's – especially the school world's – ten commandments' but that having come to this conclusion, his principles forbade him to act otherwise. He had told the headmaster as much and Dr Ridding, though understanding and sympathetic, rather prophetically declared that Lionel would not remain 'unspotted in the world' if he took such a position.[32]

Johnson cared not a jot for the world and its opinions, and the significance of this event in recalling it here is not so much its facts as its impact on Frank. For while this was probably music to Charley's ears, as a man who had struggled with his own 'true nature' and was regarded as 'compulsively and permanently homosexual' before he left Rugby,[33] for Frank it was barely believable:

> My basis of morality totters ... I cannot understand, is it my blindness? or am I right in my moral code? I should say so unhesitatingly to anyone else, but when one so infinitely above me as J... says thus, I hardly dare resist.[34]

What a quandary. Was Lionel slipping from his exalted position or demonstrating yet another example of his higher spiritual evolution? Frank's world view was always coarser than Lionel's. He had already confessed that Lionel was 'immensely above us, or me anyway, & I feel a little hopeless about him. C[harley] is satisfied & says he understands him.'[35] It bothered Frank when his own very black-and-white morality was threatened or when Lionel led where he struggled to follow. In a desperate attempt to re-establish some sort of equilibrium, he set about getting to the elusive facts, inviting a visiting Wykehamist, Hugh William Orange, to tea, to 'extract the world's view' of Lionel. It was not consoling: 'as bad as could be' was how Orange described Lionel's conduct, and 'known to the world'. To Frank, it remained 'inexplicable', though he no longer had the consolation of disbelieving what he heard.[36] He kept what Orange told him to himself. But if Frank thought it would end his and Lionel's differences, he was wrong. Lionel's letters soon became alarming in a new way. He was 'working himself up into an enthusiasm for the priesthood' and Frank 'could not help denouncing the falseness & weakness of such a position' which was based, in his view, on expediency, not faith.[37] Johnson, however, was determined that this was his right course and tried to convince his friends to do likewise: 'Why not become a priest?' he wrote to Sayle on 30 May.[38] As Lionel's differences with Frank intensified, he leaned more towards the understanding Charley: 'Do come here on the 28th of June,' he wrote, adding, 'Do you think Russell would understand, if I said I would rather have you alone this time? Don't either of you misunderstand me! but you won't, of course.'[39]

Whether Frank understood or not, he would do everything in his power to prevent it. Desperate to maintain his connection with Johnson, he tried to read the poems of Walt Whitman, which Lionel was then enthusing over, but it was not easy: *Leaves of Grass* 'breathes of nature & is a very catholic production' but Frank could not trust it 'because of the strong undercurrent of sensuality I seem to detect all thro' it'.[40] Restoring direct communication with Lionel became Frank's preoccupation. He finished his term at Oxford and, after a brief stopover at PL, set off on an epic bicycle tour (without the benefit of pneumatic tyres) around the south-east of England, culminating some 250 miles and six days later at Winchester in time for the annual Eton match. Afterwards, he talked with Lionel at length about the priesthood. They tolerated each other's opinions but remained at odds.

It soon became apparent that while at PL, Frank had again leaned on Lady John to intervene on his behalf with Captain Johnson. After Winchester, he went to London to spend summer with the Stanleys in high spirits and high hopes of a resolution. At the beginning of July, Lady John wrote to say she would write to Captain Johnson 'if there is a mutual promise not to talk of anything J's father would disapprove of'. Frank 'absolutely refused to make any condition'. Perhaps he sensed that Lady John would weaken under his resolve. He settled into life with the Stanleys with an apparently light heart. He involved himself with Aunt Maude's girls' club, went to the House of Lords with Lady Stanley, and talked with Aunt Rosalind about women's suffrage and with Aunt Blanche about all manner of things social, religious and political. Blanche took him to meet the 'very agreeable' Robert Browning and at Thomas Sanderson's new bookbinding business in Maiden Lane he was introduced to William Morris's daughter, May. Sanderson had by then married Annie, the daughter of radical politician Richard Cobden, and henceforth adopted the name Cobden-Sanderson – 'Cobbie' to his friends. Within a week came the news that Frank's stubbornness had paid off. Lady John had written and Captain Johnson agreed that Frank and Lionel's correspondence be renewed to their 'mutual advantage'. Frank wrote to his friend at once, 'my heart thrilling with a deep, silent joy'. 'At last,' replied Johnson, before at once picking up again their prior discourse. To Captain Johnson, Frank expressed his thanks, adding 'that I was not as wicked as I was painted' and received in reply the captain's hope that 'I may now depend upon you both and trust I may never have reason to regret the confidence I place in you'.[41]

The rest of the summer was spent in visits of one kind or another. Inexplicably (unless it was due to the Stanleys' intervention), the first was to Jowett at his private Oxford residence, where Frank spent a very dull week mostly alone or with Jowett's assistant while the master worked. He then returned to PL where he whiled away the hours reading Ouida and longing for Lionel: 'Dear Lionel, he is restful, & I love him with a strange yearning that feels itself unable to approach him – unworthy boy as other men dare to call him.'[42] He visited the Dicks in Winchester and found Lionel still there. They talked, but 'not much about anything – we know so well where we differ that there is not much room left for discussion'. It was an early illustration of how narrow their sympathies actually were. Johnson's whole life was spiritual and literary. He cared nothing for mathematics or science, as Frank did, or the philosophies of Mill and others that Frank discussed with his university friends. Frank, on the other hand, was finding *Leaves of Grass* 'better every time I read it'. He purchased a copy and posted it to Lionel.[43] But he would not let the matter of Lionel's ambitions drop. In August, Lionel wrote to Charley, 'Frank has just treated me to some vulgar inanities about being an Independent Minister: oblivious of things temporal and ignoring things eternal', adding a little dig at Frank's theosophy: 'Truth as an absolute known quantity or quality is not to be found: Madam Blavatsky may have found it in miraculous tea cups but hardly so as to preach it in Westminster slums.'[44]

In the autumn, Lionel returned to Winchester and Frank and Charley to Oxford. The three men kept up their correspondence – agreeing on some things, disagreeing on others – and during the Christmas vacation Frank spent a few days with Lionel's family in north Wales, before taking him to PL. Then, in April 1885, Lionel visited Frank at Oxford and was introduced to all his friends. Lionel was ecstatic at their reception and afterwards wrote to Jack Badley in raptures over the fellowship and love he was shown. He had never known such fraternity: 'Brotherhood is God,' he wrote.[45] All seemed well.

But such periods of calm were never long-lived where Frank was concerned. In May 1885, in an extraordinary turn of events, his own morality was suddenly called into question. He described in *Life* how one day without warning he was summoned by Jowett. Word had reached the master of a letter – a 'scandalous' letter – written by Frank to another undergraduate. It would be better for all, Jowett suggested, if Frank voluntarily went down for a month as punishment for such 'disgusting' behaviour and then return to sit his *moderation* exams when the dust had settled. Frank was incensed. He denied the accusation and 'being possessed by that white virginal flame of innocence' demanded to see the letter. Jowett, it seemed, could not produce it. Nor could he say what it contained; though he had it on good authority from the Warden of Merton that it existed. Frank demanded a formal inquiry. Jowett refused. Frank completely lost his temper, told him he was 'no gentleman', that he was 'behaving in an autocratic way, indefensible even in the head of an Oxford College' and that he refused to have anything more to do with him. Jowett retaliated with a year's suspension. Frank refused to accept the punishment, saying he would sooner take his name off the college books than acquiesce to such humiliation over something he had not done. He stormed out. And just like that, his Balliol career was over.[46]

Had Jowett been understanding or fair-minded like Ridding, Frank later said, they could have discussed the matter and Jowett would have seen his error. Had Frank had the cool detachment of Johnson, he might have been able to reason his position. But Jowett was obstinate and refused to accept he had made a mistake, and Frank was enraged and refused to retract his personal comments or accept the injustice. Frank left Oxford, 'accompanied to the railway station and seen off by scores of enthusiastic friends and defiantly wearing in my buttonhole the white flower of a blameless life'.

7

A Very Improper Friend

Or did he? When Santayana read Frank's account of his sending down, he dismissed his *virginal flame of innocence* as 'a cheeky lie, when so many of his readers know the facts'; the *white flower* provoked the reaction, 'Good God! No doubt he wore a white buttonhole. It was aestheticism à la Bunthorne, then prevalent in Oxford, where Oscar Wilde's influence was recent.' The whole account he declared 'a complete falsification of the events as told me by Russell himself'.[1] No doubt, the letter *had* existed – Frank had told him about the Warden of Merton finding it – but the chief point as far as Santayana was concerned was that when Lionel Johnson visited Oxford in April 1885, he had stayed overnight in Frank's rooms, that the authorities had seen them together and had declared Johnson too young to be Frank's 'natural friend'.[2]

What might have led them to such a conclusion? Aside from Johnson being almost a foot shorter than Frank – who when dressed in his loose sack coat, tan trousers and straw boater looked like 'an aesthetic cavalry officer, 6 feet tall but limp'[3] – a clue to their reaction might be found in Jowett's Greek syllabus. In *Hellenism and Homosexuality* (1994), Linda Dowling suggests that by subjecting students to Plato, Jowett had unwittingly brought into focus the sacred and erotic nature of knowledge-sharing – particularly between an older and younger man. In certain quarters this idea had flourished, and within a minor faction at Oxford, the idea that *paiderastia* was anything other than a natural extension of brotherhood was swept away, revealing male love as something more noble and ennobling than 'an exploded Christianity and those sexual taboos and legal proscriptions inspired by its dogmas'.[4] This had been the strict opposite of Jowett's intention. He had to some degree foreseen such an eventuality, but tried to control it by reasoning that the love Plato described was purely spiritual. In a letter written the year before Frank's sending down, Jowett had stated that Platonic love was 'the mystical love of men for one another – the union of two human souls in a single perfect friendship' but not necessarily to be encouraged. Such friendships 'make us know what is in us ... [but] are very likely to become foolish and only by great care is it possible to avoid this'.[5]

There is no mistaking what Jowett meant by 'foolish'. He might not have experienced this love himself, but he had previously been put in the position of having to police it when, in 1874, the critic Walter Pater, then a Fellow at Balliol, became enamoured with an undergraduate, William Money Hardinge. This episode is interesting to recall in relation to the situation Frank now found himself in, both in the accusations made and the manner in which Jowett acted. Pater was said to have written some amorous letters to Hardinge, and Hardinge to have boasted of his relations with Pater to his friends. Hardinge also enjoyed shocking friends with his erotic poetry and generally revelled in his reputation as the 'Balliol Bugger'. Whether this reputation was deserved or whether Hardinge was simply posturing is uncertain, but Jowett was made aware of the letters and acted by supposedly blocking Pater's future promotion and convincing Hardinge to submit himself to rustication for the remainder of the academic year 'without any fuss or public inquiry'. Hardinge complied and was then allowed to return in November 1874 to finish his degree. Jowett subsequently befriended him, was said to be delighted when he won the Newdigate Prize for Poetry in 1876, and Hardinge, in his gratitude for the prudential manner in which Jowett had treated him, wrote and published an appreciation of him by way of obituary.[6]

Jowett's reaction was regarded as typical. He was considered firm but fair: 'Though he did not spare you in private, he stood between you and harm in public.'[7] He believed there ought to be a statute of limitations on indiscretions: 'I am strongly against the errors of young men being visited upon them several years afterwards, if they have changed their ways.'[8]

This last comment was written specifically about Frank at a point in his future when Jowett was called upon to act in friendship. It will be considered in due course. But for the time being, the significance of Jowett's statement is that he thought it necessary that Frank 'change his ways': the question is, in regard to what? Ion Thynne's indiscretions have shown that the dons demanded to be treated with respect. Jowett, it is known, was primarily concerned with Balliol's reputation and the avoidance of negative publicity. As such, there is little doubt that Frank's explosive reaction and demand for an inquiry made it impossible for Jowett to act with anything like the sympathy he had shown Hardinge. But what remains curious is that thus far, Frank had not been proved guilty of any misconduct beyond allowing Lionel to stay overnight in his rooms. Was this, in combination with Frank's attitude, a grave enough offence to warrant a permanent sending down?

Santayana's published account reports with certainty that Johnson was the 'innocent cause' of Frank's dismissal and that the ferocity of Frank's reaction was due to the fact that the accusation involved his beloved friend.[9] In his private notebook, he recorded his thoughts about Frank and Lionel's relationship, concluding that it was in no way improper 'in the material sense'. Their relations had not been 'in the least erotic or even playful'. Rather, their effusions were 'Shelleyesque' and might have flowed from 'two Polish poets, planning a fresh creation of the universe'. They conspired against authority, 'denied the right of God or man to check the movement of their transcendental souls', but did not debase their higher commune with ignoble physical relations. He dismissed the authorities' interpretation of Frank's guilt as the 'prying, gossiping, obscene, nature' of dons 'gloating on the scandals that reached them' and 'venting their bottled rage against the rebellious youth' by pretending to 'the tenderest prudence' while 'inventing a story to suit their vilest instincts, and imposing it on the public, by innuendoes, as the sad truth'. Yet, in addition to the implication within this statement that Frank's behaviour was notorious enough for there to be stories that *could* make their way back to the dons, he also contended that Frank's 'early obscenities' *had* existed.[10] So, what else did he know or guess?

There are several notable difficulties in getting anywhere close to facts in a case such as this. Firstly, nothing was written down that could be potentially incriminating due to the consequences if it got into the wrong hands. Victorian society was repulsed by male same-sex relations. Any evidence of such was punishable by up to two years' imprisonment with hard labour, even without physical evidence of actual penetration.[11] Secondly, the diversity of relationships found in all-male schools and universities confused matters: 'There was innocence and depravity, and all the intervening gradations of distinction ... Romantic, sacrificial friendships and rabid sensual lusts all went on in the same community together.'[12] Not only that, but often the manner in which these relationships were expressed in writing was remarkably similar, whether sexual or not. Platonic love, in particular, expressed itself with 'high personal passion ... imagination exalting the soul, instead of flaming the senses'.[13] Arguably, the more acceptable same-sex relationships have become, the more the subtle distinction between the Victorian (homo)sexual relationship and romantic friendship has been lost. Conversely, Victorian propriety and laws made it imperative that homosexual practices be veiled in secrecy, with Plato and others providing a coded language that 'when combined with an ethos of spiritual comradeship' allowed 'nameless and ineffable' desires to be expressed and experienced without taint.[14] How, then, can one accurately determine the true meaning of anything written unless it be explicit?

Further difficulties arise from the fact that Frank's diaries covering his final year at Oxford have not survived. By his own admission, they were destroyed sometime between his sending down and his second court appearance in 1896; though this, he asserted, was because they were embarrassingly childish in content, not because they were incriminating.[15] Further, the diary that has survived covering the period February to July 1884 is not in Frank's handwriting. It was transcribed sometime between 1891 and 1896 by Frank's then secretary and mistress, Mary Morris.[16] This is both interesting and potentially problematic. Why would he have her transcribe an old diary if not to conceal or change facts that might publicly embarrass him? And how can such a document be relied upon? The simple truth is that on its own it cannot. The picture drawn in the last chapter of Frank's innocence awoken and his morality challenged may be based on pure fabrication. But taken in conjunction with other documents, a scenario does emerge – it will be down to each individual reader to decide the likely truth of it.

In May 1885, after his initial meeting with Jowett, Frank wrote to Lionel for advice. Lionel wrote a long letter in response.[17] Everything here quoted from it, Frank culled from the version published in *Winchester Letters*. Lionel began (somewhat surprisingly) by congratulating Frank on his sending down – 'You will now be able to assert yourself,' he said, and 'being in the right, you will be perfectly happy.' But as regards the charges of immorality against him, Lionel wanted to know, 'Do they mean to pin definite acts upon you or merely cast your general ideas and manner of life against you?' He declared himself 'very downcast' for the effect this would have on Frank's family and suggested that if the authorities could point to definite acts, Frank had no choice but to accept their judgment. If not, 'face them with Walt and Jesus'. The important thing was that Frank should not lose faith in their ideals – 'that is all'. He offered Frank the consolation of his support. 'As for Charlie,' he continued, 'this will be good for his soul: it is a tangible situation in which he must be firm one way ... Still the infinite triviality of the affair confuses me: how can the Warden of Merton and Spooner etc. actively concern themselves in the matter of your morality?'

This reference to 'Charlie' is the first indication that the charges against Frank involved someone other than Lionel and of course refers to Charles Sayle – 'Charley' – despite the variant spelling. Was it to him, then, that the mysterious letter was written? Is that why Lionel refers not just to Brodrick, Warden of Merton, but also William Spooner, Warden of New College, where Sayle was an undergraduate?

Lionel's advice continued that Frank should not be carried away or obstinate: 'Be simply indifferent: show that you cannot and will not dishonour yourself by accepting their dicta and dogmata.' He suggested Frank tell his family that his life was 'rapidly becoming impossible, without more freedom' – 'leave Oxford as soon as you can, leave everything: go somewhere, and do what you like'.

How Lionel ever thought Frank would be able to have this conversation with his guardians is unclear. When Rollo arrived in Oxford, summoned by the authorities, he gave Frank no opportunity to explain, but merely flung himself into a chair in Frank's room and exclaimed in a tragic PL tone: 'Oh, Frank.' 'If this was his attitude before he had even asked for one word of explanation,' Frank afterwards wrote, 'I had no desire to have any more truck with him, so my only answer was to say: "If you feel faint you had better have some sal volatile." That finished our relations.'[18]

Lionel's advice continued with the vain hope that Frank might 'dismiss whatever insults your own soul'. In the full arrogance of youth, he advised turning to their new prophet-poet Walt Whitman and away from the outdated bigotry of the Oxford dons, 'the hatefullest enemy of the light: the Christian virtue that is keen scented after vice'. Not that he was trying to excite Frank to 'headstrong rebellion'. If Frank's conscience accused him, then 'don't be hypocritical, don't swear you are innocent: *mea maxima culpa* is your fitting formula'. At best, he continued, if Frank was compelled to leave Oxford, 'none of your friends worth the name will consider you unclean … and then all this miserable folly will be at an end. You will be your own master legally very soon. Spiritually, really, we are always our own masters…' He asked, just once, 'Has my name turned up again?' but knew, in reality, this was no longer about him, but about whatever had happened with Charley, which would always be open to speculation.

Frank, in desperation, reached out to all those he thought might understand and be able to influence Jowett, including Dick and Dr Ridding at Winchester. He dispatched Lionel to call on Revd Dickins to secure his support; but even Lionel felt the need for clarification before so doing:

I lunch with Daker on Sunday – one question – can you answer me by then? understand me: have you technically incurred legal penalties? don't be angry: you don't suspect me.[19]

What can be inferred by this reference to 'legal penalties'? Is he implying punishment for breaking the university's rules as to conduct, or the laws of the land? If his question related to Charley, their behaviour had already drawn attention. Rollo had written to Frank as early as March 1884 objecting to the fact that Frank did not 'associate with equals' when the only one of Frank's friends he had then met was Sayle.[20] Jowett likewise had cautioned Frank on his choice of friends: 'I have not the least wish to dictate to you who shall be your friends, but I hardly think that you see the effect of some kind of friendships on yourself or on those who are the objects of them.'[21] And even more damning, his and Charley's behaviour had drawn the attention of their peers: 'They behaved sentimentally, even in public; at a concert R. & S. sate [*sic*] hand in hand.'[22]

The replies, when they came, were less than satisfactory; kind perhaps but otherwise useless. Lionel described Brodrick's as 'the most touching'; Ridding's as 'cruelly sincere … quietly satirical and practical and scarifying'. Others were 'blind, all blind'.[23] Dick sought further information, but Frank's evasive answers puzzled him – 'they don't understand it at all … Speak out, they all cry: guilty or not guilty? clear yourself, etc.'[24] But Frank either could not or would not give a clear account of himself at the risk of exposing either himself or others. Even the Daker was bemused. He was 'absolutely thunderstruck at the possibility of the charge'. He could not 'comprehend the fatuous folly of the authorities – provided that you were really, as he put it, innocent, which is a large word…'[25]

In *Life*, Frank said these men were not 'available' to help him, and in a certain sense that is true. His friends rallied, though some with more hesitation than others. Osman Edwards wrote to Lionel and 'seems disposed to take our side'.[26] Jack Badley 'confesses that he accepts the triumphant aspect now, but did not before' (Lionel's protestations on Frank's behalf appearing to have changed his mind).[27] But Harry Marillier immediately jumped to Frank's defence and went to him as soon as he was released from

Cambridge, quickly becoming the main point of contact between Frank and the friends he felt so cruelly separated from. Yet all was not quite over. After term ended and Frank's friends had returned to their family homes, Lionel wrote to Frank:

> Even far away in Wales, my dear mother has heard rumour of you ... [Dick] wrote her a magnificent defence of you, and I have assured her perturbed spirit with assertions of your true and catholic situation – without going into details. I think my people will give no more trouble.[28]

Lionel was wrong. Behind the scenes, Captain Johnson had once again been making enquiries, this time via a mutual friend of his and Jowett's, and on 5 July, Jowett had replied in 'the strictest confidence' that he considered Frank 'a very improper friend'; that he had sent him down for a year and, further, that he would recommend Captain Johnson 'forbid any further acquaintance between his son and Lord Russell'.[29] This was an extraordinary move from the man who had built a reputation based on fair-mindedness unless he genuinely believed that Frank was guilty of some immoral practice. Either way, the impact of Jowett's intervention was immediate. Within a week, Lionel had written to Jack Badley that his planned visit to Sayle was off: 'Neither can I go to Russell's.'[30] All communication between Frank and Lionel was once again banned, this time 'on pains of rejection and expulsion and disinheriting, etc'. Not only that, but Captain Johnson forbid the authorities at Winchester to pass on any correspondence Frank might try to send through them. In a final blow, Frank was asked to stay away from his beloved school. Lionel's penultimate letter sympathised and relayed the feelings of Frank's Winchester family:

> Dick is very kind – talked much to me – asserts his faith in your innocence of motives, if not in your acts – but considers himself bound in honour, as a public servant, – not to take personal feelings into account. Mrs Dick is terribly sad ... she seems heartbroken ... I have heard nothing as to Charlie, but have written to break off the visit, thinking that best. At the risk of seeming obtrusive, let me ask you whether you still think him worthy of your sacrifice?[31]

In what way exactly Frank had sacrificed himself for Sayle is unknown. Frank's only comment on the affair was a defiant letter written to Mrs Dick, in which he apologised for distressing them but said he had 'not the least intention of giving up my aspirations and hopes and ambitions, and as you say of ceasing to endeavour to do *exactly* what is right – as *I* see it':

> ... when they all reviled and abused me I had a moment when I felt as if it were no longer worth doing right and that I might as well justify their abuse. But it has passed ... You and those like you it is who enable me to bear up in spite of much misconstruing: for I doubt if even I should have the strength to stand firm if everyone disbelieved in me.[32]

As for Charley, he completely disappeared out of Frank's life until they met briefly in 1918 to share Lionel's correspondence for the publication of *Winchester Letters*.[33] He returned to New College in October 1885 apparently untainted, but carrying with him the secret that shortly due for publication was a volume of his romantic poems compiled over the summer and entitled *Bertha: A Story of Love*. He dedicated the volume to *Nostro Amori* (our love) and in it endeavoured to depict the feelings of one who had tasted 'the nectar of Love' but 'from whose hand that cup had been ruthlessly dashed'.[34] The volume, published in November 1885, was by Sayle's own admission a tribute to male love. Only one poem is dedicated – 'to E', Osman Edwards. Two more – 'Sea Song' and 'Étude en Réaliste' – were added latterly and singled out by John Addington Symonds as being the only ones with a 'virile consciousness' as if written from experience.[35] There is no evidence these or any others were written for Frank beyond timing and an obvious mutual affection. The authorities took great exception to the publication and Sayle, like Hardinge before him, agreed to be rusticated for the remainder of the academic year, returning in October 1886 to complete his degree. Charley's first action on his return was to ask Frank's old friend Maurice Davies to call. In January 1887, Davies and 'Long' Roberts obliged. Sayle took it as 'a sign that at least they had pity or at very least bore no ill will' – concerning what, he did not say.[36]

In 1893, Charley joined the staff at Cambridge University Library, where he remained for the rest of his life. His surviving diaries record his deep affection for the stream of undergraduates he befriended, often with the approbation of their parents, and with an ever-increasing disparity in age. On his death on 4 July 1924, his then intimate friend, A. C. Benson, wrote of him: 'He lived a very innocent life with books, music and beautiful young men ... what his emotions led to, I don't know. There was something tepid about it ... I expect S. was a homosexual person, perhaps of perverted fancies but blameless morals. He went about accosting beautiful girls & boys – feted them, caressed them, but did no one an ounce of harm.'[37]

Meanwhile, Frank sat and licked his wounds: 'My soul was filled with wrath and hatred and for at least six months afterwards I used solemnly to put on my [undergraduate] cap and gown every Sunday and sit in the garden and curse Jowett.'[38] But far from having finished with Oxford – and instead of removing his name from the books as he publicly declared – at the end of his year's rustication Frank wrote to Jowett asking to return. Jowett's reply was kind but firm: he could not readmit Frank to Balliol yet – 'even if I thought it right ... I am certain that the Fellows would not consent'.[39] In reply to a second appeal, Jowett regretted he could not give Frank a *bene discessit* to enable him to transfer to Cambridge with consent and approbation: if he did, he would be forced to write 'what ought to be forgotten and not written down'. He recommended Frank did not try for another college 'because your application would lead to enquiries, & if enquiries are made, to a refusal', but to wait for another year to let the dust settle.[40] By then, Frank had come into his inheritance. He would never submit to a second potentially humiliating refusal, but neither would he ever be free of the stigma attached to his name. For the time being, however, the final reflection fell to Lionel:

> It is only now that I fully realise the force of Shelley's invectives against 'custom' – how it enslaves and encircles and banalyzes – the Dicks full of love, tied by their official position – and so with all of us – none of us free agents, oppressors or oppressed: all under the domination of Frankenstein – it makes one laugh more than most other jests. And in ten years – how miserable this will seem. I am definitely cut off by facts from you and Sayle – Harry is looked upon askance – the general social communion of several others broken up – distrust and distress introduced – and for a nothing – because custom is violated and her virgin shame exposed as worthless. I can't write, I have no will to leave you with words of anything but peace – but damn the world at least.[41]

8

A Series of Adventures

On 29 September 1885, Oscar Wilde wrote to Harry Marillier:

Dear Harry,
Next week – I will be charmed – How do I get there? It sounds
  marvellous.
Why Ferishtah? Browning causa?
Ever yrs, Oscar.[1]

The letter was delivered to a semi-detached house of London brick in the village of Hampton, on the north bank of the Thames. It had been taken that summer, at an annual rent of £26, by one 'John Russell' and named (as Wilde correctly surmised) for Robert Browning's recently published volume of poems, *Ferishtah's Fancies*. Frank was not yet twenty-one and therefore too young to sign a lease, so rent for Ferishtah was paid in advance from his £400 annual allowance; and not the protestations of Rollo, nor the interventions of family friend and Lord Chancellor Lord Selborne, would reverse Frank's decision to take it as he dug in his heels and threatened concealment of the property's location if attempts were made to force him home. Frank did, however, accept Rollo's condition that he have a tutor of his guardians' choosing to live with him. They chose Graham Balfour, 'a very gentle person, perfectly upright, and of the most kindly disposition', who was a trained barrister and cousin of Robert Louis Stevenson.[2] After a wary start, the two men became good friends. They lived with two staff – a middle-aged general servant, Mrs Hall, and a boot-boy named William Harding, or 'Faithful William' as he would become known – and a cat – the first of many (Frank would never be without one again). A stream of guests called to keep alive the spirit of Oxford in the London suburbs. Ion Thynne, Edgar Jepson and others came up from Oxford, and Harry Marillier and Herbert Roberts from Cambridge; Harry it was who made the necessary invitation that would see the flamboyant figure of Oscar Wilde descend upon them on Wednesday 7 October 1885. 'Let us live like Spartans, but let us talk like Athenians,' Wilde dramatically suggested.[3] It would make a change from their usual occupations of boating on the river, or shooting bottles with Frank's derringer, or playing with the guinea pigs belonging to the girls next door.

For Frank, it was fun, but could never replace the loss of Lionel and Winchester or extinguish the self-pity that punctuated his anger at the injustice of his situation. He wrote to Mrs Dick (the only one of his elders to visit him at Ferishtah) that viewing himself objectively he'd decided he was 'such a good sort of fellow, but never able to run smoothly in harness':

> It is laughable enough, but at the same time occasionally painful; and I feel as if I should like some to know me inside, and explain to the world that I am not such a villain as I appear on the surface.[4]

He was not, he claimed, unhappy, but no number of jaunts up and down the Thames in his newly purchased steam launch, *Isabel*, would wash away the stigma attached to his sending down. For that, he needed to go further afield. Hence, in the manner in which things were then done, Frank was advised to go abroad to allow the passage of time to dampen rumours in his absence.

To this end Frank sailed from Liverpool with Balfour on HMS *Etruria* on 12 October 1885 bound for New York and a 'Grand Tour' of the United States. Over the next six months, the two men travelled over 8,000 miles coast-to-coast, by rail and steamer, observing and commenting on a country in the midst of the rapid industrialisation that would make it a world leader by the century's end.

Initial impressions were not great. Frank struggled to like New York with its 'disfiguring' billboards, loud advertisements and huge volume of traffic – mostly horse-drawn tramcars and cabs – constantly clattering through its cobbled streets. He found the hustle-and-bustle overwhelming and missed 'the dignified quiet of the lounge in an English hotel'. He called it 'a disgustingly untidy and unfinished city'.[5] Brooklyn Bridge and Central Park were open, but Ellis Island was not and the Statue of Liberty was yet to take up her station as light of the free world. Sanitary conditions had improved with sewage and waterworks, but tons of horse manure, dead animal carcasses and refuse still littered the streets. Crime rates were high, and newspapers reported that Frank would have been the victim of a 'Bunko sharp' as soon as he stepped off the boat had he not dismissed the man for daring to intrude upon him without an introduction 'without the faintest idea that the fellow was a rascal'.[6]

Boston was an improvement. There, Frank was 'most kindly and courteously entertained' in 'the American home of culture'; most notably by George Santayana, who was then an undergraduate at Harvard.[7] Frank was

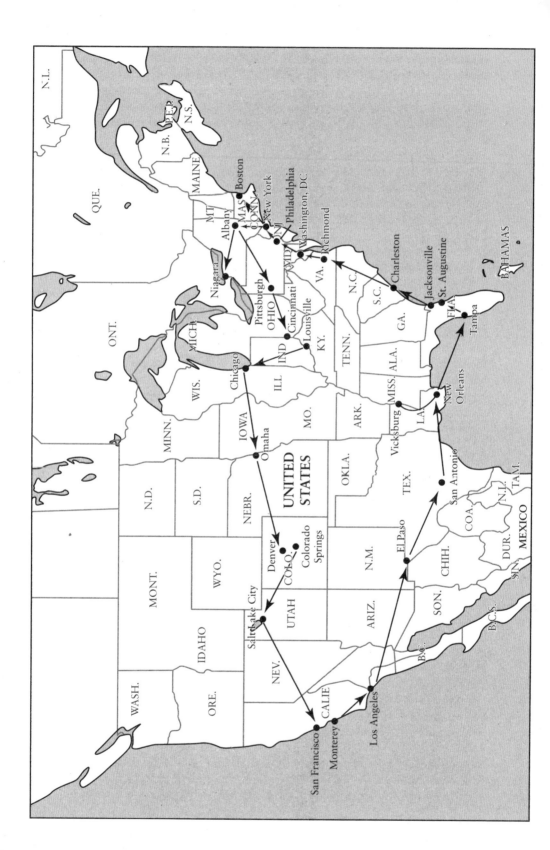

the first Englishman Santayana had ever encountered, which was significant in itself, but Santayana found Frank 'remarkable on his own account':

> He was a tall young man of twenty, still lithe though large of bone, with abundant tawny hair, clear little steel-blue eyes, and a florid complexion. He moved deliberately, gracefully, stealthily, like a tiger well fed and with a broad margin of leisure for choosing his prey. There was a precision in his indolence; and mild as he seemed, he suggested a latent capacity to leap, a latent astonishing celerity and strength, that could crush at one blow. Yet his speech was simple and suave, perfectly decided and strangely frank.[8]

The photograph of Frank taken during his tour and used on the cover of this book perhaps belies this description; as does Santayana's previous description of him being like a limp cavalry officer. Yet Santayana's captivation as Frank proceeded to seat himself, uninvited, in front of his new friend's poorly populated bookshelves, to read aloud Swinburne's *Poems* in a rhythmic, monotonous drawl that to his attentive listener made the English language 'like stained glass, an object and a delight in itself', meant that the two men were destined to be friends for life.[9] While Santayana spotted this instantly, Frank found the visit made him homesick: 'I begin rather to wish that I was still at Oxford, or saw any chance of going back there: such a sudden cutting off from all my pleasant societies and kind friends seems a little harsh,' he lamented, admitting at the same time that a man cannot 'offend his community and go unpunished'.[10]

Most other Americans Frank found uncongenial. He objected to being hailed 'Mister' and found them curt and 'only half-civilized' in their manners. With the exception of Harvard and an 'historic' visit to Walt Whitman at his humble home in New Jersey, it would not be until Frank reached French ('ergo pleasant & civilized') New Orleans and the southern colonial states that he would find American company agreeable. Many of the towns he visited – particularly Pittsburgh and Philadelphia – he found as offensive as New York. But their industry sparked his imagination. He stood at Niagara Falls 'calculating how much electricity they could be made to supply to New York & cities on route if they were kept constantly at it working dynamos'. In Buffalo, he admired a 'large grain elevator, capable of distributing grain at the rate of 20 thousand bushels a day'. In Pittsburgh, he marvelled at Andrew Carnegie's steelworks and in Chicago, went to see the 'fine pumping engines' of the city's waterworks. The Pullman Palace Car Company and the town built for its workers impressed him. Less palatable were the stock yards, so numerous as to give Chicago the epithet 'chief slaughterhouse of the world'. It was fortunate, Frank commented, that it being such a cold day 'the frost made such a steam that we could see nothing. But ugh! the smell was enough to make me all but ill.'

In early December, they headed out west by the Chicago, Burlington and Quincy Railroad, spending one day in Omaha before embarking on

Opposite: Map showing the route of Frank's US Grand Tour.

the 1,000-mile journey to Denver, where they walked the foothills of the Rockies and took sight-seeing excursions. Frank drove an American buggy to the Garden of the Gods – where he learnt that 'a horse will trot over a rotten wooden bridge full of holes without putting his feet into any of them' – and completed the ten-mile ascent to Pike's Peak on horseback to take in the 200-mile views across the plains to the east and mountain ranges to the west from a vantage point 14,000 feet above sea level. From Colorado Springs to Utah, they took the Denver and Rio Grande Western Railroad, which at nearly 2,800 miles was then the longest narrow-gauge railway in North America, rising to dizzy heights of over 10,000 feet in the Tennessee Pass. They followed the path of the Green River to the Mormon territory of Salt Lake City. Of Native Americans, Frank said virtually nothing (most likely through lack of contact) and of African Americans, apart from generally disliking the manners of those who waited on him in his various hotels, he commented only that those he later saw in New Orleans seemed 'to have a craven self-assertion ... as if in spirit they had not yet caste off the yoke of slavery'. Of the Mormons, however, he had much to say. His 'sense of injustice and indignation were very much aroused' by recent legislation against their practice of plural marriage which subjected any man deemed to have more than one wife to either a $300 fine or six months' imprisonment or both. As Frank saw it, the law forced each man to choose one wife and turn his others out as harlots; in the process turning the 'gentile' who enforced the law into a 'whoremonger pimp, and panderer'. He solicited private interviews with three women – mother, wife and daughter – all personally affected by polygamy, to fully understand their position and was interested to find them all keenly defend it. He concluded that the whole system was 'vulgar and unrefined, but certainly not immoral', taking into account the lower levels of prostitution in Mormon communities. In general, he concluded, 'Their faith intellectually is bosh – but their practice procures a community as vigorous & patient, & materially prosperous as Israel', suggesting this might be the real reason for their persecution. He was riled with the same sense of injustice that would see him take on a number of discriminatory and controversial causes throughout his political career, equally rationalised in accordance with his own self-determined morality.

Here, also, Frank had his first brush with the American press. In a humorous encounter, Frank's clothing – 'a coarse, gray and well-worn suit ... a slouch gray hat and flaming red necktie' – led a rather dubious reporter to wonder whether Frank really was an earl, or whether 'Earl' was his Christian name! Frank joked about it with another reporter in San Francisco, before cursing his 'confounded rank' and relationship to Lord John.[11] Reporters followed them everywhere. By the time they got to Texas, Frank's tolerance was exhausted. He curtly dismissed a reporter who revenged himself in print the next day by saying Frank had 'the appearance of a mudpile, and the manners of a mudlark'.

California, Frank liked. The 'delightfully lazy' inhabitants and the easy pace of life appealed to his inner lotus-eater. The 'armies of

Chinese' forever clipping, trimming, sweeping and raking around his hotel made it 'just like an English garden'. So impressed was he with their industry that he bought a Chinese boy to take home! Poor Quai Paak. The intelligent fourteen-year-old caught Frank's eye as he toured a missionary school in Monterey. Frank paid $50 for him with (so he said) the approval of his guardians back home. The boy travelled the whole width of the continent with Frank and crossed the Atlantic only to be promptly turned around and sent back again by a thoroughly disapproving Lady Stanley.[12]

On their return journey, Frank and Balfour passed through Texas (about which Frank had little to say apart from the tiresomeness of the long train journeys through 'alkali deserts, where nothing grows but cactus, & not always that'), journeyed 400 miles up and down the Mississippi (which was 'nothing but a broad sheet of filthy, muddy water, low banks & small trees crowded very close together' making the experience 'oh! so dull!') and crossed the Gulf of Mexico to Florida, where they took a small steamer up the Ocklawaha River to Silver Springs (an experience Frank actually did enjoy – 'the water is a lovely brown colour, & the fresh green of the trees which often brushed the boat on either side was delicious') before heading on towards Richmond, Virginia. In truth, Frank was tiring of his American exile and his thoughts went repeatedly to home. The river journeys suggested the idea of summer on the Thames. Frank even dared to hope that, with a little help from Mrs Dick, he might be able to convince Captain Johnson to allow Lionel to go along. But his return was still more than two long months away. Fortunately, the social demands of the old colonies kept him sufficiently distracted. In Washington he made the acquaintance of several politicians and in a wonderful period note turned up uninvited at the White House, knocked on the front door and secured an appointment for the next day with President Cleveland himself, whom Frank 'rather liked', finding him 'a rugged, firm and thoroughly *honest* man'. With Mrs Nancy Dyer, wife of the soon-to-be Governor of Rhode Island, Frank talked about Mrs Dick, whom Nancy had met when the Richardsons toured the US in 1876. She, in turn, 'really quite lost my heart' to Frank and afterwards begged Mrs Dick,

> Do try to influence him not to be so at warfare with the existing state of things in the world generally ... no one else seems to have any influence over him.[13]

Many women would find Frank attractive throughout his life; some (to their cost) would find him irresistible. But when one young lady who received him in Washington dared to suggest things were getting rather 'Darby and Joan' between them, it was time to leave: he was not ready to get tied down, and certainly not in the New World.

Back in England, Frank purchased a larger steam yacht named *Royal* – 50 feet in length, with a displacement of 11.5 tons and an advertised speed of 8 knots – and spent the summer navigating the Thames (without Lionel).

Then, in August 1886, with a small crew consisting of an engineer named Saunders, a mate called Parker, and 'Faithful William' – the boot-boy from Ferishtah – serving as cabin boy, Frank decided to cross the Channel to Belgium, where Mrs Dick was holidaying with friends. Among her party were two college men: Campbell Dodgson and Reginald Waterfield. Dodgson recorded Frank's shaky start, 'the precious yacht having stranded on a sand-bank near Margate'.[14] It was disappointing, but not, said Frank, his fault: the 'water-rat' he had taken on at Margate had been piloting the vessel. Frank had promptly sworn at him, sacked him, and, with 'the courage of ignorance' and 'self-confidence of youth', taken over as captain, teaching himself how to read charts and study tides, eventually arriving a week late.[15] He received Mrs Dick and friends proudly on board; Dodgson and Waterfield spent the night aboard before they parted company.

The next plan was more adventurous still. Frank steamed down the Kennet and Avon Canal to Newbury and spent much of the winter at Plenty & Son's watching workmen replace *Royal*'s engine with something more powerful, absorbing the atmosphere of the foundry and studying the manufacturing and installation processes involved. If his telegraphic system at PL was his introduction to engineering, his time at Plenty's was an apprenticeship for the various business ventures he would embrace in future years. But for now, he was more interested in getting the best out of *Royal* and, in the spring, tested her new engine on the Thames, around the south coast as far as Southampton and up the east coast to the Norfolk Broads.

On many of these trips Frank was accompanied by friends – principally Ion, St George and Jepson. Santayana, who was in England on what would become a habitual summer visit, also spent three days aboard *Royal* in April 1887. He would later describe the excursion fondly as the real beginning of their intimate friendship. Though rather neglected in Frank's memoirs, the importance of this friendship – particularly following Frank's severed connection with Lionel – should not be underestimated. Santayana was intelligent, observant and uncomplaining and therefore an ideal companion. His own upbringing had aspects as unconventional as Frank's and he was as independent in spirit as his new friend; though in all other respects he was as different a personality as could possibly be imagined.

Santayana was Spanish by birth but had grown up mostly in the US with his mother and half-siblings while his father remained in Spain. His mother, Josefina, had previously been married to Bostonian George Sturgis and had been left widowed with four children after only eight years of marriage. Her subsequent union with Agustín Santayana was occasioned as much by chance as necessity: they had been thrown together through their respective colonial lives. It was, according to Santayana, a rational rather than a love match and their subsequent decision to live on different continents appears to have been equally so: Josefina had long been committed to an American upbringing for her Sturgis children, while Agustín's loyalty was to Spain. He wanted his son to have a quiet and stable Spanish home, but the joint facts of his family's difficulties and the growing awareness of the comparative limitations of a Spanish education for the precocious 'Jorge', conspired against him.

Within three years of Josefina's departure, Agustín took the nine-year-old Santayana to Boston, left him with his mother, and returned home alone.

It was a culture shock for the young Spaniard. Urban Boston, puritanical in outlook, was a world away from the native simplicity of the ancient city of Avila. To begin with, Santayana spoke no English. When it came, it was with a 'purity of diction' that was neither American nor English but somehow 'mid-Atlantic'.[16] He felt alien, found early friendships difficult, described himself as 'solitary and unhappy, out of humour with everything that surrounded me, and attached only to a persistent dream-life, fed on books'.[17] At school, he cultivated a natural detachment, enabling him to take a certain pleasure and interest in the goings on of those around him, amusing himself with disinterested observations. Like Frank, he found affinities with the other men at university, but unlike him, remained somewhat formal and (interestingly reminiscent of Lionel) aloof. His early experiences and observations brought him to the conclusion – just as they had Lionel and Frank – that he needed to formulate his own moral code by which to live:

> I am ashamed and truly repentant if ever I find that I have been dazed and false to myself either in my conduct or in my opinions. In this sense I am not without a conscience; but I accept nobody's precepts traversing my moral freedom.[18]

The combination of these factors would form the basis of his philosophy. While he would always feel Spanish at heart and respect his Roman Catholic upbringing, he would never align himself to any country (though he lived in many), any cause, social or political, or any professional organisation. It was a fundamental difference between him and Bertrand, whom Santayana admired but later criticised for becoming embroiled in political activism. In fact, both Russells differed from Santayana in this respect. Frank attacked things head on and revelled in 'emotional strife and struggle', believing it brought out his better qualities, while Santayana described himself as 'never better entertained than when neglected'. As such, Santayana welcomed the freedom that Frank's absorption in his own affairs naturally afforded. The success of their friendship, he would say, was that he proved himself 'a sympathetic figure in the background ... capable of receiving impressions' without needing to make them.[19] He was not, therefore, 'a nuisance'; and in return, got to experience something of 'the frightful quotidian morass' that shaped Frank's life 'without getting his boots dirty'.[20]

That April, 1887, impressions received were marked, many and varied. Santayana watched Frank talk with workmen aboard *Royal*, flirt with a waitress (and a cat) at an inn and give the briefest attention to Lady John's letters before letting them casually fall to the floor 'as if into eternal oblivion'. He listened as Frank commented on newspaper reports, made complaints about the state of the world, his foolish relations, the folly of government, or the unfairness of bad weather. These things, Santayana observed, were 'the just perceptions and judgments of a young god to whom wrongness was hateful on principle, but who was not in the least disturbed about it in his own person'. They were admirable expressions of 'a transcendental spirit, fixed and inviolate in its own centre'.[21] He wrote to a friend at Harvard,

> I don't tell you anything about my adventures with him because I have to maintain with you my reputation as a philosopher, and in this respect I have quite lost my reason. When I am safely in Spain again, and can treat the matter objectively, I will make a full confession of my fall – from grace and self-control I mean and not into the Thames, although this also is mortifying enough.[22]

Poor Santayana! His fall into the Thames was pure slapstick. At Frank's suggestion, he had attempted to board *Royal* by running along the boat-hook, as Frank with his catlike agility had just then so easily demonstrated. Santayana knew he shouldn't, but Frank insisted. Santayana hesitated, wobbled and succeeded in falling into the river, pulling Frank in after him. Frank went 'head over heels, with a tremendous splash, which caused great laughter among the Sunday trippers lined up on the shore ... [and] flew into an indescribable rage', letting out an 'inexhaustible flow of foul words and blasphemous curses'.[23] Cut to the quick, Santayana assumed he had irrevocably humiliated Frank, but Frank it appeared had a short memory for such things and never mentioned the episode again. Normal relations were resumed and in another letter to America, Santayana enlarged on his admiration for 'the ablest man, all around, that I have ever met', describing Frank as a 'splendid creature' about whom 'I know I am making a fool of myself'.[24]

His fall 'from grace and self-control' and his 'making a fool of myself' were expressions he asked his friends not to misconstrue. He was referring specifically, he said, to allowing himself to be swept along by Frank's formidable and irresistible ego and talked to with the same insolence with which Frank spoke to servants and not minding. He was not (as he obviously thought they would or perhaps *had* concluded) talking about 'country matters'.[25] But while appealing to friends is one thing, controlling biographers it seems is quite another, and his comments (perhaps inevitably) provoked in the late 1980s speculation about his sexuality in the 1880s that now seems idle and irrelevant. Santayana's letters demonstrate an attraction that quickly turned into a deep devotion, but nothing more. Frank would not be aware of it for many years and would never reciprocate to the same degree.[26] He was incurious about Santayana's life and career and needed no great unanimity with him as he had with Lionel. He did, however, quickly take him into his confidence and – no small gesture on his part – demonstrated his respect for him by taking him to Winchester in June 1887 to show him his beloved school and introduce him to Mrs Dick. After which, the two men parted: Santayana to Germany, where he was studying, and Frank to the Norfolk Broads with St George and Ion Thynne.

It was at this time too that Frank relinquished Ferishtah in favour of Broom Hall – a rather neglected but much larger property in Teddington, further up the Thames. The house was situated about 200 yards above Teddington Lock. Though it hasn't survived, descriptions of it suggest it was an old-fashioned red-brick building with generous frontage, spacious without being large, and set in its own grounds. Frank spent a portion of his inheritance modernising it, wiring it for electric lighting, acquiring appropriate furnishings and filling its library with his father's books, his school classics and the latest scientific and engineering manuals. As a finishing touch, he brought in the Williamses – his parents' old servants – to run the place: Mrs Williams (his mother's beloved Lizzie) became housekeeper, Isaac was promoted from gardener to butler, and their two eldest daughters – Kate and Ellen – became housemaids.

This achieved, Frank began his next great adventure: a madly ambitious year-long Mediterranean cruise in *Royal*.

Setting off from Dover on 18 August 1887 were Frank, Ion and Jepson, with a crew of five and the inevitable ship's cat. Frank's previous engineer, Saunders, had proved too fond of drink and had been let go in the spring to be replaced by two men in their twenties: John Cockerton and Thomas Moyse. The only member of the original crew was Parker, retained as mate. Jim Cruden was employed as ship's boy and, at Cockerton's suggestion, William Aylott replaced Frederick Kast as cabin boy (Kast having held the position briefly after 'faithful' William left to join the Navy).

Both Frank and Jepson wrote accounts of their voyage and it is interesting to note how they differ in accordance with their respective personalities. Frank's is factual (greatly assisted by the logbook he'd kept), recording the dates on which they arrived and left each place, when and where people embarked and disembarked, the difficulties they faced with navigation and their aggravations with locals and crew. Jepson's is frivolous and reads more like that of a lads' holiday, embellished with colourful accounts of their various antics. Together, they make an arresting picture of a grand expedition that took them on a 3,000-nautical-mile round trip to Naples.[27]

Leaving Dover and skirting the south coast to Shoreham, they passed the pier head late on 23 August, setting a course for Cherbourg. Somehow in the night they drifted and when land was sighted the next day it was that of Alderney, some 23 nautical miles west of their intended destination. Oh well, said Jepson, no man becomes a sailor in a day; but Frank was disgruntled until he learned from other skippers that this was not uncommon for a Channel crossing. He relaxed and managed the next leg to Jersey without event. There they stayed two weeks, waiting (according to Frank) for the fine weather necessary to facilitate the safe navigation of the inhospitable coastline that would take them around Brest and on to Bordeaux. According to Jepson, the delay was planned for a family visit and gave Frank enough time to fall in love with the young lady Jepson himself had wooed the previous year. Ah! sighed Jepson, if only she had returned Frank's interest and they had married, undoubtedly, he and not Mr MacDonald would have been the first Labour Prime Minister! But she was engaged to an officer of the garrison, and 'on such things as army men do the Destinies of Nations turn!'

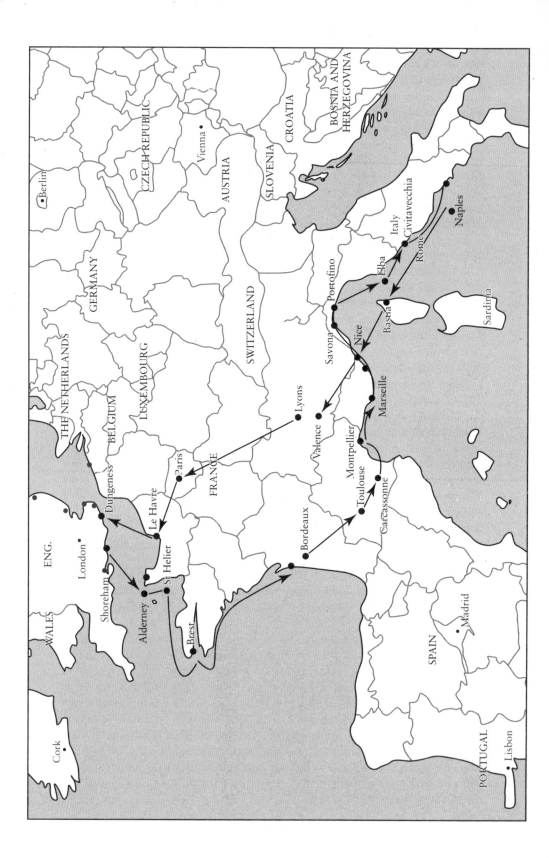

On 8 September, they departed for Brest one man down – Ion having left them to return to England. Frank set a course for Belle Isle (which they narrowly missed running into) before making a beeline for the mouth of the Gironde, nearly running down a fishing boat on route and arriving with no more drama at Bordeaux. 'But what a city! What wines and what food!' exclaimed Jepson. It was enjoyable, agreed Frank; particularly their excursion to Arcachon, where (Jepson explained) they explored the lagoons in the company of the president of the Bordeaux Yacht Club, ate oysters, swam in the river and frequented an amusing little music hall (a pastime Frank was known to detest).

After lingering there for a week, they embarked on the next leg of their journey, crossing France by canal to the Mediterranean port of Sète in the Gulf of Lion; first via the Canal Lateral and after Toulouse via the Canal du Midi. For this, Frank reported, they unstepped their mast and shifted their weight to bring *Royal* down at her head. At 50 feet, they just fitted into the admirably managed and perfectly kept locks. But ah! there were so many of them, complained the restless Jepson – one every few miles. And the lock-keeper was always at lunch, and the gates were *so* slow to open and the locks *so* slow to fill that each one meant an hour's delay. Jepson took to stripping off and swimming along behind *Royal* to burn up his frustrated energy. At the first big town they came to – Agen – Frank recorded the peculiar sensation of traversing the 32-foot-high aqueduct spanning 40 feet across the Garonne; Jepson, that they were mistaken for spies in the café where they went to play dominoes on account of Frank's Teutonic appearance. At Carcassonne, while Jepson enthused about the architecture, the theatres and galleries they had visited, Frank noted that 'the ship's boy fell overboard twice'. Then, when Jepson's restlessness (combined with a wager that he could not outstrip *Royal* for speed) found him running along the bank of the canal, underdressed and alone in the French countryside and arrested by a gendarme in search of an escaped convict, each man claimed himself the hero of the hour. To Frank, it was his air of pomposity and violent gesticulations, along with his French roared in an English accent over their insult to his friend, which rendered the gendarme 'paralysed with fear' and secured Jepson's release; to Jepson, it was his refusal to be led away and his determination that he would sit by the canal bank and allow the appearance of *Royal* to prove his story or hear what the British Consul had to say about it! Either way, it is highly doubtful that the villagers who gathered round to see the commotion were still talking about it fifty years after the event as Jepson claimed!

Skirting the Gulf of Lion, they arrived in Marseille at the beginning of October. Here Ion rejoined them and Parker was dismissed for drunkenness and replaced with a man named Linton. A new propeller was fitted to *Royal* and during the delay they frequented the *Café Glacier* on the Canebière, where they played dominos and drank rum sorbet cocktails, following local advice not to moor *Royal* too close to land if they wanted to avoid thieves and to not walk through the city without a revolver.

Opposite: Map showing the route of Frank's Mediterranean cruise.

At the end of the month, the weather turned foul and squalls that blew up as they rounded the coast to Cannes tossed the little boat about, threatening to sink her. It left both passengers and crew shaken and resulted in a bout of drunkenness that saw Moyse hit Cockerton and bloody his nose and the ship's boy, Cruden, desert through cowardice after Frank threatened to throw him overboard if he did not pull himself together. At Monte Carlo, heavy losses at the tables resulted in Jepson having to pawn his gold cufflinks. Frank 'lost all he wished to' – Jepson did not know how much but did witness £150 disappear in the space of ten minutes. A gloom settled over the party. At Savona, after a couple of drunken episodes – one in which Ion 'bethought himself of a wife' and nearly ended up on the wrong end of her lover's stiletto, and another in which he mounted a fountain in the marketplace to deliver an English 'revolutionary harangue' (fortunately unintelligible to most of those listening) – Frank thought it better that they part company and sent him home. The rest persevered along the Italian coast in short trips, necessitated by inclement weather and fortified by warm rum, eventually arriving at Civitavecchia. From there, Jepson and Moyse returned home. Left alone with a diminished crew who became increasingly harder to motivate as they sank further into drunkenness, Frank decided to give up the unequal struggle and on 15 December 1887 laid *Royal* up in Naples harbour, left Cockerton and Aylott on-board and returned home for the winter.

On 6 May, Frank, Moyse and a new mate, Bowles, returned to find (perhaps inevitably) that the engine had not been maintained and that Cockerton and Aylott had spent the majority of their winter carousing with the crew of other vessels in port. Frank's account of the return journey suggests multiple issues, especially with Cockerton, who apparently connived in the disappearance of the ship's cat, resorted to much drunkenness and threatened on one occasion to desert (and was only prevented from so doing by Moyse stealing his boots!). By the end of the month, they had crossed back to Marseille and taken on a pilot to help them navigate the Rhone. On 2 June, Santayana joined them at Valence as they travelled northward by river and canal – a journey which by all accounts was the most relaxing and 'lotus-eating' of them all. Frank and Santayana spent three weeks together without boredom or a cross word between them and with little aggravation from the crew, before parting company in Paris. From Le Havre, Frank re-crossed the Channel to Dungeness, the crew were paid off at Dover, and he arrived back at Broom Hall, proud of his achievement but no doubt exhausted, on 3 July.

There, he settled into the life of an aristocrat a little too strapped for cash to live in idleness.[28] He involved himself in the setting up of an engineering business in the grounds of Broom Hall with up-and-coming inventor James Swinburne. But if he thought this the pinnacle of his adventures as a young man, he was mistaken. He had not been home a year and was busily distracted with his new venture when one day a visitor was announced – an attractive and well-dressed lady of forty-four, accompanied by her twenty-year-old daughter, slender, sweet and demure. They called in the belief that they knew the gentleman residing at the hall, or perhaps were mutually acquainted. They were mistaken? They apologised. But could they stay and look over the grounds? They shared the young earl's passion for the river and would be only too happy to return the compliment if he would care to call on them one day soon at their residence in nearby Walton.

In no time at all, Frank found himself writing to Santayana with the news that he would soon be a married man:

> Could a happier eventuality have occurred? Did I not often say that marriage was my best hope of salvation...? Though no doubt the thing is common enough & may be seen every day, still the difference is that the touch of a warm human love has come to *me*, and swamps and sweeps away all cobwebs & ash-heaps in my brain ... If I ever told you I was satisfied with my situation before, it was a lie & a mere vain attempt to deceive myself.[29]

At last, real contentment was within his grasp.

9

Material for Incandescence

In Mrs Dick's parlour in November 1889, former prefect Captain Bray read Frank's palm and reported the following:

> [His] life to be compared to an ocean steamer driving through a heavy sea. Threatened at twenty or thereabouts, but character stronger than circumstances. Will weak, as in many strong characters, easily ruled – affection strong, but likely to be a trouble. *The* characteristic of the hand is that the marriage threatens to be the most troublesome feature of his life ... I foretell fifteen years of trouble in connection with his married life which will eventually end with his death at the age of forty.[1]

Given the fact that Frank's sending down occurred in his twentieth year and *was* the consequence of strong affections, one wonders what, if anything, he made of this prediction; not only concerning his early demise but (more pertinent just at that moment) the likely failure of his forthcoming marriage, then just three months away. His friends had kept a watchful eye over him in the interim. He had not long returned from his epic Mediterranean tour when Lionel Johnson wrote to Santayana, 'I incline to think it time for his drama of life to become critical in some way ... he does not appear to progress.'[2] Doubtless Frank never would progress again in a manner Lionel would admire, though their loyalty to each other never wavered. Indeed, as early as September 1886, Frank had told Dodgson that Lionel 'would not find him interesting now' as he has been 'in a state of mental torpor for the last year' – a condition somewhat relieved by his involvement with James Swinburne.[3]

Swinburne had ventured into electrical engineering in 1880 when Joseph Swan selected him to set up and manage a manufacturing plant for his incandescent lamp in Paris, following which he returned to England to become a technical assistant at Crompton's dynamo works in Chelmsford. By 1889, Swinburne had established himself as an inventor with thirty-three registered patents and numerous published articles on the design, manufacture and operation of a wide range of electrical equipment and was looking for the means to develop his latest invention: the *Hedgehog Transformer*. To this end Swinburne and Co. came into being, with himself as senior partner, draughtsman and technical director, Harold Sherwin Holt as manager, and Frank filling 'the humble but necessary position of taking care of the accounts and correspondence'.[4]

The company set up in a wooden shed in the grounds of Broom Hall in order to take advantage of Frank's electricity supply and in 1890 moved to their own buildings near the railway station in Teddington. Swinburne proposed Frank for membership of the Institution of Electrical Engineers and they started marketing the *Hedgehog* as 'rapidly superseding the clumsy, inefficient, closed circuit transformer', a claim that Swinburne failed to realise in anything but theory. Nevertheless, the company diversified into wattmeters, voltmeters and galvanometers which they took to the Electrical Exhibition at the Crystal Palace in 1892. But these, like many of Swinburne's electrical inventions, proved 'commercially problematic' and the company failed to generate sufficient sales to be profitable.[5]

Frank, however, had thrown himself into the endeavour and was revelling in his new status as a gentleman of business. He had also maintained close links with Plenty's of Newbury, becoming chairman when it was incorporated in 1890. There was a marked change in him. Early in 1889, Dodgson reported to Lionel that Frank was 'very amiable & much more civilized than he used to be'.[6] On the surface he seemed fulfilled; deep down he still was not.

It was in the spring of that year that the previously mentioned uninvited callers changed the course of his life, if not for the fifteen years Captain Bray predicted then certainly for the next dozen. Maria Selina Elizabeth, Lady Scott – known to friends as Lina[7] and to more intimate acquaintances as Bo – and her daughter Mabel Edith, whom she affectionately nicknamed Babs, called under the pretence that they were known to Frank and quickly secured the promised return visit:

> I went to Walton and found the ladies living in a tumble-down, rambling, creeper-clad but rather attractive house called 'The Hurst', and I was petted and fussed over there in a very attractive manner. There were other visits, there were launch expeditions together...[8]

These not only included 'Bo' and 'Babs' but also Lady Scott's elder daughter, Lina Mary, known to the family as Giddy, who two years previously had married stockbroker Dick Russell (no relation) and lived in Windsor. The Dick Russells were frequent visitors at The Hurst and equally welcoming. Soon, Lady Scott announced that she was thinking of installing electric lighting. Would Frank look into it for her?

> I threw myself into the project with enthusiasm ... In consequence I naturally became a frequent visitor to the house, and the acquaintance rapidly developed.

Frank became part of the family:

> We were always having meals together, making expeditions together on the
> river, driving together, or playing lawn-tennis, and it was not long before
> I began to look upon Mabel with a growing affection.

She was 'exquisitely beautiful, particularly in her figure', which was slender
and athletic. She was lively and fun-loving, played the banjo and violin
and was admired by all who knew her. Indeed, Frank's attentions were not
the first she had received. In 1884, when Mabel was just fifteen, she was
rumoured to have caught the eye of Lord James Douglas, brother of the
Marquess of Queensberry and uncle of the soon-to-be infamous 'Bosie',
who made several proposals, all of which she declined. Yet while Douglas's
advances were rejected, Frank's were apparently not quick enough:

> So one evening, when we were alone, Mabel explained to me that we were
> getting rather conspicuous, and that people were beginning to talk, and she
> thought it would be better that we should not see one another again. The
> dodge is an old one, but it worked perfectly, and I left the house an engaged
> man.

Yet all was not quite as it should be:

> I remember very well that the next day when I went down to see my old
> friend, Mrs Dick, at Winchester, I felt quite clearly in my heart that the
> thing was a mistake ... but I was very lonely, not at all happy, and Mabel
> was certainly very attractive, so I took no steps.

His misgivings concerned the Scotts' *modus vivendi*. They moved in very
different circles and 'lived like butterflies', taking 'a flighty and almost loose view
of things' which contrasted sharply with Frank's principled, moral outlook. But
in his loneliness, Frank pushed his doubts aside and took Mabel to Winchester
for inspection. Her reception was polite though not particularly encouraging.
She was 'much what I expected' in her general appearance, concluded Mrs
Dick's daughter Margaret, who was of a similar age, yet she detected no
particularly strong affection between them: 'to all intents and purposes I should
think they were out for the day together,' she wrote.[9] Frank's friends were
blunter. Dodgson thought her 'uninteresting, though pretty: the ladies said she
painted too much' and on hearing of their engagement concluded,

> I suppose the pipe and grey flannel shirt will have to be sacrificed at the
> altar of Hymen. She is said to be rich: Swinburne & Co. have fitted up her
> mother's house with electric light: the spark appears to have found material
> for incandescence.[10]

Even the eighteen-year-old Bertrand found her 'very nice by nature, but from
education utterly without firmness or moral courage'. She was submissive

and in the habit of pronouncing everything 'sweet', which was annoying, even if she did play a good game of tennis and sang 'most beautifully'.[11]

What, then, was the appeal, for a man for whom brotherhood and intellectual discourse had been so important just a short time ago? Was Frank's lethargy and loneliness so consuming that such flattery to his ego and feminine pampering as these ladies bestowed were enough to convince him he was in love? In one sense, yes: the Scotts answered a deep need in Frank that had been there since his mother's death and filled for a long time by Mrs Dick. It had been compounded by the rejection and bitterness he felt after the Oxford incident, which he confessed 'might well either have driven me to desperate or riotous wickedness or suicide' had he not worked it off.[12] It was the same need that had led him to seek out Mrs Williams for his housekeeper and was now passing not so much to Mabel but to her mother, Lady Scott.

Lina was quick to perceive this. She recognised the young man's loneliness and offered him empathy and intimacy to secure him for her daughter. They shared stories of their sad pasts (for Lina, too, had a tale of woe) and they became close and confidential friends in sympathy with each other against a harsh, cruel world. As such, when questions were raised within Frank's family about Lina's reputation and warnings issued that she was 'rather too well known in society, and had rather too coloured a past', instead of 'sheering off' as he said he intended, Frank leapt to her defence. He believed her wholeheartedly when she said she had been misrepresented by gossips. But because the accusations came from the Stanleys, not the Russells, Frank felt obliged not to dismiss them out of hand without first challenging their veracity. At Lady Stanley's suggestion, he agreed to let St George investigate:

> I was informed that Lady Scott's husband, Sir Claude Scott, the banker, had left her, that she had had an intrigue lasting many years with another man which was notorious, and which had ended in an action by her resulting in a compromise for a considerable sum, and that since then her life had been practically that of an adventuress.

The Scotts emphatically denied the charges and Mabel, showing another side to her 'sweet' character, went on the warpath in her mother's defence, telling Frank that Lina would prove her innocence. Lady Stanley, she said, should be ashamed of herself:

> It is so *sad* to me, anyone being so unjust and uncharitable ... We have now proved that it was poor mother's sister, who she never speaks to, that was on the Houseboat. Mr Lane Fox told us it was mother. Poor thing! only another instance of the unfairness of people...[13]

Mabel vowed to '*squash flat* all sweet mother's enemies'. Lady Stanley 'will be made to suffer for the lies she has told'. She began gathering statements from the family outlining Lina's history and announced her mother's intention of publishing in the newspapers a document drawn up by her solicitor to prove her innocence. Then Lady Stanley would have 'the consolation before she dies of seeing 2 or 3 people ruined, which mother has always tried to prevent'. If Frank would stand by them, she promised to take good care of him when they married 'as long as you are in a good temper with me'.[14]

Nothing could have been more certain to have the opposite effect than intended than this attack by the Stanleys. That Lina, who had shown Frank only love and kindness, taken an active interest in his future and sympathised about his past, should be thus wrongly accused by his own family was more than he could bear. He aligned himself more firmly with the Scotts than he otherwise ever would have. Even when the undeniable evidence of Giddy's involvement in a scandalous nullity suit reached him, he would not be moved.[15] On 26 December, a little over a month before the wedding, with the squabble now spreading to the Russells, Frank wrote to his uncle Henry, Lord Villiers, vicar of St Paul's, advising him that as he refused to call on Lina, and as 'her quarrels are my quarrels', he and Mabel would not marry in his church. 'You have treated disrespectfully a woman whom we have every reason to love and honour above the rest of her sex,' he wrote.[16] But Frank was no longer an objective judge, and the facts (had he known them) might well have alarmed him had he been considering a friend's position instead of his own.

Lina was the daughter of Henry Charles Burney and his wife, Cecilia. Henry's father, William Burney, was founder of the Royal Academy at Cold Harbour, Gosport, where Henry assisted him. After William's death, Henry moved his family to Richmond and set up his own military college on Little Green, where Claude Edward Scott, eldest son of the 3rd Baronet of Lytchet Minster, registered as a pupil. Undoubtedly this is where Lina and Claude met, and when she was sixteen and he twenty-one, they married. It could have been an advantageous match for Lina – the Scotts were bankers, founders of Scott & Co., Cavendish Square, and owners of the palatial Sundridge Park in Kent. But the marriage was contracted without their knowledge or consent. Claude's incensed father posted a notice to the effect in the London papers and altered his will, settling his son's inheritance on the next generation and leaving Claude a modest £300 annuity but nothing more.[17] The marriage failed, and in 1875, Lina filed for a judicial separation on the ground of Claude's cruelty.

The legal position as regards separation and divorce was then quite different. Marriage was considered a sacred contract which could only be broken by faithlessness. It could not be dissolved by mutual consent. Rather, one person had to be guilty and the other innocent. As such, under the terms of the 1857 Matrimonial Causes Act, a husband could only sue for divorce on the ground of adultery. In such a case, he would be released from the marriage and could at the same time claim damages against the man with whom his wife had cheated. Legally, his wife was his property and therefore if she was seduced by another man quite literally became damaged goods. The law recognised that in such a situation a husband should be suitably recompensed. The same did not apply to women. A wife needed to be able to prove *aggravated* adultery – that is, adultery compounded by another offence, such as desertion, cruelty, bigamy or incest. She had no right to sue for damages, but was free to remarry if the court ruled in her favour. However, at the discretion of the court, a divorce could be refused if there was evidence to suggest either that the two parties had colluded in bringing the suit, or that the complainant (the plaintiff) was also guilty of a matrimonial offence. If only a 'lesser' crime – cruelty or desertion – could be proved or a wife could prove *only* her husband's adultery, the court could award a *judicial separation* and order the husband to pay alimony. This option allowed them to live apart but not remarry. It was largely seen as a means of protecting vulnerable women against violent husbands or husbands who abandoned and failed to provide for them. Desertion had to be of two years' duration before an action could be brought.

In the case of the Scotts, Lina's first petition included a claim of adultery against Claude with Lady Frances Pelham-Clinton, in addition to cruelty in the form of his habitual use of offensive, insulting, blasphemous and threatening language against Lina and their children, alleging that he 'frequently threatened [her] with pistols and has struck her and has twisted her arm and has assaulted and beaten her'.[18] Lina had long known of her husband's affair, which would be proved in a later suit, but this quickly became irrelevant. Claude countersued, with the allegation that Lina had also committed adultery with no less than five co-respondents, one of whom had 'communicated to her a venereal disease'.[19] From each he claimed £1,000 damages.

The implication was immediately obvious: the respective guilt or innocence of either party was immaterial. Many reputations would be harmed if this came to court, and Lina's most of all. She would never recover from the suggestion that she was a serial adulteress. Every day the scandals of the divorce courts were printed in London papers, removing specifics regarded as too risqué for the family breakfast table but otherwise recounted verbatim. Regional papers picked up the stories and reprinted them, sometimes embellishing them, sometimes reporting more graphic details for their less prudish readers. Press cutting agents were employed to hunt down stories from newspapers nationwide so that nothing would be missed. Society gossips spread stories like wildfire. Stigma was immediately attached to participants without any consideration of the facts. There was no way this would pass notice, disappear or be forgotten. The Scotts compromised, each withdrawing their accusations of adultery, and when the case came to court in July 1876, it was an action for judicial separation on the single ground of Claude's cruelty, which Lina won. The court gave her custody of the children and ordered Claude to pay alimony of £520 per annum plus a quarter of any money thereafter derived from stocks and securities 'only so long as the said Dame Selina shall lead a chaste life'.

The couple parted and within four years Claude was dead and Lady Pelham-Clinton named as his executrix and sole beneficiary. With him died the alimony. The provision that Claude's father had made for his granddaughters in his will meant that on coming of age at twenty-one, Giddy and Mabel would receive a sum of approximately £26,000 each. Until that time, the money was held in trust with a dividend paid for their upkeep and education. Lina got nothing and was faced with a dilemma. Her daughters were then just sixteen and eleven respectively. If she wanted them to marry well, she needed to maintain a lifestyle that would attract high-class suitors, but that would mean living beyond her means. The £1,600 p.a. she received by order of Chancery for her daughters' maintenance while still minors was insufficient. She could mortgage her life insurance policies and borrow against her children's trust fund, but it would still not be enough. And as the only work available to her would have been something demeaning of her position, such as lady's companion or nurse, her only hope, if she wanted to fulfil her ambition, was to marry well again herself.

Enter Captain John Edmund Philip Spicer. His family resided in Walton and he was an officer in the 1st Life Guards at nearby Windsor. In 1883, his father – who had made his fortune as partner in the Combe Delafield Brewery – died, leaving John his prestigious estate, Spye Park in Wiltshire. It is not clear when he and Lina first became involved, but in 1885, she brought a suit against him for breach of promise to marry. She told Frank that she had lavished money on Spicer, only to find that when she was free to do so, he would not marry her. She sued, and on the day the case was due to be heard, settled for a reported £6,500. The truth of her claim and the nature of their relationship is obscured by lack of surviving documentation, but society would have assumed Spicer's desertion was more likely due to his having discovered something unsavoury about Lina than anything he himself might have done.[20] Yet, despite everything that would follow, Frank would always believe Lina's version of events. He presented Mabel's statements of her mother's innocence to his family as 'proofs'. They forged ahead with their wedding plans undeterred; but it was far from plain sailing.

Frank took a London residence for the ladies at 48 Eaton Square, Belgravia. The wedding was set for 6 February 1890. At Frank's insistence, the service would be held at midday in St Peters, Eaton Square and presided over by Revd Dickins. Invitations were sent out. Some of Frank's friends sent regrets: Santayana was in America and Lionel doubtless was never really anticipated, but Herbert Roberts, Frank's Cambridge friend, whom he had seen often in London that winter, would be sorely missed. Harry Marillier agreed to be best man and to stay with Frank at his lodgings on King Street for the week beforehand. So far so good. But there remained unresolved the question of introductions. On New Year's Day, an indignant Frank noted in his diary that Aunt Maude still refused to make Lina's acquaintance. Relations with St George were also strained and it was still uncertain which members of his family would consent to come to the wedding breakfast hosted by Lina after the service. Bertrand sent Frank an 'impertinent' letter on the subject. It was not until three weeks before the day that Frank could finally say most of his family were coming, or until the week before that the situation was significantly eased by Lady John writing to Mabel specifically asking to be introduced to Lady Scott at the church.

Then there were Mabel's changeable moods. She and Frank bickered throughout January, and on several occasions Mabel appeared less than excited about her forthcoming nuptials, often preferring Giddy and Dick's company over Frank's. His diary is punctuated with references to how nasty or nice Mabel was being, his own mood seemingly dependent on whether she was 'irritating' and 'hysterical' or 'sweet' and 'attentive'. On two occasions they had huge arguments – the first at the beginning of January, when in a fit of rage Mabel told Frank he could not tell her what to do as he was not yet part of the family, unlike Dick; and a second, spanning the two days before the wedding, in which a 'half crazed' Mabel 'in a vile & filthy temper' told Frank she did not want to see him, but was going to dine with Giddy and Dick instead.[21] Mabel seemed to realise very early on that the best way to antagonise Frank was by putting the interests of others before him.

The whole situation was compounded by poor health. Agatha had already declared herself too unwell to attend and Lina often appeared to be on the cusp of going down with something or other. Then on 7 January, Frank was diagnosed with 'flu. He spent the next few days feeling weak and 'seedy' and being nursed back to health by an attentive but somewhat under-par Lina. By the 19th, Mabel too was ailing. She quickly developed a chest infection and it soon looked unlikely she would be well enough for the big day. If Frank had been at all superstitious, he might have asked himself whether this were not the start of the marriage troubles foretold by Captain Bray. The vicar of St Peter's called at 6 p.m. on the eve of the wedding in the middle of Mabel's tantrum and found 'everything in a fearful upset' and Frank 'quivering with rage & excitement'. Giddy, 'dear girl', saved the day, taking Frank to her lodgings to dine with her and Dick. Afterwards, Frank went back to King Street to find Harry waiting for him and the two men sat up together, talking.

Finally, the morning of the wedding arrived. Frank breakfasted with Harry and saw his old friend Maurice Davies, quickly followed by Dr Godson, who came to tell him that though Mabel would be able to go through with the ceremony, he would not yet declare her fit for the honeymoon – she must stay at Eaton Square a few more days. This time, Frank was 'not a bit upset'; an 'unnatural calm' had come over him. He began dressing casually at 11 a.m. and half an hour later set off with Harry for the church. He greeted his guests – among them Benjamin Jowett, who, in the month following Frank's engagement, had received him at Balliol, and with whom (on the surface at least) Frank had made his peace.[22] At ten past the hour, Mabel arrived. She wore a dress of ivory silk draped with *mousseline de chiffon* and trails of orange blossom. Under her Honiton lace veil, bordered with a thick ruche of ostrich feathers, was the requisite wreath of orange blossom, popularised by Victoria some fifty years previously and still the height of fashion. She walked up the aisle to a choral procession, accompanied by Lina. A pageboy in white satin court costume supported her veil, and seven bridesmaids – all in white satin with ostrich feathers at their throat and wrists and carrying little bunches of Neapolitan violets – followed behind. Frank was deeply moved:

When the music began it went thro' & thro' me & I shook all over. But when Mabel had reached the chancel & I stood beside her, I quite recovered my composure. In a moment, so it seemed to me, we were married & the ring on her finger.

Afterwards in the vestry, the principal members of both Frank and Mabel's family witnessed the signing of the register. Not only Lady John, but also Lady Stanley and Lyulph were introduced to Lina and 'made themselves charming'. Aside from Uncle Henry, the only person notable by her absence was Maude. Then back at Eaton Square, the breakfast went off without a hitch, though Frank thought it rather dull. By 3 p.m., everyone had gone and Lina, Giddy, Dick and Frank had tea together. Dr Godson returned to examine Mabel, who was 'very good & bore up wonderfully & did not cry'. Frank declared himself 'thoroughly happy & contented'. But the following night, Mabel took a turn for the worse. She woke shrieking with pain and spent the next hour lapsing in and out of consciousness, terrifying Frank with assurances that she would die. The diagnosis was pleurisy, and in a rare expression of his affection for her, Frank made one last entry in his diary: 'Never have I had such an awful time or felt so frightened – the very heart seemed torn out of me at the bare idea of losing my precious darling as soon as she was mine.'

Mabel would recover – slowly. They would honeymoon at the Imperial Hotel, Torquay, eventually leaving on 20 February and returning the following week to Eaton Square to start their married life. Broom Hall, which Mabel thought 'gloomy', would be relinquished in favour of Amberley Cottage, 'an ugly half-finished villa in a new jerry-built quarter of Maidenhead'.[23] But their troubles were only just beginning. Of the dozen or so predicted years of misery associated with his marriage, Frank had so far lived through less than one. And though Captain Bray might, in one sense, be relieved to hear that his powers of prediction were not infallible – that Frank went on to live well beyond his fortieth year – the accuracy of his prophesy regarding Mabel would very soon be borne out; though doubtless not even he envisaged anything like what was about to happen.

10

To Love, Honour and Obey

The marriage was a disaster. Mabel returned from the honeymoon weak and listless. She insisted her childhood nurse remain in her service and complained bitterly about demands Frank made on her, declaring herself too unwell to manage the household accounts or supervise deliveries. Yet she was always well enough to accept social invitations. Frank reproached her for her shortcomings. He thought Lina hadn't exercised sufficient restraint over her whims and was determined to mould her into the useful, practical sort of wife required by an earl and man of business. But he lacked Lina's soft touch and failed to coax out of Mabel anything like the level of obedience or submission he desired. His tactlessness only roused her resistance. In the first few months of their marriage, they locked horns repeatedly over their differing ideas as to their respective roles and responsibilities. In frustration, both appealed to Lina to smooth things over. And perhaps, with her powers of persuasion, she might have succeeded had there only been these few simple domestic differences to resolve. But even before the ink was dry on their marriage certificate, deeper divisions emerged concerning those thorniest of issues: money and sex.

Protection of the family fortune was paramount. When any two noble families united through marriage, steps were taken to ensure the newlyweds were amply provided for but did not reduce the family's overall standing by frittering away their inheritance or making risky investments. A marriage settlement drawn up by the fathers would direct how their money could be spent – how much on property, for example, or for personal allowance – the bulk of the fortune being held in trust. Requests to release additional funds had to be approved by its trustees. The settlement became legally binding with the signing of the marriage certificate and, until 1882, everything in it would then become the husband's. If the marrying woman had any influence, she could protect her portion from an extravagant or financially unsavvy husband by settling everything she was entitled to on any potential children and receive for herself an allowance known as 'pin money'. This was for current use only: she was not entitled to save it or dispose of it in any way other than as her husband directed. The passing of the 1882 Married Women's Property Act changed this. A wife's inheritance became her own and she could direct what happened to it; although pin money was still subject to the same restriction, and arguably the long tradition of male dominance cast such a shadow over the practical application of the law that many women continued to settle their portion as before.

As such, Frank assumed, as he visited his own solicitor the week before his wedding to settle £10,000 of his inheritance on any children from their marriage, that Mabel would be doing likewise with her £26,000. Yet Mabel and Lina were determined that only £20,000 would go into trust. They insisted also that any dividends be paid directly to Mabel and that on Mabel's death, the capital be used to provide an income for Lina (or Giddy if Lina pre-deceased her), with Frank having no interest in it at all (though curiously there was a provision that up to three-quarters of the capital could be settled in favour of a husband or children from a second marriage if there was one). Frank's solicitor, Richard Du Cane, argued for alterations that would have allowed Frank some of the income or inheritance, but failed. As a result, Frank declined to have anything to do with the final document. The ladies, he said, remained mysterious about it until after the wedding when they finally confessed their real financial position. On 13 February, Lina revealed to Frank not only that she had borrowed £7,000 to lavish on Captain Spicer but that ever since she had 'borrowed and borrowed' and was now 'penniless'. She had squandered everything to secure good marriages for her daughters. She had pawned her diamonds to pay for her electric lighting: 'I ought not to have done it, ought I? But I wanted you here. I always, always liked you.'[1]

How must Frank have felt to learn that he had been so manipulated? How much worse must it have been to learn further that Mabel had debts of her own amounting to some £3,000, accumulated in anticipation of her coming-of-age and the release of her trust fund? And how unsurprising that Frank would later view all the Scotts' actions from the moment they met as a 'deliberate plan of campaign' to secure him for his fortune, just as he claimed they had formerly planned but failed to entrap William, Earl Craven, whose father had died leaving an estate worth over £173,000.[2] Sensing his potential rage, Lina pleaded with Frank to 'write me no harsh letter; the past is past ... I shall let this house at once and go out as a nurse and earn my living'; unless, of course, she could 'soon meet someone who will pay back my income and marry me'.[3] In the meantime, Frank was cornered. He was forced to lend the ladies money to help them out of their predicament and to agree, against his principles, that Mabel borrow a further £1,500 to satisfy her creditors. Neither could his anger be given free rein: his cornering was partially of his own making. Not only had he ignored his family's warnings in taking Mabel for better or worse, but in the process he had incurred the wrath of another who was even then threatening to sue for breach of promise to marry.

Kate Williams – the playmate of his youth and maid at Broom Hall – had been Frank's mistress since 1887 and believed that, in the course of his seduction, Frank had promised marriage. Doubtful though this was given their respective positions, Frank had made no secret of the intrigue among friends. Santayana recalled an episode in which Kate and her sister had accompanied them on a trip on Frank's launch; Kate sitting 'silent and dejected' in the stern next to Frank, her hair loose and dishevelled as he said he liked it, while her sister, the 'bright-eyed' Ellen, 'moved about with the freedom of a member of the family'. Santayana questioned whether they were *both* Frank's playthings.[4] But whatever his relationship with Ellen, Kate was decidedly unimpressed by the announcement of his engagement to Mabel. A week before the wedding, she sent Frank a threatening letter saying that unless he gave her mother £100 a year, she would make their affair public.

This situation was not unheard of for a man in Frank's position, and there was really only one of two ways to deal with it: pay up to keep the young lady quiet or engage a lawyer to see her off. Frank chose the latter, writing in his diary, 'Shall George Lewis her.'[5]

George Lewis was a solicitor of high renown. Of Jewish-German descent, he had been articled to his family's firm Lewis and Lewis of Ely Place, Holborn, becoming a solicitor in his own right in 1856. Through marriage to his German cousin, Elizabeth Eberstadt – a confident, lively, and somewhat acerbic young woman who developed a reputation as a society hostess – he then found himself representing the eclectic stream of artists, writers, actors and politicians who passed through the doors of her salon. Lewis quickly became the lawyer of choice in the upper echelons of society, representing all five defendants in the famous 1890 Baccarat Scandal involving the Prince of Wales. He fought doggedly for his clients, making it his practice to engage on their behalf the leading barristers of the day. Yet while his skill in gathering evidence gained him the reputation of being 'not so much a lawyer as a shrewd private inquiry agent', greater still was said to be his capacity for keeping many of his high-profile clients out of court.[6] Further, he had an almost photographic memory, barely ever made notes and was consequently regarded as the most discrete lawyer in London, refusing even to write his memoirs for the secrets they would inevitably reveal. Oscar Wilde described him as, 'Brilliant. Formidable. Concerned in every great case in England. Oh – he knows all about us, and he forgives us all.'[7]

In 1879, the Lewises had taken a house in Walton-on-Thames, becoming neighbours of Lady Scott. Lewis had drawn up Mabel's marriage settlement. He was, therefore, the natural choice to defend Frank against Kate Williams; especially after her family started sending Lina anonymous 'disgusting' letters 'unfit for *anyone* to read'. By his instigation, a temperate letter was sent pointing out to Kate the possible legal consequences of her actions. When that proved insufficient, detectives were employed (probably by Lina). Not those of the recently established CID (1878), but the key-hole kind – that strange breed of mostly down-at-heel characters sent to spy, intimidate and dig up dirt using the most un-Holmesian of methods. They proved more effective. On 25 February, Lina wrote to Frank, 'Isn't it a blessing she is gone? She might have had a baby, and people would have said it was *yours*, born before its time, nasty beast.'[8]

Meanwhile, Mabel, who knew all about Kate but had been protected by her mother from the more sordid details, was having problems of her own. She had suffered since puberty with 'dysmenorrhea' – an antiquated clinical term for painful and difficult periods, strongly associated in the minds of Victorian doctors with hysteria and caused (according to the wisdom of the ancient Greeks) by an ill-behaved wandering womb. Mabel suffered enormously. Her doctor prescribed morphine to sedate her, but had nothing to address the cause. Lina wanted a second opinion. On 1 April, she wrote to Frank, 'Where there is such pain surely there must be something wrong.' Possibly Mabel was pregnant, or thought she was – she had planned a stay at The Hurst, 'because London is so very bad for anyone who is going to have a baby' – but ultimately there was no child: it was either wishful thinking or she miscarried.[9]

Like many young women, an understanding of sex and the rhythms of her own menstrual cycle seem to have eluded Mabel. She had previously told her mother she was 'horrid frightened of the results of marriage' – a fact Lina duly passed on to Frank.[10] Her health had already been used as a reason to end a prior engagement to a young aristocrat named Edward Fitzgerald, which had been announced in January 1888.[11] Mabel suffered from back pain which she claimed was the result of a riding accident, but was later dismissed as 'hysteric'; as were the mood swings that led to her vicious arguments with Frank. Poor Mabel Edith! It would be another twenty years before Marie Stopes would write that a woman's symptoms were an expression of frustration that could be relieved by a satisfying sex life and an understanding husband; and Mabel's problems, once associated with hysteria, would always be regarded as her fault.[12] Frank, with equally as little understanding, would remain hurt and confused by her fluctuating moods, while Lina would continue to mollycoddle her, unable or unwilling to educate her. Later, Mabel would claim that her innocence regarding sexual matters was shattered by revelations about Frank's behaviour prior to their meeting.

For a while they struggled on, apparently only able to stop bickering when in company. In February and again in mid-April, Herbert Roberts came to stay and recalled an enjoyable few days with Frank, Mabel and Lina, singing at the piano and going to the theatre. Then, at the beginning of May, came the first evidence that Frank and Mabel's problems went deeper than mere lovers' tiffs, with an episode that would soon become known as the 'Albemarle Incident'.

Frank was to be presented to the Prince of Wales at the Queen's Levée on 6 May at St James's Palace. He and Mabel had taken rooms at the nearby Albemarle Hotel where Mabel assisted him into court dress for the occasion. Frank left with the assumption that she would be there to help him undress on his return but found instead only his manservant waiting for him. In Frank's absence, Mabel had lunched with a female friend of whom Frank disapproved and was late returning. During the course of the ensuing argument, Mabel told Frank she was sorry she had ever married him. Frank told her she could 'go to the devil' and rang the bell for her mother. On Lina's arrival, he apparently said, 'Here is your saintly daughter, you can take her away as soon as you like' and stormed out, leaving Mabel 'without a farthing in my pocket and not caring what became of me'.[13]

The details of this event and much more besides would ultimately be disputed in the divorce court, but from the letters and telegrams that passed between them, it is clear that Frank returned to the hotel the next day where he obviously expected to find that Mabel had not taken him literally. He was wrong. She had gone to Lady Salisbury's and sent a telegram to say she would return by 9 p.m. Frank waited for two hours, and when she did not show he went to Walton to find she was not there either. The following day, he received a telegram from George Lewis asking to meet him. Frank refused and instead wrote to Mabel:

> For God's sake put an end to the awful situation you have created. All last night I waited at the Albemarle for you ... I have looked for you all to-day, but you have concealed your address. I can only beg and pray you to return to your proper position by my side.[14]

He was shocked and horrified at the thought of solicitors being involved in their quarrel and asked her to join him at PL the following day where he would wait for her. Again, Mabel did not appear. Instead she wrote demanding an 'ample apology for your desertion, and for your cruel treatment to me since our marriage. I have stood it until my health is broken and my spirit too, but you *left* me, and so the responsibility rests *entirely* with you.' Her doctor, she continued, insisted she go to the seaside for a month to be 'quite at *peace*' and, though she was acting on her own volition, if Frank wished to write and 'promise to be kind and gentle in the future ... kindly address to Mr. Lewis, 10, Ely Place'.

The mention of Lewis and the careful wording of the letter, with recognisable legal terms, reveal the extent to which Mabel, acting on her own volition or not, had already taken advice. She quickly followed this with a letter to Lady John, in which she stated that 'the time has now come when I must tell you of the unhappiness of my married life through the treatment of Frank'. She was '*terrified*' of him, she wrote, and appealed to Lady John for understanding: 'I *must* uphold myself, as I have done no wrong, only Frank, so no one must suffer but him.'

Lady John immediately sympathised. They arranged to meet, but with both women claiming to be too unwell to travel, it never happened. Instead, Lady John wrote offering friendship, but impressing upon Mabel the extent to which her actions threatened to ruin her reputation and chance of happiness. She suggested Mabel and Frank *both* had something to forgive the other and reminded Mabel that marriage vows 'cannot be lightly set aside'. In the eyes of God and the world, the course she was taking was 'terribly serious'.

The letter appeared to do the trick. Just as Lady John had previously brought Frank to remorse for attempting to impress Buddhism on Lionel Johnson, she now succeeded in bringing Frank and Mabel together for a difficult interview which resulted in the 'ample apology' Mabel sought. On 11 May 1890, Frank wrote,

> Dearest, dearest Mabel, ... I do not think, darling, that you can know how deeply, truly, honestly and devotedly I love you, and how awful it is to hear the things you said yesterday. I know my manner is disagreeable often, and I am afraid I have been harsh and cruel to you and not remembered how tenderly and with what gentleness you have always been treated. Dear heart, what can I do more than say how dreadfully grieved I am and beg and pray you to come back to me ... I will never reproach you for all this misery, I will go down on my knees to you and ask your pardon ... Be merciful as we ourselves must hope for mercy from God for our faults...

For a few weeks, things seemed better. Mabel followed her doctor's advice and went to Brighton with Lina. Frank visited them on the understanding that Mabel must not be 'worried'. When apart, they wrote to each other and Mabel playfully signed her letters 'your affectionate little wife'. Towards the end of the month they visited friends in Essex, then spent several days at the Grand Hotel before returning to Eaton Square. As soon as they were home, the old problems resurfaced. First, it was Kate Williams with another threat of litigation. Lina stoked the flames by suggesting someone was giving her money to fight. This was followed by more disagreements. Frank refused an invitation for Mabel to visit an old family friend, Captain Hargreaves, in Ascot, considering Hargreaves an unsuitable acquaintance. Mabel accused Frank of excessive control, both of her movements and finances: the dividends from her trust fund were being paid into their joint account at Child's bank, for which Frank held the only chequebook. In the midst of a bitter argument, Frank sat down to write to his solicitor that he would do nothing more to help Mabel with her financial difficulties unless she 'consult me personally when she is calm'.[15] The following day, Mabel again appealed to Lady John in confidence, recounting how, when she asked to see the letter, 'He flew at me, Granny dear, got hold of both my arms, and almost broke them, and cut one of my wrists so that it bled very much, and I quite thought he would kill me.' It was the second time Frank had used physical violence against her, she claimed; the other time being four nights previously when he had struck her and 'raised a big lump on my chest'.

The next evening, they argued again. Mabel took herself off to bed, leaving Frank in his study. In the middle of the night, she woke to find herself lying naked on the floor with Frank standing over her. She screamed for her nurse and clung to her in fright, threatening to throw herself from the window if she should be left alone with him a moment longer. She would not stay to listen to his explanation that she had fainted and he was trying to rouse her. She spent the rest of the night with her nurse and in the morning left for Walton. Frank followed and spoke with Lina. It was decided, for everyone's sake, that Frank would stay with her and Mabel would go to PL to recuperate.

From the safety of her new retreat, Mabel wrote to Frank saying she hoped someday 'everything will come right' and that he would 'do nothing I should not wish you to during the time I do not see you'. She did not elaborate on what that might be, but finished by asking him to send her some money, signing herself 'your affectionate Wife, Mabel'. Frank's reply was formal and businesslike. He did not plead for her return or apologise for his behaviour. He simply stated that he would allow her £80 a month while they were apart which would be paid into an account of her own 'on the understanding that you do not run up any bills of any kind whatever at any shop ... and pay all your own expenses'. When she regained her strength, they could decide 'calmly and rationally whether we are capable of living together or not'. Mabel formally accepted his proposal. In consultation with her doctor, it was decided she should stay quietly at PL for three months, during which time Lady John would take responsibility for her and Frank would stay away. Lady John wrote to Lina that she would keep 'poor dear Mabel' quiet. Agatha wrote to Frank that 'we all avoid talking of what is sad and painful in the past ... and pray for a better and brighter future for you both'. Only in private did they voice their own concerns, as the eighteen-year-old Bertrand's diary reveals:

> It is most fortunate, as Aunt Agatha was saying, that [Mabel's] nature is not a deep one; if it were, she must be almost broken-hearted by the prospect of life-long misery which is apparently all there is before her.[16]

Away from Frank, Mabel regained her strength. She entertained the Russells at the piano and played lawn tennis with Bertrand, made short trips to Windsor to visit Giddy and to Walton to see Lina (when she was sure Frank would not be there). Frank, meanwhile, leased Amberley Cottage in Maidenhead for £160 p.a., and continued on the presumption that it would soon become their marital home. Santayana visited and found him comfortable. Meanwhile Mabel quickly tired of PL and before the end of June used the pending visit of Lady John's stepdaughter, Georgy, as an excuse for a prolonged stay with Giddy, from where she returned permanently to Lina in Walton. Frank was unhappy with the arrangement, but Lady John begged him not to make trouble: she did not believe that Lina would 'exert any but a good influence in a matter she has so much at heart' and Mabel would continue to visit PL, from where they would keep an eye on her. It wasn't enough. Almost as soon as Mabel arrived back at Walton, she started wanting things 'settled for my future' such that, even as Frank was writing asking for decorating decisions for Amberley Cottage, George Lewis was attempting to secure her an increased allowance. Lady John begged Mabel to desist and Rollo was sent to dissuade Lewis from further action. They both conceded. Mabel turned her attention instead to the wedding presents, writing to Frank to negotiate which she may have, while simultaneously writing to Rollo to arrange a family interview to discuss terms of her return.

It is difficult to know for certain what was going through her mind at this time; whether she was simply pushing her advantage or actually preparing for a life alone as she oscillated wildly between protestations that she was ready to return and exclamations that she was too afraid to even see Frank, who was now in her eyes 'a dangerous man'.

July was a tense month. 'Naughty little *Babs*' demonstrated her frivolousness by encouraging the Russells to take up her pet name (they refused) and Frank proved difficult to control. Mabel pushed Rollo to recruit senior men in the family for a group consultation. George Howard (by then Lord Carlisle) declined, saying he had previously tried to exercise influence over Frank and, having failed, felt it would be 'entirely useless' to try again. He suggested Lyulph might be the better Stanley representative, having not already spoken to Frank 'recklessly'. Once again, the only person to step forward of her own volition to offer her services was Mrs Dick, who wrote to Mabel on 28 July. She prayed Mabel would not stay away long, spoke of Frank's loneliness and devotion and tentatively suggested that their problems stemmed from age and inexperience. She advised, 'live under the same roof, *even* in another part of the house' so Mabel could gradually accustom herself to Frank. She offered friendship, inviting Mabel to Winchester. But Mabel was affronted by Mrs Dick's 'unwarrantable liberty' in writing to her so: it was not 'ladylike'. Agatha agreed and advised her not to talk to anyone outside the family: Mabel was getting all the help she needed already. The Russells were indeed doing their best and continued throughout to support, encourage, sympathise and advise while the Stanleys remained remote. Despite having more practical qualities and a worldlier outlook, they chose not to intervene. Perhaps their initial disapproval of the match naturally excluded them. It is certainly difficult to envisage the formidable Lady Stanley having much patience with Mabel. She and Maude visited Mabel once at PL, they wrote both to her and Frank to sympathise, but did no more.

At the beginning of August, Mabel spelled out her position to Agatha: either Frank owns up to his bad treatment of her, apologies and begs forgiveness – again – or she would seek the protection of the law. Rollo, still persevering with the proposed family interview, met Mabel at The Savoy to hear her side in private first; yet even he was beginning to doubt his capacity as mediator. Lina had taken a cottage at Bray, just upriver from Amberley Cottage, and earlier that week Frank had witnessed Mabel, Lina and a party of friends picnicking on the bank of the Thames as he steamed past in his launch. On seeing the group, he had assumed that, far from being quiet and regaining her health as she had promised, Mabel was living the high life. In a temper, he'd called out to them, 'Put the wine on the bank, that is *all we want*!' and then continued on without waiting to hear who the guests were or what the occasion. Rollo heard Mabel's side of the story at The Savoy. Rather unwisely he over-empathised, revealing more than he had intended of his own experiences of being on the receiving end of Frank's temper, and afterwards had to repair the damage, asking Mabel not to 'exaggerate your fear of F. or think he looks angry, when it may only be chagrin or annoyance', reminding her: 'I rely on you to keep silence respecting anything which would cause trouble if repeated.' Agatha had arranged with Frank for the family interview to take place the following week, 12 August. Mabel arrived with Giddy at the appointed time, but Frank did not show. He had heard that Mabel had had a further consultation with George Lewis, in light of which he felt further discussion was futile and had engaged a solicitor of his own.

Alfred Percy Doulton of Vandercom & Co. was less of a celebrity than George Lewis, but hard-working, thorough and dependable. The son of a Liberal MP and grandson of Sir Henry Doulton of Royal Doulton pottery fame, he had been practising since 1879. He already handled Frank's financial affairs, and by mid-July had taken over negotiations with the Williamses. Lina claimed a long-standing friendship with him, but his loyalty to Frank was unswerving and he seemed amply able to resist her interferences, which continued with a stream of letters offering her assistance with Kate should he need it. Lina also wrote to Frank, guiding him back towards Mabel. By 20 August, it looked as if her efforts were succeeding. Frank agreed to receive Mabel's list of demands for her return, which were as follows.

Lina must live with them for six months. Frank must provide her with a room of her own. Her maid should sleep in an adjoining room. Mabel should be allowed to visit Giddy whenever she liked and have Giddy and Dick to stay. She should have her own income and be allowed to go to 'any house I am invited to', whether Frank wanted to go or not. Frank must promise to treat her kindly and 'never be harsh'. If he could concede to all this, there would be no need for the family interview, Mabel would come to Amberley Cottage for a visit with Lina on 30 August and move back permanently on 16 September; but not before, because she had arranged to visit an old friend in Scotland.

Frank took his time to reply, finally sitting down to it ten days later; the day Mabel and Lina had intended to visit. He began by saying he would be guilty of 'moral cowardice' if he did not express how grieved he was at the tone of her letter, but as he strongly felt it his duty to smooth matters he would let it pass and attend to her conditions. He readily agreed to everything except her freedom to accept any invitation and to having Dick Russell in his house. As her husband, he was held responsible for her actions; and he suspected Dick of talking about him in public. He hoped, however, that by his other concessions Mabel would see that his motives were good. In turn, he would endeavour to forget those things she had done that he found bitter and hoped that together they might learn 'mutual tolerance and forbearance without which a peaceful married life is impossible'.

Were such negotiations likely to succeed? We can only surmise. Before Frank's letter arrived, events took over. Mabel had a cheque dishonoured and on trying to cash another was told there were no funds in her account to meet it. She cancelled her visit and demanded an explanation. Frank, it appeared, had taken her desire to control her own income literally and cancelled her £80 standing order. He now reminded her that it had always been conditional on her staying out of debt and remaining at PL: could she say she had done these things? He had agreed that the dividends from her trust fund would go directly to her after she had demanded her 'own money': if she had not accounted for the fact that the next payment would not be until October, that was not his responsibility. Further, her instruction to George Lewis to get her an additional £1,000 a year, as far as he was concerned, 'swept away and annulled my previous existent terms'.

Mabel was furious. She set about writing to anyone who would listen that Frank had left her destitute again. But it was not until Frank received a chastising letter from Maude Stanley that it finally dawned on him that Mabel had assumed he had engineered the situation to embarrass her. He wrote assuring her that he had asked the managers of both their banks to inform her of the change of arrangements. Mabel didn't believe him: it seemed impossible that two managers from two separate banks would both fail to carry out his instruction. Maude appealed to Frank to send Mabel money to tide her over: 'You married her with a full knowledge of her bringing up and what you might expect from her different notions of life to those of the women in your own family.' It was too late. Mabel fixed on this incident as the excuse she needed to separate permanently. She had already begun widening her net to secure the sympathy of friends and had succeeded in procuring that of Frank's best man, Harry Marillier, who had visited her in early September, heard her side of the story and written to Frank in a 'stinging strain' to voice his disapproval, favouring Mabel with the sentiment, 'Poor little woman ... But I *never* thought it was a bed of roses you were making for yourself.' By mid-September, Mabel had resolved that it was her 'earnest wish' that she and Frank should separate permanently. She informed Frank in writing on the 20th. He replied that her accusations of cruelty were a 'product of your imagination ... I have given up far more for you than you could ever realize – while you have repaid me by renouncing your duty as a wife and making an open scandal of your name.' A scramble for allegiances ensued which produced the following:

Maude wrote to Frank expressing her distress that Mabel would sue for separation but her thankfulness that he could answer all her accusations. Lady Stanley excused both herself and Lyulph by politely refusing to engage with Mabel, while expressing the opinion that 'patience and forbearance on both sides might have healed the breach'. Lady John wrote somewhat ambiguously that she would always do her utmost for both Mabel *and* Frank 'who I have loved so very very dearly from his birth that darkness in his lot must be darkness in mine'. Agatha and Rollo waivered somewhat nervously in the centre ground, unwilling or unable to take either side convincingly and reiterating to Mabel their primary concern, that she should 'do all that is possible to keep what is most discreditable and vile from being brought forward, and that *no more* than is necessary to your object will be submitted'. Harry wrote to Agatha and received such a timid reply that he feared 'the Russells are going to shirk taking an active part'. He warned Mabel that 'most of them are rather slender reeds to lean on and will shift the burden round to anyone else if they can'. Lina somehow managed to convey her equal allegiance to both, accompanying Frank to Winchester where she 'got rather pitched into by Mrs Dick'. And Santayana, of course, remained unequivocally loyal to Frank, receiving from him the most uninhibited expression of his feelings towards Mabel at this time:

> Fancy me married to a vulgar music-hall termagant! Me! My dear fellow – so *very* much out of my line!! A woman who has hysterics, makes scenes, wears borrowed jewels, accepts presents from strangers, calls young men by their Christian names, likes to see herself in newspapers and shop windows, goes to Aquariums, Piers and music-halls, etc., etc. And yet because she dresses well, and don't drop her h's, there are people who think she's a lady. Bah! I'd sooner have married an honest kitchen maid.[17]

With or without the assault from Mrs Dick, Santayana found Frank's continuing to see Lina incredible. When he visited Amberley Cottage in July 1890, it had surprised him that Frank had a photograph of Lina on the mantelpiece of his largely unfurnished study, but nothing of Mabel. What Mabel thought of this arrangement, he did not like to guess. He assumed that as she said nothing, she must not object. It soon transpired that Mabel had more pressing matters to worry about. As news spread about their separation, letters from friends arrived, intending to be supportive but in one particular instance revealing 'facts' about Frank that would have dire consequences.

In November 1890, Lady Cardigan, widow of the infamous commander of the Charge of the Light Brigade and a lady of dubious reputation whom Frank had already refused to meet, wrote,

> Dearest Babs, I got your little note and was sorry not to see you yesterday ... Did you know that Lord R. had been expelled from Oxford for malpractices? Did you know of his taking a Chinaman to the upper storey of his Grandmother's house in Dover Street, which Chinaman was cleverly shipped off afterwards quietly to his own Country by the Honble. Lyulph Stanley? You never ought to have been allowed to marry such a man – so says everyone. His character is well known, but it is no use crying over spilt milk. You can't divorce him, so the judicial separation is the only means left, but I do hope your mother will have no communication with him; it would look as if she condoned his treatment of you, & must have the worst possible effect. She really never ought to speak to him again. When we meet I will tell you more.[18]

On the same day, Mabel heard from another source that Frank had visited Kate Williams. She was horrified. Perhaps Frank was, as Lina suggested, only trying to settle his case with her quietly, but Mabel was unconvinced. She appealed to Agatha to tell her the truth about Oxford, bemoaning the fact that she did not know it before her marriage. She wrote to Lady Stanley asking directly if she knew that Frank had seen Kate and if the accusations about Oxford and the Chinaman were true. The Chinaman was, of course, Quai Paak, the boy Frank had brought home from California, and therefore his presence at Dover Street was perfectly accurate. But Lady Stanley refused to dignify Lady Cardigan's scandalous insinuation with a reply. Mabel took her silence to mean that everything she had been told by her friend was true. Why else would the family not deny it?

On 29 November, George Lewis filed Mabel's petition for a judicial separation. In it, the events of their short married life were described in such a way as to allege that Frank had 'habitually treated [Mabel] with harshness and cruelty and been violent in his conduct towards [her] terrifying her and injuring her health'. In asking her to look over the accounts, he had compelled her to 'remain up till two and three o'clock in the morning' and 'when unable to complete them has called [her] a useless uneducated woman and an ungrateful devil'; in asking her to take in deliveries he had 'insisted upon her standing in a cold cellar ... whilst the wine was being counted over, knowing that [she] had barely recovered from Pleurisy'; at the Albemarle he had 'ordered [her] to dress him for the levee and whilst doing so he cursed her' and on his return had 'compelled her to help him to undress when he again used insulting language and told [her] to go to the Devil and handed her over to her mother'; on the occasion when they argued and she had grabbed the letter he was writing to Doulton he had 'violently caught hold of [her] by her arms and forced bracelets into her wrists and made them bleed and injured her arms'; and on the night of the fainting incident, he had 'insisted upon [her] getting out of bed when she fainted with terror. When [she] recovered consciousness she found herself marked and in great pain and she took refuge with one of the servants.'

In addition, there were accusations that he had 'insisted upon [her] going every morning to put paper in the men servants' water closet and to see that it was clean which made [her] sick and ill' and that on another occasion, after she had gone to bed, he had 'insisted upon [her] going downstairs when he caught hold of her by the wrists and made them black and blue forced her down on to her knees and used offensive language to her'. On 6 June, he had 'in a violent passion seized [her] by the shoulder and shook her raising a large bruise', after which he 'struck the wall violently marking the wall with his knuckles'. On this occasion he 'raved about the boudoir and told [her] he was looking for a pistol and that he would shoot her or himself'. All this, and the insulting language he used towards her, and the contempt he showed her before the servants, had seriously injured her health and she had been compelled under medical advice to leave him.[19]

The language is common for petitions at this time. In order to be awarded a judicial separation, Mabel not only had to prove herself the innocent party, but also that Frank's cruelty satisfied the legal definition of the term, meaning there must be 'danger to life, limb, or health, bodily or mental, or a reasonable apprehension of it'.[20] It was her only option. She could not claim desertion because they had agreed to live apart with the approval of both their families, and though she might suspect his motives in visiting Kate Williams there was no evidence of adultery. Neither could she wait to see whether in due course evidence would materialise: a petitioner had to bring suit without 'unreasonable delay' and as she and Frank had not lived together since June and there were no accusations of cruelty since then, she risked a petition on this ground being thrown out if she did not act quickly.

Frank's team, in preparing their defence, asked for greater clarification on certain points. The resulting 'further and better particulars' filed on 12 January 1891 contained a shock that none expected. Aside from the additional information that the insults had happened at dinner, or that by calling her 'a beastly barren woman' and threatening to shoot her, or tying the cord of his dressing gown around his own throat as if to kill himself, he had undermined her nervous system, there was the following startling paragraph:

> That in addition at 48 Eaton Square the Respondent insisted upon a man named Roberts sleeping in the house for three or four days and nights, and after the Respondent had undressed, going up to Roberts' bedroom remaining with him for several hours, and again in the morning. Upon the petitioner expostulating with him upon his conduct, the Respondent told the Petitioner to go to the Devil and mind her own business.[21]

Further, was the allegation that Frank had told Mabel he would turn her out of the house if she did not allow Roberts to visit and had compelled her to extend Roberts a further invitation, during which the same behaviour was repeated.

Frank considered most of Mabel's allegations puerile and easily defendable, but this was something else. Was she actually accusing him of an 'unnatural crime' with Roberts? If so, it was preposterous. Whatever Frank's past actions might suggest, anyone who knew Roberts would instantly dismiss any notion of a homosexual liaison between them. Frank wrote to Roberts at Bath College, where he was then a mathematics master, to warn him what was coming. Meanwhile, Doulton applied to the court registrar to have the statement struck out on the grounds that it did not represent an act of cruelty and contained a veiled accusation that should either be made clear or withdrawn.[22] The registrar refused, saying he did not think an imputation could be put on it. Roberts' family disagreed: 'Whatever Messrs. Lewis may mean,' his brother wrote, 'as long as those words remain as are, there is a dirty insinuation about them.'[23] The Russells, fulfilling Harry's prediction that they would turn out 'rather slender reeds', withdrew their support from Mabel, refusing one by one to communicate with her. Mabel tried to defend herself, insisting that she would have said nothing about it had Frank's team not pushed for particulars and apparently quite at a loss to understand what charge they thought she had brought that was so despicable. When Harry wrote to Mabel asking if it were true that she was bringing charges against Frank and Roberts, she somewhat confusingly replied,

> I assure you I have brought *no* charge against Mr. Roberts. Any charge I bring against Lord R. I am in full position to *prove*, both from my own personal knowledge of him, the evidence I hold of his relations, & servants at Amberley Cottage ... I should recommend any man with self-respect, after what I know now, to avoid his companionship. I am most humiliated to think I should have lived with a man, even for 3 months, with such a shocking character ... but I am in the hands of clever men of the world, who, I feel sure, would not bring charges against *Ld. R.* unless they could prove them.

She denied she was responsible for a recent front-page article in the French newspaper *Le Figaro* which stated quite categorically that if Mabel won her action, Frank would find himself facing charges of a criminal nature. She genuinely seemed bemused by what had happened and, perhaps getting cold feet, made one last attempt to draw Lady Stanley's assistance. It was not her wish, she wrote, to act vindictively or bring the case into open court 'if some arrangement could be made to protect me'. Maude sent the letter to Frank in the hope it might influence him to reopen private negotiations, but Frank took it as 'a very serious sign of weakness'. He cut communication with Lina and wrote to Doulton, 'I am delighted to perceive how timorous they are getting, and am wholly of the opinion that consistent firmness on our part is the one way to crush these reptiles.'[24] He instructed his solicitor to write to Mabel's that he refused to consider any proposal until they took the petition off the file. They declined.

Yet even with all the momentum apparently with Frank, as the expected July date for the trial approached, there were times when he wavered. He had already recognised that '*if they venture into court* it is a struggle for life: one *or both* of us will leave our good name behind us', and in his darker moments the thought occurred that it could be him. There were 'other things' he had told Mabel 'from a sense of honour and which she would never have learnt from anyone else' which if they came out under cross-examination might lead him to suffer 'social penalties'.[25] He turned to the Russells for support, writing to Lady John, asking if he could visit – 'I shall go mad if I can't talk to someone' – and to Agatha, lamenting that he had heard nothing from them for so long and offering the closest thing to an apology they would ever get: 'I behaved atrociously to everybody 6 years ago, and now the girl I loved and trusted is going to make me smart for it.'[26]

As July came and went, the whole family was in limbo as they waited on tenterhooks for the case to appear on the daily lists. Mabel made one last attempt to clarify what she meant in her statement about Roberts, 'namely, that during his visit to Eaton Square, Lord Russell neglected me shamefully, leaving me his young wife for hours, to be in Mr. Roberts' society'. If this was really all she had intended to allege, writing so to Harry would have no impact on the proceedings, which continued unaltered. Agatha also made one last attempt to influence Frank: 'How we all *long* that this misery might yet be settled privately and quietly … I wd. do anything desperate on my own responsibility … but *what can I do*? Tell me if you think of anything.' She invited Mabel to PL to speak with her quietly about the action, but was disappointed. Meanwhile Lina begged Doulton to convince Frank to see her, firmly planting the blame for the breakdown in negotiations on Lady Cardigan. She appealed to Frank directly to settle out of court 'for *my sake*, who you have always had such affection and friendship for'. But there was no halting proceedings now. The stage was set, the players engaged, their lines rehearsed, their costumes chosen. The papers anticipated the spectacle they were about to see. After only four months of married life and a further eighteen of drama, the performance that started on 6 February 1890 at St Peter's church in Eaton Square would begin its second act on the stage of the Divorce Court on 1 December 1891.

11

In the High Court of Justice

On that gloomy, overcast Tuesday morning, Frank made his way along London's Strand towards its intersection with Chancery Lane and Fleet Street and the building that was to become so familiar to him: the palatial Royal Courts of Justice. The new home of the high court had been built to coincide with some sweeping reforms to the British judicial system and opened by Queen Victoria in December 1882.[1] Behind its intimidating façade of finely chiselled Portland stone, over a footprint of some 5 acres, the monumental Gothic structure housed nineteen suitably sombre oak-panelled courtrooms around a vast cathedral-like hall. It's 700 additional rooms allowed all the business of civil law to be carried out under one expansive roof for the first time. As a young man of twenty-six, Frank stood at its entrance and wondered what fate awaited him inside. A timid man may have shuddered at the prospect, but Frank firmly believed truth was on his side and took courage.

At the same time, hurrying towards the building from the opposite direction, sharpened pencils at the ready, were Fleet Street's court reporters. Their readers eagerly anticipated news from courtrooms I and II – home of the divorce division – and there was plenty to be had. In nine years, its judges had issued on average some 350 decrees annually to applicants desperate to sever the Gordian knot that tied them into unhappy marriages. Few of these were greeted with such anticipation as the so-called *causes célèbres*, which revealed the foibles and failings of those of the highest social strata. Pressmen from the popular papers jostled for position with their broadsheet counterparts, ready to take down every word. Their efforts would be recounted (with only subtle discretionary modifications) under sensational headlines in multiple editions throughout the day, while the broadsheets' serious, instructive, meticulously detailed accounts would appear the following morning. On every street corner billboards and street vendors invited passers-by to read all about it. Frank would later recall that for the duration he was tortured not by the trial itself but by the horror of seeing his name in large letters on posters all over the city: 'I had always shrunk from publicity,' he confessed, 'and felt as if I was being skinned alive in public.'[2]

Such was the fascination with its dramas that the divorce court's regular players became household names. Judges and barristers were caricatured in *Vanity Fair* and were as renowned for their performances as were the leading stage actors of the day. A select few came up against each other time and again, commanding fees that guaranteed them an annual income of between £15,000 and £20,000, and holding a celebrity status to rival that of their famous clients. Almost as soon as a *cause célèbre* was announced, speculation would begin as to its sparring partners. In the case of *Russell* v. *Russell*, scheduled for 10.30 in Court II that morning before Sir Charles Butt, president, lead counsel were named as Sir Edward Clarke QC for the petitioner and, for the respondent, a namesake (but no relation), Sir Charles Russell QC; the two men were perhaps the best known and most highly respected barristers of their day.

That George Lewis chose Sir Edward to represent Mabel is not surprising. They had a long-standing working relationship and Sir Edward was at the height of his career, holding at the time the office of solicitor general. Instantly recognisable by the 'ample and distinctive whiskers' covering his jowls and the fur coat in which he always arrived at court, he was an earnest man of inexhaustible energy who had raised himself from humble origins to become a great advocate. The son of a silversmith, he had pursued an ambitious path to liberate himself from his father's trade, winning a clerkship at the India Office and thereby a bursary to study law at King's College. He was called to the Bar in November 1864 and quickly demonstrated a natural eloquence, powerful memory, 'high standard of honour and genuine devotion to principle'. He was said to possess an 'incomparable lucidity'; his skill in summing-up left little doubt as to the correct verdict. He believed it 'better to be moral than amusing, and good-hearted than either', was 'too eloquent to be dull, too serious to be flippant', had 'more sentimentality than humour, and ... was not ashamed of being demonstrative'.[3]

Sir Edward had taken his first brief from George Lewis in 1871 and 'took silk' to become QC in 1880,[4] becoming in the same year a Tory MP. He was knighted in 1886 and became solicitor general, holding the position for six years. In 1890, he secured a famous victory for Captain O'Shea, proving his wife's adultery with the Irish Nationalist Charles Stewart Parnell. His opponent had been Sir Charles Russell, whom he had faced many times across the courtroom. Indeed, such was their popularity that, by 1891, whenever the services of one was retained, the other would often follow.

Sir Charles was from County Down and proud of his heritage. When advised early in his career that he could add £500 annually to his earnings simply by dropping his Irish brogue, he refused. His ambition to be a barrister brought him to England. He entered Lincoln's Inn in 1856, was called to the Bar in 1859 and quickly recognised as having 'a clear head, a strong will, an imperious temper, and an independent spirit'. He had a domineering personality and rough demeanour. He abhorred scandal and was intolerant of 'stupidity, folly, verbosity, and affectation' in his juniors. He too rose quickly through the ranks, taking silk in 1872, becoming a Liberal MP in 1880 and the first Catholic attorney general since the Reformation in 1886 and 1892–94. In later life, he would join the nobility as Lord Russell of Killowen, become a Lord of Appeal and eventually Lord Chief Justice of England. As a barrister, he built his reputation on the great pains he took with every case. He never came to court unprepared and took few notes, keeping his eye instead on the action unfolding before him. He was not naturally eloquent, but knew instinctively which points to seize upon, watching every turn of the jury and changing his line of attack with alarming rapidity. He was described as an 'elemental force' and no great respecter of persons. His very appearance was said to be intimidating – 'the manly, defiant bearing, the noble brow, the haughty look, the remorseless mouth, those deep-set eyes, widely opened, and that searching glance which pierced the very soul'. The tenacity with which he would drive his point home was legendary. In cross-examination, he did not try to manoeuvre his witness, but would go straight to him, 'take him by the throat and drag him' where he wished him to be.[5]

On this occasion, Sir Edward and Sir Charles were well matched with their clients also. If anyone could elicit sympathy for Mabel regarding Frank's alleged abusive treatment, it was Sir Edward; if anyone would give her accusations the short shrift they deserved, it was Sir Charles. Sir Edward's junior counsel was Lewis Coward, who had supported him in the O'Shea case. With Sir Charles came the intimidating line-up of divorce court specialist Frederick Inderwick QC, the soon-to-be knighted Frank Lockwood QC, William Robson – who would take silk the following year and be much involved with Frank's future litigations[6] – and William Compton Smith. Frank was clearly sending the message that he meant business.

For Mabel, too, the point-scoring began long before Sir Edward rose to make his opening speech. The 'clever men' in whose care she had placed herself had paid the additional fee to have a special jury, comprising men of a higher social standing than in a common jury, in the hope that their sympathies would be more readily stirred by the refinement and delicacy of the ladies. The ladies themselves had been carefully directed in their deportment and dress. The press – in this case, the *Star* – reported that the 'beautiful' Countess Russell, 'simple, smooth-faced, soft eyed' and dressed in blue velvet, with a boa and a spreading hat, came to court supported by her mother and sister. Lina wore 'an open fur coat, with the tiniest of French bonnets fixed at an angle at the back of her curled head' and had 'a much more opulent style of beauty than her daughters'. She 'occasionally refreshed her nerves with a sniff at a great gold-lidded vinaigrette'. Frank, meanwhile, peered out from behind his little steel-rimmed spectacles, looking more like an 'assistant board school master' than an aristocrat.[7]

In his opening speech, Sir Edward emphasised the short duration of the Russells' marriage and the separation necessitated by Frank's conduct. He spoke of the family's interventions in securing 'expressions of penitence' for his behaviour and described how the majority of Frank's actions might be considered trifling had Mabel not been 'extremely weak' at the time of her marriage – a condition for which her husband lacked sympathy. He did not know, he said, what 'peculiarities' Frank suffered from, but he was in the habit of treating his wife with 'utter want of consideration'. He was likewise in the habit of acting 'with great cruelty' to his cats, pulling them along on strings and, on one occasion, throwing one up to the ceiling several times 'until it was half killed'. Mabel had remonstrated with him and he had replied that it was necessary for him to 'lick the cat into shape, and he would do the same for her if she did not mind'. Trivial though this may seem, this kind of behaviour on a daily basis, he asserted, amounted to cruelty.

Sir Edward then summarised the key events in Frank and Mabel's short married life. To his executive mind, the episodes described in Mabel's petition organised themselves neatly into 'incidents': there was the 'accounts incident' in which Frank kept her standing for hours over his books, the 'cellar incident' in which she was made to check off the delivery of his year's supply of wine, and the disagreeable 'incident' at the Albemarle Hotel, when in his anger he made her turn out her pockets and left her there without a farthing. There was the 'incident' in which he forced her to her knees in his office, and the 'pistol incident' in which he 'raved about the boudoir of their house' like a maniac, threatening to shoot them both. During the 'bracelet incident' he had caught hold of her violently, and during the 'fainting incident' she had been forced to take refuge with one of her servants. In addition, there were the numerous name-calling incidents and the incidents in which he spoke to her with contempt before the servants. Each one, when added to the next, would make life 'exceedingly trying' for any young woman, 'especially one in bad health'.

Then there was one more serious matter about which they would hear: the 'Roberts incident'. He read aloud the paragraph from the particulars. It was 'an unusual, and a serious paragraph' and one which 'carries with it a very serious suggestion against Earl Russell'. But, he said, he was not there to make that suggestion; only to say that by repeatedly leaving his wife alone to spend time with Roberts in his bedroom – no matter what he was doing there, which might have been something 'perfectly innocent', such as 'spending the night in mathematical exercises with the head mathematical master of a college at Bath' – it was nonetheless 'great cruelty' and 'distressed her extremely'. After the 'cheque incident' Frank showed no real repentance and Mabel became convinced she 'could not safely resume marital relations with her husband', for which they would bring corroborative evidence. Sir Edward concluded by saying that he was aware that there were cases where 'wives were hysterical, and that some force was necessary on the part of a husband', but in Mabel's case 'there was not the slightest ground for that supposition'. She was entitled therefore to the full protection of the law. He called on Mabel to give evidence.

Mabel made her way demurely to the witness box. In a 'meek, almost inaudible voice' she confirmed the facts of the marriage and respective settlements and gave details of Frank's behaviour which she said 'troubled and stressed me very much'. Of the incident when she was forced to her knees she elaborated,

> It was half-past nine. I had gone to bed early because I did not feel well. I went down to Lord Russell's library. He said, 'I suppose you have been sulking upstairs, and will say that I have made you ill by quarrelling this afternoon.' I said, 'I don't wish to continue the quarrel.' He bullied me, and said I was a beast, and that he hated me. He called me a barren brute. I asked him not to be insulting to me. He seized me by the wrist, tearing the lace off my jacket and forced me on to the floor on my knees.

A gentleman had then called and Frank had left her on the floor saying, 'Stop there and don't dare move until I come back', but the maid came and took her back to bed.

With regard to the Roberts incident, she said Frank had 'ordered her to bed' after dinner. He followed at about 11 p.m. having already undressed in his dressing room. She asked if he was coming to bed. He said no, he was going to Roberts' room. The same thing happened for the next two nights. Each time, Frank did not return until 3 a.m. When she remonstrated with him, 'he told me to go to the Devil and mind my own business'. In a quiet, injured tone she said Frank was always unkind to her when Roberts was there, never allowing her to speak much. She had been greatly upset to discover that Roberts had stayed with Frank at Amberley Cottage in August or September 1890 – she wasn't sure which – and confirmed that she had refused to go there, but stumbled over whether Roberts' presence was the cause and Sir Edward gently let the matter lie.

With regard to the incident at the Albemarle, she recalled 'in her little resentful way' that Frank had called her 'useless', had said he was damn sorry he married her and wished she were dead. He'd demanded she turn out her pockets and give back the money and pocket-watch he had asked her to look after, which he supposed she had stolen. Afterwards, he'd refused to admit that *he* had been the one to leave and said if Mabel did not return to him 'the family would not know me, and that I should be ruined'.

On the occasion of the pistol incident, they had been arguing and Frank had rushed out of the bedroom into the boudoir where she found him 'ransacking the drawers of the writing table' looking for a pistol to 'shoot himself with, or me, he didn't care'. When she told him that there was no occasion to shoot anyone, he took her by the shoulders and 'shook her like a rat' before venting his rage in a 'very plebeian manner' by punching the wall. When they separated in June and she asked him not do anything she would not like while they were apart, he'd said it would 'depend how he felt'.

116

She came to see that she could not return to him with any hope of happiness or safety.

Sir Charles then opened his cross-examination by asking if, up to July 1890, Mabel had ever really contemplated returning to live with her husband:

A: I hadn't made up my mind.
Q: I didn't ask you if you had made up your mind, did you contemplate it?
A: I do not think I did.
Q: Then when you wrote with the terms [of your return], did you not mean them?
A: I wished to do all I could.

This first exchange set the tone for the rest of it. There would be no soft touch from Sir Charles, no gentle coercion to get her facts right. He immediately went on the offensive over Roberts, asking why Mabel had not mentioned him when she outlined the terms of her return; to which she replied that she did not then know that Roberts had again stayed with Frank. Sir Charles wasted no further time in broaching his most important question:

Q: Now be good enough to see that you understand my question before you answer it. When you introduced the name of Mr. Roberts into your petition, and when you referred to it to-day, aye or no, did you intend to suggest (to use my learned friend's expression) any imputation upon your husband, or upon Mr. Roberts – aye or no?

Sir Edward immediately objected that it was not reasonable or relevant, but the judge disagreed and Sir Charles put his question again:

Q: When you introduced the name of Mr. Roberts, did you, or did you not, mean to make an imputation upon that gentleman, and upon your husband, aye or no?
A: I did think it very strange that Lord Russell always left me for Mr. Roberts.
Q: Aye or no. Did you, when you introduced his name mean to make an imputation upon Mr. Roberts and upon your husband, aye or no?
A: [Hesitation] Yes.

There were audible gasps around the courtroom, but Sir Charles barely drew breath. He pressed his advantage by drawing the confession from a rather confused Mabel that she knew there had been an application to strike out the allegation on the ground that 'an allegation, if meant to be injurious, ought to be made specifically', but could not remember when she heard of it. Her representative had stated that no imputation was intended by the paragraph except that Frank had 'cultivated Mr. Roberts' society'.

What about her letter to Harry Marillier in which she said she made no charge against Roberts?

A: Well, I do not think I have brought any charge against Mr. Roberts at all.

Sir Charles pressed her to confirm she had sent Harry newspapers clippings which she said revealed Frank's true history (but which mysteriously never materialised, despite applications to produce them) and read aloud the letter in which she stated she was 'in the hands of clever men of the world'. She acknowledged writing it.[8]

He turned then to other matters, securing only denials from Mabel that she had ever suffered from hysteria or had torn the lace of her own nightgown, or (to the amusement of the court) that she had soundly boxed Frank's ears after the pistol incident. At the same time, he forced admissions that health issues caused her to break off her engagement to Edward Fitzgerald; that the wine delivery had only taken fifteen minutes; and that she had known Frank disapproved of 'Mrs K' when she lunched with her on the day of the Albemarle incident. He then returned to the subject of Roberts, pushing her for a second time on whether and when she had made suggestions of impropriety. Eventually, Mabel said that after their final separation, she 'heard from the family things that made me think and feel sure'.

Q: I think I have got it at last. Then, until some things that you subsequently heard, you had attached no importance to this incident about Mr. Roberts?
A: How could I?
Q: I am not asking you how you could. It is not for me to answer questions...

Who, then, were the family members who had suggested impropriety? Mabel would rather not say. Sir Charles pressed her, Sir Edward intervened, but the judge again supported Sir Charles and Mabel was forced to answer:

A: I say it very much against my wish to bring their names in. But you force me. It was the Dowager Countess Russell, Lady Agatha Russell, the Honourable Rollo Russell, and I have also had a letter from Lord Carlisle.

The day's business ended with Frank's barrister having apparently secured two very significant admissions: that despite her counsel saying it was not the case, Mabel *did* mean to accuse Frank and Roberts; and that the source of this information was Frank's own family. But he had pushed her hard and, in so doing, had won her the sympathy of the press. The *Belfast News-Letter* said it was impossible not to feel 'for the soft, gentle-faced' twenty-two-year-old 'as she feebly, nervously, wrestled with the trying and exhausting cross-examination' while her husband 'sat in the well of the court ... "adding up", as it seemed, the net result of her evidence'.

The second day began with the popular press reporting that Countess 'Babs' arrived in court looking much brighter, having added to her blue velvet gown 'a glimpse of white handkerchief peeping out at her breast'. She was apparently relaxed as she retook the stand, but soon wavered under Sir Charles's insistence that the Russells had never said 'one word to suggest in the Roberts incident there was a grave crime'. Not about Roberts, she conceded, but about 'things connected with [Frank's] past life'. She could not say exactly *when* they told her these things – and Sir Charles was not going to give her the opportunity to say *what* they might have said – but it was most definitely after their separation, during her stay at PL.

Was, then, her admission at the close of day one an exaggeration? Did she suggest – aye or no – that it had anything to do with her state of health? Was it not true that she had written Frank 'affectionate' letters, though she had no intention of returning to him? Was it not also true that at this time she was being pressed by creditors and had met with Frank's solicitor to arrange to borrow money to repay them at his suggestion? Might not her precarious financial position be the real reason for her continued affection towards her husband? All Mabel could say in reply was that her doctor prescribed the period of separation, that she could not remember the exact timing of her meeting with Doulton and her affectionate letters were written 'to be kind'.

Concerning the cheques incident, Sir Charles questioned whether in fact there was any mistake on Frank's part. Was it not the plain state of things that she had sent him a letter requesting to manage her entire income? Yes, she conceded, and set about explaining which cheques had been paid in, which had not, how her dividends had not paid until October, and her consequent embarrassment which, it appeared to her, Frank would have predicted. The judge intervened – it seemed such a small point, was it worth following up in such detail? Yes, indeed, said Sir Charles, it is the cause of these whole proceedings. And to substantiate his point, he read the exchange of letters between Mabel and Frank, Mabel and Doulton and Frank and the bank managers. Perhaps that was a misjudgement on his part. The judge concluded at the end of it that Frank's explanation to Mabel did not look like a mistake at all, but 'an intentional matter' and 'a justification of what had taken place'.

Thereafter, the change of tone in Mabel's letters, the requests for her belongings and her share of the wedding presents, all seemed reasonable. Sir Charles was reduced to trying to disrupt Sir Edward's re-examination with jibes that Mabel's assertion that Frank threw the cat ten times towards the ceiling before landing it on top of the wardrobe was 'too absurd' to be believed; with taunts that if she had indeed asked the butler to send the pistol to Teddington, it was ridiculous to suppose Frank would look for it in Walton; and with objections to Sir Edward trying to get in evidence of what the butler told her, because, said Sir Charles, *he* had not asked to know – this 'clever lady' had put it on him. To the disappointment of the whole court, Mabel was allowed to stand down with what the butler told her 'forever unknown', though with the acknowledgement that 'through her long examination she had been sustained by a full-sized sense of her grievance'.

Much of the afternoon was then taken up with other witnesses called to attest to the minutiae of the case. Dr Godson of Grosvenor Street – the 'well known ladies' physician' – was called to attest to Mabel's declining health which he ascribed to her 'living unhappily', and to deny that she was hysterical or nervous. On the contrary, she was 'very strong-minded' – an active young woman who liked riding, boating, and driving. Then when a Dr Izod was called to collaborate Godson's evidence concerning Mabel's dysmenorrhoea – which, he was pleased to tell the judge, was *not* an impediment to marriage – a confused discussion took place between lead counsel, a juryman and the judge as to whether there was a difference between 'spasmodic dysmenorrhoea' and 'dysmenorrhoea with spasms' and if so, which was most severe and which it was that Godson had said Mabel suffered from.

Next, Giddy, in a tailor-made grey dress and black feather hat and boa, looking pale-faced and nervously biting her lip, took the stand to attest to her sister's illness on her return from her honeymoon and her scratched wrist after the bracelet incident. Finally, two of Mabel's servants were brought forward to attest to Frank's rough handling of her; the second of which, Mabel's aged Nurse Vale, had the rapt attention of the whole court when she testified to entering Mabel's room to find her 'absolutely naked' and very 'agitated and excited' on the occasion of the fainting incident, but admitted under cross-examination that Mabel had not complained that Frank had 'ill-used her'. She wept bitterly when Mr Lockwood read aloud a letter she had written to Mabel in which she had asked her if the sin of separation – 'for so it is' – was really her only option: 'I allways [*sic*] thought darling you ment [*sic*] to go back and try to do what is right.'[9] In an act of sympathy, Mabel stepped forward to help her venerable old servant down from the witness box.

After a short adjournment, Sir Charles opened for the defence by asking the jury to consider why they were there. Why did Mabel need a judicial separation from a man she was already physically separated from? In his opinion it was obvious that her motives were pecuniary, but that lacking any 'real materials' by which to convince the court of Frank's cruelty, this 'clever and engaging woman' had manipulated the innocent society of friends into a very serious charge. Her counsel said he was not there to make that charge. Who was, then? And how could they, the prosecution, take it other than as a grave charge? Through the 'devilish contrivance' of that paragraph, Frank was forced to come to court to defend both his reputation and that of the innocent Roberts who could not bring counsel to defend himself. It was 'impossible to resist the conclusion,' said Sir Charles passionately, 'that this lady, having committed herself to that vile statement – vile in itself and dishonest in the way it was put forward' – had not 'deliberately perverted that part of the account' to the possible ruination of Roberts had he not been esteemed by his college friends and superiors. 'The whole story was one of gross exaggeration.'

Sir Charles had not finished his speech when the court rose at 4 p.m., but he had whipped up a storm; though to whose advantage was not immediately clear. As Frank left the court, a large crowd assembled around him. Several policemen endeavoured to keep it moving, but when an acquaintance of Frank's joined him and the two men began talking confidentially, a large mob of 'roughs and spectators' gathered and whispers circulated that the acquaintance was Roberts. There were some 'ugly rushes' followed by shouts of 'Who killed the cat?' and 'What price Roberts?' The two men crossed the street and walked quickly along Middle Temple Lane, but the crowd of 200 to 300 followed them mewing and crying 'Puss-Puss!', 'Roberts!' and 'Oh, the dirty man!' and they were forced to flee through the Temple and up Fleet Street, where they hailed a cab and drove off up Chancery Lane 'amid a storm of groans and howls'. Mabel and Giddy, meanwhile, slipped away quietly to the Savoy, to join their mother who had been notable by her absence all day. What, one wonders, would the crowd have made of the letter she had sent in her stead that morning had they known of it? It was marked 'private' and addressed to Doulton. It begged him not to put her in the witness box. She had already refused Sir Edward and had heard that Sir Charles now intended to call her:

> ... surely Lord Russell does not wish me to perjure myself, and he knows perfectly I should be bound to say what is true. He *must* remember one of the mornings Mr. Roberts was staying in Eaton Sqre. and Dobson was putting breakfast on the table that I said if he and Mr. Roberts made such a noise over my head I must change my room and he said they were bear fighting. How can I deny such a thing to shield him when his wife and Dobson heard me say it.[10]

The following morning, Frank was joined at his solicitor's table in the packed courtroom by Lyulph Stanley and Roberts. Mabel sat with Giddy and George Lewis. Lina was nowhere to be seen. Sir Charles continued his speech by addressing the ancillary issues of the case. A different light would be thrown on it, he said, when they got the real facts. He went through them one by one – the pistol, bracelet and fainting incidents – checking them off as he went. Was that everything? No! The cat! He had forgotten the cat! The court erupted as Sir Charles continued:

> He was not an admirer of cats himself, but Lord Russell was. Did they believe he had thrown this cat to the ceiling, striking it on the head about 10 times? A cat had only nine lives, and the 10th blow would probably have finished it. (Loud laughter.) They had not heard, however, that the cat did come to an untimely end. It might be alive and flourishing, and it might be the father of a large family for all he knew. (Laughter.)

Even Mabel and Giddy laughed. But joking aside, said Sir Charles, it was his contention that they would not believe that Frank had treated his wife in an 'unmanly' manner. He pointed to the fact that they had separated on good terms and that Frank had subsequently stayed with Lina while Mabel was at PL; representatives of which – Rollo and Agatha – were in court and would be heard. The jury would find him not guilty of the charges because an adverse verdict would not only besmirch Frank's reputation, but 'would affect a name which has been one of credit in the history of the country'. He then stunned the expectant courtroom by calling Roberts to the box.

Roberts' duration there was brief. After a quick overview of his career, his introduction to Frank and early visits to the Scotts, he 'denied absolutely' that Frank was ever in his room 'undressed'. When they sat up talking, Frank wore a smoking jacket and they were in his study on the ground floor. His cross-examination was, in the circumstances, briefer still – the latest they sat up was 2 a.m., Mabel went to bed at eleven, breakfast was at eight; after which Frank went to work.

Following Roberts, Frank took the stand, remaining there for the rest of the day and the early part of the next. He was examined by Mr Inderwick in a manner Frank later described as a 'masterly performance'. Throughout, he felt 'like a swimmer who is being supported in the water by a strong hand'; an old hand, in actual fact, well practised in the delicate art of examination-in-chief, who got everything he wanted 'without any leading questions or any hesitation'.[11] Frank, naturally, contradicted Mabel in almost every detail but remained relaxed and genial throughout, entertaining the crowded courtroom with his candid replies.

Yes, he was annoyed to discover his wife's debts had not been paid off before their marriage. No, he never kept her standing for hours over the account books: there were only five or six entries in her handwriting. She would sit at the table trying to add them up. (Laughter.) There was no pretence whatsoever for saying it took hours. No, he never directed her to look after the servants' offices, but had asked her once to see that the water closet on the ground floor was properly supplied. The servants had the right to use that facility. No, she did not complain about counting off the wine delivery and he did not tear the lace on her jacket or force her to her knees – *she* had torn the lace *herself* in her ravings. And it was 'absolutely false' that he went up to Robert's room and stayed there until 3 a.m. or compelled Mabel to write and request his return.

At the Albemarle, *she* had asked to dress *him* – she was anxious he should look smart for the occasion. His objection to Mrs K was that she was a divorced woman who very much deserved to be divorced (sensation!) – and yes, it was true they argued on her return, but he did not leave her without any money – quite the opposite – he had got out his pocket book, but Mabel had said to her mother, 'I don't want any of his dirty money' so he had put it away. (Laughter.) The argument concerning the pistol started because he did not want his wife to go to the house of a gentleman in Ascot who openly kept a mistress (sensation!); and it was not true that he ransacked the boudoir for it because he knew it had gone to Teddington to be warehoused. On the following afternoon they were on good enough terms to enjoy a game of lawn tennis. He could not remember if Lina was in trouble with her creditors again at the time, but it was not an uncommon thing. (Laughter.) On the occasion of the bracelet incident, the injury was caused by him trying to get back the letter he had been writing to Doulton which Mabel had seized. It was true she boxed his ears before leaving the room. (Laughter.)

On the occasion of the fainting incident, he was very frightened. He had done all he could to revive her with eau-de-Cologne, burnt feather, etc., and eventually resorted to throwing a basin of water over her. He removed her nightdress because he had opened the window and was afraid she would catch cold. He wrapped her in the eiderdown, but when she came to, she became immediately hysterical and in jumping up the quilt fell off her and that was the moment the nurse came in. He tried to calm her by saying, 'Don't be so violent, darling', but she turned on him, saying, 'D—— you, do not call me darling.' She took up the soap dish and threw it on the floor, then made for him with the poker (laughter), but the nurse intervened and took her away.

He was ashamed to say he had used the word 'barren' once, but it was in fun and not meant to be offensive. They were alone at the time. Mabel asked him never to use it again and he had not. He was never unkind to the cat and never spoke rudely to her in front of the servants.

Frank was then cross-examined by Sir Edward and had been warned that he was 'the most deadly cross-examiner in England'.[12] But Frank's pedantic Stanley streak made him equally as fastidious about details – a fact which he later admitted must have made him 'as trying a husband as Mabel could have had to put up with'.[13]

He could not say a compromise had not been suggested by Mabel, but it was not done through her solicitor, so was therefore irrelevant. And the downturn in her health was more likely because she had been unused to restraining herself before the marriage than as a direct result of the marriage. He had exercised control in this respect. On their honeymoon, for example, when she drove him in a pony cart on wet, slippery roads, he convinced her to continue though she was nervous and he could not then drive:

Q: Why did you not consider her condition, and indulge the fear, even if it were unreasonable?
A: How could I indulge it? I was trying to soothe her. She did not ask to get out.
Q: Was that a case of early restraint?
A: No; I do not call that restraint.
Q: Her restraint was something more severe than that?
A: I should say restraint was restraint.

Frank said that, being unaccustomed to it, Mabel rebelled, making *herself* upset and excitable in the process.

Q: What had you to restrain her about?
A: I wanted to restrain her to six cigarettes a day. (Laughter.)

Frank did not remember that he had ever taken the accounts of the electrical business to Eaton Square, but if he had, he certainly had not asked Mabel to work on them. When Sir Edward pointed out that there were no 'coils' and 'volts' in household accounts, Frank said neither would they be found in electrical accounts – 'wire was sold by the pound and not in coils, and volts were not matters which could be bought or sold'. His general mode was not to *order* his wife, but to *ask* her – though often even that irritated her – and then they would argue, and his arguments were cogent (laughter), and sometimes she would give way.

As regards the Albemarle incident, the servant who came to dress him was the butler who was in court that day (but never called). The mention of servants naturally brought Sir Edward in a roundabout way to Kate Williams and he asked if it were true that at the time of the fainting incident Frank had re-employed one of his former servants against Mabel's wish that he should 'drop all connection with the past and the Williamses'. Frank said he had. The servant was Moyse, his former engineer on *Royal*. He was a good servant and nothing to do with the Williamses. Sir Edward then asked him directly if he had seduced one of the Williams' daughters. He had, some three or four years ago, seduced Kate, who was then twenty or twenty-one. The relationship continued until a couple of months before his engagement. He had arranged to pay her mother £1 per week and, after his engagement, the young lady brought an action for breach of promise which Frank settled for £500. Mabel knew all about it – he told her himself (some applause).

After several further questions concerning the fainting incident – why, for instance, Frank had not called for help earlier if Mabel had been in a faint for forty minutes (A: it didn't occur to him it would last that long) – and what he had to say about the nurse's evidence that she heard Mabel speaking in a pleading tone with him before she entered (A: he wouldn't have called it pleading, her voice was very loud and her manner violent) – he asked Frank his age. He was then twenty-six.

Q: In 1885, you went down from Oxford?
A: Yes.
Q: Were you *sent* down from it?
A: I was.
Q: For what?
A: A complaint was made that I had written an improper letter.
Q: To a man or a woman?
A: To a man, I suppose; but I never saw the letter, and never knew what was in it. I never knew the details. I challenged investigation at the time, but never obtained it.
Q: Were the circumstances of your leaving Oxford known to your relatives and friends?
A: Yes, I suppose they were.

Given that Sir Edward denied he intended any imputation on Frank and Roberts' activities, it was curious he mentioned Oxford at all. It gave

Sir Charles the opportunity in his re-examination to ask Frank, had he taken his own name off the college books? (A: Yes); had Jowett subsequently received Frank and attended his wedding? (A: Yes); and which of Frank's behaviours had Mabel known about? Frank had told both her and Lina about Kate, but had not told Mabel about Oxford:

Q: Why?
A: Because Lady Scott told me not to do so.

Loud applause broke out around the auditorium. The final question of the day was asked by the judge himself: did Mabel know that the gentleman in Ascot had a mistress in his house? Certainly, Frank replied, she and Lina told him themselves. The crowd erupted once more. The day had ended well for Frank, with the promise that the next – the last of the proceedings – would be even better.

That day, for nearly an hour, a crowd waited in the rain for the courts to open and an 'ugly rush' at the Strand entrance gave police 'considerable trouble'. Sir Edward further cross-examined Frank with questions concerning entries in his diary, but the entries were brief and Frank had little difficulty in claiming he could not remember why on one specific day eighteen months previously he had written 'M. suspicious', or, on another, that there was 'much upset', and the net result was that the prosecution concluded their interrogation on a weak note. The situation was compounded when the judge returned yet again to the by-now-infamous paragraph concerning Roberts and the application for it to be struck out, declaring that if it had come before him he would have made short shrift of it; that at the very least it should have been recorded as a charge of 'gross indecency'.

Sir Charles furthered their advantage by securing from Frank the declaration that he had sacked the butler because he was 'frequently drunk and violent to the maidservants'. Further, that the relationship with Kate had not been known in Teddington, where she still lived with her family, until her name was mentioned in court the previous day by Sir Edward. Thereafter, the several other defence witnesses were quickly got through, and their various testimonies – Dr Rushworth's that Mabel was certainly hysterical, and three of Frank's maids who all said they had never seen Mabel anywhere near the vicinity of their water closet or heard Frank speak rudely to her – all seemed rather academic, and Sir Charles delivered his closing address with confidence that the case now stood in a very different position than when Sir Edward had given his 'detailed and elaborate' opening speech some four days previously.

Mabel, he said, had been spoiled and possibly 'her being subject to great pain had tended to increase the family's indulgence'. She had sought to 'terrorise' Frank with vain threats of exposure and brought to court an 'odious charge' and calumnious stories from his past to prejudice the jury against him. Crueller still, Kate's reputation had been 'ruthlessly sacrificed' for the same contemptible purpose. It was a 'natural and generous impulse' on the part of those present that Frank's explanations were greeted with applause and if, after the jury had heard all the evidence, they were not prepared to 'scout a claim based on exaggeration, misrepresentation, deceit, and malice' nothing he could say would induce them to do so. He resumed his seat 'amid considerable applause'.

Sir Edward then appealed to the jury in a 'calm, light, argumentative style' to return their minds to the evidence his learned friend had clearly forgotten or passed over. The real issue of the case was that this couple were married on 6 February 1890 and by the time Mabel left on 12 June, she was 'a woman of broken spirits, nerves, and general health'. He did not know whether to be glad or sorry that the Roberts incident had not been struck out: if it had, he would have been relieved not to have to deal with it; but by the same token, Frank would have been denied the opportunity to clear his name, which he and Roberts had amply done. In his own questioning of Mabel, he had, as far as he could, 'dissociated her from any charge of that kind', but Sir Charles, 'knowing the advantage of an affirmative admission, pertinaciously cross-examined her on the subject and got the admission of which he had availed himself so largely since'. He had asked, what are we here for? But everyone knew that if Mabel continued to live away from her husband on her own income she would 'expose herself to censure; that the world would believe she must be in fault'; and Frank was content to see her 'exposed to sneers, temptations, and the difficulties which such a life involves'. Sir Charles had tried 'to alter the position of the parties by forcing the charge from her'. He hoped the jury could see through this device and 'relieve from her the burden of living with a man who cared nothing for her health and happiness'. At the end of his speech, there was more 'emphatic applause' and 'stamping of feet' and the judge was forced threaten the offenders with a fine or imprisonment to restore order.

At 3:50 p.m., the judge began his summing-up. Much of what he said favoured Frank. Though he did not agree with Sir Charles that Mabel's only object was money – Sir Edward was quite right that a woman who could no longer live with a cruel husband was entitled to their protection – some of her charges were uncorroborated and he told the jury they must dismiss these from their minds. These included the accounts and cellar incidents, the fate of the cat, and the assertion that Frank instructed her to take care of the servants' water closet. This, in particular, he felt, was not only uncorroborated, but had been disproved: was it possible that in a house of six or seven servants such a thing could have gone unwitnessed? If this allegation was false, it was 'wicked and malicious' and invented with the purpose of injuring her husband. In which case how could the jury trust anything she had said? Frank had admitted he had placed restraint on his wife and to do so violently was wrong; but there was such a thing as proper restraint and they must ask themselves whether in restricting her to six cigarettes a day, or preventing her from entering certain houses, whether he had not a right to do so. In relation to events in his past life, he asked them to consider why these had been introduced?

This left only the Roberts incident. That paragraph should never have been allowed to stand as it was and the prosecution dared not stand by a bold, straightforward charge of base criminality or gross indecency. It was not his opinion that a judge should direct a jury in 'a manner so colourless as to conceal his own views' when he had 'far greater opportunity of weighing and testing evidence than any juryman can have'. And it *was* his view that Sir Charles was right to confront the Roberts issue. But while he was the sole judge of the law, they were the sole judges of the facts and he asked them to consider whether Mabel had told the truth or sought to deceive them. If they decided that it was not true that Frank had visited Roberts in his room in the small hours, then either Mabel 'has sworn to that which she *knows* not to be true, or to that which she *does not know* to be true'. In either case, what is the value of her evidence in any of the other dozen or twenty subjects on which she had spoken and what becomes of her case? And if that charge is not true, why was Oxford referred to except to make them believe Frank was 'addicted to such practices'? Do you suppose, he asked the jury, that Professor Jowett – 'a man of the highest distinction and of the highest consideration' – would have attended Frank's wedding or received him if he thought any imputation rested on his former pupil? It was his own opinion that the events at Oxford were 'open to disproof' and it was a 'strong thing that it should now be cast in his teeth'.

The jury retired at 5.15 p.m. and returned fifty-five minutes later. When asked if they found Frank guilty of cruelty, the foreman's pronouncement – we do not – was met with cheers inside the court, and further outbursts 'again and again renewed' in the corridor outside. After receiving his friends' congratulations, Frank made his way out onto the Strand, where he was greeted by loud cheers (intermingled with some slight hissing) from a crowd of some 200 to 300 people, 'waving their hats and handkerchiefs in approval'. Mabel and Giddy had quietly slipped away when the jury retired. ·

12

The Cachet of the Court

Frank was exhilarated. He had been completely vindicated and his satisfaction was palpable in the letter he afterwards wrote to Santayana: 'The dramatic intensity of the last two days was marvellous,' he told his friend, wishing he could have been there to witness the 'glorious experience' for himself and enclosing 'representative' newspaper cuttings.

> The general feeling is one of great satisfaction with the verdict –
> 1. of my friends that I shd. have cleared the Oxford cloud & all the later Scott slanders & insinuations.
> 2. of the enemies of the Scotts that their unbroken career of success shd. be checked & themselves so utterly confounded.
> 3. of political people that the honour of a great name should be maintained.
> 4. of honest women that so foul a blot on their sex as Mabel Edith should have won social ostracism & loathing by her vile arts.
> 5. of men in general that women should not have it all their own way in law courts.
> 6. of socialists and Radicals that a Peer who works should have defeated a Peeress who did not.[1]

Harry Marillier had made up with Frank after hearing Mabel's testimony and others no doubt felt as Frank suggested. Still, the 'general feeling' was not exactly as he would have it. Certainly, there was a consensus that the result was the only possible one and the Scotts had acted dishonourably, if not dishonestly, but their confoundment was only temporary and Frank, as the *Pall Mall Gazette* commented, did not exactly emerge a 'hero'.[2] The press found many more points of interest to comment upon than the six he listed and the cross-spectrum of opinions when taken together offer not only a critique of the Russell case but a fascinating insight into the moral preoccupations of late Victorians.

At one end of the journalistic spectrum, the most respectable broadsheets (notably, the *Times*) chose to report events but not comment on them, reflecting both a general revulsion at the goings-on in the divorce court and a more particular issue with anything relating to same-sex activity. H. G. Cocks talks about this in *Nameless Offences* (2010). By endeavouring to provide across-the-board, detailed, transparent reporting while avoiding anything that could be regarded as morally corrupting, factions of the press ended up creating a form of discourse which 'simultaneously referred to homosexual desire, and tried to cover all traces of its existence with circumlocution and evasion'.[3] This sensibility, which disqualified the use of plain English for subjects of a homosexual nature, created enormous confusion. In the Russell case, Mabel Edith's cross-examination by Sir Charles could arguably be considered an example of this: did Mabel understand Sir Charles' question well enough for her positive response concerning Frank and Roberts' bedroom antics to be judged a direct accusation of sodomy – aye or no?

Those papers that did comment took a highly moral standpoint, using editorials to extrapolate the lessons that could be learnt from the proceedings to justify their reporting. The *Morning Post*, for example, said there was nothing 'either edifying or desirable to bring under public notice' about this case before adding nearly two columns of comment to the numerous it had already dedicated to the previous four days' reporting. Its major concern was the 'grave danger' of 'the practice of bringing charges which, so far from being substantiated, are withdrawn almost without an apology' and the potential effect on a gentleman's reputation should such practices continue. Sapping character by innuendo was evil, it proclaimed, and required reprobation.[4]

Only the satirical *Vanity Fair* dared to suggest that the real reason for the extensive coverage of *causes célèbres* was their entertainment value. 'If the happiness of many – even at the expense of the few – is the principle aim of the philanthropist, that individual ought to rank the diversions of the Divorce Court very high amongst the beneficial factors of the world,' it suggested, before taking a swipe at the rise of the predominantly middle-class 'Mrs Grundy' type who devoured its offerings 'on principle' and with great 'personal self-sacrifice' so that 'she should be alive to every foible of human nature in its sinister developments, in order that she may point a moral to the budding minds she seeks to shield from like contamination'. Thank heaven for Mrs Grundy! – that she alone was strong enough to silence the disapproving voices that clamoured for such cases to be heard *in camerâ* and thereby rob the press of their favourite pastime of passing judgment on the court once the court had passed judgment on the case.[5]

With Frank having been found innocent of the crime, the principal thing left to deliberate was who to blame for the slander. Taking a paternalistic stand, the *Post* concluded that the lawyers were at fault, turning the Russells into the latest victims of 'the unhealthy social craze which nowadays prompts people to drag their daily lives through the mire of public criticism'. Echoing Lady Stanley's opinion that with a little common sense the whole thing could have been avoided, it suggested that 'the average number of *really* unhappy marriages in this country is in all probability extremely small' and that most couples, though not 'ideally suitable', managed to rub along together quite nicely without 'bringing any broken hearts for dissection' by lawyers.[6] The more outspoken papers went further. Said the *Star*, the so-called 'honourable gentlemen' of the supposedly 'honourable profession' had, in their handling of the Roberts incident, perpetrated 'one of the dirtiest tricks of the lowest pettifogging attorney' by not specifically naming the charge implicit, which would have enabled Roberts to defend himself.[7] The Roberts incident was universally condemned as despicable, both in its implication and the manner in which it was used. Nothing could more clearly express Victorian attitudes towards homosexuality than the words chosen to express their disgust: the accusation was 'gross', 'vile', 'foul'. Nobody believed for one minute that the offending particular was brought, as presented, in innocence of the implication; and both the *Star* and the *Pall Mall* further singled out Sir Edward as the key culprit, 'who took the case into court in this abominable shape knowing well that he had nothing behind' and as solicitor general should have set a better example.[8] Only the *Dundee Courier*, in its belief that Clarke had previously advised Mabel *not* to bring the case to court in this form, actively defended him for discharging 'a most difficult duty in the best of taste'.[9]

Sir Edward also came under attack for his cross-examination of Frank in relation to Kate Williams. The minor and short-lived society journal *The Dwarf* asked if there was 'anything more base or cowardly' and found it 'incredible' that there were lawyers prepared to do it. It was a 'wanton piece of cruelty' to mention her by name when neither 'Mrs K' nor the Ascot gentleman who supposedly kept a mistress had been so shamed. This, they said, was a class issue. Who cared what happened to Kate Williams after shame had been brought upon her and her family by 'a diabolical desire on the part of Lady Russell's friends, to connect the earl's name with infamy'?[10]

In actual fact, the Williams issue was ongoing at this point. Kate had taken advice and a notice had appeared in the *Standard* on the last day of the trial stating that Griffinhoofe and Brewster of New Inn Road had been instructed to make it known that their client 'indignantly denied' that Frank had succeeded in seducing her and that steps were being taken to prove this slander.[11] A reply – which was essentially a non-reply – from Vandercom & Co. was printed two days later, after which the matter passed from the public domain. But Frank's letter to Santayana of 19 December 1891 reveals that Kate was trying to get campaigning editor W. T. Stead of the *Pall Mall* to take up her story – unsuccessfully, as she 'naturally failed to obtain the 'virgin' certificate'.[12] Whether behind this rather coarse comment Kate's silence was obtained at further expense to Frank is unknown. What is known is that he remained on friendly terms with Mrs Williams at least and the family as a whole never again appeared as 'servants' on a census. From April 1891 they were described as 'living on own means', housed in a very nice villa in Teddington and Isaac Williams passed as a gentleman on his other two daughters' subsequent marriage certificates.[13]

As regards Roberts, for those who did not blame the lawyers, there really was only one culprit: Mabel Edith. Rollo had warned her with some prescience that if she brought such charges she would be thought 'rather vindictive' for referring to things not in her own experience.[14] In defeat, the press condemned her a liar. The disappointed *Shields Daily Gazette* commented that 'when a woman, and especially a woman of position, goes into a witness box, there is a disposition to believe all that she says', but that Mabel had acted 'in a manner that is quite incomprehensible' and would henceforth be remembered as 'one who endeavoured to destroy her husband's character on evidence that neither judge nor jury would believe'.[15] More damningly, the strictly conservative *St James's Gazette* declared that, whether she had told those lies out of hysteria, 'which we take to be the legal term for natural and acquired nastiness', or because she wanted Frank's money was irrelevant. Mabel had shown herself to be

> ... a young woman, badly brought up and improperly trained, who had apparently plunged into all the silliness of that sort of fashionable life which may not be exactly loose but is rather more than fast, who has shattered her nerves with morphine and cigarettes, and who was accustomed to associate with people of doubtful conduct and evil reputation...

Her 'hysterical dislike' of her husband was therefore unsurprising. They refrained from speculating on whether she had brought the action for 'malice or money' or had been 'honestly, though woefully mistaken' in her charge, but offered the view that anybody who knowingly brought such false testimonies 'deserves to be whipped at the cart's tail'.[16]

Other criticisms – of which there were many – largely focused on Mabel's frivolity and the distasteful idea that, had she won, she would have become Frank's life-pensioner, 'restored to the gay and vacuous pursuits to which her tastes inclined her, while he hid his head a disgraced and socially banished man'.[17] It was actually incredibly difficult to find any paper that spoke well of her after the 'revulsion of public feeling' that resulted from reports of day two of the trial.[18] At best, the *Blackburn Standard*, which restricted its comments to her 'sweet beauty' as against Frank's 'cynical smile', expressed the opinion that 'hysterical persons seldom look as intelligent' and expected that one day she would make a 'devoted wife and mother'.[19]

If this be the case, it can only be assumed that *The Dwarf* hoped it would not be in the image of *her* mother. In a bid to show where 'the chief mischief lay' it re-ran a story from the previous year in which it had chronicled the court experiences of the Scotts – Lina's with Captain Spicer and Giddy's mysterious nullity suit – before asking whether 'Babs' would have the same success. Alongside, it printed a facsimile of a letter Lina had written in response to the original article 'deeply grieved' that they should make 'such an attack on my sad life' and asking for a reporter to come and hear her story in the hope that they would regret their action. *The Dwarf* agreed, but Lina went quiet. So now, they provocatively expressed the hope that she, having 'reached the acme of her worldly ambition' by obtaining an earl's coronet for her daughter, should realise 'her duty now lies in straining every nerve to render her child worthy of the honour' to 'wipe out the foul miasma of the miserable past' and provide a 'pure and healthy' home for the now divided couple.[20] Lina didn't respond; and given *The Dwarf*'s standing it would have been of little consequence had not *Truth* picked up the story and added to their list the fact of Lina's judicial separation from Claude and several more minor misdemeanours which subsequently got reprinted in papers nationwide.[21]

Frank, on the whole, fared much better but did not get off completely scot-free. Several papers with middle- and working-class readers commented that the case would have been 'of no public interest' if it had been of 'some unillustrious Mrs Jones' and that the glimpse it afforded into the lives of the aristocracy was 'unpleasant' at best.[22] The more radical *Liverpool Daily Post* condemned the aristocratic breed as 'more essentially vulgar' than the educated middle-class and predicted their downfall.[23] Other than that, there were some rather benign comments regarding Frank's 'injudiciousness' (*Pall Mall*), his 'shortcomings' (*Telegraph*), his 'absence of worldly wisdom' (*Post*) and one somewhat more disapproving observation in the *Star* on the 'vexatious control' he had used to attempt to break Mabel 'as he breaks his horses or his dogs', which was not so much a criticism of Frank as the 'spirit and tone' of the whole trial, which assumed that his actions were 'just and reasonable': '"You use your authority with her?" "Yes." "Quite right." ... The inequality of it all is hideous.'[24] The enlightened *Star* also published, later in the week, a letter from women's campaigner and social reformer Josephine Butler, who asked what the court's reaction would have been if it had been Mabel who had admitted being in another relationship two months before her engagement? Her prediction was that Mabel would not have been praised as Frank had for confessing his 'trifling irregularities' but would have been condemned as 'a fallen woman, not an errant fool'.[25]

The severest attack on Frank (and the one that gave him most trouble) came from the 'scurrilous rag' *Hawk*, edited by Augustus Moore – brother of writer George Moore – to whom it quickly transpired Mabel had given an interview after the trial. The tone of the resultant article which appeared on 8 December was immediately set by Moore's opening comments, in which he said that it was 'quite certain' Frank had 'left Oxford under a cloud the blackness of which it would not be polite to penetrate', and that if Mabel had been able to prove her charges against him 'there is very little doubt that she would have been entitled to a separation from a man who would have been as big a brute as ever darkened the sunshine with his shadow'. And yet, she had not; and now Frank was 'being made a hero for the very negative quality of not having been proved a brute'. The case left many questions unanswered: why had none of the Russells been called to refute Mabel's assertion of what they told her? Why weren't Lina and the butler called in relation to the Roberts incident? Why did no one seem to know anything about the 'disgusting letter' referred to in the Oxford incident? And why didn't anyone seem interested in what it was that had caused Mabel to throw the soap dish, menace Frank with the poker or threaten to throw herself from the window?[26]

These are reasonable questions in point of fact if not point of law and, in conjunction with the answers Mabel gave *Hawk*, worthy of some consideration – though an answer to the question surrounding the fainting incident will always remain elusive. It would not matter that Santayana would later write in the margin of his copy of *Life* that Mabel's fainting in the first place covered 'a terrible unmentionable accusation, involving all R's past', or that this was interpreted by Santayana's biographer as Mabel hinting at Frank's 'unusual sexual demands';[27] or that immediately following this incident Mabel became so terrified of Frank she would never be alone with him again and sought multiple ways to justify separating from him; or even that his third wife, Elizabeth, would on one occasion describe Frank's advances as 'sadistic'.[28] Mabel did not bring a specific allegation, the 'pleading tones' heard by her nurse were refuted on oath by Frank and her subsequent fear of him dismissed as hysterics. Mabel made no further comment on the incident in her interview.

She did, however, comment on the butler, Spink. She said the defence could not call him because Frank's discharging him for drunkenness had discredited him as a witness. She claimed this was tactical on Frank's part, that Spink was not a drunk but that Frank had been concerned about the evidence he might give. The fact that Spink was still in Frank's employment at Amberley Cottage when the census was taken in the April before the trial and then let go sometime after it was decided the case would come to court does seem to suggest this; as does the fact that Spink left Frank's service with a reference, enabling him subsequently to be employed as butler to a retired civil servant living in the rather salubrious Mandeville Place, Marylebone. But without his evidence, none of this can be verified and 'what the butler saw' will always remain a mystery.

With regard to the Russells, Mabel said she had presumed that after Sir Charles had pressed her so hard with regard to Roberts, he would have called them to refute her claims. He had not. There was no reason why he should. The defence would have had nothing to gain from so doing, having already heard negative testimony from Frank and Roberts concerning the episode and observing that the prosecution brought no corroborative evidence to support Mabel's claim. But astonishingly, in this interview, Mabel claimed that had Sir Charles done this, she would have produced the Russells' letters 'making the charges which I referred to' and that the only reason this was not done was because she had previously promised them she would 'say as little as possible' about Frank's immorality. If she had not done this, she declared, 'I could have won'.[29]

As for the Oxford incident, Mabel claimed she had not known it would be referred to, that it could not be followed up because Jowett was dying and therefore in no position to attend court, but that she did not believe he would have testified that he had sent Frank down 'without proper evidence'. Of course, it is impossible to say what a man would or would not have testified given the opportunity and Jowett was never asked to give a deposition. But seemingly he did intervene on Frank's behalf behind the scenes. At the end of September 1891, Lyulph Stanley had written to his old master concerning Frank's case, saying he thought it unjustified and Mabel's fault. He also said,

> I think Frank has very much changed for the better in late years and is heartily sorry and ashamed of all the old aberrations. I should be glad to see him helped...[30]

Jowett's reply is not extant, but the following month, Lady Stanley wrote thanking him for his friendship. After the case was won, Jowett replied that he was glad of the outcome and expressed the opinion previously quoted that the errors of young men should not be visited upon them if they had changed their ways: 'Let them begin again under brighter auspices, and be helped by their friends.'[31]

How exactly Jowett helped – whether through direct communication with the judge, Sir Charles Butt (with whom he was on friendly terms), or in another manner – is another unknown. Jowett would die in 1893 having never passed another comment on the subject. But even so, it still seems remarkable that in his summing-up the judge specifically referenced Jowett's attendance at Frank's wedding and Frank's visit to Balliol after his engagement as somehow proof of his innocence regarding the Oxford incident. And clearly the cloud over Frank's name had not completely dispersed. Just four days after Mabel's *Hawk* interview, *Vanity Fair* published an article entitled 'A Glimpse at Lord Russell's "Past Life"' in which an 'old friend' directly addressed the improper letter.

The lengthy article is another curiosity. It begs the question why it was felt necessary and on whose authority it was written if, as Frank said, his name had been cleared and public opinion was so unimportant to him. It claimed Frank was 'neither a saint nor a monster', but 'one whose nature was coarsened and twisted and very nearly ruined by the joint efforts of others'. The first of those 'others' was Jowett. It explained that when Frank was at Oxford there was 'a sort of Buddhistical, Theosophical, neo-Platonic, Walt-Whitmaniac, Brotherhood of Man cult' which Frank and his friends followed. It resulted in their taking friendships so seriously, that they would talk of 'loving' where ordinary men would say 'liking'. It was 'mawkish and even sickly, if you like'. It seemed so to the author then, and 'seems so to Lord Russell now', though at the time he took it seriously and it became his religion. But it was the author's opinion that, had it been brought to Jowett's attention, this 'rather puerile extravagance of affection in phrase and manner' would have been taken exception to; and yet, 'Mr. Jowett, incredible as it may seem, never saw the letter himself'.

From there, the article adhered to Frank's version of events before blaming the subsequent rumour-mongering and Frank's inability to clear his name for turning him 'more or less' bad for a time, resulting in two summers 'indulging in wild follies' and the affair with Kate Williams. 'The very indefiniteness and mystery of the Oxford cloud made it difficult to dissipate,' said the author.[32] And this is a valid point, picked up by Cocks in *Nameless Offences*: that the

Victorian secret of sex was an open one that 'did not conceal knowledge, but "knowledge of the knowledge"', preventing 'a more general investigation and general discourse that would have had disturbing consequences for class privileges and social boundaries'.[33] Had it not been so and Jowett had been confident of Frank's guilt, he would have exposed him. Sometimes, this secrecy worked against a man, but sometimes it protected him and worked in his favour – as Frank's victory in court demonstrates – at the price of there always hanging over him a cloud of suspicion.[34]

Second only to this mystery was that of Lina. Why had she not been called? Mabel told Moore that her mother had been too ill to attend court; that she had had an 'attack of haemorrhage' and Dr Godson had advised that it would kill her if she did. She would have given 'most important evidence' and they had hoped it would have been taken by commission but was not. Why, she could not say. This is at odds with what we know Lina told Doulton in her private correspondence: that she declined to give evidence when approached by George Lewis and then asked not to be put in the witness box by Sir Charles. Why would she do either of these things? If her assertion that she knew about Frank and Roberts 'bear fighting' in Roberts' bedroom is to be believed, then by refusing to testify Lina abandoned her daughter to her fate by withholding vital evidence. Was this simply a case of split loyalties? Did she believe Mabel would not need her testimony, that the Russells would be forced to testify in her daughter's favour though she herself was not? If so, it is an incredible assumption given the statements of those 'slender reeds' as soon as the particular concerning Roberts was filed. Or was she in the unenviable position of having to choose between supporting her daughter's bid for separation against leaving Frank open to charges of gross indecency with a potentially far greater penalty? For if Mabel had won her case, there is little doubt that Frank's behaviour would have been investigated and quite possibly have come before the Central Criminal Court, just as did Oscar Wilde's four years later after he lost his libel case against Lord Queensberry. Whichever way you look at it, Lina's actions benefitted Frank at Mabel's expense.

But what if Lina's claim was false? Why say it in a private letter to Doulton? Had the defence really thought she would sacrifice her own daughter by giving evidence in Frank's favour? If so, it begs the question, what would make her loyalty to Frank so strong when he had shown so little care and consideration of Mabel? Lina had handpicked Frank for Mabel and was fond of him – professed, in fact, to love him as much as she did Mabel. Mabel's deep attachment to her mother meant Lina spent an inordinate amount of time with the young couple – both together and separately – and Frank wrote fondly of 'darling Bo' in his diary; a little too fondly perhaps.[35]

A final interpretation is that Lina was not called because she knew something that made her a dangerous witness for *both* sides. She and Frank had always had a confidential friendship and it is not impossible to suppose that implicit within her statement that she would perjure herself if she did not wish to harm Frank was the threat that she would be forced to tell the court what she knew about other matters if called: Oxford, for example. Frank had already stated under oath that he had told her everything about it (though which version of events?), and their letters clearly show that Lına had also been involved in some dubious way with the Kate Williams affair.

If any or all of these considerations leave the impression that, far from the women having it their own way in court, the odds in this instance were stacked in Frank's favour, or that there was much that was *not* said, or that Frank's answers had been less than completely truthful, it would not be for the first time. Santayana's response to Frank's letter quoted at the beginning of this chapter, lauding his own performance and success, has not survived; but Frank's subsequent reply has:

> I thought the papers would interest you. I cannot however agree with you that my evidence was not strictly accurate. Both Doulton and I have read it through since carefully and are agreed that nothing could have been more careful and true.[36]

The care cannot be doubted; the truth remains to be seen, but is at this point academic. Despite Frank's exhilaration at his victory and Mabel's indignation at her loss, one fact remained unchanged: they woke on the morning following the trial still married. And after everything that had transpired, was it at all possible to believe that either of them wanted to be? Yet even as they turned their backs on the old year, brushed off the horrors of their very public performance and looked ahead to what the next might bring, Frank received a startling letter that would mark the beginning of the next act:

> January 1892
>
> Dear Frank,
> Notwithstanding the cruel way you have treated me, I have made up my mind to try and live with you again, with some substantial person to protect me. I, therefore, wish to know if you will receive me.
> Yours affecty.
> M.R.[37]

13

Conjugal Rights and Wrongs

Early in 1892, Frank wrote to George Bernard Shaw, a man he would come to know well through the RAC and Fabian Society. In this, their first correspondence, they shared their views on marriage and divorce, perhaps triggered by a private member's divorce bill presented in the Commons on 10 February.[1] It is an interesting discourse, with Shaw taking the position that, it being so difficult to get any political party to 'meddle' with the marriage laws, the only practical solution was to advocate 'free unions' to force the upholders of the marriage contract to 'lighten and loosen the chains in order to prevent their falling out of use altogether'. Marriage to a partner one comes to dislike, he said, is 'penal servitude of the worse kind' and if people only realised this before committing themselves 'they would face anything in the way of social ostracism sooner than run such a risk'.[2] Given Frank's recent experiences, one might have expected him to agree, but he seems never to have lost his belief in the desirability of some kind of marriage bond. He told Shaw that his position on free unions was 'cowardly on the part of the man on account of its unfairness to the woman':

> Very few men have such nobility of character and very few women such whole-souled devotion as to prevent such a union being broken sooner or later. And when it is broken the chief hardship falls on the woman.

Yet, he said, 'I do firmly believe that any relaxation of the marriage laws if supported by popular opinion, must be conducive to morality'.[3] Over the coming years, Frank would have ample opportunity to demonstrate his adherence to both positions.

He didn't respond to Mabel's letter asking to return. Neither did he react to her *Hawk* interview. From the end of the trial until March 1892, the only contact seems to have been between the couple's solicitors, arguing over costs. The judge had ordered Mabel to pay; Mabel declared herself unable to do so. The law required that, at the start of a case, the husband put down a bond to cover such a situation and Frank had duly deposited £350 with the court in July 1891. He had also been ordered to pay Mabel's £48 solicitors' bill, due to her swearing she could not afford this either. Additionally, Mabel had opened an action against Frank in the Queen's Bench Division claiming her right to the balance in their joint bank account, which, she said, represented dividends paid from her trust fund. Frank suggested they cry quits – that Mabel keep the bond to pay her court fees and he pay her solicitor's fees and keep the balance of the account – but clearly Mabel thought she could do better and continued to pursue him for everything before finally settling as Frank had suggested. How, one might ask, is this behaviour conducive to a desire to reconcile, if that was what she really wanted? The short answer is that Frank did not believe that *was* what she wanted. He believed what he had always believed and what Sir Charles had argued during the trial: that Mabel was just after his money.

Consideration of an amended clause from the 1857 Matrimonial Causes Act tends to substantiate Frank's view. By the terms of the original Act, a married person deserted by their spouse without cause could file a petition for restitution of conjugal rights. Though open to both sexes, it was more often employed by wives. A judge heard the case, and if he found in her favour then the husband was ordered to return. If after two years the husband failed to do so, he was guilty of desertion and his wife could either apply to the court for a writ of attachment, which would subject her husband to a term of imprisonment, or for a judicial separation on the ground of desertion.

In 1882, a case came to court that demanded an amendment to this rule. Georgina Weldon, a colourful character who had already made full use of the courts in bringing suit against people she thought responsible for having had her committed to a lunatic asylum (it was in fact her husband), filed for restitution as was her right. The court found in her favour. Her husband recognised his duty to support her and promptly provided her with £500 a month, a house to live in and two servants to attend her. He could not, however, concede to live with her, believing that so doing would bring 'certain misery on us both'. His wife replied that he should 'bow to the inevitable', and, when he still refused, applied to the court for a writ of attachment, committing him to prison. The judge, while acknowledging that Weldon had provided for his wife, was forced to conclude that under the terms of the 1857 Act he had not fulfilled his duty to her, giving him no alternative but to issue the writ, though he thought it an inappropriate sanction. Parliament responded swiftly with the 1884 Matrimonial Causes Act – passed without debate or comment in either house – which abolished the sanction of imprisonment and substituted it with the discretionary power of the court to make financial orders. Weldon was spared his incarceration, but more significantly, *all* wives suddenly had the immediate right to file a petition for judicial separation on the ground of desertion after only *two weeks* if an order for restitution was not complied with, and potentially receive lifelong alimony from their absent husband; or, if he cohabited with another woman in his absence, for divorce, if she could prove adultery too.[4] Frank considered Mabel's true intention was to force him into such a situation.

Correspondence between them resumed on 8 March when Mabel wrote asking if they could meet 'to discuss our position and our future'.[5] Frank replied that if this was 'the first sign of sorrow' for the wrong she had done him, he was pleased to have it, but would need 'some expression of sincere penitence' beforehand. Mabel said she wanted to show him 'certain documents in her possession' and offered that if he could prove their 'shocking accusations' unfounded she would willingly apologise. Frank refused: he must have it in writing that she did not believe the accusations *before* he would meet her. At this impasse Lina once again intervened, suggesting that as she had 'protected' Frank throughout, she had earned the right to ask him to hear Mabel. Frank authorised Doulton to do so on his behalf, but Mabel had lost patience. On 31 March she wrote to Frank: 'I think now the position resolves itself into this. Do you intend to make any provision for me in the future as regards money?' If not, she should be 'compelled to go on to the stage'. Frank's reply was emphatic. Had Mabel not settled her mother's debts before their marriage she would still have £26,000 yielding an annual income of £1,000. As it was, she had £600, which should be ample to live on 'if you live quietly'. The blame for their separation was hers. She was impenitent and grasping. He had been on the cusp of instructing Doulton to offer her an allowance, but after the *Hawk* interview had felt obliged to cancel the instruction. If she now showed repentance, he would allow her to return. To suggest the necessity of stage work was 'absurd'. If she embarked on that path, it would not only hinder their reconciliation, but would be 'from love of notoriety' not necessity.

Mabel was incensed. She regretted 'not one single shilling' used to repay her mother's love and devotion. But the non-payment of some dividends had reduced her income to £500 and out of that she now had to support Lina as she was 'forced to live with her'. She would not apologise until Frank's relatives 'come forward publicly and explain' what they told her about his past life, which threw 'a strong light on much of your conduct towards me, which up to that time had been equally horrifying and inexplicable'. She was going to perform in an amateur stage production in aid of the National Lifeboat Institution the following week, she said, and without an allowance would be compelled to go on the regular stage thereafter. If Frank did not reply within a day or two, she would conclude he intended to do nothing and would take one of the 'very good offers' made to her.

Perhaps Mabel thought a public declaration that she was taking to the stage would shame Frank into submission. If so, how little she knew him. The announcement in *Lady's Pictorial* that the amusing 'skit' *A Pantomime Rehearsal* would be performed on 11–12 April with the expectation that Mabel would subsequently take to the professional stage left him unmoved. Neither did it look like the event would springboard Mabel into a glittering stage career. *The Era* declared it a 'thin and wearisome affair'. The skirt-dancing routine which Mabel performed with Giddy (and which Frank later described to Santayana as 'not so open as a cancan, but a deal more suggestive'[6]) was 'of a very elementary order' and the 'flummery of encores and flower presentations was decidedly overdone', making it hard to suppress the thought that the costly bouquets handed up across the footlights pandered to the cause of personal vanity at the expense of charity; though 'it is sometimes very difficult to distinguish between the two'.[7]

Frank's subsequent letter, dated 15 April, simply advised Mabel that, in the light of her 'most cruel attack' on his relations and lack of remorse, 'I must decline any further correspondence'. Desperate, Mabel demanded to know *immediately* what, if anything, Frank would give her. Though Frank did not know it, her situation had suddenly been made acute by – of all things – the untimely death of her mother's florist.

On 14 April 1892, the executors of the will of one Charles William Buck of Covent Garden filed a petition for bankruptcy against Lina for non-payment of her debt. It came before the bankruptcy court on 27 July. Lina's finances were astonishing. With the exception of a few larger items and a bill for £103 owing to Messrs Swinburne & Co. and proved by a certain Earl Russell in respect of an electrical installation at The Hurst in 1889, her debts comprised unpaid hotel bills, dressmaking and millinery accounts and general household expenses to the tune of £14,358, of which £3,768 was unsecured.[8] Lina had previously offered to pay back her creditors at the rate of 5s in the pound, but now declared herself unable to do even that. Gathering as much pique as she could muster, she made a most entertaining witness (despite her woes), declaring that her furniture could not be sold to pay her debts as it had all been made over to Mabel on her marriage, that she did not dispute the debt to Swinburne & Co. but had rather thought it cancelled out by the very expensive dressing-bag she had given Frank as a wedding present, and offering then and there to surrender to the barrister the diamond brooch she was wearing, despite it belonging to Mabel. 'No one regrets more than I the position I am in,' she declared. 'It will be the best endeavour of my life to pay everybody in full.'[9] Whether she ever achieved this is unknown, but nonetheless, records show it was not until December 1895 that she was released from the scrutiny of the trustees appointed by the judge to oversee her financial affairs.[10]

None of which stopped her, as 'the only small link' between Frank and Mabel, continuing to appeal to Frank's better nature. 'You believed everything you were told of me once,' she wrote to him in a lengthy appeal; why should it be any different for Mabel? 'Come forward like a man' and earn her love and respect, 'before it is too late'.

The letter almost occasioned some progress. Frank conceded that Lina could take Mabel's documents to Doulton and Mabel agreed, as long as they did not leave her mother's hands. The outcome of the meeting, however, was inconclusive. The letters Lina took were copies in her own handwriting and meant very little without statements from the Russells to substantiate them. Mabel compounded matters by writing to Rollo, blaming the Russells collectively for her problems and threatening them with the one thing they feared most: exposure. Unless they recognised her publicly, she would reveal the things they told her about Frank only after she was tied for life. Rollo denied telling her anything: '*You told me* of "dreadful things" which some friends of yours in London said of [Frank] ... and I simply told you not to listen.' Meanwhile, Frank wrote to both Rollo and Agatha for unequivocal answers to questions of his own: Had Agatha told Mabel or Lina that he had been turned out of either Oxford or Winchester for 'misconduct of a particular kind', or that he was not fit for a woman to live with? Had Rollo told Mabel that he entirely approved of her leaving him, or that he had once 'kicked a pet dog to death'? For her part, Agatha denied everything; but poor Rollo was forced to admit that after denying any knowledge of Frank's alleged cruelty to cats, he 'unluckily added, you had when quite young, ill-treated a dog, but since then I had never known you to be cruel to animals'. And Rollo – upset beyond belief by the 'perversions and inaccuracies of statements so freely & recklessly made with reference to myself and others' – asked to be excused any further communication on the subject.

Then, just as the Russells withdrew for a second time, two things happened that would have a bearing on events that can only be described as farcical. First, Mabel's uncle Bertie, who had been living for some years in Belgium, returned to take up her cause and, second, Frank fired his coachman.

Bertie Charles Scott was the younger brother of Mabel's father, Claude, and by no means a stranger to the courts, having tried and failed to divorce his first wife for adultery in 1871, succeeded with his second in 1883, and (despite being well catered for by his father's will) been declared bankrupt the same year. Perhaps he thought these experiences would fit him for the task, but his interventions were largely ineffectual. After Vandercom & Co. declined to discuss Frank's business with a third party, Bertie insisted his solicitor, Arthur Wellesley Peckham of Valpy & Co., 19 Lincoln's Inn Fields, take over from George Lewis as Mabel's legal representative. Peckham promptly set about trying to change the whole tone of negotiations by bluntly asking Vandercom what Mabel could expect to receive in exchange for her apology. You misunderstand, replied Vandercom, our client requires an apology *before* he will consider any proposal. No, we don't, retorted Valpy, if *your* client will not reward *our* client for doing as *he* wishes, he clearly has no desire to resolve this very 'unsatisfactory position'. Vandercom declared they had nothing more to add and the stalemate was resumed.

Meanwhile, Frank's coachman, Walter Rowe, blotted his copybook and was summarily dismissed. He immediately contacted George Rich, another of Frank's ex-servants then employed by Mabel, telling him he had information concerning Frank that might be of interest. On 16 October, he was summoned to Giddy's house in Windsor to be interviewed by Mabel and Lina. He had been fired, he told them, for refusing to touch his cap to a Miss Morris, who was 'a typewriter in the employ of Lord Russell'. His lordship drove her about the country in his coach.[11] Rich and Rowe were immediately dispatched in the company of a Mr Sabine to Teddington to spy on Frank. How they managed to come back empty-handed is a mystery, for Mary Morris, who lived in Teddington with her mother, was indeed Frank's secretary and had been his paramour since at least the summer of 1891.

Santayana later recalled that he first met Mary at Frank's house on the South Downs that summer. In this he was mistaken. He *had* stayed with Frank, but it had been at Amberley Cottage (the house on the South Downs was still some years off) and on that occasion, Mary was not there. He eventually met her in 1895. First impressions were not great. Frank afterwards wrote to him,

> You did not appreciate Mary – it was the fault of her timidity and of the hurried way in which you saw her. Kindly suspend your judgment as you will see reason to change it...[12]

But Santayana never disliked Mary:

> She was a clean honest young woman, reasonable, docile, with a good complexion and a copybook hand. She was the absolute slave and adorer of her lord and master, and juster to him than his other lady-loves.[13]

No photographs of Mary survive, but she leaves a definite impression on events over the next few years and, from her actions and history, Santayana's seems a fair appraisal. She was born to John and Ellen Morris in Putney on 27 May 1870, the middle of five children and their only daughter. Theirs was a nautical family. John's father had been a master mariner and John was a midshipman in the Royal Navy before leaving to captain ocean liners across the Atlantic. The family had done well. By the time Mary was born, they had a house in a very nice Georgian terrace wrapping around the corner of Putney Hill and Richmond Road where they lived with three servants. When John left the Navy in 1881, the family relocated to Liverpool and Mary was sent to the All Hallows Orphanage in Ditchingham, Norfolk – a High-Church Anglican establishment that educated children of upper-middle-class families who expected to have to earn their future living. Mary's father being away at sea qualified her for a place, with the fees he paid supplementing the free education of local upper-class orphans. The sisters provided a homely environment and expected their pupils to go into further education or become governesses.[14] In Mary's case, All Hallows equipped her for a secretarial post at Swinburne & Co. Her handwriting first appeared on their headed notepaper in January 1891.

Mary appears to have become involved with Frank soon after. She received dictation of letters to Doulton concerning Frank's private life sent from Amberley Cottage from April 1891, and in March 1894 Frank confessed to Bertrand that he had been 'hypothetically engaged' to her for three years.[15] Perhaps Mary's presence goes some way to explaining why Frank reciprocated Lina's use of detectives by setting his own on Mabel. If he could prove her adultery, he would be free to marry Mary. But Mabel was always with her mother, who chaperoned her 'even to hotels where the young man of the moment occupied the adjoining room' if Santayana is to be believed,[16] and Frank's detectives came back similarly empty-handed.

The next move, in fact, happened quite by chance. Mabel and Frank bumped into each other at Paddington Station one morning in early December, talked briefly and agreed to meet again in a couple of days, each in the company of another. Mabel gave Frank the impression that the Roberts charge in the first suit was 'all a mistake' and the fault of 'that brute' Sir Edward Clarke.[17] She afterwards wrote him a friendly letter in anticipation of their meeting. But Frank replied saying the meeting would only take place if he got his apology first – and, while she was at it, a letter to Roberts apologising for and withdrawing her accusations. He was even good enough to suggest exactly what she should write. On file, there is a heated reply to this dated 13 December, threatening to publish every document Mabel had in her possession and be damned! It is in Lina's handwriting but professes to be a copy of a letter from Mabel which Frank later swore he never received and which reads very much like an angry outburst of Lina's. Mabel's actual reply was more controlled but still demonstrates the extent of her exasperation: 'Dear Frank,' it begins, 'You certainly are difficult to understand...' It suggested she show him her documents and hear his side of the story in return; after which 'when all is ended you can prosecute anyone you please if the things are untrue'. Frank declined.

The year ended with a Christmas card for Frank from Lina with the message, 'God grant this time next Xmas all will be forgotten & you are with people who love you'; and for Mabel, with an attempt to convince Frank's equally immovable uncle Lyulph to attend an interview with her uncle Bertie, who was pushing her to get her documents published 'by an editor who is sorry for my miserable position'. If forced to go along with his advice, she told Lyulph, 'Frank will have to sue people and the thing will never end ... I hope you will appreciate the good faith this letter is written in from my own heart'. Lyulph did not:

You seem to me to singularly misunderstand your position when you assume that after the past litigation you have any right to demand explanations from your husband. You have done the upmost to blacken his character and you have failed.

1893 was a very bitter year for the Scotts. A further letter from Mabel to Frank only elicited the response, 'You have passed the limits of human endurance ... I shall take no notice of any [future] communication from you.' And Lina's detectives continued to disappoint. A letter to a Richard Dickinson on 1 February asking him and his colleague – the gloriously named John Spackman Horniblow – to meet her at Valpy's the next day was followed with the request that if they had any good news, they would write immediately: 'How strange if you are the person to bring [Frank] to justice,' she wrote confidently. 'Anyone who proves anything will not only get my thanks but enough to start them in life, for although we have enough evidence to hang any ordinary man, it is not quite sufficient for our purpose.' Her optimism proved misplaced; the ten shillings it cost her, wasted. Dickinson soon became a nuisance. He had already asked Lina for clothes and money, had no fixed abode and his credentials were dubious at best. Lina eventually left him to Valpy, who after several polite attempts to put him off finally resorted to insisting that he 'please don't trouble us any more'; on which instruction, Dickinson attempted to switch sides and wrote to Frank, with as little success.

Thereafter, both Frank and Mabel attempted to restore some semblance of normality to their lives in their very different ways and with varying degrees of success. In March, Mabel appeared at Windsor county court, this time being sued by a general contractor for non-payment of his £24 bill for the turfing and laying of a tennis court at the cottage in Bray; and throughout the following month, mother and daughter were often spied on the river by reporters for the *South Bucks Standard*, who were finally rewarded for their vigilance when, at the end of April, they published the rather underwhelming story that Mabel in her launch *Lurline* and Frank in *Isabel* had both been 'in Marlow Lock at the same time!'[18] Frank, meanwhile, having ceased to be a partner in Swinburne & Co. in July 1892, had set up his own company of electrical engineers so that he might become 'more of a director and less of a clerk'.[19] He co-authored an article for *National Review* entitled 'Electricity in Country Houses' to promote the newly formed Russell & Co. of 11 Queen Victoria Street, in which he advocated the use of electricity to stimulate the growth of vegetables, fruit and flowers as a means of getting homeowners to club together to finance generating stations at mutually convenient points.[20] It didn't necessarily bring him the kind of publicity he was hoping for – *Smart Society* rather cruelly commenting that perhaps his devotion to science explained 'his lamentable inexperience with the ways of human nature, particularly when of the feminine gender'.[21]

For the summer season 1893, Lina, Mabel and Giddy took a houseboat at Bray Reach and smothered it in flowers, representing 'the height of fashion'. They were often seen on the river in their 'pretty little electric launch' and in August, Mabel led a committee to organise the Bray Amateur Regatta, which attracted a large audience and comprised 'an interesting programme of aquatic sports' led by Giddy.[22] Mabel, dressed to match her sister in a white drill skirt, muslin blouse and sailor hat trimmed with black cock-tail feathers, coxed for the winning team in the sculling race alongside her brother-in-law, Dick, and Lina, wearing a similar white tailor-made costume, presented prizes. Frank meanwhile preferred to let Amberley Cottage for the season and spent his summer dipping a toe into politics for the first time. Though he had taken up his seat in the House of Lords in 1887, he had not as yet made use of it. He chose as his first public foray the Irish Home Rule question, writing a public letter to the Secretary of the Royal Dublin Society voicing his inability to appreciate their reluctance to trust themselves in the hands of their own countrymen when any English government could damage them equally as well.[23] He followed it by voting in favour of the Irish Home Rule Bill at its second reading in the Lords in September that year – one of only forty-one Peers to do so.

Then, in August, at Bertrand's request, Frank took Santayana to Cambridge, for the specific purpose of introducing the two philosophers at a pleasant lunch discussing philosophy, poetry and art. Bertrand had been at Trinity College since September 1890 and the change in him as he approached his coming-of-age made him more interesting to Frank. Until that time, Frank had considered him an 'unendurable little prig'.[24] Now, Bertrand had completed his Tripos and was embarking on his philosophical career while trying to solve the more pressing problem of how to win the affections of Miss Alys Pearsall Smith.

Alys belonged to a wealthy Philadelphian Quaker family who lived at 'Friday's Hill' near Fernhurst, Sussex, neighbouring Rollo's residence. The Russells had been occasional visitors there and Bertrand had fallen secretly, instantly and hopelessly in love with Alys at their first meeting when he was only seventeen and she twenty-two. By means of a most philosophical courtship, Bertrand set about convincing Alys first, of the wisdom of marriage in general; then of the wisdom of marrying him. The next step was to convince Lady John. Her reaction was strikingly similar to that of Amberley's declaration of love for Kate. She tried to divide them, summoning Alys to PL to secure from her a promise 'not to let anything but simple friendship arise'.[25] Their engagement, therefore, remained a secret – even from Frank, who was back in Cambridge in March 1894 with Mary and her mother. Mary was to sit the entrance exam for Newnham College 'to polish up her education and make her fit to be a Countess'. It was 'very like the Russells to think College a good preparation for wedded happiness!' commented a sceptical Santayana.[26] Bertrand, having been told of the affair and introduced to Mary, wrote his impressions to Alys, describing her as 'in no sense a lady and very dull and not even pretty', but with enough 'force of character ... to stand [Frank] if they ever bring it off'.[27]

Mabel, meanwhile, had been completely ostracised by the family. The Russells ignored her appeals, and by the time she wrote to Lady Stanley in September 1893 saying she had been 'offered a salary of £100 a week to go to America to act' they really must have all just wished she would go, however unlikely the assertion. Their wall of silence began to have the desired effect. As 1893 drew to a close, the constant stream of letters dried up and the Scotts were left to their own devices and the plague of detectives that continued to buzz annoyingly around the fringes of the affair, just enough to irritate and keep the lawyers busy while they waited for Mabel to make her next move. The moment finally came on 19 March 1894, when Dick Russell thrust a letter into Frank's hands at Taplow railway station. Frank ignored it and on 10 April 1894, Valpy's clerk served Frank with a petition for restitution of Mabel's conjugal rights on the platform of the much busier Paddington station.

The petition was quite straightforward: Mabel had written to Frank asking to return, Dick Russell had put the letter into his hand, Frank had not responded. Now Mabel asked for the assistance of the court to order Frank to take her back. Frank's team decided that the best form of defence was attack and answered Mabel's petition with a shocking answer alleging that her petition had not been presented *bona fide* insomuch as Mabel 'has alleged and still alleges' that Frank 'has been guilty of the crime of *sodomy*', has 'falsely and maliciously' stated and published the allegation and, when so called upon, refused to retract it and apologise, persisting in her allegation; and that this, along with her prior allegation that Frank had been guilty of physical cruelty to her, amounted in themselves to acts of cruelty on her part. They therefore pleaded for Frank to be judicially separated from Mabel.[28]

This was a bold but risky strategy. The impasse of the previous two years had meant that Frank had only seen copies of the documents Lina had taken to Doulton and did not know whether Mabel had anything more. He had not seen, for example, Lady Cardigan's letter in which his reputation was thoroughly besmirched. In bringing this answer, his team were attempting to take advantage of Mabel's lack of apology to force her to bring out into the open 'every single shadow of a suggestion or insinuation, every scintilla of rumour, every scrap of paper' that might imply Frank's guilt, but only at the risk of further harm to his reputation.[29] Their hope was that because Mabel was asking for restitution, she would have to produce this material and *at the same time* say she did *not* believe it, to avoid appearing inconsistent and weakening her own case. In addition, if she *were* to openly say her former accusation was *not* true, she would leave herself open to the question of why she had not publicly retracted it previously – especially in the face of the *Hawk* interview, in which she had said that she *could* have won. Further, in legal terms, the wording of the answer dared to make plain the accusation only previously insinuated. Never before had the blunt term 'sodomy' been used in relation to the Roberts incident, and in coming from Frank – who was now forcing Mabel into defending a false allegation she claimed she had never intended to make – it turned the whole case on its head. Seeing the danger, Mabel's team instantly tried to get the answer struck out on the ground that Frank was not claiming his health or well-being had suffered as a result of Mabel's actions, thereby not meeting the definition of *legal* cruelty. They failed, appealed, and failed again. The case would come before the court and both sides set about ordering the disclosure of documents to ascertain its exact shape. Valpy also filed an application for alimony pending the suit, which Frank was ordered to pay at the rate of £550 p.a., plus an additional £88 in solicitors' fees incurred by Mabel since the end of the previous trial.

The gathering of letters, the taking of statements, the sorting and organising of four years' correspondence, the occasional fracas – as when Frank accused Lina of deliberately running into him in her launch on the river, with the suggestion of very offensive and 'unmanly' language used on both sides – quite aside from any business coming into Russell & Co., should have been more than enough to occupy Frank. But in the midst of all this, Frank suddenly found himself in another upheaval, as the opening paragraph of the twenty-first chapter of *Life* tantalisingly reveals:

> In 1894 I had become well acquainted with a very charming and attractive lady of artistic tastes who stimulated my admiration for Sarah Bernhardt. We constantly went together to see her magnificent performances, and in that emotional atmosphere we very soon thought that we were in love ... I did not, however, altogether approve of her principles, and I did not think that our temperaments were at all likely to suit in any serious union, and so I decided to run away before my feelings were too deeply involved. And naturally I ran to America...[30]

Who was this mystery woman? Frank did not name her. She simply appeared as an anonymous precursor to a three-week sojourn in America, from which he said he returned 'cured of my infatuation'. It could not be Mary. Though she is not mentioned anywhere else in the memoirs, she had by this time been on the scene for three years and would remain so for several more yet; and the description is hardly fitting. There have been suggestions that it referred to an early encounter with Elizabeth von Arnim, Frank's third wife, to whom he was supposedly introduced that year by Maude Stanley.[31] But, though Elizabeth was a fan of Sarah Bernhardt, she had just had her third child when the renowned stage actress was in England that summer and had returned home to Germany by the end of July, rendering Frank's flight to America redundant. It fell to Santayana to reveal her true identity. Next to the paragraph in his copy of *Life* Santayana wrote,

> If this is Agnes Tobin, he went to America to see her people! He had her photo and that of Mary Morris always in his pocket. Laying them one day before me, he asked which I should incline to: and I very truthfully said: *Neither!*[32]

Agnes Tobin was the third of twelve children born to an Irish Catholic lawyer and his Chilean wife who were settled in San Francisco. She was fluent in French, German, Italian and Spanish, read both Latin and Greek, and from the 1880s had crossed and re-crossed the Atlantic many times, travelling widely in Europe, but favouring England. In later life, she achieved some renown for her poetry and translations of Petrarch's sonnets. When Frank met her as a thirty-year-old, there was said to be something about the sensitive, delicately featured Agnes that demanded attention. She was 'lovely in her features and in her gestures, her voice low and dark but limpid, beautifully dressed and jewelled, cosmopolitan, many-languaged, witty as well as wise'.[33] Santayana disagreed. He found her uninspiring and far from beautiful; but then Frank's own graceful stature was by this time also starting to give way to an expanding midriff and he was already suffering acutely from the varicose veins that would plague him for the rest of his life.

When Frank called in on Santayana that August and explained that, far from racing across the Atlantic to flee her, he was actually on his way to San Francisco to seek her family's approval for the match, Santayana interpreted Agnes's interest in his friend as some kind of 'divine vocation, to capture a superman, to tame him, to save his soul, and to become a British peeress'.[34] Certainly, her hold on Frank was strong: she 'plays on me like a flute', he told Santayana.[35] In an early example of a pattern that Santayana witnessed time and again, Frank appeared to have neither the desire nor inclination to 'suppress or sacrifice' his passion once roused. Neither, in coming clean to Mary about Agnes and Agnes about Mary, did he see 'the absurdity of asking one lady-love to sacrifice herself for another' when he was free to marry neither!ated[36] But Agnes's brother, Dicky, did see it, and though he gave Frank 'the loveliest of lovely times' as 'only Americans can',[37] Frank left San Francisco disappointed, having been 'thrown back' in his quest for Agnes. 'Let it lie ἐν γούνασι θεῶν (on the knees of the Gods),' he wrote philosophically to Santayana, and returned home to find that Agnes had chosen to physically distance herself from him by taking off to France.[38] Would he follow?

For once, the Russells inadvertently came to Frank's aid, making the decision for him. Bertrand had been sent all over the place by Lady John during the summer, in a bid to separate him from Alys. He had been to visit his mother's brother, Algernon, in Rome, where he was then Papal Chamberlain; and to Penrhos, North Wales, where Lyulph had a home. Now, in a further echo of his father's fate, he was to go to Paris for three months at the invitation of the British Ambassador, to take up a temporary post as honorary attaché. Lady John hoped that, where this gambit had failed with Amberley, it would succeed with Bertrand and he would forget Alys. But Bertrand had refused to promise he would not write to Alys while away; in fact, quite the opposite – Bertrand was determined to keep up 'a constant flow of words between them', and they wrote to each other twice and sometimes three times a day.[39] At a loss to know what else to do, Lady John sent Frank to 'talk' to him.[40]

With the dual purpose of possibly seeing Agnes and of helping his brother, Frank arrived in Paris on Saturday 13 October 1894. Bertrand was not particularly overjoyed to see him. Their relationship was difficult and, over the course of the next few days, Bertrand's letters to Alys revealed his oscillating attitude towards his older brother.[41] On Saturday he wrote, 'He's very exacting as a guest and lets one know if he's not satisfied.' On Sunday, 'It was really quite nice seeing him again, he *is* a pleasant companion, in small doses.' By Monday, 'I *shall* be glad when he goes. I hate him and half fear him ... I dread his comments if he should know me as I am.' On Tuesday, he wrote, 'He gives me a sense of perpetual discomfort, like a hair shirt.

I feel the hard rock beneath his soft outside, and it makes me perpetually on tenterhooks for fear of what he will say next.' 'I was afraid thy brother wld. spoil thy happy content in thy daily routine,' Alys replied. 'He is a dreadfully oppressive person, & fills up the whole horizon in such an exacting way.'

Over the course of the next week, much of the brothers' conversation was relayed to Alys and commented upon. It surprised Bertrand to learn that Frank was 'rather afraid' of him too, 'because I never let myself go, & one felt me coldly critical inside'. Alys said it explained why Frank didn't attempt to interfere with Bertrand and domineer him, 'because he seems fond of thee. But his being afraid of thee keeps him from going too far.' It interested Bertrand that 'each of us thinks himself all fire and passion and the other an icy lump of cold reasonableness'. Frank had expressed the opinion that Alys had an 'American hardness, by wh. he means not submitting completely to the husband, & not being sensual. He says American women only love from the waist upwards – thee can imagine I don't open my soul to him!' Perhaps Frank's comment was influenced by having been jilted by Agnes, but Alys was not at all intimidated: 'I don't think he will be much bother. And it will always be amusing to help him out with [Mary].' Yet 'the fear of his brutal words' made Bertrand keep Frank at arm's length.

Despite this, they did find some sympathy. Frank told Bertrand that Mabel had manipulated him into marriage, saying if she hadn't been 'so damned pretty he would never have got drawn in'. 'Poor wretch!' sympathised Bertrand. 'The memory must be very bitter. He is in great trepidation lest she shd. win her case for restitution.' Alys agreed it would be awful to have to live with Mabel again, but Frank was 'an awful fool to let himself be caught by such a girl'. Frank did not tell Bertrand about Agnes, however, despite writing to Santayana from Paris that he had tried to see her. Perhaps the habit of secrecy learned at PL was difficult to break. Or maybe it had something to do with the fact that Frank had only just recently asked Bertrand to persuade Alys to recommend Mary for membership of the Pioneer Club – a progressive club for women in London – in a letter written from San Francisco, while he was busy trying to convince Dicky of his commitment to Agnes!

Frank returned to England feeling he and Bertrand had been 'unusually confidential' ('It was the wine!')[42] and in full support of his brother in the face of their grandmother's disapproval. He stood best man at Bertrand and Alys's wedding on 13 December 1894 (despite some trepidation about the Quaker ceremony), which Lady John, Agatha and Rollo did not attend. By the beginning of 1895, it looked as if he and Mary had weathered the storm – but not with Frank as *completely* cured of his infatuation as he claimed, nor through any noble gesture on his part. Agnes had 'retired into an inscrutable silence' which, Frank confessed, was a painful blow to his vanity. Yet, 'to return to Mary free of entanglement was a great and intense pleasure: she presumes on it … although she will never credit me with an elevated feeling. Is that because she *does* or does *not* know me?'[43] Neither was the status quo resumed without the severe testing of Mary's 'whole-souled devotion';

then only twenty-three (six years Frank's junior), she had taken on the dual responsibility of caring for him and bettering herself in a bid to feel worthy. She wrote to Santayana from Newnham College that 'although my boy is the very best and dearest on earth he is most troublesome and wants a great deal of managing'. Agnes may have withdrawn, but Mary still felt her threat: 'I would give anything if it was in my power to alter this but it is not ... If I were one third as noble, generous and trusting as he I should be better able to brighten his life which has been very sunless. I do my best and only hope that it will not be a failure.'[44]

As the choppy waters of Frank's increasingly turbulent love life seemed for a time to settle, he at least was happy. In contrast to Santayana, who was feeling his age, Frank declared, 'I go on getting younger.' Once again, the turmoil had done him good. He would not agree with his friend that Agnes had been an 'evil influence'; she remained a 'sweet angel' whom he would always love 'tenderly and paternally – or more'. And the woman he was left with was, he said, 'a brick'.[45] She would need to be. In a few short months, Frank and Mabel's case would come to court and its outcome would have a bearing on them all.

14

In the High Court of Justice, Again

At 10 a.m. on Thursday 4 April 1895, the players gathered once again in Court II of the Royal Courts of Justice for the second act of *Russell v. Russell*. Though the subject was familiar, its aspect had completely changed and some key casting decisions had been necessary to meet the new requirements. Out had gone the principled Edward Clarke and the remorseless Charles Russell, to be replaced by two new 'silks': the colossus of the divorce court, John Murphy, and the rather dapper Sir Henry James. Retaining Sir Edward after his controversial handling of the Roberts incident would have been out of the question, even if he had been available. But he was then otherwise engaged in Oscar Wilde's prosecution of the Marquess of Queensberry for famously (mis)libelling him a 'somdomite' in his disgust at Wilde's relationship with his son, Lord Alfred 'Bosie' Douglas. It was pure coincidence that these two very high-profile cases both involving accusations of sodomy came to court at the same time. Wilde's case against Queensberry opened at the Old Bailey on 3 April and was instantly a huge sensation. Over the next fortnight, the cases appeared alongside each other in newspapers on a daily basis, and Wilde's arguably influenced Frank's in public perception. Whether the opposite is also true is little considered.

The 'fatherly, round-bellied' John Patrick Murphy led for Mabel.[1] Murphy had followed his father to the Bar in 1856 and taken silk in 1874. He was considered one of the divorce court's most experienced, thorough and diligent advocates. Weighing in at twenty stone, he was also probably its largest. Universally popular, he used the full magnitude of his presence and popularity to good effect – particularly in representing ladies, for whom he often 'almost drew tears from the jurymen'. He had both 'forensic vigour' and the ability to 'roar as gently as a sucking-dove', and was formidable and genial: a prime example of 'what an honourable Barrister should be'.[2] Outside the courtroom he was a keen singer; he had reportedly performed as a tenor in the first Handel Festival at the

Crystal Palace in 1857. With him were Charles Frederick Gill – 'the finest mouthpiece on the circuit'[3] – William Tyndall Barnard – who later became senior registrar – and Rollo Frederick Graham-Campbell – whose stellar career at Bow Street earned him the distinction of becoming its longest-serving magistrate.

Leading for Frank was Sir Henry James. He had been called to the Bar in 1852, taken silk and become an MP in 1869, made solicitor general in 1873 and attorney general in 1873–4 and 1880–5. A principled man, in 1886 he turned down the position of Lord Chancellor rather than be party to the possibility of an Irish home rule government. He had a profound respect ('perhaps too profound'[4]) for persons of high rank and counted many among his friends. Yet against Murphy, Sir Henry must, at first glance, have appeared slight and nervous. He had an unfortunate 'uneasy and restive' manner, and despite a solid reputation and the occasional 'masterly display of argument', was never considered spectacular.[5] His genius ('in so far as he had any') was likened to that of a solicitor's clerk who 'understood how to make a bill of costs'. He was 'as anxious and as careful over a fourpenny piece in his verdict as over the verdict itself'.[6] It was this quality that ideally suited him to Frank's case. He would be fastidious over the minutiae, picking away at the definition of legal cruelty with his 'penetrating intellect' and dogmatic manner. Though it was thought he sometimes threw in the towel too quickly and negotiated cases he could have won, he was also considered a 'shrewd and profound jurisconsult'.[7] He was suave and dignified but his seriousness made it 'hard to associate him with any sort of flirtation however mild'.[8] He was immune, therefore, to womanly wiles. One contemporary described him as like 'a hedgehog, which when rolled into a ball presents a most formidable array of irritating little spikes, but which a terrier who knows his business can in a moment unroll, toss into the air and dispatch'.[9]

Fortunately for Sir Henry, his opponent in this case was no terrier and whatever backbone he lacked was amply provided not only by his client but also his junior counsel. Robson had returned for a second round and with him were Henry Bargrave Deane, another divorce division stalwart, and Arthur Llewellyn Davies, older brother of Frank's Balliol friend Maurice. The judge for the occasion was Sir Charles Edward Baron Pollock, the last of the great legal barons and, if not a great judge, certainly a 'kindly and considerate one'.[10]

As a whole, it was a prestigious cast of legal characters that settled in for the next seven highly anticipated court days.[11] This was the first time a petition for restitution had been brought by someone who had previously sought a judicial separation, and the uniqueness of both parties' positions drew legal as well as public interest. Frank, 'spectacled and sedate', arrived with Lyulph; Mabel came with Lina, both dressed entirely in sombre black. Though Mabel's petition for restitution had triggered the proceedings, the purpose of the trial was for her to defend Frank's charge of cruelty. Hence, Sir Henry opened for the prosecution with a sweeping condemnation of Mabel's 'repugnant' accusations. The suit, he said, was not brought in good faith. Her true purpose was not to be reunited with Frank, but to publicly secure an allowance Frank had never privately refused her. For she knew that if she won her case it would be a 'moral impossibility' they could live together again. How could they? Every time Frank took her hand, every time he sat near her, would he not feel she was his accuser? Frank was entitled therefore to resist her suit and did so on the basis of *her* cruelty – a cruelty not physical, but 'calculated'. For there could be no greater cruelty than that a man's wife should reiterate charges against him of criminal conduct that the 'fullest inquiry' had found false. It was a 'heartless wrong, and an unretracted wrong'. If she was now going to say she did not believe it, it would be for the first time.

Sir Henry called Frank to the witness box to be examined by Robson, but before he could say very much, Mr Murphy raised a point about the wording of Frank's answer. If taken literally, he said, *all* the details of the first trial would have to be gone into again, not to determine their veracity but to discern whether Mabel believed them when she filed suit. A long and tedious debate ensued which lost most of the audience in all points except Murphy's declaration that he was instructed to say – 'though perhaps it is late' – that Mabel was now satisfied that the charge relating to Roberts was 'without foundation', though there was 'great excuse' for her having believed it when she said it. By the end of the first day, the rather underwhelmed crowd – not realising the implication of Murphy's statement – left court wondering whether anything sensational was to be revealed.

When the following morning the session began with a report that counsel had agreed overnight that there would be no rerun of the scandals of the first trial (or any further mention of the unfortunate cat) it must have occasioned some disappointed groans. Further, when most of Frank's evidence proved equally tedious as he confirmed or denied receiving letters or making statements without elaboration, many must have regretted not going to witness the Wilde trial instead. Thank heaven then for Mr Murphy, who, almost as soon as he stepped forward to cross-examine, put a letter into Frank's hand and asked him to read it quietly to himself. It was then passed to Sir Henry, and then the judge; and a furore ensued when he suggested that, though he had no intention of reading it aloud to the court, the jury should read it. Sir Henry strenuously objected, and that told the expectant crowd that there was something in it of substance. Tension mounted further when Sir Henry, leading Frank's re-examination, elicited from him the following facts: that he had never seen this letter before; that it was written by a lady still living who was known to him; that never once had Mabel alluded to its existence; that it had not been disclosed, but that Doulton had got wind of it about six months previously; and that its content was 'absolutely false'. The mysterious letter was put away, but the experienced observers of courtroom dramas were not concerned: they knew it would resurface and sat back contentedly as one by one the Russells gave evidence for the first time.

Lady John – then eighty – was too frail to attend court; and Agatha, who at forty was passing through that 'critical period of life' and just recovering from 'flu, was also excused.[12] Their depositions, therefore, had been taken at PL in December. Interestingly, given the number of times Mabel had written of the things supposedly said to her by the Russells, her solicitors tried to block them as 'unnecessary, irrelevant and immaterial'.[13] Perhaps they sensed the Russells would deny everything Mabel said they had told her. This, of course, is exactly what happened. When the depositions were read out in court, it was shocking to hear the grand matriarch, Lady John, forced to deny saying to Mabel, 'What an awful man your husband is ... He has always been a bother & a disgrace to the family' or that she looked upon their marriage as 'a miracle from heaven & hoped it would reform him & make him a better man' or that she never liked Roberts ('I have never met him') or that Mabel shouldn't allow Frank to have any of his college friends stay as Frank had been 'turned down from Oxford for disgraceful conduct with men' which was 'almost too shocking to talk about'.

Poor Lady John; it must have been a most distasteful and difficult interview. It pained her to say she thought it 'most unlikely' she'd told Mabel that Frank had caused the family much anguish. When asked whether he had, she'd replied, 'Please don't ask me.' To then be asked whether she had told the Scotts that Rollo's reaction to Frank's sending down was that 'the best thing he could do would be to blow his brains out' was especially hard. 'Oh, good heavens, no!' she'd answered and subsequently appeared quite shaken by the suggestion of other things she could not remember having talked about. It was impossible to recollect, she'd said, if the subject of Oxford ever came up, but that 'one has to answer things when said'. And when they finally arrived at the subject of the Chinese boy, she'd denied 'with warmth' that Frank had concealed him at Dover Street or that Maude had ever brought him to PL. She knew he had been sent home but had had 'nothing to do with it'. With rising indignation at the suggestion that Frank had been 'sent out of the country after Oxford' and was looked upon as a 'perfect outcast', she'd asked for it to be added to the record that when Frank went down from Oxford he 'came to this house and stayed here'.[14]

Agatha's deposition shows her similar discomfiture. When asked what were the 'charges' that stopped her seeing Mabel in February 1891, she'd said that the decision was Rollo's and that she had asked 'not to know' details. She categorically denied ever talking about Frank's past with Lina or Mabel – a fact that was called into question when it was revealed that the letter she had written to Mabel on 13 July 1891 in which she had said 'we cannot help feeling – all of us – that everything said at the trial about Frank's past life can only be said by your wish' was only 'practically' her own. It was written at Frank's instigation to prevent Mabel 'raking up the past' after Agatha had expressed the desire to do something 'desperate on my own responsibility' to correct that which she was forced to concede looked very much like evidence she *had* talked to

Mabel about Frank's past: another letter asking Mabel to 'think over all our talks together, when we begged you, and you "promised faithfully" to do your best not to bring forward what was unnecessary'.[15] The point was further compounded by Frank's examination-in-chief, when he clearly answered that he was referring to 'Oxford and the other things' when he asked Agatha to write to Mabel to prevent her 'raking up the past'. Nothing was made of this. Murphy declined to cross-examine and any pressure that might subsequently have been put on Rollo for the evidence he was about to give in court was lost. As such, there was little for Rollo to do except confirm that the 'discreditable and vile' things he had asked Mabel to keep out of court were things *she* had told *him*, not the other way round; and his cross-examination went no further than to give him the opportunity to deny that he had ever advised Frank to blow his brains out.

Also passing without challenge was Frank's assertion that Jowett had never seen the mysterious 'improper' letter which had triggered the Oxford incident. This was a fact that had been voiced only once in Jowett's lifetime, by Frank's 'old friend' in his article in *Vanity Fair*, and never before by Frank, who had had ample opportunity to do so on oath at the previous trial. In addition, Mabel's assertion that she'd known nothing about Oxford until the Russells enlightened her was weakened by the subsequent evidence of St George, who said that the subject of Oxford *had* come up at his interview with Lina before the marriage, that Mabel was present when Lina said she had 'things' she could use against Frank if Lady Stanley refused to meet her and that when he'd responded that Oxford was ancient history, there was no indication from Mabel that she did not know what they were talking about.

Of all the prosecution witnesses, the most entertaining was Frank's disgraced coachman, Walter Rowe, whom, it transpired, Frank had subsequently re-employed. His testimony centred on two keys points: why he had been sacked and what had happened at his subsequent meeting with Lina and Mabel. The forty-year-old servant took some time to get his evidence straight. When he did, he claimed he didn't know why Frank had let him go, but that 'everybody has a right to change their servants when disposed'. He had told Lina and Mabel this and showed them the reference Frank had given him. Lina had offered him a good situation if he could tell her anything of interest about Frank. She spoke of 'immoral purposes' and asked him if Frank had ever 'made any overtures' towards him, because 'he is a very immoral man, and has been guilty of that sort of thing'. Rowe claimed Lina also asked, 'Did I know anyone his Lordship had interfered with?' after which 'a deal more conversation took place' and Lina instructed him to go to Teddington with George Rich to spy on Frank. She gave him a sovereign, but he did 'very little' to earn it.

There had been much muttering and laughter throughout Rowe's examination, but Mr Deane was satisfied he'd got what he needed and was about to hand his witness over to Murphy for cross-examination when Rowe, clearly enjoying himself and fearing he might not get another opportunity, suddenly blurted out,

> ... but I have not quite finished (laughter) – the young man on board the 'Royal', his Lordship put a rope around his waist and towed him aft the 'Royal'.

Much hilarity and confusion ensued as both counsel and judge struggled to understand whether Rowe, in relaying another of Lina's astonishing claims, was suggesting she had been talking about *a* boy or *the* boy – 'a floating buoy, or a living boy?' – and, when it transpired it was a real boy, whether Rowe had thought Lina 'mad' for saying so ('I should not like to say that she was') or whether it was natural. ('No, I thought it was rather unnatural.' (Laughter.)) It would have been more unnatural still if Rowe had actually managed to blurt out the whole of Lina's comment, which had been that the unfortunate boy had been towed aft *Royal* 'to hide his guilt' after Frank had committed an 'unnatural offence' with him.

Mr Murphy asked about Rowe's discharge. Had he been entirely honest about his reason for being so? He had; though he thought it rather hard as he had given good service. (Laughter.) And then there followed another kerfuffle over whether Rowe had or hadn't touched his hat to 'Miss Morris', whether Frank had or hadn't objected, and whether or not that wasn't in fact the real cause of his dismissal. Rowe said not; and when asked why Frank had taken him back, replied, 'Well, he could not better me, I suppose, that was about the truth of it' (loud laughter), before appearing confused by Murphy's insinuation that, in taking him back, Frank had secured himself a valuable witness. Hadn't he told the ladies that Frank was on intimate terms with 'a certain woman'? – 'Never in my life!' Hadn't he also said that Frank had fathered his maid's baby? – Again, 'Never in my life!' But, Rowe volunteered, Lina had said 'she would make it worth my while if I could find out'.

Over the weekend, the papers were full of the Wilde trial which had concluded on Friday with Queensberry's acquittal. They preferred to speculate on Oscar's fate than the Russells', with the *Star* going so far as to report that the whole Russell case was really a question of law and therefore of little interest.

The following week started with little to challenge this opinion. As the prosecution rested, Mr Murphy submitted that they had failed to make a case for the petition of restitution being submitted *mala fides*. Further, that Mabel's actions did not constitute cruelty as the law defined it since Frank's health had not suffered; that she was under no legal obligation to apologise for anything she had said or done; and that therefore, there was nothing to go to the jury. In Sir Henry's reply, he recognised that he was stretching the definition of legal cruelty. In these times, he said, information was so quickly circulated that a man's reputation depended on what was said of him and the old definition that depended on physical harm *must* be modified; the only question was, by how much? Baron Pollock appeared to agree. He further ruled that Mabel's withdrawal of her accusation concerning Roberts meant the case must continue. The issue of cruelty would, therefore, go to the jury, along with the question of Mabel's *bona fides*.

It was not a satisfactory conclusion for Mr Murphy, who had attempted to arm himself with strict adherence to the law as it had been practised by the ecclesiastical courts long before the civil court had been given jurisdiction. He told the jury that the case was really a question of whether a husband could get rid of a wife and his obligation to support her simply because she had made some allegations against him. It had been presented to the court as if Mabel were the malefactor and Frank the accuser, but from the final day of the last trial until an order for alimony had been made by this court, Frank had not contributed a farthing towards his wife's maintenance.

The mystery letter from day two – simply referred to as 'the letter from Lady X' – was then produced and given to the jury to read. It was still not read aloud. Murphy pointed out that up to the point at which the charge against Frank was 'dragged' from Mabel in the first trial, there had been no cruelty on her part. Further, he asked the jury to consider what cruelty there had actually been since. It was a painful fact of the case that Mabel and the Russells disputed what they had told her concerning Frank's character. He invited Mabel to step forward and give evidence.

Mr Barnard opened Mabel's gentle and not overly long examination-in-chief towards the end of the day with a direct question: 'Do you believe there is any truth in the charge against your husband and Mr. Roberts?' Mabel clearly answered, 'No.' She'd only answered as she had in the first trial because she was 'bullied into it' without really understanding what she said. She countered just about everything denied by the Russells and refuted St George's claim that Oxford had come up in her presence at his meeting with Lina.

The following day was completely taken up with Mabel's evidence. In an attempt to recreate something of the effect of the first trial, she had chosen (perhaps unwisely) to dispense with her plain attire for the occasion in favour of something a little more frivolous. She arrived at court wearing 'a big spray of lilies of the valley and a dainty lace edged kerchief peeping shyly from her beaded bodice':

> At her throat was a gold coronet shaped brooch set in pearls and the letters
> of her pet name which an admiring world has learnt ere this to be 'Babs'. It
> contrasted oddly with the 'envy, hatred and malice and all uncharitableness'
> which has been so prominent in this case.[16]

As a married woman of twenty-five, 'Babs' no longer enjoyed the sympathy of the press. Even before the hearing began, the London *Figaro* had voiced the opinion that there was 'a good deal of natural disgust in society' towards Mabel, who had 'lost caste' by attempting to reunite herself with Frank after bringing 'the most abominable charges it is possible to conceive' against him.[17] It is difficult to see how emphasising her frivolity would help her counter this perception. With her integrity already in doubt, she now needed a strong performance to lay the ghost of her disastrous cross-examination at the first trial.

With 'the mysterious instinct of court crowds, the court filled up speedily' as Sir Henry stepped forward to begin his cross-examination. He proposed, he said, to go through all the events in chronological order – it being so difficult otherwise to get the facts straight. In so doing, Sir Henry proved that every single one of his 'irritating little spikes' was sharpened and pointing directly at Mabel. He pulled apart every word of her letter to Frank after the meeting with St George, delving fully into the implication of her statement that there 'ought not to be secrets between us' to prove that she knew more than she let on. When he extracted the admission that she couldn't remember what she had thought was then 'worrying her to death' or what it was about Frank's past that needed clarifying, he knew he had scored an advantage. And when Mr Barnard objected that Sir Henry was questioning Mabel about a letter that had not been disclosed and ought to have been, the hedgehog turned his little spikes on him, dismissing it as a 'small grievance'.

> Mr Barnard: It is a very great grievance.
> Sir Henry: It is the best you have got, I admit.

From there, Sir Henry skipped quickly over the marriage to the separation and the substance of what Lady John had supposedly told Mabel, concluding that it seemed unbelievable that a lady of such high character would ever stoop to say such things. Finally, he turned his attention to Roberts. When had Mabel first come to the conclusion that there had been 'anything improper' in Frank's conduct with him? Once again Mabel had difficulty answering. It had been after speaking to the Russells at PL, but what exactly she believed at that time she seemed unable to verbalise. Use of the word 'sodomy' was so indelicate as to be unthinkable. In the end, Sir Henry suggested splitting the accusation into two possible interpretations – 'a crime' and 'some impropriety' – enabling Mabel to say that she never thought there was 'a crime' – even after receiving Lady X's letter or when she was 'bullied' into making the charge in the witness box. But she still found Sir Henry's little jibes off-putting.

> Q: When you said just now that you had been bullied at the last trial into making the charge, of course, you were referring to the present Lord Chief Justice's cross-examination?
> A: Yes, I was.
> Q: You were bullied into making the charge?
> A: I consider I was.
> Q: What charge were you bullied into making?
> A: The charge of neglect.

Q: What, bullied into making that charge, when you always made it? Do
   you tell the jury you were bullied into the charge of neglect and cruelty
   only?
A: I do not know really, I am so nervous.

Mabel was invited to sit, to take an adjournment. Sir Henry expressed
himself personally very sorry she had to be subjected to this, but after she
had recovered herself, asked in disbelief whether she had not heard her
husband being hooted at in the street after she had given her evidence? Did
she not read the newspapers afterwards and understand the inference taken
from her answers? – No, she did not.

At last, it was time to address Lady X's letter. Sir Henry wanted to
know whether this 'Lady X' was a particular friend, an 'intimate' friend
to whom Mabel would look for advice. No, came the answer, but she was
a friend she had known for many years. Was it not true that Frank had
refused to know her before the wedding? – Yes, it was true; but she did
not exactly understand Frank's objection. She thought it was 'something
about her life'.

During the course of his questioning, Sir Henry 'accidentally' let slip
the lady's name – just once – and the *Star* jumped on it (as much as they
dared), revealing that she was in fact 'Lady C_____'. The following day
they reported with glee that the accidental slippage seemed 'doomed to
make trouble'. *Burke's* and *Debrett's*, they suggested, had been put to full
use on the mystery and an intelligent telegraphist had innocently expanded
the X and C to Lady Cross, which was wrong, but likely to cause just as
much trouble. The real answer, of course, was that 'Lady X' was Lady
Cardigan, whose letter to Mabel of 21 November 1890 had spoken of
Frank's 'malpractices' at Oxford and the Chinaman he had secreted in
Dover Street.

There could not have been a single gentleman of the special jury who
had not heard something of this lady. Her reputation was infamous and
she had proudly signed the letter 'A. Cardigan & Lancastre'. She had been
born Adeline Louisa Maria de Horsey in 1824 and before her marriage to
the Earl of Cardigan had been linked to several men, including the Infante
Carlos, Count of Montemolin, the Carlist claimant to the Spanish throne.
In her late twenties, she was thought to have given birth to an illegitimate
child. Everyone in society was 'very shy of her' and it had been Lady
Stanley's opinion at the time that it was 'very desirable' for society that
the truth of the rumour should be 'settled one way or the other'.[18] When
Adeline subsequently became involved with Lord Cardigan, he was still
married but living alone. Their unchaperoned walks around Hyde Park and
twenty-seven-year age gap were a huge scandal. When Cardigan's wife died
in September 1858, leaving him free to marry, his family refused to receive
her; Queen Victoria declined as well. When the couple offered invitations
across all society to a great ball, 'nobody came'.[19] After Cardigan's death
she married Don António Manuel de Saldanha e Lancastre, subsequently
styling herself the Countess Cardigan & Lancastre (though strictly speaking

she was not entitled to use both titles together). Now, Mabel was forced to admit not only that she had adhered to the words of a notorious gossip, but that she had not sought from Lady Cardigan the foundations of her statements, nor insisted that Lady Cardigan be subpoenaed to attest to them. Mabel had not communicated with her for years and did not know where in the world she then was.

From this uncomfortable revelation, Sir Henry moved on to another, forcing Mabel to admit that she had allowed the *Hawk* interview to be published containing references to letters from the Russells 'stating the charge' that she knew did nothing of the kind; that she 'never thought very much' about the effect of it and had been 'too unhappy to care' at the time whether it would hinder a reconciliation with her husband. She had not become aware of the inference put on her charge, she said, or fully understood the nature of the suggestion made in Lady Cardigan's letter until the spring of 1894. Prior to that, she had continued to believe that though Frank was not guilty of 'a crime' there was still 'something'. She was not asked what it was that made her suddenly aware, and she did not say. But when she claimed she did nothing to retract the charge once the light dawned on her because she thought these proceedings would give her ample opportunity to publicly apologise, it sounded hollow; and when she further admitted that the real reason she had felt indisposed to apologise to Roberts sooner was because 'she did not like him', she appeared malicious. Her assertion that Roberts' visits – during which they sang together at the piano – had been less than pleasurable sounded weak as Sir Henry suggested their voices would not 'blend very well now'. And when Sir Henry then challenged her to produce 'anything you have got prejudicial to Roberts', poor Mabel could only say that she was not sure she had anything, she must have made a mistake and was sorry. Her final claim – that she had never met Lina's detectives or read their reports herself or known anything of their content – prompted Baron Pollock to plead, 'Do yourself justice.' She could not. But her mother was in court, she said, and she would tell them. It was she who had employed them (with your sanction, added Sir Henry).

The final day of evidence began with a very brief turn from Giddy, who was called upon to swear that she was not present at the meeting between her mother, sister and Rowe. She was very pretty, said the *Star*, but not a patch on Lina, who was next in the box. The fifty-year-old dame outshone both her daughters, in a 'velvet gown, of the colour of Parma violets'. With all the aplomb of a Wildean matriarch she confidently dispatched questions concerning the Russells and countered all Rowe's claims about their 'unnatural' interview. She denied that Rowe and the detectives had failed to produce evidence because there was nothing to find, but because they were inept: 'I do not believe in detectives,' she pronounced, which was comical given that she had employed so many.

When it came to her cross-examination, Sir Henry, who had so easily outwitted Mabel, was positively confounded by Lina's self-possession, which did not slip even in the face of the most indelicate challenges. His apologetic probing as to whether she had ever been bankrupt elicited a quite unperturbed, 'Oh, yes.' Thereafter she gave more performance than evidence, her witty and evasive responses rarely resolving themselves into anything resembling facts. When Sir Henry asked if she'd known about her daughter's charge against Roberts, what it inferred and whether she believed it, she very carefully replied that she had known, but 'did not wish to believe it to be true'. That is not the same as *not* believing it, the judge pointed out, and only after much equivocation did she finally settle on the answer that she neither believed it *nor* wished to believe it. *Ever.* On little else would she be so categorical. Concerning the detectives, yes, she had employed them to follow Frank, though she never bore him any ill-will but always 'sincerely' loved him. In which case, Sir Henry wanted to know, what had she meant by writing to Dickinson for any 'good news' concerning Frank. Would 'good news' be his innocence or guilt?

A: I suppose of his guilt.
Q: That would be good news to you, madam, if he was guilty?
A: No that would not have been good news. I wished him to live with his wife.

Then what did she mean by writing to them in such a way? Well, it was the 'awkward situation' she found herself in which could not be resolved *without* Frank's guilt. Her daughter was living with her when she should have been with her husband. Therefore, she 'did not feel justified in *not* having detectives, in case there was anything'. Following her logic was a challenge. Pinning her down to whether the guilt she referred to was with men or women was another, until she finally decided that 'certainly not men – only women' was the appropriate response. And so, she had written to Dickinson for her 'good news' and declared it would have been strange if *he* had brought Frank to justice, not just because Dickinson was a 'disgraceful man … almost a broken-down gentleman' but, she revealed, with perfect poise, because he was her cousin.[20]

Throughout the rest of their exchange, Lina disguised misdirection with misapprehension, becoming positively slippery when Sir Henry asked about the evidence she had 'enough to hang any ordinary man', feigning first an inability to recognise what might be construed by such a comment, then saying she could not remember what evidence she had, then that it was a privileged conversation that took place in Peckham's office, which the judge said was no defence. Finally, she declared, she would not tell an untruth: 'Detectives never prove anything. (Laughter.)' Flamboyantly, she turned to address the jury with haughty self-deprecation:

A: I am sorry, Gentlemen of the Jury, I really forget what happened – what that meant … I am not a very good-tempered person. I do say I was in a passion when I wrote that.

Q: With Lord Russell? Or with whom?

A: With the whole thing. I was in a passion with my daughter ... [for] coming back and living with me when she ought to be living with her husband.

Q: But, Lady Scott, you have great experience in the world, and you know it is a very serious matter...

A: Then I apologise for it.

Q: To whom?

A: To Lord Russell.

Q: It is the first time you have ever done so.

A: I have never had a chance before.

And thus, the question of what actual evidence she had against Frank was deflected again. Sir Henry tried to come at it from another angle. Frank had to be guilty of something if her daughter was to get her divorce. Certainly, but Lina preferred she would go back. What? Even though Mabel would rather die than return to him?

A: I have heard lots of ladies say that.

Q: You have heard lots of ladies say they would rather die than go back?

A: Yes; and they do go back and are very happy afterwards. (Laughter.)

Q: ... to husbands ... whose footsteps terrify them?

A: I have heard them say much worse than that. (Laughter.) ... It is my firm opinion, Gentlemen of the Jury, it is every woman's duty to try...

Was Mabel then a virtuous woman and Frank a virtuous man?

A: Virtuous woman, certainly; virtuous man – I do not know what men's virtues consist of.

Q: You are very hard on us, Lady Scott (laughter): is this the result of your personal experience?

A: It is a long time since I have been married.

How many detectives had Lina employed, Sir Henry wondered? There had been ten, she thought, with a new one employed each time one came back empty-handed: 'When one did not bring any evidence, and I had paid him, I was not going to employ him again.' And how many had been set up for life? None, because she had no money to do so. It was true, she *had* promised she would, but 'ladies often promise things they do not fulfil'. (Laughter.) It was indeed a costly business, she agreed, but she came into a little money now and then.

Q: Not kept back from your creditors, I hope, to go to detectives?

A: Yes. The money has been run away with by detectives.

Q: How gratifying to your tradesmen and others who supply you with flowers and dresses?

A: Oh, they do not mind, I think. (Laughter.)

Lina's coy response, made 'with a complacent look at her Parma Violet velvet' was too much for Sir Henry. 'I think I must leave it,' he said, admitting defeat. But Lady Scott was not quite finished. Under Murphy's direction, she was permitted a final comment on her interview with St George. It was he, she said, who had first told her that Frank had been sent down from Oxford. She never asked St George why he told her and, she realised, she should never have listened to him because Frank had said 'he was an interfering bother to the whole family, a meddling man who meddled in the family's affairs'. But listen to him she had, and afterwards went to see Frank's tutor at Oxford to hear what he had to say; and, though she never spoke to Jowett, that is how she came to allow Mabel to marry Frank. Turning for the last time to the jury, she told them how she had thought it all 'a sort of joke'; that Frank had been 'turned down for practical joking, or something of that kind', and that she had only received St George because 'Lady Stanley of Alderley made a disgraceful remark about me, which I expected her to apologize to me for, and Gentlemen of the jury, I trust that you—' But Robson cut her off: 'I think you had better not make any speeches. Mr. Murphy will do that for you fairly well. (Laughter.)'

Lina left the box having clearly stated that which she'd said would have been perjury had she been forced to say it at the first trial, but having evaded much more. Baron Pollock decided that 'given the importance of the case' and the lateness of the hour they would adjourn until after the Easter recess. In Frank's view, it could have all been settled that day if the judge were not an 'idle old lazybones', but it was of little consequence:

> Everything has gone perfectly and it does not matter much whether we get the legal verdict or not: my character is vindicated to the fullest extent...[21]

The papers were strangely quiet over the recess. Without a verdict and with much still happening in the Wilde case – with Oscar's committal at Bow Street on 19 April and anticipated appearance at the Old Bailey scheduled for the following week – there was little to say about Frank, and no inclination or available space in which to say it. Easter, then, was relaxing. Frank spent it at Amberley Cottage with Mary and Lionel Johnson where Wilde's case was of greater concern than his own. 'This Oscar affair is awful,' he wrote to Santayana: 'Alfred Douglas is a great friend of Lionel's and he is dreadfully distressed.'[22] Perhaps it was fortunate that the press did not know about this tenuous link between Frank and Oscar, or that Wilde had been a guest at Frank's house in Hampton during the aftermath of the Oxford incident. The column inches might have freed up quickly enough if they had.

On Tuesday 24 April, the court reconvened. In his closing address, Mr Murphy said it had been a brave attempt by Sir Henry to revolutionise the divorce law, but that they could not separate a couple simply for quarrelling: couples quarrelled every day. He attempted to distance Mabel from Roberts by pointing out that the 'terrible things' she had heard were not about him, but about Oxford, and that Frank had refused to communicate with her on this. As regards *Hawk*, he said it was for them to decide if this one incident, apart from everything else, was sufficient for them to award a judicial separation, given that Frank's health had not suffered as a result. It was true that Mabel had made some foolish statements, but it was simply not true that she had continued to repeat her original charge.

By contrast, Sir Henry's speech was impassioned. He rather dramatically suggested that if Frank had not brought these proceedings, Mabel's charges would have made him an outcast, unable to 'associate with any human beings in this country'. He did not believe she didn't understand the nature of her charge until 1894: the summing up of Sir Charles Butt in 1891, for which she was present, could have left her in no doubt. In her cruel attempt to drag 'the great and honoured name of Russell to the dust' she had not hesitated in referring in *Hawk* to letters from the family she knew did not exist and to suggest that if her mother had given evidence the result would have been otherwise. Her conduct and that of Lina beside her had inflicted 'the greatest amount of moral cruelty'. In her 'perverted mind' she had created notions of Frank's behaviour that were without a shadow of foundation. She must be condemned by every right-minded person for her actions – 'for the cruel wrong she had inflicted on the man she now said she believed to be quite innocent of the charge'.

On the last day, Baron Pollock spent more than two hours summing up and covering the 'new and important' question in this case: what is legal cruelty? For the only thing that could prevent Mabel being entitled to restitution would be if the jury found her guilty. To assist the jury, it was necessary to draw their attention to the manner in which the law had been interpreted and applied down the years. He told them that roughly a century ago it had been observed by Lord Stowell that in cases involving cruelty there had always been either some actual physical harm or some threat to life or health. He quoted specifically Lord Stowell's words: 'What merely wounds the feelings is in few cases to be admitted.' However, he did not think Lord Stowell could imagine cases of tyranny or cases where there were charges of gross offences which would equally render married life unbearable and, after giving a few examples, suggested that 'there must be some limit to the old rule on this subject'; the only question was what that limit should be.

The members of the jury must ask themselves, what was Mabel's state of mind that she could believe charges against her husband 'imputing to him more guilt and more misconduct than should have been implied from the mere facts themselves'? The family had investigated the Oxford incident. Professor Jowett, 'one of the most distinguished men who has been known to Oxford in modern times', had invited Frank back and attended his wedding. All this was known – and more, as Lina herself had enquired of the facts of Frank's tutor. It was, therefore, in his opinion extraordinary that this was used as a basis for one of the most remarkable things he had ever heard, in or out of court: the Roberts incident. Echoing Sir Charles Butt's summing up in the first trial, Baron Pollock concluded that the jury must ask themselves whether anyone 'with a grain of common sense or good feeling could have ever twisted these facts into a charge of a man having committed an abominable offence? To my mind it is past belief.'

With regard to Lady Cardigan's 'cruel' letter, he asked them to consider that Mabel could have asked Lina, who apparently had 'a knowledge of the world that is not common to many women', to help her as to what was meant. He pointed out the 'intense contradiction' between Mabel and the Russells and the lack of evidence to substantiate her claim. He suggested her feeling 'bullied' into making the charge showed nothing more than her lack of courtroom experience and that the rights and wrongs of the *Hawk* interview were immaterial. The important question was, how far could she have supposed the information given by Frank's relations supported her charge? They had Frank and Mabel's letters to help them. If they thought Mabel's letters honestly written by a woman believing the charge against her husband and prepared under certain circumstances to forgive, then they would pause before finding those letters part of the evidence of cruelty. But if they thought they were written with a view to reaching some sort of compromise to extort money from her husband (which, he said, did leak out towards the end of the correspondence), then it was not for him to say what conclusion they should arrive at as to their verdict (though, really, they could not have been in much doubt). Though this case was a 'first impression', it did not prevent them giving a verdict; however, in enlarging the law they should consider it very carefully.

On this final comment, the jury retired. It took them all of twenty minutes to decide: Mabel had not acted *bona fide* and was guilty of cruelty.

Frank was delighted, writing to Santayana that 'the general public were quite unable to appreciate the legal difficulties in our way and had made up their minds we must succeed. We were by no means so certain.' But Baron Pollock's summing up had placed them 'in a legal position of such strength that no appeal can possibly dislodge us'.[23] It certainly seemed to be the case. Frank's *white flower of a blameless life* shone brighter than ever. The press had bigger fish to fry. As Frank and Mary celebrated, Oscar Wilde – the 'true' face of sexual depravity, against whom Frank was a paragon of virtue – was brought before judge and jury at the Old Bailey. At the first attempt, the jury failed to return a verdict. At the second, Wilde was convicted and sentenced to two years' imprisonment with hard labour. Despite Wilde's eloquence on the Hellenistic concept of male love, public hostility towards homosexuality proved disastrous for him, while for Frank the gamble of raising and challenging the ugly spectre of an unwarranted and unsubstantiated accusation of the same morally offensive behaviour, written in bold plain English, had paid off. The abhorrence of homosexual practice 'served to reinforce [Frank's] contention that his wife's accusations constituted legal cruelty' and secured the verdict in his favour.[24] But one significant thing remained unchanged: though now legally separated, neither he nor Mabel were free to remarry. For all the rights and wrongs and all the legal wrangling, the most pressing question for them both was still how to slip the Gordian knot for good.

15

Will No One Rid Me of This Pestilent Wife?

All conjugal rights and wrongs aside, 1894–5 saw several major changes in Frank's life. First was his entry into local politics. In 1894, the Local Government Act brought district and parish councils into being. Frank stood in Cookham, Maidenhead, and credited Bertrand's fiancée, Alys – who campaigned for the Vestry of Westminster[1] – with infecting him with a 'pernicious electioneering spirit'. He positively enjoyed 'hobnobbing with workmen, & Rate collectors & all sorts of curious people' and was duly elected on 17 December.[2] He became chairman of Cookham parish council and, by default of his election to the district council, a guardian of the poor responsible for the administration of Maidenhead workhouse. Alys didn't win, but the papers didn't make too much of it. They preferred instead to report that when the contest was at its peak, Alys slipped away to submit to the infinitely more feminine occupation of becoming Mrs Bertrand Russell.[3]

Full of reforming zeal, Frank launched himself into his new occupation: mapping out and defending public rights of way as a parish councillor, overseeing maintenance of roads as a district councillor, and questioning outdated barbaric practices in the workhouse as a poor law guardian. In total, he spent six years in service to these councils and by the end of only the first month had added to his portfolio of titles 'Justice of the Peace for Berkshire'. In an early example of his inclination to stick up for the underdog, he used his influence at Maidenhead petty sessions to challenge what he saw as the often perfunctory and unimaginative sentencing of prisoners by many of the magistrates with whom he worked.

So much did Frank enjoy his new-found career that in February 1895 he stood for election to the much larger and more influential London County Council (LCC) as Progressive candidate for West Newington alongside the editor of *Reynolds's Newspaper*, W. M. Thompson. Backed by the Liberals, the Progressives were in the ascendancy, having dominated the LCC since its creation in 1889. Both Frank and Thompson won easily and Frank wrote immediately to Santayana of his new post 'of some responsibility and distinction'.[4] He was clearly proud to be taking his first steps in the family business, having already found a home at two bastions of liberalism: the National Liberal Club (NLC), which he joined in 1889, and the salubrious Reform Club on Pall Mall, where he became a member in 1894. His politics positioned him towards the left of the party, though not so far as to consider himself a socialist. Indeed, in response to a series of articles in *St Stephen's Review* in March 1892, in which he was named as a one-time member of the Oxford branch of the Socialist League, Frank had immediately written to the editor categorically stating, 'I am not now, and never was, a Socialist.'[5] He would not always feel so inclined.

His business interests at the time were testament to his assertion, though Russell & Co. had proved something of a disaster. In a growing market, Frank had found it difficult to compete and in 1895 gave it up as a bad job at considerable personal financial loss. By the autumn, the only thing he had left to show for his endeavours was his telegraphic address – OUKETI – which he had decided to keep, perhaps thinking it a wry joke given his circumstances.[6] Not that the experience had dampened his enthusiasm for business. He continued to be chairman of Plenty's of Newbury, whose fortunes rose and fell but were secured by their providing steam-launch engines for the Admiralty; and in 1895, Frank accepted the chairmanship of the London board of the Portuguese Companhia do Nyassa.

It was then common practice for companies to employ aristocrats as figureheads and reward them accordingly for their advertising value, but Frank's involvement with Nyassa was a little more hands-on. Nyassa was one of several companies formed to take over the 'administration and exploitation' of Mozambique from the then effectively bankrupt Portuguese government.[7] It had early ambitions to develop the region through a proposed railway system linking the Indian Ocean and the Great Central Lake System of Africa. Its directors, however, were far more concerned with financial manoeuvres between its London and Lisbon offices, such that their influence in Africa was slight. In June 1895, Frank was sent to Lisbon for six weeks to mediate (or, as he put it, 'to browbeat the Portuguese Government into recognizing our half of the Board and disowning the other half'[8]). He turned out to be not very diplomatic. The Conde da Lavradio took personal exception to his comments and challenged Frank to a duel. Frank dismissed it on the ground that Englishmen don't fight; their subsequent accusations of cowardice gave him not 'a moment's uneasiness'. Only later did he learn that Portuguese duels were in fact 'innocuous and bloodless', involving a 'correspondence of incriminations' in the press, not pistols at ten paces.[9]

Mary and her mother had accompanied Frank to Portugal, and on their return Frank and Mary set off again, this time with Mary's brother as chaperone, on a tour of Gloucestershire and the Wye Valley. Frank would travel all over the south of England with various companions when motor cars became his obsession in the early 1900s, but on this occasion they were in a 'light four-wheel Scotch dog-cart' pulled by a pair of horses in which he calculated they could cover 100 miles in a week quite comfortably.[10] They stayed for a week in a cottage in a remote village a few miles from Frank's childhood home of Trelleck and then explored the Cotswolds, returning via Witney and Woodstock and registering in various country hotels as 'Turner & party' so as not to excite attention.[11] Both Lionel Johnson and Santayana were invited to join them.

In many respects, this was an enjoyable time for Frank. With Agnes gone, Mary settled at Newnham and new ventures to distract him, he was happily dividing his time between Maidenhead and London. He had taken a *pied-à-terre* at 2 Temple Gardens, just off the Embankment, and was often to be found dining at the NLC. During evenings he played whist in the card room or frequented the smoking room on the top floor – affectionately known as the 'vestry' for the small circle who used to assemble there. Here, he met a host of characters whose names would crop up at intervals throughout his life, most notably John Sargeaunt, a well-loved classics scholar and master of Westminster School who published works on the poems of Virgil, Pope, and Dryden; and John J. Withers, who would take over as Frank's solicitor on Doulton's death in 1904, and whose firm, founded in 1896, still operates as Withersworldwide. There was only one ever-present thorn in Frank's side: Mabel Edith.

At the end of the second trial, Baron Pollock had reserved judgment on the matter of costs and an allowance for Mabel. On 27 April 1895, it came before him again. Mabel's barrister, Mr Barnard, argued that the £900 p.a. income from her trust fund had been severely hit by reduced interest payments, such that it was now only £171. Frank's income, meanwhile, was declared as being between £3,500 and £4,000. Barnard wanted the £550 pre-trial alimony to be made permanent, but Frank's barrister disputed the huge drop in her income, claiming it to be nearer £500. The judge deferred judgment to give Frank's team another week to see if they could accept the declared figures.[12]

Both figures do actually correspond to statements made by each party prior to the suit, but the reduction in Mabel's income was less about dividends than the extortionate amount of interest she was paying on loans. Since her separation from Frank she had borrowed heavily and her interest alone amounted to some £560 p.a., even before the principal sum was repaid.[13] With the additional reduction in dividends, Mabel's income was as declared, but Frank's team still demanded to see Mabel's bank book before they would budge. Their win in court had put them in a very strong position, for Mabel was now officially the guilty party and must not be seen to be rewarded for her crime. She must shift her expectations. Lina's bankruptcy, however, made her position critical and Mabel instead decided to try to extricate herself from the position of malefactor. On 3 May 1895, she lodged an appeal against the verdict. All further discussion of costs and allowance was put on hold until after an appeal court judgment.

The appeal as filed asked the judges to consider two courses of action: either set aside the jury's verdict on the ground that no legal cruelty had been established, or order a new trial on the grounds of non-direction or misdirection of the jury by Baron Pollock on nine specified points. The case came before the appeal judges – Lords Lopes, Lindley and Rigby – on 28 June 1895. In addition to the above, Mabel's counsel highlighted the lack of any detrimental effect on Frank's health caused by Mabel's supposed cruelty, pointing out that 'passionate language or conduct that hurts the feelings is not cruelty'. They cited twenty-six cases from between 1785 and 1886 to support their claim. They thought the question of cruelty ought not to have been left to the jury. Further, they pointed out that neither the ecclesiastical court nor the divorce court had ever 'acted on the footing that an appellant for restitution of conjugal rights must come with clean hands'. They asked the judges to make allowance for the fact that the *Hawk* interview had taken place a matter of days after the first trial and that no further repetition of the charges had been subsequently made. They also pointed out that Frank's accusations of Mabel's cruelty had only come as a result of her petition for restitution, some four years after the event. Frank's team responded that their client should not be penalised for being an 'unusually strong man'. Thereafter they stuck to their original assertion that Mabel was only after his money and suggested the court would not 'countenance a species of blackmailing which would be punishable by penal servitude'. After three days in court, the judges determined that as it was such an important case, they would retire to deliberate their verdict.[14]

On 7 August, some four weeks later, their judgment was read by Lord Lopes. He justified the 'anxious care' they had taken over it and quickly revealed their conclusion that Mabel had *not* acted *bona fides* in bringing the Roberts charge. Her subsequent repeating of it made her crime all the more reprehensible and her declaration that she wished to return to Frank 'incredible'. Her conduct therefore was 'indisputable': her actions constituted 'high moral offences'. But was it legal cruelty?

Lords Lopes and Lindley agreed that Baron Pollock had not adequately defined legal cruelty, leaving the jury 'somewhat at large'. Lord Lopes therefore took the opportunity to define it thus: 'There must be danger to life, limb, or health, bodily or mental, or a reasonable apprehension of it, to constitute legal cruelty.' This definition he based on *Evans* v. *Evans* (1790) – the case Baron Pollock had cited in his summing up. Lord Lopes interpreted Lord Stowell's comment – that 'what merely wounds the feelings is in few cases to be admitted' – not as meaning (as Baron Pollock had interpreted it) in *very few cases* it is allowed but as meaning *never*. And as the 1857 Matrimonial Causes Act bound them to adhere 'as nearly as may be confirmable to the principles and rules on which the Ecclesiastical Courts have hitherto acted' they felt a compunction to jealously guard the definition of legal cruelty as Lord Stowell had defined it and they had now reiterated it, and to adhere to his further comment that 'no amount of want of civility, rudeness, insult, or abuse, however gross, which did not affect life, limb [etc.]' should be considered legal cruelty. After citing numerous other cases to substantiate this conclusion and to reinforce the assertion that 'necessary protection' was to remain 'the foundation of all separation', Lord Lopes added that 'the difference of the sexes makes no essential difference in the principles' and that they were not prepared 'in the face of such a consistent body of authority arrayed against it' to authorise a departure from the accepted definition. In his and Lord Lindley's view, interpreting Mabel's actions as legally cruel would not only change the definition but open up a new ground for separation – viz. by the simple *accusation* of a marital offence – and this they could not do. It was a matter for the legislature, not the courts.

Lord Rigby, however, disagreed. 'For myself,' he commented, 'I can imagine no case of repeated insult and indignity more atrocious.' Nor did he agree with his colleagues' narrow interpretation of Lord Stowell's words, highlighting the fact that in summing up *Evans* v. *Evans* Lord Stowell had also said: that which constitutes cruelty must be both 'grave and weighty, and as such shew an absolute impossibility that the duties of married life can be discharged'. Lord Rigby interpreted these words as inferring that that which is 'grave and weighty' need not always be physical violence, though 'what falls short is to be admitted with great caution' and such cases are 'very exceptional'. Neither did he feel 'constrained' by a definition of legal cruelty that required physical violence to make it so, and said that in the Russells' case it was sufficiently clear that 'disputes would inevitably arise between this ill-assorted pair', that Frank would feel 'under constant and reasonable apprehension of the repetition of the infamous charges already made' and that married life could not be resumed without raising the prospect of a state of personal danger to one or the other party as a result.

With a 2:1 majority determining that Mabel's behaviour did not constitute legal cruelty, Lord Lopes declared that they had no alternative but to overturn the judgment of the court below and deny Frank's right to a judicial separation.

That still left the question of Mabel's petition for restitution. It was a 'startling proposition', Lord Lopes said, that one ruling should naturally determine the other. It required 'careful examination'. The judges had scoured the histories and could not find a single case in which a decree for restitution was refused when a decree for separation had been declined. They had been forced, therefore, to go to the wording of the 1857 Act for guidance and had found some flexibility there. The Act stated that the court 'may decree', not *shall* decree, that a husband be forced to return to his wife on pain of prosecution if he had abandoned her 'without lawful cause'. They also recognised that the Act did not specifically state the *nature* of the behaviour (beyond adultery or cruelty) that would be deemed a bar to restitution. The wording of the 1884 amendment to the Act had also to be considered. It had neglected to include the phrase 'without lawful cause' when it stated that if a respondent refused a restitution order a separation could be instituted, but they did not think it was intended that it conflict with the original Act in this matter. They therefore determined that it was quite within their remit to consider

Mabel's behaviour independently of Frank's counter-suit and concluded that their overturning of Frank's judicial separation did not naturally entitle Mabel to restitution if they deemed her behaviour justified Frank's absence. And this, they ruled, 'even at the risk of being thought somewhat illogical'.[15]

Here was a legal muddle apparently full of contradiction. In ruling as they did, the appellate judges justified Frank and Mabel's separation but did not sanction it. It left the pair in a worse position than they had been to date: separated, but no longer judicially so; legally, as married as ever. Without evidence of Frank's reaction, we are left to imagine his feelings as his prior confidence in the strength of his legal position was swept away. For as of this moment, *neither* was cruel, and with their separation justified, neither would ever be able to prove the other's desertion. As a result, nothing but a change in the law or proof of adultery on Mabel's part would ever legally separate them. Corseted by the letter of the law, the judges had manipulated it as far as they could to produce evidence for the required result; though it is difficult to see how they could have done otherwise. It is ironic that the opposing viewpoints of Lords Lopes and Lindley on the one hand and Lord Rigby on the other were justified by Lord Stowell's same summing up 100 years previously. It has led commentators to conclude that what steered the judges' interpretation 'must have been, in the long run, the views of each individual judge as to the social implications resulting from one view as opposed to the other'. In which sense, they were just as much corseted by the necessity to uphold the condemnation of Mabel's accusations of homosexuality, which were egregious enough to successfully defend a restitution order, while simultaneously not declaring them 'grave and weighty' enough to widen the definition of legal cruelty and thereby allow 'the full flood tide of all degrees of matrimonial unhappiness to sweep in'.[16] For Frank and Mabel, the only hope was the lifeline thrown to them by Lord Rigby's dissent, which came with leave to appeal to the House of Lords on the ground that their case involved a point of law. It was their last legal option.

The deadline for appeal was 7 September 1895. On that day, Mabel duly lodged her appeal with the judicial office. It was presented to the House on 12 November. On the same day, Frank lodged a cross-appeal. It is unclear whether he did this fearing that Mabel might not have the financial resources to see her appeal through, but that does appear to have been the case. Her legal bills were already monumental. Her costs as filed by Valpy & Co. from the filing of the restitution petition in March 1894 to the end of the appeal case in August 1895 came to over £7,000.[17] Her petition to the Lords was subsequently dismissed for failure to deposit the necessary bond to secure her costs. After concerns were raised by the judicial committee as to whether Frank's cross-appeal should be dismissed along with it or for having been submitted after the deadline, and doubts expressed as to whether Mabel would be able to afford to defend Frank's appeal if it were allowed to proceed and he should win, it was finally decided that Frank's appeal would go forward and be treated as an original appeal, replacing Mabel's at his own expense.[18]

If Frank had thought the civil courts slow, the House of Lords judges easily surpassed them. The case did not get its first hearing until 30 June 1896, some nine months later. It was then heard by the Lord Chancellor (Lord Halsbury), the four Law Lords and four additional Appeal Lords. On this occasion, Frank was represented by Sir Robert Reid QC, with Messrs Robson and Bargrave Deane in support. Messrs Murphy and Barnard continued to represent Mabel. After two days hearing arguments from counsel – largely similar to that which had been put to the appeal court – their lordships reserved judgment. After hearing further from Mabel's counsel on 14 July, they once again reserved judgment. When it got to November and still there was no prospect of an imminent verdict, the celebrated criminal judge Sir Henry Hawkins was heard to quip that the case 'has got into the House of Lords, though when it is coming out nobody knows'.[19] It would not in fact be until 16 July 1897 – nearly two years after Mabel's original petition had been lodged – by which time much had happened and Frank's patience had worn thin.

In December 1895, Frank went to Syracuse, Sicily, to look at an old monastery for sale in Taormina. Returning on 2 January, he wrote to Santayana, 'I am not sure yet whether the idea is mad or sane and shall submit it to Mary's common sense for a decision.' The idea spoke of a positive attempt to carve out a future with Mary, even if it meant living part of the year abroad. The rest of the letter conveyed his frustration:

> Doulton tells me he has written to you – the activity and fatuity of the Scotts are a marvel. But I begin to feel inclined to exclaim, 'Will no one rid me of this pestilent wife?' For it is really getting a nuisance. Lena is, I think, insane … I am getting very impatient with my lonely life … I never know when I may boil over bursting all restraints, and adopt some desperate expedient for cutting the Gordian knot. It would be foolish, but is not this present state criminal?[20]

Mary was committed to Frank, but the etiquette that demanded their relationship remain secret and they go everywhere chaperoned had been taking its toll for some time. The 'desperate expedient' Frank refers to had, in fact, first been mentioned to Bertrand in Paris in 1894, when Frank had admitted considering 'a scheme for getting domiciled in Chicago so as to get a divorce by the law of Illinois'.[21] American divorce laws differed from the English and from state to state, with some more liberal than others. Illinois, along with Utah and South Dakota, were once regarded as the easiest places to obtain what was known as a 'migratory divorce' – a divorce obtained somewhere other than a person's usual place of domicile. The foolishness of the move was that such divorces were often legally dubious outside the territory in which they were granted, which was clearly not ideal. But this letter raises two more immediately pressing questions. What, in the meantime, had the Scotts been up to, for Frank to suddenly declare Lina 'insane'? And why had Frank's solicitor, Doulton, written to Santayana? Fortunately, Santayana kept Doulton's letter. Its revelations were shocking. 'The Scotts,' he had written, 'are now adopting a new tack':

> They have actually the audacity to hunt up the crew of Lord Russell's yacht (the 'Royal') with the view to making charges of a disgusting nature against him, as long ago as 1887–8. I need not describe their methods to you, as probably you know them – suffice it however to say that they appear to have got hold of one or two disreputable characters.

Doulton asked Santayana to tell him what he knew of crew members Parker, Cockerton, Cruden, Aylott and Linton; to advise whether he had ever witnessed or heard of 'any immorality' by Frank with any of the crew; and whether he had been contacted by a detective named Littlechild.[22]

Santayana, in fact, did not know of the Scotts' recent methods. Though he had met Frank and Mary in Woodstock in September 1895, he had returned to America by the time Frank first knew for certain what they were up to. That news came in a letter from *Royal*'s former cabin boy, Frederick Kast, in which he told Frank that a detective acting for Lina had been searching for him. An advert had appeared in the papers asking,

> Will Mrs. Kas [*sic*], formerly of Kingston-on-Thames, or her son Fred, please send their address as it may be to their advantage to S.G.L., Box 349, Willing's, 125, Strand.[23]

Kast's brother had responded and now the detective was on his way to India to locate Fred, who was then a soldier with the Chitral Relief Force. He wanted to know from Frank 'what to do or say'.[24]

Thus it was revealed that only five days after the appeal court ruling, Lina had taken matters into her own hands. Learning from previous mistakes, she had employed the services of a more credible detective, former DCI John George Littlechild, who had run Special Branch for ten years from 1883 to 1893 when he retired to become a private investigator. He had spied for the prosecution during the first Wilde trial and was well respected. Lina sent him to hunt down William Aylott, the cabin boy on *Royal* when Frank undertook his Mediterranean tour in August 1887. Aylott was known to Lina for subsequently being employed by Swinburne & Co. on the installation of her electrical lighting at The Hurst in 1889. Littlechild quickly tracked him down to Atley Road Board School in east London, where his father was caretaker. Aylott spoke to Lina and afterwards made a formal statement on 12 August 1895; as a result of this, Lina sent Littlechild in search of Kast.

It was unfortunate that Frank did not receive Kast's letter until 19 November. It had been written on 1 September, but Kast, not knowing Frank's address, had sent it to the Hogarth Club, where Frank was not a member. As soon as Frank got it, he replied, telling Kast that his letter confirmed rumours that Lina had been sending detectives about 'with the object of trumping up false charges of infamous conduct' against him. He did not 'intend to tolerate any longer this loathsome conduct of my wife and her mother' and would do his best to bring them to justice. He advised Kast that if a detective should approach him he should take his name but otherwise not speak to him. He reminded Kast that though he had not considered him 'a model boy' during his employment it was nothing compared to the 'filthy practices they now wish to accuse you of', and he hoped Kast would tell them 'in the strongest terms' that he did not intend to be made 'a cat's paw for their false and filthy accusations'. Frank was reminding Kast (though not in so many words) that, as the law stood, sodomy was a crime for *both* participants. He advised Kast to stay put and 'continue honourably in your service of the Queen'.[25] It was too late.

On 7 October, a telegram had been sent to Kast's commanding officer requesting Kast return home to his supposedly sick mother. An initially uncertain Kast was soon convinced by Littlechild's envoy, David Smith, to give up his post on the promise of £500 and £1 a week for life. By 13 December, Kast was in Bombay, awaiting his passage home. He wrote back to his regiment that he had been put up in 'the best hotel in Bombay. Seven rupees a day, everything found except strong drinks. So you can bet I am doing the heavy.' He signed himself 'F. Smith, but still the same Kast'.[26]

Kast arrived back in London on 23 December 1895 and made a formal statement in a solicitor's presence a week later. It contained 'the most filthy and ridiculous details ... charging Russell with b——[buggery]'.[27] Ridiculous or not, Frank was clearly unnerved. For not only had Kast's re-emergence triggered Doulton's letter to Santayana, but Doulton's clerk, Ellis Eyton Baines, had been promptly dispatched to Bombay to intercept Kast, arriving, rather infuriatingly, the day after Kast's ship sailed.

Fortunately for Frank, Kast's arrival appears to have been something of a non-event and all went quiet. Frank wrote to Santayana on 9 February 1896 that the 'two boys whose souls [the Scotts] have purchased at a price' were clearly not proving as compliant as Lina might have hoped. With confidence that the thing had gone away without any action on his part, Frank quipped, 'It was a very determined effort of Lady Scott's but I am not surprised at its collapse – it is naturally hard to get a witness prove himself a perjurer by confessing himself a sodomite.'[28]

Throughout the summer, the situation remained relatively unchanged despite word occasionally reaching Frank of the 'large sums' the Scotts were having to pay to keep their 'unreliable witnesses ... in affluence and hiding'.[29] June saw the House of Lords appeal hearings already mentioned and another hearing that, while not wholly unexpected, Frank thought an unnecessary waste of time and money.

On 15 June 1896, Herbert Ainslie Roberts – he of the 'Roberts incident' – sued Mabel Edith for libel.[30] The sole object of the action, as stated by his counsel, was to 'put an end forever to the pain and annoyance he had been caused' by the persistent repetition of the charges against him. Roberts sought an unconditional written apology from Mabel and an undertaking that she would never again repeat the charges either directly or by insinuation. Should she decline, he asked for 'such substantial damages' as the court felt would demonstrate his undisputed innocence. A document had been prepared with acceptable wording and, after some discussion, Mabel's counsel stepped outside and returned with it signed. The court awarded damages of forty shillings plus costs against her. It was hardly the £3,000 the *South Wales Echo* suggested Roberts had in mind, but he left court vindicated and content. His name would never be linked with Frank's again.[31]

Also, around this time, Frank found a somewhat less drastic solution to his domestic arrangements with Mary. He saw advertised for sale a house on the South Downs that had once been used as a semaphore station, conveying messages from naval ships docked at Portsmouth to the admiralty in London. It was being used as a summer retreat by the wife of a British diplomat. The name given to it was Telegraph House. Employing a similar shorthand to that used for Pembroke Lodge, Frank would always refer to it as 'TH' and it would become his most treasured possession.

Frank is rather vague about when exactly he bought TH, but his marital squabbles with Mabel and his secrecy concerning Mary hardly make that surprising. He could not openly say he took the property so that he and Mary could be together, but that is almost certainly the case. On 13 August 1896, Santayana wrote to a friend that Frank had 'bought a little cottage for his "cousin". Her mother was there to give respectability to the party.'[32]

Frank first visited the property 'in November' – probably 1894, when an advert for 'A Government old Telegraphic House' with 2 acres of grounds, 700 feet above sea level, appeared in the *Standard* priced at £600.[33] Frank secured it sometime between then and summer 1896 with one acre for £450, promptly buying the second acre from a neighbour after completing the purchase and realising it wasn't included. The positioning of TH on the South Downs is exquisite. It sits nestled beneath Beacon Hill, with the rolling downs rising up above it to the rear and falling away gently in a capacious lawn extending into woods at the front. It is private and secluded, yet its expansive prospect gives an air of freedom not dissimilar to his childhood home, Ravenscroft. In the years Frank spent at TH, he would become as fond of the downs as he had been of the Thames and would make extensive alterations to the property, including erecting a tower from which the Isle of Wight could be seen on a clear day. It was his first property purchase and he glowed with pride: 'I surrounded it with a wire fence to show that it was really mine.'[34] Mary and her mother moved in and Frank visited at weekends, concealing his true identity from the servants and villagers so that Mrs Morris would appear to be the legal tenant and Frank her daughter's beau. Mary surrendered her place at Newnham, leaving without Tripos, supposedly to go to the Daughters of the Cross at Carshalton, Surrey, but really to TH to await her lord and master.[35] This part of Frank's life at least, though not public, was at last secure.

Everything else was characteristically turbulent. In November 1896, Roberts sent bailiffs to Bray to collect his unpaid forty shillings from Mabel.

Lina was livid. She thought she had seen Frank watching from his yacht and afterwards wrote cautioning him to 'take care not to go too far'. To Roberts she wrote that if he did not leave off molesting her daughter 'it will only end in sorrow to yourself, as now she has protection in papers in hand'.[36] Kast, it would appear, who had been hidden away in Hastings under his assumed name, had been appeased with a settlement after threatening to return to the army and was fast becoming Lina's star witness. Far from being idle, she and her new friends had been very busy indeed. Within a week of her letter to Roberts, she was ready to show her hand. Santayana was staying with Frank at Amberley Cottage when on 17 September 1896 an envelope arrived containing two documents detailing in no uncertain terms Frank's alleged immoral behaviour with *Royal*'s two cabin boys – Aylott, who at the time was nineteen, and Kast, then just sixteen years old. The documents were unsigned, but typed at the bottom were the names 'Cockerton, Aylott, and Kast'. Included with them was a declaration signed by Lina saying that she was compelled to circulate this information 'to protect her pure and holy daughter who had been so foully wronged'.[37] Frank raced to show Santayana. 'This time it's a prosecution for criminal libel,' he declared, 'and Lena goes to prison!'[38]

On Frank's behalf, Doulton applied to Bow Street for arrest warrants for the culprits, but failed due to lack of evidence of publication. As a result, he placed an advertisement in several London papers and sent his clerk, Baines, to locate and interview Cockerton and Aylott, to see if they could be made to incriminate themselves. It was not difficult. On 25 September, at his home in east London, Cockerton readily admitted signing the original libels at the office of solicitor Bernard Abrahams in Soho. In addition, Cockerton told Baines that he supposed Lina had caused the papers to be printed and circulated and that he had assented to Abrahams doing what he liked with them. Baines then saw Aylott at Atley Road Board School and he admitted likewise, adding that he thought the papers were to be sent to the judges at the House of Lords. He told Baines that he had gone to Abrahams' office at Cockerton's request.[39] Doulton took the information back to Bow Street, but still the magistrate ruled that there was insufficient evidence of publication.

Finally, an Arthur Carrez, 'a vendor of indecent literature and purveyor of rubber goods' near Leicester Square, came forward in response to the advert to admit responsibility for the printing of the libels.[40] He made a formal statement at Withers' office on 7 September, in which he said he had been introduced to Lina in mid-August by a Mrs Ida Franklin who lived above his shop and ran a massage business there. She introduced Lina to him as her sister.[41] Lina asked him to print 500 copies of two type-written documents. He took them to a Mr Parris of Greek Street, who did the printing, while he (Carrez) undertook to correct the proofs. Then at the beginning of September, Carrez received a telegram from Lina from the Grand Hotel, Brighton, asking him to visit her there. She gave him a list of names and addresses where she wished the copies to be sent. A few days later she appeared at his office with a wooden box in which were 500 copies of another five-page document which she wanted sent out with the others. He put them all together, and took 400 complete sets to an Edward Wallet, a translator in Chinatown, to envelope, address and post. Lady Scott paid him in total £13 for his work, out of which he paid Wallet £2. Wallet corroborated Carrez's statement, saying he had addressed and posted 350 sets in total, and enveloped a further fifty, on which he wrote 'Private and Important' but no address. These, he gave back to Carrez, who delivered them to Abrahams (with the exception of one copy, which mysteriously made its way into Wallet's pocket and was later produced at Bow Street like a rabbit out of a hat).[42]

Frank had his evidence of publication at last. But before he could do anything with it, he received a startling summons to appear before Winchester borough magistrates on a charge of indecently assaulting Kast within that city in June 1887, some nine years previously.

Frank chose Charles 'Willie' Matthews to go with him to Winchester as his advocate. Outside the courtroom, Matthews was known as a cultivated, witty, highly sociable man; 'a delightful combination of Etonian, Bohemian, courtier and lawyer' who counted Edward VII and George V among his friends.[43] Inside, he had a 'dramatic' style, no doubt engendered by his being raised by actors.[44] His face was 'feminine', his voice 'high and thin', and his delivery 'carefully rehearsed and prepared'. These peculiarities increased his effectiveness. 'It was impossible not to listen to him,' said fellow barrister Edward Marjoribanks, who applauded 'the pathos he could put into a single sentence'.[45]

Frank no doubt hoped a little of Matthews' wit and charm would work its magic on the Winchester magistrates, but it soon transpired there was little for him to do. The pair arrived, along with Santayana and a dozen or so supporters who crowded into the packed court, only to discover that the charge had been struck out on the ground that the offence took place outside its jurisdiction. Matthews 'got up melodramatically and with fearful grimaces and pregnant inflections' declared himself unsurprised that the case had been withdrawn, but would not comment on the reason for it, saying 'no doubt more would be heard of the matter in due course'.[46] Instead, he and Frank sped back to Bow Street where, this time, Frank's application for warrants was successful. At 9 p.m., Detective Inspector Alfred Leach found Lina at Limmer's Hotel, Hanover Square, and presented her with a warrant. 'Thank God it has come to this,' she declared, before pointing at Mabel sitting opposite and saying, 'She has no father and brother and I will fight for her till death.'[47] The following morning, Detective Sergeant Arthur Hailstone arrested Cockerton as he left his house. Cockerton also went willingly, saying, 'I have been expecting this. What I have said is what I have been told by others, and as there was more than one instance I was obliged to believe it.' As they passed the Bank of England on the omnibus on the way to Bow Street, Cockerton saw Kast walking along the street and told the detective he would be wanting him too. He hailed Kast to join them. DS Hailstone conveyed them both to Bow Street where they were formally charged. Kast said nothing, but DS Hailstone reported that the two men 'seemed pleased' with the course of events.[48] Aylott escaped arrest by being abroad.

Thus, on 10 October 1896, Maria Selina Elizabeth, Lady Scott, fifty-one; marine engineer John Cockerton, thirty-two; and Frederick James Kast, twenty-six, formerly of the 1st Battalion King's Royal Rifles, stood shoulder-to-shoulder in the dock at Bow Street charged with criminal libel. George Wade Wallis represented Lina, and Arthur John Edward Newton represented the men. Little is known about Wallis, except that he was Newton's partner in a practice neighbouring Abrahams'. Newton, by contrast, was well known as a 'talented and thoroughly dishonest solicitor'. He invariably wore grey silk gloves because, he said, it stopped him getting his hands dirty.[49] He had represented Lord Arthur Somerset in the Cleveland St Scandal (1889) and Oscar Wilde. The whiff of homosexual intrigue, therefore, hung about him long before his introduction to Cockerton, Aylott and Kast.

Over the course of the next two days, the magistrate, Mr Lushington, heard the case. Of the libels, the only one thought suitable for reading aloud was a page addressed to the House of Lords appeal judges; the rest were considered indecent. The document asked their lordships to read the enclosed statements which show 'that certain crucial and important facts have been wilfully or accidentally kept back'. The authors were prepared to prove the statements 'up to the hilt' and requested their lordships exonerate Mabel from all blame. It concluded, 'We beg to assure your Lordships that we only wish as Englishmen that justice should be done to Lady Russell who is an innocent woman – (signed) William Aylott, John Cockerton, Frederick Kast.'[50]

Matthews declared it a 'gross contempt of court', signed by the three men but not Lina, though she paid for the printing (and interrupted his speech by shouting from the dock that she was prepared to answer for it). It disclosed, he continued (ignoring the interruption), 'a maliciousness that was almost beyond human comprehension' and was contrived through the employment of the bookseller, Carrez, to whom Lina had written, 'You are so clever I want you to find me a rich American gentleman to help me through all these expenses with a view to marriage. I have had plenty of good offers, but must get riches.'[51] The statements had been sent as far afield as France (to *Figaro*) and America (to the *New York Herald*) and had been broadcast wholesale to Frank's friends and associates. Matthews asked for satisfaction for his client.

The defendants all pleaded not guilty and reserved their defence. Mr Lushington, without any equivocation, duly committed the case for trial at the Old Bailey, setting bail at £1,000 for Lina and £200 for each of the male defendants. Lina's was immediately paid by Thomas Harrison Lambert of 44 Buckingham Palace Mansions.[52] The men were not so fortunate and were remanded in custody. Once again, Frank wrote to Santayana in triumph:

What do you think of it? Warrants on Friday night – committed for trial on Monday! and the evidence! and Matthews' speech! quite irregular but very telling. Have we not done well? it has all gone swimmingly.[53]

Meanwhile, William Charles Aylott, twenty-eight, who had not 'fled the country' as Matthews had suggested but was working 'in the service of a lady of high position' in Algiers, came back voluntarily when he heard of the case and presented himself at Bow Street on 10 November.[54] He pleaded likewise and was remanded in custody with his fellow defendants.

The date was set for the trial: Monday 23 November 1896. By admitting to the publication of the libels and reserving their defence, the only course of action open to Lina and her motley crew was to put in a plea of justification; that is, to attempt to prove that the libels were not in fact libellous, but true statements. There were risks for both sides. In the central criminal court, the stakes were high. As Oscar Wilde had so amply demonstrated, a verdict in favour of one party left the other open to conviction, the threat of a torturous prison sentence and a reputation destroyed.

16

Hell Hath No Fury

So deeply is the mythology of the Old Bailey etched into the British psyche that it needs little introduction, unless it be to clarify two points that would appeal to our pernickety protagonist: one, that the name does not officially refer to a building at all, but a street; and two, that the building so nicknamed was not always the iconic Portland stone monolith that now stands on the corner of Newgate Street and Old Bailey under the outstretched arms of Lady Justice.[1] On the cold, bright morning with which we are concerned, Frank and Lina arrived at a much more austere brick building, still umbilically linked by a tunnel known as 'dead man's walk' to the stark, rusticated brick fortress that was Newgate Prison. The prison was redundant but the court still very much bustling, drawing large crowds to its dark panelled courtrooms, not minding the oppressively stuffy atmosphere and inadequate gas lighting.

It was to Old Court – the original and largest courtroom – that our cast was summoned on 23 November 1896. Lina, on removing her fur coat, 'lit up' the gloom in a 'light flowered bodice with dark sleeves' and fashionable small black bonnet perched on top of her ample head of hair. Her white gloved hands hung over the edge of the dock. In one, she gripped the large gold-stoppered bottle of smelling salts she would cling to throughout.[2] There she stood with her ill-assorted conspirators, facing the judge across a sea of barristers, lawyers and officials, boxed in by the jury and witness stand. Every available space on the press benches and in the public gallery above had been filled by an all-male audience – the charges deemed too gross for ladies' delicate ears. Frank sat at his solicitors' table in his now all-too-familiar frock coat and red necktie. The only concession he made to the gravity of the proceedings was to swap his usual mid-grey for something a little darker. Otherwise, he appeared unconcerned by the change of venue and the new cast of legal characters required for a criminal action.

Leading for Frank on this occasion was Sir Frank Lockwood QC, who as solicitor general had successfully prosecuted Wilde in the same building just eighteen months previously. He was a big, burly man of ruddy complexion who, at over six feet tall, cut an imposing figure. Called to the Bar in 1872 and taking silk in 1882, his success as an advocate was attributed to his manner, 'which was at once striking and engaging'.[3] He was popular both inside the courtroom and out. Outside, he was considered an entertaining after-dinner speaker, always ready with an amusing tale. Inside, he was famed for sketching the scenes around him – an activity in which he was constantly employed – on his brief, in notebooks, on slips of paper, sometimes even into the woodwork. As an expression of high spirits, it delighted everyone without detracting from the business in hand. He was joined in court by 'Willie' Matthews, his junior in the Wilde trial, Travers Humphreys, and Arthur Llewellyn Davies.

For Lina was John Lawson Walton QC who, earlier that year, had secured record damages for his client of £12,000 in a civil libel case.[4] The son of a Wesleyan minister, he held radical views and his services were put to good use over the years by various trade unions, both in the courts and the Commons, where he sat as Liberal MP for South Leeds. In 1905 he would be knighted and become attorney general. With him were Messrs Geoghegan and Lowenthal.

Finally, for the male defendants, was the hot-tempered, often indiscreet, dramatic and emotional 'Great Defender' Edward Marshall Hall. Marshall had been called in 1883 and quickly found his home at the Old Bailey, where his style of advocacy can best be described as mercurial. 'He never had a plan of campaign, or, if he did, he never was faithful to it', often appearing to know as little as anyone else in court what he would say next.[5] He was yet to be knighted or become the famous defender of the Camden Town or 'Brides-in-the-Bath' murderers (1907 and 1915 respectively). When this brief was offered him, he had tasted success, but had just then been convalescing from pneumonia and, after a year's absence, is said to have accepted 'with much legal ground to recover'.[6] His junior counsel was Percival Clarke, son of Sir Edward, the prudent prosecutor for Mabel in the first trial.

Hearing the case was Sir Henry Hawkins, whose illustrious career at the Bar peaked with his cross-examination of the Tichborne Claimant in the longest-running civil case in British legal history. He became a judge in 1876, possibly as a result of this performance. Once a skilled and ambitious advocate, he was admired as a judge but considered ruthless and made enemies. His features were described as 'rigid and inflexible' and many found his humour cutting. Behind it lurked 'an element of cruelty' and a doubt that 'the sorrows of the victim ever very much moved him'. One contemporary suggested, 'I can conceive no greater motto for his coat-of-arms than "Vengeance is mine"'.[7]

With Lina having quite openly stated that her purpose in publishing the men's statements was to reveal Frank's character to the world, the prosecution's task was to convince the jury that the statements were malicious lies, secured with bribes, as an act of vengeance against a man who refused to be manipulated for his money. Initially, it didn't look too difficult. In his opening speech, Sir Frank Lockwood emphasised the fact that, in the 1895 trial, Lina had sworn Frank innocent of her daughter's charges concerning Roberts. Now, he said, it would be his task to reveal that, months before that application, Lina had in her possession 'every statement and every charge which any of these men had made' and that while she was endeavouring to obtain restitution for her daughter, she was at the same time gathering these stories against Frank. Lina listened with a fixed 'cynical smile' as Sir Frank told the court he thought it would be hard to believe there existed 'any woman – any mother – in this world who is so low and so debased a thing' that she could be party to renewing cohabitation between her daughter and Frank if he had been guilty of the conduct ascribed to him in the statements of these men. He read to the court the statements as they were recorded at the office of Bernard Abrahams.

Though read out in full, their precise wording is uncertain. Some 400 copies were printed and broadcast by Lina, but not a single one appears to have survived; not even the one that made its way into Mr Wallet's pocket. Further, Victorian prudery extended into the court system – at least where homosexuality was concerned. Not only were plain terms such as 'sodomy' and 'buggery' not used in open court, they were avoided wherever possible in court documents 'as though even the clerks could not bring themselves to refer to the acts by name'.[8] Of the 52,000,000 words used in recording the 100,000 trials in the *Proceedings of the Old Bailey*, only 200 were used to describe this twelve-day hearing, where others were described in exhaustive detail. In the court books there are only the basic facts. In the central criminal court file of depositions, there are only those relating to the arrest of Lina and the three men. It is as if, on the conclusion of the trial, there was a clean sweep to ensure that, even for posterity, nothing but the broad facts of the case would remain. As such, all that can be relayed of Aylott and Kast's statements are the details which appeared in the self-censored press, from which can be ascertained the following.

Frederick Kast stated that when he was fifteen he acted as cabin boy on *Royal* and that 'certain alleged acts' of a 'gross character' were enacted upon him by Frank in Winchester, Southampton and the Norfolk Broads.[9] In June 1887, when *Royal* was lying at Southampton, he had gone to Winchester to meet Frank to collect the crew's wages. There, on a railway bank at the side of the station, Frank had sexually assaulted him. Kast told Cockerton and Dutton (then an engineer aboard the vessel) what had occurred. Afterwards, in the Norfolk Broads, he was assaulted again. He subsequently left Frank's employment in July 1887 after being left behind when sent ashore to fetch Frank's tobacco pouch from his club. He alleged that shortly afterwards, Frank sent him a postcard addressing him as 'Dear Fred' in which he asked him to rejoin the yacht for an excursion to see the French Exhibition. Kast said he declined in consequence of what had happened.

William Aylott's statement charged Frank with 'attempted misconduct' while the yacht was lying in the Rhone on the outward leg of the Mediterranean tour. He stated that on one occasion, Frank had asked him to sleep in his cabin 'for company' and that the cabin was also shared by a pilot who was helping them navigate the Rhone. After Aylott had turned in, Frank asked him to open a porthole and, while he was reaching over to do so, 'caught hold of him' and they 'struggled'. He also said that he and Frank argued constantly:

> Once he threw an ink pot at me and I threw it back. Another time we had a set-to in the cabin. He twisted my head round, and I hit him and left him on the settee gasping. On another occasion I took up a coal hammer to throw at him. This was witnessed by Mr Lane-Fox. In spite of all this, the Earl kept me in his service. I believe he feared what I might say about him.

John Cockerton stated that on Jubilee Day (21 June 1887), Kast came on deck to prepare breakfast and 'made a communication to him'. He said that this was not the first time he had heard of such behaviour. In early 1887, he was told by a waterman in a public house in Hampton that Frank was in the habit of 'kissing and caressing a boy known as "faithful William" as if he was a girl'. He also stated that Frank was in the habit of treating *Royal*'s cat cruelly, throwing it overboard and leaving it to 'scramble up the mop as best it could'.

There could be no mistaking the seriousness of these allegations, particularly those of Kast. Even without his original statement, his status as key witness for the defence and the multiple references to his allegation being 'far graver' than Aylott's imply that Kast was accusing Frank of full penetration, which, if proved, could have left both men open to a charge of sodomy (punishable under the 1861 Offences Against the Person Act by penal servitude for life or not less than ten years) or, failing that, the lesser crime of gross indecency.[10]

To all these events the men had fixed dates, to which, Sir Frank said, he intended to hold them 'hand and foot'. He asked the jury to watch for 'any attempts by the defendants to shift their ground'. There was a tone 'something like exaltation' in his voice as he suggested that Kast, in particular, would have to abandon 'material parts of his statement' when it was shown that the incident he alleged to have taken place in Winchester could not have happened on the date stated and that he had mistaken their route to the Norfolk Broads.

The news that Frank would be first in the witness box the following morning brought Lina to her feet. The judge rounded off the first day by allowing her bail 'for her convenience' but under strict instruction not to discuss the case with anyone. The men he remanded in custody and sent to Holloway.

Next morning, Frank arrived ten minutes before time 'with the air of a man to whom the witness box is no novelty'. The 'youthful looking' Lina, not to be outdone, had swapped her flowers for a dress of pure white chiffon with lace bodice, sable collar and light grey bonnet with black aigrette. The judge took his seat. But before proceedings could get underway, there occurred 'one of those little scenes that he dearly loves' – a letter, addressed to the foreman of the jury, by '*One Who Knows*'. These anonymous letters were a common feature of the Victorian court, especially in *causes célèbres*. They were never read out in court or given any credence, but where many judges regarded them as a nuisance and consigned them to the bin, Justice Hawkins appeared to relish those sent to his court. He would make light of them, playfully speculate as to who the author might be or what they knew that was so important they needed to inform him of it personally. Then, suddenly, he would turn cold and issue a stark, clear warning that if he discovered the culprits their meddling would find *them* in the dock. Of all things to have survived from this trial, these letters have – filed away with the depositions, as if with some future intention of identifying, finding and prosecuting their authors. Outside court they were opened and read, and as a set they offer uncensored insight into public opinion surrounding the trial – at least among those with strong enough views to put pen to paper. This first one sympathised with the foreman in his difficult task but suggested that if he only knew Frank as the author did, he would have no difficulty in coming to a 'speedy and righteous conclusion', exclaiming,

> Alas for the peerage which is defiled by contact with such a scoundrel! – an adept in the horrible vice which has made Oscar Wilde's name a bye-word, though without any of the latter's redeeming qualities … Do *your* duty like men! Don't be gulled by the sophistries of a mountebank like Lockwood, but by your verdict, consign his cur of a client, (if not to a felon's dock) at least to well merited oblivion.[11]

Others, it shall be seen, ran along similar lines.

Frank entered the box and Willie Matthews took him through the various dates, persons and places of his yachting adventures described in chapter eight. It was a somewhat tedious affair, punctuated by odd moments of bated breath, such as when Frank was asked directly whether he had kissed and cuddled 'faithful William' like a girl ('Most decidedly not; neither then, nor at any other time'). Lina, with pencil, notebook and smelling salts in hand, intently scribbled down every word – of sleeping arrangements, of passengers getting on and off the boat, of payments to the crew – handing down a stream of missives to her counsel. The wages themselves were immaterial but the timing of their payment was not if the prosecution were determined to be meticulous about dates. Frank produced his account book to prove that none of the crew were owed wages at the time in question and his diary to account for his movements in Winchester, which included meeting Santayana on 19 June after lunch and taking him to dine with the Richardsons before taking tea with Revd Dickins and returning to the Richardsons' for the night. On the afternoon of 20 June 1887, he returned to the yacht in Southampton in readiness for a trip to the Isle of Wight for the Queen's Jubilee celebrations.

The prosecution's fastidiousness afforded Marshall Hall the first of many clashes with Justice Hawkins. As Sir Frank had predicted, Marshall intervened requesting to change one of the dates of the alleged offences, claiming personal responsibility for entering it incorrectly in the plea. He had mistaken the date of the Jubilee and wished it corrected. Justice Hawkins rather sternly objected to the request being made in the jury's hearing and even more strongly to Marshall's next suggestion that his entitlement to do so came from Sir Frank making 'such a deal' of dates which were a mere technicality. The judge found Marshall's comments 'disrespectful to me and insulting to Sir Frank'. Marshall apologised and retook his seat. But the jury had heard his comments, which was all he wanted – to disrupt an otherwise impressive turn by Frank as he confidently refuted other dates, contradicted Aylott's recollection of their course and denied that he ever allowed his staff to strike him or harmed the ship's cat.

For day three, Lina swapped her white chiffon for beaded black crepe and a little black velvet bonnet. The effect, said the *Star*, was like 'a change from morning to night'. Said the *News of the World*, all her 'striking costumes' had a 'carefully studied effect' and looked both 'remarkably expensive and elaborate for a bankrupt prisoner'. Today's was extra special, for Lina knew what was coming. Unlike her male companions, she declined her proffered chair, but stood in anticipation in the dock, eyes riveted on Frank as Willie Matthews rounded off his examination-in-chief. What she was waiting for – what, perhaps, the whole crowded courtroom was waiting for – was Frank's cross-examination. Yet when Lawson Walton rose to begin it, his questions were of such an unexpected character there was mild confusion in the gallery and consternation at the prosecution's table. Lina's grip on the dock tightened as she leaned forward to capture every word of Frank's replies.

First, Walton wanted to know when Frank and Lina first became acquainted. Then, how long they had corresponded after the first trial and whether Frank 'entertained very high esteem and a very deep affection' – even 'extreme affection' – for her. 'High esteem, for a certain time,' conceded Frank; following which he felt 'sorry for her'. 'Ha!' exclaimed Lina from the dock; but Frank could not be made to revise his answer. So, Walton put into his hand a letter he was forced to admit he had written to Lina on 20 December 1889, during the tumultuous period before his and Mabel's marriage. 'My Darling,' it began – 'Keep right and well, my sweet' – and ended, 'God bless you, darling: you are the best of women, and I shall always love you. Give Mabel a kiss for me.' It was signed, 'Your loving and devoted friend, Frank'.

Walton asked if Frank's words were sincere; if they were words of esteem? Yes, said Frank, and sympathy. Walton then produced another, dated 30 January 1889 – a week before the wedding:

Dearest, – Parting with you seems harder and harder to bear. I do not see why you should not come to Paddington [from where he was departing on his honeymoon], and come quite alone. I should like to give you a last hug my darling – my angel. Bother! I am beginning to cry.

There were sniggers around the courtroom that became open laughter when the judge, looking at the original, commented, 'I do not see any appearance here of tears.' The letter concluded, 'I cannot write any more ... I cannot see the paper. Good night, my darling.'

Walton wanted to know whether *this* was 'a sincere expression of your feeling towards the mother of the lady whom you were about to make your wife ... written six days before the marriage?' Yes, said Frank, no doubt. The next letter produced was also his, but he denied dating it 4 February – two days before the wedding:

> Dearest, – The sooner I see you the better I shall be pleased. Of course, I always love to see you ... Come soon, my lovely one ... – Ever your loving, Frank.

Walton then produced a book Frank had given Lina in November 1889, thinking it might be 'useful to her' – *The Imitation of Christ* by Thomas à Kempis. He read aloud the inscription: 'For my dear Bo, the truest woman and most faithful friend I have ever known. – From your loving Frank.' These words, Frank admitted, though 'rather exaggerated', were also sincere; as was his defence of her to Revd Henry Villiers that she was 'a woman whom we have every reason to love and honour above the rest of her sex'. Walton then asked, was it true that on the day before his wedding, Frank had deposited two deed boxes with his bank with instructions that they should be delivered to Lina in the event of his death 'at once without waiting for probate'? Frank replied that he had not remembered doing so, but the letter immediately produced to the manager seemed to confirm it. Walton left the court to wonder what was in the boxes and moved on to Frank's relationship with Mabel, wanting to know if, after their separation in May 1890, Frank really was anxious for her return. So far as Frank could remember, he was. How then could he explain another letter marked 'Not for M', written in May 1890, telling 'Bo' he would not go to Brighton and asking her to escort Mabel instead. Mabel was not being 'actively disagreeable' but 'the stony-hearted, self-righteous saint has not shown an atom of kindness or softness' and 'it would be a relief to get rid of my curse for a few days'. Walton asked, was Mabel a curse or a beloved wife? She was both, said Frank; his feelings changed on a daily basis according to her behaviour. But a further letter to Lina written after the separation and dated 17 June 1890 seemed to suggest that his feelings were stronger elsewhere and more consistent than he wished to convey:

> Dearest, – ... I wish you would be as though Mabel did not belong to you ... I want you at Maidenhead. I am tired of feeling that anybody is a curse, and does not care two straws for me. A bad wife is a curse to any man, and will ruin his life.

The following week, he wrote:

> Dearest Bo, – ...come here to me for a continuous visit of at least three months. If you speak a word of this to your daughter or fail to accept

this invitation, I shall know that you have been lying and love me no more than that false woman does ... Oh Bo, if you only realised what my love is worth you would not blindly and contentedly throw it over, and with it all your chances of peace and happiness in this life.[12]

Under further questioning, Frank continued to assert that it was possible to love his wife *and* consider her a 'hard-hearted fiend'. The fact that he spoke so strongly was testament to the depth of his feelings, he claimed. Neither was it his fault these letters had not been read at the previous trial – they were in Lina's possession. He had ceased to love Mabel, he thought, towards the end of 1890 or early 1891 – at which point Sir Frank rose and asked what possible relevance any of these questions had to the case in hand. This question, Walton said, he could answer with ease. He wished to reveal the differences between Frank's evidence and his private letters and to exonerate Lina, who had been described as 'a blackmailer, briber, and conspirator'.

But was that all? Was there not an ulterior motive in the extensive reading of these letters which appeared in full in papers across the globe? The *Sporting Times* was at no loss as to what they were supposed to infer from them, and on page one of their next edition daringly printed the following verse entitled,

THE POLITE LETTER-WRITER GONE WRONG.
(Vide Scott-Russell Case).
My precious – my darling – my sweet!
Show sentiments wide of a flaw,
When duly addressed to the wife of your chest;
But —— not to your mother in law![13]

Under re-examination, Frank professed that he had only written to Lina in this manner because the Scotts habitually did so; an explanation which is borne out by other extant letters but which misses a fundamental difference in the manner in which Frank addressed himself to Mabel, which was, on the whole, less effusive. These letters add significance to Santayana's comment that when he first went to Amberley Cottage in its partially completed state in July 1890, the only thing of note in Frank's office was a photograph of Lina. They raise questions about the true meaning of Lina's protestation in her letter to Frank of 21 November 1889 that she had given him Mabel, the person she loved best on earth, 'against all my own interests' – and this, undoubtedly, is what Lina intended when she handed them over to her counsel. Later, in his summing-up, the judge declined to comment on them, saying only that they were 'of a character almost unprecedented. I cannot understand them.' He did not have the benefit of Frank's diary for 1890, which was kept meticulously until his wedding day and then suddenly ceased, and which reveals in repeated entries that all the time he and Mabel were squabbling on the run-up to their wedding, his feelings for Bo were indeed deep and unvarying. She was his 'loving Bo' who came to visit him alone and whom he convinced to go to Torquay with him in January 1890 where, living up to its name, their presence was noted by the *Observer*, listed among recent arrivals at the Imperial Hotel while Mabel appears to have stayed in London.[14] The corresponding pages in Frank's diary have been torn out. 'Very sweet' was how he described Lina when she accompanied him alone on a later train journey; 'very sweet' was also how he described Mabel when she was loving and attentive. At the wedding, he 'nearly cried once or twice when I looked at my darling Bo & thought how she would be left alone'. She looked 'lovely & bore up splendidly'. Mabel just looked 'ill'.[15]

During the writing of Ronald Clark's *Life of Bertrand Russell* in the 1970s there was some suggestion that Frank had spent his wedding night with Lina while Mabel lay ill.[16] Entries from Frank's diary seem to contradict this and Alys Russell defended his reputation in the face of the public use of these letters by writing to a cousin, 'No-one here seems to have put the construction on Lord Russell's letters that there was a liaison between them.'[17] Santayana did. He suggested that 'the touch of warm human love' that Frank had written to him about had not been Mabel's but Lina's. He may not have slept with her on his wedding night but 'she had overwhelmed him – their letters prove it – in a torrent of effusive sympathy and affection … a [mother's] love enveloped him, mixed with all the arts of sensuous seduction' and having thus seduced him, she 'planned something heroic: to give Russell up as a lover, resign him to her daughter, and keep him only as a dear, dear son and as a source of income'. In all this, 'Mabel Edith was insignificant' and the only reason Lina did not foresee that the match was doomed to failure was because she was blinded by her own love, was in 'such a welter of emotion and excitement that she was incapable of clear observation or judgment'.[18] The only question as far as Santayana was concerned was the extent to which Mabel was cognisant of the affair. He assumed fully – that she accepted her mother's gift of an earl for its title and consequence, with good grace and eyes open, not doubting for one minute that it was anything other than a gesture of sacrifice and love.

What, then, would Lina's likely reaction be when Frank refused to provide for them as she had planned? Did she feel, as Santayana suggested, 'grievously injured'? Did this motivate her to bring forward all Frank's letters and have them read out in court for the world to hear? Lina's actions strongly suggest that it was she who was the woman scorned in this bitter feud, not Mabel. It was enough to make her wish to publicly humiliate Frank – with his love letters and the statements of his former crew. But was it enough to make her bribe the men to invent them? This, the court still had to decide.

Day four began with another anonymous letter to the foreman. Again, it was not read aloud, but the court was much amused by the fact that the envelope was addressed 'O.H.M.S.' which, the judge supposed (it being a Friday), was done to ensure it reached the foreman before the weekend. The foreman joked that they would not know where to find him on Saturday. No, said the judge, but *he* would know where to find *them*; and what he would do if he did! The author, however, appeared not to have cared very much what the judge thought, said or did. Instead, he begged to say Frank had 'frequently behaved in a *most disgusting* way with young men and boys (whether the judge likes it or not)' and that people with Frank's 'depraved tastes ... ought to be burned!!' It was signed, '*Not a bugger*'.[19]

Continuing his cross-examination, Walton asked if it had not been incumbent on Frank to seek a retraction of the now infamous *Hawk* article, but Justice Hawkins thought not. It was a scurrilous paper, the whole of which was 'beneath contempt'. What about the equally infamous Lady Cardigan letter? For the first time in a law court, Frank was asked to account for the return of the Chinese boy, Quai Paak. He could not account for it, he said. The boy was in his service, but he had not been responsible for his return or even asked for the reason behind it. Neither was he conscious of any impropriety in employing him.

> Q: You know that if there were impropriety it would be of a very gross
>   character, and you really tell the jury that, though you were conscious
>   of no such impropriety, you never demanded an explanation from
>   anyone as to why they had interfered between you and your servant?
> No answer.

Frank was then asked about the letter he wrote to Kast in India. Walton wanted to know if it might not be perceived as threatening Kast in saying he would be accused alongside Frank as a 'willing accessory'. Frank did not think so. Nor did he think his letter would have prevented Kast returning, but it would have kept him out of the dock.

> Q: I accept your answer. You think, then, if he had not refused to accept
>   your advice he would not have been in the dock?
> A: I think he would have been warned not to be bribed.

Frank could not deny that Baines had been sent to India, but did deny it was to prevent Kast's return and that his own trip to Italy to inspect the Sicilian monastery might have thrown him in Kast's path. The steamer on which he travelled stopped at Malta en route but he had not expected to intercept Kast there because Kast's ship did not call at Malta, but at Brindisi and then came straight home.

Though Frank's answer wasn't directly incriminating, this was a dangerous line of questioning. To the press, who described Walton's performance as rather lacklustre, it did not yet perhaps signify, but it wasn't lost on the prosecution who realised that before the trial ended, they would have to bring witnesses to prove beyond doubt that Frank had made no attempt to prevent Kast's return to England.

Marshall Hall, meanwhile, was keen to take over Frank's cross-examination on behalf of the men. He ascertained that Kast had been employed by Frank for only five weeks, Cockerton for thirteen months and Aylott for two years. He wanted Frank to have to admit that certain aspects of Kast's statement were true, so took him through various points concerning the geography of Winchester and the location of his friends' houses as they were mentioned in Kast's statement. After which, he turned his attention to Frank's past. How long had Frank been in the habit of keeping a diary? 'Some years.' He had not shown any of them to Lina but admitted that some had been kept in the deed boxes he had deposited at Child's bank before his marriage. These boxes he had subsequently retrieved from the bank and some of their contents had been destroyed. He could not remember whether among the destroyed items was the diary for 1885 – his final year at Oxford. So Marshall Hall asked for it and Frank, trying to maintain an air of nonchalance, authorised Doulton to retrieve it knowing full well he would be unable to do so. The diaries that had been destroyed, he told Marshall, were not done so because they were of a seriously incriminating character, but because 'they were childish'. Other items destroyed were 'bundles of letters' of no great importance.

Q: What! Letters deposited with your bankers of no importance?
A: Certainly.

They were 'personal papers' Frank had thought would be safer at the bank than at home, he said, denying that it was because he wanted them safe from observation. What about this, then? Marshall asked, holding up a little book which had just been handed to him by Lina's solicitor. It was an engagement diary for 1888–9 which Frank had left at The Hurst and Lina had kept. Should it have been returned to him, perhaps? Frank did not say so and, after his counsel intervened, Marshall put the book away, leaving the court to wonder at its significance. As it never rematerialized, it must be assumed Frank was merely being goaded.

But the diary for 1887 *was* of interest. The Winchester pages were left blank. That, said Frank, was how he knew he was there: the diary was irregularly kept. Santayana was with him anyway and would be called to collaborate. Were, then, asked Marshall, Kast's charges pure inventions – or perhaps he should say 'impure inventions' – and where in the world was Ion Thynne, whom he understood to have been subpoenaed as a witness? Frank replied that Ion had been in England but had returned to Buenos Aires because his daughter became sick. Ion would have testified that he had shared the after-cabin with Frank the whole time he was on board, contrary to the men's statements. Marshall could not believe the prosecution would let such an important witness go. Frank said, they did not *let* him go, he went. And they did not attach much importance to it at the time as they were not then aware that the defendants would plead justification. Frank objected to the subsequent suggestion that entries made in the logbook for 28 June 1887 (the date they had set off for the Norfolk Broads) and 11 July 1887 (the date of their return), though both made at the same time, had been fabricated to place Ion in his cabin at the time of the alleged assault on Kast.[20]

The next question concerned Frank's actions on receipt of Kast's letter. Had he not sent a lady detective with Doulton to see Kast's mother? No, it was Mrs Williams, his old housekeeper, whom he'd sent to find out what Lina was up to. And what about Aylott? What did Frank think of his character? Aylott was, said Frank, 'a notorious liar' (laughter). Yet Frank had employed him as a valet after he ceased to be his cabin boy. Was lying a necessary quality for a valet? asked Marshall Hall. That, interposed the judge, 'depends upon the person whom he is valeting' (laughter). Frank said he did not mind Aylott's lies; he took no notice of them. He had not considered him a dangerous liar. He had given Aylott £3 and a good character when he left because he did not want him to be without a position. He had not thought him capable of lying to the extent that he now did, however, without being paid for it. One lie in his statement was that Frank asked him to bring his bed into his cabin: *Aylott* had asked *him*. There were few things he would not have asked. The whole story about the porthole was 'pure invention'. But Frank did have to admit that Aylott once threatened to bring an action against him 'after I had thrown him overboard in France'. (Sensation!)

Q: What did you throw him overboard for?
A: Insolence.

There followed some discussion as to whether or not this was the correct way to treat a servant before Justice Hawkins reminded them they were not there to try an action for assault.

Q: Have you ever, as Aylott asserts, thrown your cat into the sea?
A: Yes.
Q: Was that for insolence too? (Laughter.)

No, said Frank, it was for a bath; he denied that there were cries of 'shame' from spectators on the bank. Marshall concluded his cross-examination by asking Frank to confirm for the benefit of the court that the men had never approached him for a penny by way of blackmail.

Sir Frank Lockwood then gave Frank the opportunity to controvert some of his opponents' insinuations and to repeat once again his by-then well-rehearsed explanation of his sending down from Oxford. In addition, Frank explained, he had sued neither the *Hawk* nor Lady Cardigan for their libels because he was not a rich man and had already spent between £10,000 and £15,000 in legal fees to the end of the restitution hearing. The judge quipped that Frank might not be rich but perhaps Lady Cardigan was, and that his expenditure ought to have given him an appetite for more. It was a humorous exchange on which to end a gruelling examination.

Frank had spent more than three long days in the witness box. Though towards the end he was 'rather tired and not very clear', he reflected, 'I kept my end up and was able to deal adequately with every suggestion made.'[21]

Above left: 1. Lady Frances Anna Maria Russell, 'Lady John', 1865. (Gloucestershire Archives)

Above right: 2. Lord John Russell, 1877. (Bertrand Russell Archives)

3. Lord and Lady John surrounded by their children (L–R) Willy, Rollo (seated), Georgy, Amberley and Agatha – outside the summerhouse at Pembroke Lodge, 1863. (Bertrand Russell Archives)

4. Lady Henriette Maria Stanley, *c*. 1863.
(Bertrand Russell Archives)

5. Before Bertrand:
Amberley, Kate,
Frank and Rachel
on the veranda
at Ravenscroft.
(Bertrand Russell
Archives)

6. Frank and Rachel, 1870. (Bertrand
Russell Archives)

Right: 7. Maude Stanley, 1863. (Bertrand Russell Archives)

Below right: 8. Agatha Russell, *c.* 1890. (Bertrand Russell Archives)

Below: 9. Frank, *c.* 1877. (Bertrand Russell Archives)

Lord Russell

Above left: 10. Frank at Winchester, 1881. (Winchester College Archives)

Above right: 11. Frank's first crush: John Sanders Watney, 1883. (Winchester College Archives)

12. Lionel Johnson at Winchester (far right), 1884, aged seventeen. Campbell Dodgson (standing, left) was six months younger than Lionel and Hugh William Orange (seated, centre) a year older. (Winchester College Archives)

Right: 13. An 'aesthetic cavalry officer'? Frank as he was when he first met Santayana. This photo was taken in Salt Lake City in December 1885, the year of Frank's sending down from Oxford.

Below right: 14. Lionel Johnson, the same year, 1885. (Winchester College Archives)

Below: 15. George Santayana, *c.* 1886. (Columbia University, Rare Book & Manuscript Library)

16. A Ferishtah Group, 1886–7. L–R (back): P. U. Henn, Ion Thynne, Charles 'Long' Roberts, Frank (in fashionable boater), Edgar Jepson. L–R (front, sitting): Osman Edwards, Herbert Ainslie Roberts.

Above: 17. Steam Yacht
Royal.

Right: 18. Mabel Edith,
Countess Russell, as she
appeared in *The Sketch*, 28
February 1900.

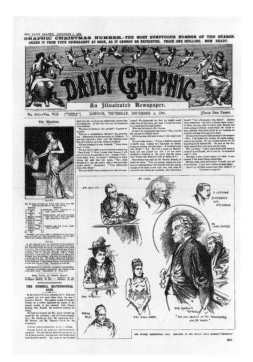
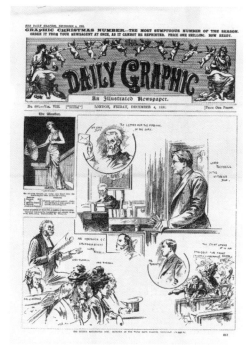
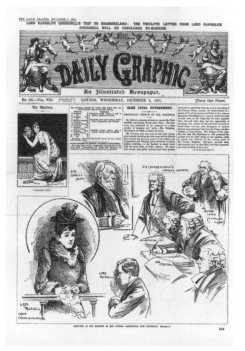

19–22. The Russells' Matrimonial Suit, 1–4 December 1891, drew large crowds, made headlines across the globe and the front page of *The Daily Graphic* each day. (Bertrand Russell Archives)

23. Bertrand ceases to be a 'prig', graduating from Cambridge in 1893. (Bertrand Russell Archives)

24. Frank in his early thirties, portrait by Russell & Sons, Baker Street. (Bertrand Russell Archives)

MIDDLE GATE
Winchester College 1898.

Will you and all your Family come to

Mr. & Mrs. Richardson's Christmas Party,

in School, on Monday, December 26th,

4 to 6.

Theatricals and Singing.

25. George and Sarah Richardson – Mr & Mrs Dick – as Frank knew them in later life. The Dicks' house in Chamber Court was on the first and second floors to the left of Middle Gate, just out of this picture. (Winchester College Archives)

WHO ARE THE

PROGRESSIVE

CANDIDATES

FOR

HAMMERSMITH ?

Printed and Published by the Swan Electric Engraving Co.
116 Charing Cross Road, London, W.C.

EARL RUSSELL

Is the able representative of a name honoured alike in Liberal tradition and the history of our times. He truly maintains the devotion of the Russells to the cause of the people, and has always been ready to enter into public work by direct and popular election. He is a Guardian and District Councillor for Maidenhead, Parish Councillor for Cookham, and is J.P. for Berks. He has performed admirable service by insisting that the proceedings of the Board of Guardians should be open to the Press and the Ratepayers, by preserving public foot-paths and preventing encroachment on Common Land. He served on a Joint Committee of the House of Lords and Commons in 1893, and was largely instrumental in rejecting the claims of the Telephone Companies, and making electric tramway traction cheap and practicable. He also served upon a Committee of the Board of Trade appointed last year to investigate and improve the ventilation of the Metropolitan Railway Company's tunnels.

Earl Russell has for three years been a leading member of the London County Council, and has entered heartily into the detail work of the Council. He has served upon the Highways, Asylums, Appeal, Water, Standing Joint, and Parliamentary Committees, and is now Chairman of the Highways Committee. He has also been for two years Chairman of the Hanwell Asylum Committee. He advocates the establishment of a Municipal steam-boat service on the river Thames, and from his three years' experience, is keenly anxious that the Progressive Policy of the Council should continue.

[TURN OVER

26. Frank campaigns for Hammersmith in the 1898 LCC elections. (Private collection)

27. Mabel takes to the stage, performing in *A Runaway Girl* at the Gaiety Theatre. *The Sketch*, 8 March 1899.

28. Mrs Somerville after becoming Mollie, Countess Russell, *c.* 1910. (Private collection)

29. The 'Russell' House in Glenbrook, Nevada, winter 1899, sketched by Mollie's son, Stanley Watson. (Private collection)

30. Earl Russell tried by his peers for bigamy in the House of Lords, 18 July 1901, centrefold from *Illustrated London News*, 27 July 1901.

Left: 31. Frank's felony becomes an Ogden's Cigarette Card. (Bertrand Russell Archives)

Above: 32. Telegraph House on the South Downs, after Frank's renovations, *c.* 1909. (Private collection)

Below: 33. Mollie goes on tour for the Women's Freedom League, 1909. (Private collection)

34. 'Elizabeth', *c*. 1910.
(Courtesy of Ann Hardham)

35. Bertrand Russell,
mathematician, philosopher
and political activist, 1916.
(Bertrand Russell Archives)

Above: 36. 'Mollie of the Sussex garden' with one of the Russells' beloved Maltese terriers in the greenhouse at TH, *c.* 1914. (Private collection)

Right: 37. Elizabeth in the 1920s, with some of the more 'dear & perfect' dogs of her life, after her escape from Frank. (Bertrand Russell Archives)

Below right: 38. Frank and unknown companion in front of his top-of-the-range 1924 15.9hp Humber. (Bertrand Russell Archives)

39. Frank outside his beloved TH. (Bertrand Russell Archives)

40. Telegraph House today.

Interestingly, unlike his other trials, Frank described little of these proceedings in *Life* and nothing concerning his performance in the witness box beyond this one comment. On only one single issue did he reflect with dissatisfaction. Whether Kast had been bribed or not, Frank wished readers of his memoirs to know that it was not until he was sitting in the train at Fenchurch Street station, en route to the steamer bound for Sicily in December 1895, that he discovered his and Kast's paths might cross at Malta, and that he could not therefore have been trying to intercept him on his return from India. Why he felt it necessary to clarify this point some twenty-eight years after the event, only Frank can say. Perhaps it was simply another expression of his famed Stanley pernicketiness. Perhaps.

Next in the witness box was Frank's 'self-possessed' cousin, St George, who told the court he had no recollection of Aylott taking up the coal hammer to strike Frank. He was the first of an impressive group of allies called to corroborate Frank's movements in 1887 and the alleged events of 1888. Though Ion had decamped, Edgar Jepson was still on hand; and though Frank felt it highly improbable that any evidence Santayana could give would make a material difference, he was determined to give it; as were Revd Dickins – Frank's beloved *Daker* – and Mrs Dick, who told Santayana defiantly, 'We would all perjure ourselves for him.'[22] Santayana thought the act 'hardly necessary, but the readiness showed the right spirit'.[23] The valiant woman proved more than a match for Marshall Hall's provocative questioning, too. Do you suggest, he asked her, that you *know* Lord Russell slept at your house every night from Thursday to Monday?

A: Well, I did not put him to bed.
Q: That no doubt was his misfortune but not his or my fault ... You assume because he was asked to stay he slept there?
A: He could not go sloping about because [their house being within the school grounds] we are all locked in. (Laughter.)[24]

But perhaps the most astonishing evidence of the day came from Arthur Carrez concerning the printing of the libels. Though the court was amused to hear that he had assumed when Lina asked him to find her a rich American husband she was joking, they were sobered by his account of the manner in which he was employed, and not least by the production of the list (written in Lina's hand) of persons to whom the libels should be sent, which was read out in court. There were 'hundreds' of names on it. The *Post* printed a list of those most recognisable for their readers to spend the weekend considering. Their diversity shows more clearly than anything how determined Lina was that it should reach into every corner of Frank's life.

There were members of Frank's family: St George, Bertrand and George Howard, the Earl of Carlisle, whom Mabel had tried to draw into sympathy with her early on in the separation. Also, the most senior member of the family, the Duke of Bedford, and Edward Bootle-Wilbraham, 1st Earl of Lathom, who had married into it in 1860.

There were people with whom Frank came into regular contact socially and in his daily business – secretaries of clubs, managers of hotels and restaurants, lock-keepers, tradesmen and even stationmasters on Frank's known train routes – many of whom, Lina probably hoped, would not be averse to spreading a little malicious gossip. Likewise, Lady Cardigan and *Hawk* editor Augustus Moore. For business associates, Lina had picked out Sam Lewis (who had requested Frank's involvement with the Nyassa Chartered Company) and the Secretary of the Stock Exchange. From the House of Lords were the heads of the oldest aristocratic families in the Dukes of Portland, Devonshire, Somerset and Richmond, as well as people of influence – not only the Lords of Appeal but also Sir Spencer Ponsonby-Fane, who was then controller of the Lord Chamberlain's Office. The Somersets, of course, had themselves been on the receiving end of unwanted press attention when Lord Arthur Somerset, son of the 8th Duke of Beaufort, had fled to Paris in the wake of the Cleveland Street scandal. Others on the list must also have been selected for their involvement in *causes célèbres*: Sir William Gordon-Cumming, who was at the centre of the 1891 Royal Baccarat scandal; Sir Charles Dilke, who was co-respondent in the 1886 Crawford divorce case; and Sir Henry Tichborne, who had defended his right to the title of 12th Baronet against the Tichborne Claimant. One or two MPs were also targeted – including Sir Henry Farquhar (also a member of the LCC) – along with some prominent military figures and pressmen – most notably, the *Telegraph*'s Clement Scott, an outspoken critic of immorality in the English theatre. Other names on the list included the then master of Balliol, the headmasters of the top public schools and three masters of Bath College, where Roberts taught. As Frank was known to none of these personally, their addition strongly suggests a purely vindictive motive.

When the court reconvened the following Monday, it was to the delight of another anonymous letter. The judge and foreman made much of it being in a lady's hand. Perhaps the foreman had an admirer? But later, when it was opened, it transpired that the author wished nothing more than to express herself alarmed at the judge's apparent bias. Likening it to *Wilde* v. *Queensberry*, she'd decided that Frank was the real criminal – 'the man who for three days this week has polluted the witness-box, while the innocent parties have to stand their trial' – and that Justice Hawkins was protecting him. She begged the foreman to 'do your duty independently and unflinchingly', signing herself, 'A Married Woman'.[25]

It soon became clear, however, that aside from the judge's influence, the person most likely to impact proceedings was James Scott, medical officer at Holloway, who came to court that morning to announce that Frederick Kast had been struck down over the weekend with pneumonia and was too ill to attend. Kast had first complained of feeling unwell on Saturday and had rapidly declined. He now had a temperature of 104°F. The matter was discussed, and it was decided to adjourn the case for a week. Cockerton and Aylott were declined bail, while Lina, now showing signs of a similar illness, was returned to her residence in town. Within an hour, it was announced that Kast was desperately ill and his family and friends had been called to his bedside. The following day, the defence applied for his deposition to be taken in prison and it was reported that Sir John Bridge, magistrate at Bow Street, would oblige. Sir Frank immediately objected on the ground that his client had not been personally informed, but Sir John overruled him. Dr Scott, however, declared Kast too ill for a long interrogation and advised that the interview should not proceed.

The following week, Dr Scott again appeared at the Old Bailey to say that though Kast had rallied a little, he was still far too ill to attend court. His weakness was such that it would most likely be three weeks before he could continue. Lina's condition had turned out to be little more than a chill. The case was postponed until 4 January, and Cockerton and Aylott were granted bail at £200 – a sum neither could ever hope to raise.

It was a tense time. Few occupants of Holloway had ever provoked such concern over their well-being as did Kast that week with daily reports of his condition in the press. Very soon the waiting was over. Frederick Kast was announced to have died at 12:24 a.m. on Friday 11 December in the prison infirmary. The following day, Lina's benefactor paid Cockerton and Aylott's bail. Their friend's death had at least secured them that.

The following Monday, Holloway hosted Kast's inquest. The City coroner heard evidence in the presence of solicitors Newton, Wallis and Doulton. Various prison warders testified that Kast had never complained before he became ill and that that he'd had 'every attention paid him'. There was a fire lit in the infirmary day and night and no discernible draughts that could have affected him. It was also sworn that Kast had told infirmary warders he had previously suffered from ague when in India. The warder on duty when Kast died stated he had come on duty at 10 p.m. the previous evening and seen that the deceased was in a 'hopeless condition'. He'd sent for Dr Scott, but not until three minutes before Kast's death.

A juror: You knew he was dying; he was not a prisoner, was only on remand, and yet he was left in this way. Then the doctor arrived after death?

A: Yes.

Dr Scott confirmed that the travelling to and from the hot courtroom in the prison van combined with the state of anxiety naturally weighing on Kast would have adversely affected his health. The coroner returned a verdict of natural causes, with the recommendation that 'more suitable arrangements' be made in the infirmary for the comfort of its patients. It was a verdict that led to criticisms in *St James's Gazette* of the practice of remanding prisoners, innocent until proven guilty; this was especially relevant given that Lina – against whom the charge was arguably more serious – had been allowed bail. But as regards the trial, the most significant and newsworthy aspect of the inquest was a comment by Phyllis Vincent, Kast's sweetheart since the previous January, who had visited him every day at the prison since his illness:

Coroner: Is there anything else you wish to say?
A: Only that he told me he was speaking the truth in the case.

Her mother had heard him say it too.

Wednesday 16 December was Kast's funeral. Lina sent a wreath, with the message, 'With deepest respect and sympathy for one of England's truest and bravest soldiers, who died in the course of justice.' Mabel sent another, simply expressing 'deepest sympathy and regret'. Frank sent nothing, but received death threats. The words spoken with Kast's dying breath worked on the public's imagination. On 23 December, when Amberley Cottage was almost completely destroyed by fire, it was widely believed to have been caused by an incendiary device planted by some dubious-looking men who had been seen 'prowling about' the property several days earlier. Frank would later explain it as 'accidental and due to the carelessness of some painters' who were decorating some rooms he had recently added to the property,[26] but the idea that Lina was somehow involved took hold, to such an extent that even Alys insisted 'it was undoubtedly she', adding that Lina had even 'tried to bribe [Frank's] servants to poison him'.[27] In the season of goodwill, this bitterest of feuds raged on.

17

The Protestations of Lady Scott

Only two things were left unchanged by Fred Kast's untimely death: Frank's attitude – he arrived at court on 4 January 1897 looking as unconcerned as ever – and Marshall Hall's determination that Cockerton and Aylott should continue to get as determined a defence as he could muster. Everything else was undeniably altered. The case must continue, but the situation was unprecedented. Never before had a key witness and defendant died halfway through a trial and the players were a little lost; it was as if their script had been significantly rewritten and they did not know their lines. Lina felt it most keenly. She took her seat dolefully, having donned 'a costume of black velvet with a trimming of jet and bonnet to match ... strongly suggestive of mourning'.[1] She was undeniably pensive. Over the next few days she complained of weakness, struggled in and out of the dock afflicted by lumbago, appeared tense and agitated in turn, and on this particular day, as the jury reassembled, 'appeared to lapse into a state of great mental depression', now and again wearily supporting her head on her white gloved hand. The only supremely confident voice on the side of the defence was the one that counted least. The *Former Acquaintance of the Earl*' who penned that morning's anonymous letter suggested that it was not necessary to *see* a man commit a crime of this kind to be certain of his guilt – 'His conversations and general comportment among his intimates, are pretty safe indications by which to be guided' – and voiced the opinion that Frank was not yet 'out of the wood':

> ... this coroneted importation from Sodom [will] meet with his desserts. He made a huge blunder, whoever advised him to stir up this horrible cesspool. It is too late for repenting of it now.[2]

It was too late for repenting of anything now, but Marshall Hall was determined that one fact at least should not pass unchallenged. When Dr Scott retook the stand, he asked him about Sir John Bridge's attendance at Holloway to take Kast's evidence. Was it not the case that defence counsel had pressed for it not to be taken? Justice Hawkins questioned how that was relevant. It was, said Marshall, 'useful for the purpose for which I require it'. 'For prejudice?' suggested the judge. 'For justice!' retorted Marshall, determined to secure an admission that Kast had been well enough to give his statement. A 'short statement', conceded the doctor; but Frank's counsel had said they would need two hours to cross-examine (effectively preventing *any* statement being taken). Marshall also found it suspicious that Sir John Bridge never insisted on seeing Kast for himself, but the judge was having none of it: Dr Scott's statement would have been, and should have been, sufficient to guide Sir John's decision. He called on the prosecution to continue with their witnesses.

Edward Wallet testified as to the mailing of the libels. He was not cross-examined. Bernard Abraham's clerk testified as to the signing of the statements and was only briefly cross-examined as to his absolute certainty that the documents signed and the libels were one and the same. Doulton's clerk, Baines, gave evidence as to the questioning of Cockerton and Aylott. Cross-examining, Marshall asked if Baines questioned the men to get evidence of publication without telling them it would be incriminating. When Baines said he had, Marshall observed, 'Your experience in the criminal procedure is not very great.' He could not think of a single police constable who would have dared to have done it. (Laughter.)

Thereafter, various of *Royal*'s crew came forward to discredit the men's statements. William Parker, mate onboard for the expeditions to Norfolk, Southampton, and the first leg of the Mediterranean tour, didn't remember Kast but testified he had seen Cockerton and Aylott since they became involved with Lina. They'd told him there was 'plenty of money to be got' if he joined them. He'd told Cockerton he was 'a fool to draw himself into such trouble'. Almost word-for-word he told Aylott the same. Thomas Moyse, Frank's faithful engineer, testified that Kast was let go because Moyse refused to share his cabin due to Kast's poor hygiene. He saw Kast once afterwards at Broom Hall; he seemed down on his luck and Moyse gave him a shilling. John Bowles, who had been employed as mate for the last leg of the Mediterranean tour, put Aylott in Frank's cabin as he'd stated, but said that the French pilot had not slept in with them. They all swore they had never heard accusations of improper conduct against Frank. William Harding, by then a gunner in the Royal Navy, cut a fine figure in his uniform when he stepped forward to deny knowing he was referred to as 'faithful' until long after he left Frank's employment, though it came as little surprise to him when he did hear. More importantly, he remained 'faithful' to the end by denying that Frank had ever acted improperly towards him.

None of these men were cross-examined at any length, though it was established that despite some minor misdemeanours, they all left with clean slates. And somewhere along the line, the fact that other crew members did not come forward to give evidence was lost. Neither Cruden, the ship's boy, nor Linton, the dismissed mate employed for a short stint between Parker and Bowles, were called, despite Doulton having written to Santayana about them. More crucially, Dutton, whom Kast had said was present when he told Cockerton of Frank's assault, never materialised. Perhaps the defence intended to call him, but if so they never mentioned it. He is, in fact, something of a mystery, not being mentioned in anything other than Kast's statement. Frank does not name him in any account of his travels.

Sir Frank then called two witnesses whose testimonies were intended to show the real reason for Frank passing through Malta at the end of 1895, where it had been suggested he hoped to intercept Kast. Whether they achieved this depends very much on how devious one considers Frank to be. Rowland Pickering, solicitor, testified that he represented the owner of the monastery in Sicily that Frank was looking to purchase. He had arranged Frank's inspection of it, but as he dated all negotiations as being in December 1895 and January 1896, *after* Frank had received Kast's letter, his evidence did not completely exonerate Frank, just as it did not explain why Baines had subsequently been sent to India. The monastery purchase fell through because 'the property needed too many repairs'.[3] The second witness, Henry Henley of P&O, testified that the *Caledonia*, on which Kast travelled, was not scheduled to call at Malta and had not been advertised as so doing, although this was unusual. Normal practice was that P&O vessels from India did stop there. Henley assented when Walton put it to him that 'anyone who did not see the advertisement would assume that the *Caledonia* would call at Malta'. Collectively, the testimonies of these witnesses reveal at best that Frank was telling the truth; at worst, that he had simply taken the wrong boat.

Finally, two witnesses were called to address the incredible alleged assault on Kast near the railway station in Winchester in June 1887. Their testimony was less ambiguous. George Tanner, assistant clerk to the city justices, who had taken Kast's statement on 30 January 1896, said that Kast had appeared with Cockerton and a local solicitor named Scotney. They'd produced a written statement which had on it neither name nor address but detailed the alleged assault. Tanner could not produce a copy of the statement, but recalled asking Kast to name the victim. Kast named himself and Cockerton added, 'Yes, but he don't recollect much about it, it's so long ago.' Tanner then asked for Kast's address. After some prompting Kast gave Cockerton's. Tanner asked when the offence took place. Cockerton again answered, 'It was in July – no, it must have been August', and when August was recorded, changed it to June 1887. On being asked for particulars, Kast said that Frank had walked him back to the station, they'd 'sat down on the railway bank, and there the act was committed'. Kast could not recall the exact spot where it happened and therefore could not say whether it was within the city boundary. His statement was taken to the magistrate who issued the summons.

Justice Hawkins could not refrain from commenting that the whole episode suggested 'a very loose way of doing business'. Even more incredible was the evidence of Superintendent William Felton, who had served the summons on Frank. The day before the hearing, he said, he had been contacted by Scotney who informed him that Kast had now found the spot and offered to lead him to it. En route they passed Revd Dickins's house and Cockerton pointed it out, but Kast said he couldn't be sure it was where he'd met Frank all those years previously without going inside. Cockerton told the superintendent that they had a list of all the people Frank was likely to have called on in Winchester and it would be safer for Kast not to commit himself until he was sure. They would have a look round in the morning and come and report back when they found it. Cockerton had also asked the superintendent, as they walked, how far the city boundary extended, and the accompanying PC where various roads they passed led to. The PC replied that he didn't know, because the superintendent had 'previously instructed him not to know anything'. When they arrived at the spot it was discovered to be 900 yards outside the city boundary. Collectively, these witnesses succeeded in making it look as if Cockerton and Kast had invented the whole thing. The *Pall Mall* reported themselves amazed that any credence should be given to the case at all when this was the 'story on which this whole trial virtually hangs'.

Here, the prosecution rested, satisfied with their performance. It was clear, continued the *Pall Mall*, that 'no money and no pains' had been spared to present a 'complete case'. In addition, on this same day, Frank had the gratification of seeing Arthur Carrez, the man responsible for printing the libels, appear at the County of London Quarter Sessions, indicted for selling indecent photographs. On 9 December, as Kast lay dying, two undercover policemen had gone to his establishment on an anonymous tip-off and purchased some items. They had returned on the day Kast died with a warrant and removed hundreds of photographs and books. Carrez had been arrested and remanded in custody and now found himself sentenced to a further month's imprisonment under the terms of the Obscene Publications Act.

At last it was the turn of the defence. Thus far, said the *Pall Mall*, Lawson Walton had not 'shone greatly' in this trial. His cross-examination had not been brilliant and his few objections not sustained. Marshall Hall's was indeed the stronger performance. But finally, it was Walton's turn to speak on Lina's behalf. Over the next four hours, he made a 'lofty effort' to defend that which in its *modus operandi* was largely indefensible. He focused on the inescapable fact that it would be impossible for the jury to clear both the stain on Frank's youth and early manhood and, at the same time, find the two surviving men innocent. He found it telling that the prosecution had not charged Lina with publishing the statements knowing them to be false, but only with the lesser crime of enticing the men to concoct them. He highlighted the different social standing between Frank and Cockerton and Aylott, who, having none of Frank's advantages, had nothing to recommend them beyond their hitherto unblemished characters that would now be permanently clouded by association. And Kast had died under such a cloud. His story, removed by death, was now a blank. Walton was not entitled to tell them what Kast would have said.

He did, however, emphasise that Kast had not recanted one word of his statement though he knew he was dying – a fact of great weight to a Victorian audience.

Walton then considered Lina's position. We have heard most of it before – the love she professed for both Frank and Mabel, her role as peacemaker in their troubled marriage, etc. – but the letters between her and Frank were new and Walton justified their use. A 'superficial cynicism' might attach some 'dishonourable intrigue' between Frank and the mother of his affianced wife by their tone, he suggested, but in reality they revealed the extent to which she had taken this lonely and depressed orphaned young man under her wing, extending to him the sympathy and affection of his own mother, had she survived. Yet those feelings had been destroyed by Frank's actions. Lina's opinion of him had changed as she heard him tell previous juries how desperate he was to have his wife return to him, having written of her as a 'stony-hearted self-righteous saint', a 'curse' and a 'fiend'. The outcome of the last trial, Walton suggested, must have seemed to Lina a gross injustice and made her determined, whatever the outcome of the Lords appeal, that the world should know what she had learnt of Frank's character. These stories she believed to be true. How could she not? They had been told to her by Frank's chosen servants, who had walked away from their employment with characters unblemished. Of course these men had to be supported after they came forward; but there was no evidence of the large sums being paid as the prosecution suggested. Of course there were mistakes in the dates concerning events ten years back by men who were then boys and who did not keep diaries or barely even took up pencil and paper. But their statements must not be dismissed on such technicalities or because of a 'natural abhorrence' to their subject. Lina may well have acted 'ill-advisedly', but he asked the jury to consider the 'significant collocation' in time between the incidents at Oxford (1885), the Chinese Boy (1886) and Kast's account of events at Winchester (1887). All of these he went over again in detail, paying particular attention to the repeated use made of Jowett's apparent forgiveness of Frank's sins. Jowett was a Christian man, he said, who would not have wanted to see Frank's character permanently stained, but his actions were not proof of Frank's innocence. And the fact that a man in Frank's position walked away from Oxford accepting the lack of inquiry was scarcely believable. He asked the jury to look at each of these events in the light of the other, and then add to them Frank's actions in attempting to prevent Kast's return and his evidence being taken. Were these the actions of an innocent man? By their verdict, he asked the jury to endorse the view he had submitted on Lina's behalf: that Frank's actions had compelled her to act as she did through a sense of duty to her child.

The applause that broke out was quickly suppressed. Marshall Hall then spoke on behalf of Cockerton and Aylott. Despite his convalescence and long absence from the courtroom, Marshall had been on fighting form throughout the trial and this afternoon was no exception. He opened on the offensive, drawing the jury's attention to the deplorable death of Kast and the 'unfortunate error of judgment' on the part of the prosecution in objecting to his statement being taken. He read from the statute by which the deposition of a dying man can become evidence, verifying that it was at the discretion of the doctor, but suggesting that the rest of it – which specified that a statement could be taken if the witness was 'willing and able' – was idle if all the opposing side had to say was that their cross-examination would take 'two or three or six hours' to defeat it. Sir Frank was instantly on his feet and the judge strongly objected to the implication. But an unapologetic Marshall Hall launched into a condemnation of the judge's decision at the start of the trial to bail Lina but not the men, which, he said, would (unintentionally) have inevitably prejudiced the men in the jury's eyes.

The following morning, Marshall continued in a similar vein. The case could not be allowed to fail, he said, over the matter of dates. Again, he pressed his application to amend the original plea. Sir Frank, unusually supporting Marshall Hall, said he had no wish for the case to fall apart on a technicality, but the judge was adamant. The dates would stand. Marshall Hall then asked the jury, in the light of his learned friend's lack of objection (and somewhat overruling the judge) to reconsider Kast's statements as if they read that the Winchester incident happened 'at some time in June' and the other incident 'somewhere on the Norfolk Broads'. Would they then not be corroborated by the evidence of others? Why would Kast invent such a story? Men did not commit perjury for the sake of a few pounds. These men came forward to help an undischarged bankrupt with bailiffs at her door, knowing there was no money to make them rich, out of a sense of chivalry, 'which was not dead when there were men in humble life who would come to the aid of a woman in distress'. He asked the jury to compare the men's actions with Frank's. How could Frank justify writing to Kast warning him of the severity of 'the practices they now wish to accuse you of' if he were an innocent man? There was not 'one tittle of evidence' that Frank knew when he wrote this of the allegations against him (though, arguably, his knowledge of the Scotts would have been sufficient to alert him to their general flavour), and it was 'inconceivable' that Kast, in India, would have heard anything of Frank's private life (although, again, Frank's previous hearings had been reported by the press in detail worldwide). Marshall questioned again why Frank had not brought an action against *Hawk*; and when the judge suggested that if he were going to ask that he might as well ask why Frank did not bring an action against Lady Cardigan, Marshall retorted that he could not imagine *anyone* not bringing an action against Lady Cardigan! He questioned what it was in Frank's character that compelled his wife to say she would rather die than live with him and asked the jury to compare the 'mysterious and unfortunate' events in Frank's life – which his own uncle had described as 'vile and discreditable' – with the 'unblemished and unimpeached reputation' of the men before them.

The 'vigorous attempt' at applause from the gallery, which caused Justice Hawkins to threaten to clear the building, demonstrated the command with which Marshall Hall had spoken. But it quickly became clear that, so far as the outcome of the case were concerned, the most significant action had already played out behind the scenes. The judge, who had authority over the law of evidence, had been considering how Kast's statements could be used in light of his death. As Marshall Hall retook his seat, Walton asked the judge to reveal his decision. The judge ruled that Kast's statements, though adverted to by Frank in his evidence and resting in part on sworn information given before the magistrate's clerk in Winchester, were inadmissible as evidence of the truth of his deposition without his supporting testimony. In which case, said Walton, owing to Kast's death, he had no further evidence to present in support of Lady Scott. He retracted her plea of justification.

The announcement sent shock waves around the courtroom. Even those whose attention had lapsed during Marshall Hall's pontificating quickly understood that the defence case had collapsed. Everyone agreed that Kast's death had created an unprecedented situation, but now the defence and bench took different standpoints on the necessity and advisability of throwing in the towel. Both the judge and the prosecution were keen for the hearing to continue. The judge suggested that if part of the libel could still be proved, they could go ahead on that basis alone; he would simply remove the burden on the defendants to prove anything relating to Kast's evidence and charge Lina, Cockerton and Aylott with proving only that to which each had individually sworn. Walton, however, was not satisfied. He argued that the lack of Kast's statement would leave Lina compromised as it essentially corroborated those previously made by Cockerton and Aylott. If he were to be corseted by the rules governing evidence as the judge had interpreted them, he would not consider it good legal practice to continue. To substantiate his position, he cited prior cases in which it had been determined that if one part of a plea of justification failed, the whole must fail and a guilty verdict returned. Sir Henry refused to accept this and suggested an adjournment to allow counsel to discuss the predicament with their clients. When they returned, it was to a packed courtroom – into which also came Mabel for the first time, dressed head-to-foot in black, rushing forward to grasp and kiss her mother's outstretched hand. Frank, it was observed, was so deep in conversation with his own counsel as to be oblivious to Mabel's near presence, while Lina was clearly very agitated. Her grip tightened on the rail and her face flushed as she turned from Mabel to her advisers, arguing with them and waving a piece of paper on which she had apparently written some comments she wished to make. 'Not a word,' her solicitor was heard to command as the court settled.

There was a tangible air of suppressed excitement as Messrs Walton and Hall stood in turn to announce that they meant to go ahead with the withdrawal of the plea. The judge, who had previously refused to amend the plea as to dates, now eagerly impressed upon them his willingness to do so to take out anything relating to Kast's evidence; but this time it was they who were determined – 'however lamentable it may be' – that it could not be done. Sir Frank voiced the opinion that if his learned friends were determined on this path – which, he hastened to add, was not the prosecution's fault and beyond their power to influence – he only regretted that they had chosen to do it just as the accused were to have gone into the witness box to be cross-examined. The inference incensed Walton, who appealed to the judge to confirm that they had been duty-bound to continue until he had spoken concerning Kast's statements – Marshall Hall dramatically adding that if it were true that Frank could not control events, neither could his clients control 'the hand of death that had robbed them of their chief witness'. The rising irritation of all concerned became infectious. Lina turned to speak 'emphatically and angrily' to Cockerton, who remonstrated with her to be silent, but she would not be told and continued 'shrilly and sharply', 'I am not going to! I am not going to!'

It fell to the judge to restore order. A long and circuitous legal discussion ensued. Finally, the judge was forced to accept the defence counsel's decision, but only after stating in no uncertain terms that he wished it to be understood that his offer to amend the plea had been sincere and ensuring that in refusing it the defence were acting with deliberation and not under the supposition that his sentencing would be nominal. This duly noted, a guilty verdict was entered and the jury dismissed. The judge deferred sentencing to the following day. Walton again applied for Lina's bail. She was 'very ill', he said; but apparently she was not so ill that she could not compete with Marshall Hall in an appeal for bail for her fellow prisoners. 'Where they go, I go!' she declared, gesticulating wildly and expounding her opinions freely to any and all who would listen as Justice Hawkins granted bail without hesitation for all three equally for the first and last time.

The following morning, the rush to the galleries was 'a little more noisy than normal'. The gangways were crowded, the seats usually reserved for those with court business filled with strangers. Even the jury box was invaded; chief among its occupants was the foreman, who came to hear the case out. After Walton's comments regarding Lina's ill health at the end of the previous day, rumour circulated that she would not come to court to receive her sentence, but at 10.30 sharp, in she came, supported by her two daughters; all three were dressed in black outfits bedecked with large black feather hats. Depending on which paper one read, she either limped back into the dock, a victim to her lumbago (*Star*), or approached it defiantly and with an air of cheerfulness, as she kissed her infinitely more distressed daughters and whispered to them, 'Now I go to get my reward' (*Standard*). Concerning Frank's attitude, there was no disagreement. Though his frock coats were darkening by the day (today's was 'sombre black'), his mood was not. It was repeatedly remarked upon that he was 'all smiles' as he entered the courtroom with Bertrand. And little wonder. His barrister, having appealed to the judge that the sudden withdrawal of the plea did not sufficiently allow Frank the public vindication of his character (which was, after all, what the proceedings were all about), was given the opportunity to speak on his behalf. In so doing, he focused on just one issue: 'faithful' William, whose story had been completely ignored by the defence. Of all the allegations, said Sir Frank, this was the one that they might have been expected to pursue and yet they had not asked Frank a single question about it, or challenged Harding on his testimony, or made any reference to him during their speeches. Marshall Hall tried to defend this by saying it was not gone into because it had only been a rumour, but that Cockerton would have proved it in his testimony. It was another idle comment. They had thrown away the chance for Cockerton to be heard, and with it that of other witnesses who were in court to testify that the men had not been offered bribes for their statements. All that remained was for the judge to sum-up and pass sentence.

It was with 'compressed lips and stony stare' that Lina heard Walton, in mitigation of her sentence, give the judge his assurance that she promised never again to publish the statements she had been unable to prove as a result of Kast's death, though the men stood by them as true, withdrew not one word, nor wished to shirk their responsibility for having made them. It was not, however, to be her last word on the subject. Amazingly, despite reservations, Justice Hawkins allowed Lina to address him at Walton's request. Looking pale and clutching in a firm grip the piece of paper on which her statement was written, Lina spoke in a clear voice, saying she would accept any punishment the judge cared to hand down, knowing the 'terrible wrongs' her 'good, sweet, honest' daughter had suffered and believing everything told her to be true. For nearly seven years their mouths had been shut and she hoped no one there with daughters would see them similarly suffer. 'I do not fear imprisonment,' she maintained, only that Mabel 'should be deprived of the only protector she has in the world' and that 'something will happen to her'. She placed herself entirely in the judge's hands, vowing, 'Whatever I suffer I shall suffer gladly.'

Lina's voice wavered as she spoke of her daughter and Mabel turned towards her mother with a look of gratitude as she told of her sacrifice. It was all very touching, but the judge was unimpressed: 'If the object of withdrawing the plea of justification was to get rid of testimony that would be subjected to cross-examination, merely for the purpose of having a word or two of vindictive comment uttered at the last moment, all I can say is that I feel a little more surprised than I had been.' Lina received these remarks with 'tragic gesticulations' and thereafter maintained an unceasing murmur of half-audible comments throughout his summing-up.

If this had been a civil action for damages, Justice Hawkins began, then those damages might have been considerably increased if the defendants had pleased to file a plea that they did not mean to try and prove. As it was, the charges in these libels imputed misconduct that would have unfitted Frank for decent society if proved and warranted the severest punishment. They were published and broadcast wholesale with the purpose of prejudicing Frank and influencing the House of Lords. It was not a new crime – there have always been 'scurrilous, bad, wicked people' who insinuate all kinds of things in the attempt to influence suits – but it was difficult to imagine a greater crime.

Frank sat self-possessed, listening, while the circumstances of his upbringing and youthful misdemeanours were relayed to the court; Lina, with increasing agitation as the judge worked his way through the friendships Frank had made at Winchester with people who had come forward to testify for him, the forgiveness he had earned from Jowett, his adventures on *Royal* and the misconduct thereon of which he was now charged. Finally, he arrived at the 'evil day' on which Frank made Lina's acquaintance, which, he said, marked 'the beginning of all this unhappiness' and was largely the result of her influence.

'Thank you, my Lord,' Lina blurted out, unable to contain herself longer.

The judge ignored her and, passing over the 'unprecedented' letters Frank had written to her, arrived at the marriage and the difficulties therein. 'Wickedly, cruelly', the acts of friendship between Frank and Roberts were converted into charges of the grossest impropriety; and by the end of 1890, some 'wicked persons' had approached Mabel with 'calumnious suggestions'.

'Not me, my Lord!' broke in Lina, applying the bottle of smelling salts to her nostrils while her solicitor and junior counsel made concerted efforts to persuade her to maintain composure.

One such 'arch, unscrupulous, and slanderous' person, the judge continued, was Lady Cardigan, who had succeeded in poisoning her young friend's mind.

From there, he took the court through the outcome of the first two trials and arrived in due course at Lina's letter to the detective Dickinson, her 'evidence enough to hang a man' and ultimately, her arrest and the opportunity afforded her, should she have chosen to avail herself of it, to state on oath her defence before the magistrate at Bow Street.

Instantly, the court was in uproar. Marshall Hall was on his feet: 'No, my Lord; with great submission, that is not so.' Lina shouted from the dock, 'We had not, we had not.' Marshall attempted to explain that the magistrate had not allowed the defendants to give evidence at the committal, but the judge was certain he was right. 'I don't believe that,' he told Marshall, 'it is not so stated.' The affronted barrister, choosing to interpret the judge's comment as 'an assault on his personal honour' began 'ostentatiously to gather up his papers and made to leave the court' saying, 'I cannot take any further part in these proceedings.' The judge was forced to apologise. He had not meant any insult. Marshall was quickly mollified, but not before his excitement had infected Lina, who started 'wildly beating the front of the dock with her white gloved hand'.

'I will not be detained here any longer,' she declared, excitedly. 'I will go to prison. I will have my sentence, and then I will go. I will not stand here any longer. I won't put up with it.'

It was only with great difficulty that Lina was convinced to keep quiet, but her unbridled agitation was only too apparent.

'Kast, unfortunately, is dead,' continued the judge.

'Yes, very unfortunately,' retorted Lina.

And as the judge droned on in solemn tones, disputing the necessity for the withdrawal of the plea despite the fact, and deploring Aylott and Cockerton's boasts of the money they would get for their statements,

Lina 'gave way to a still more vigorous display of passion, gesticulating first with open palms on the ledge of the dock, then with closed hands, and accompanying these motions with rapidly uttered and only partially coherent sentences'.

'I never would have published them had it not been for my beloved daughter,' she moaned.

The judge, seeing nothing to be gained in remonstrating with her, continued undisturbed. 'I have thought what I ought to do,' he said. 'It would be idle of me to impose a fine ... I remember it was said yesterday you would not have the means to pay.'

'To pay what?' asked the miserable woman, who now seemed scarcely capable of following proceedings.

'In the circumstances I will deal with you as leniently as may be.'

'Thank you, my Lord.'

'I have the power to inflict more punishment – a great deal more,' said the judge before announcing to the court that, having taken into account the amount of time the male prisoners had already spent in custody, he would imprison all three for a term of eight calendar months.

A 'piercing scream' went up from Mabel. Lina seemed to stagger, but quickly recovered herself and began again declaiming from the dock: 'Thank you, my Lord, I am much obliged to you.' Clapping her hands and repeating over and over, 'Every word is true, every word is true.' Justice Hawkins finally lost his composure. 'Remove that woman,' he commanded. 'I will not allow you to stand there making statements of that sort,' he told Lina, as, all vestige of self-control lost, she was led away by warders; her fellow prisoners followed silently behind.

Mr Walton quickly pressed the question of the terms of Lina's imprisonment. Her health was fragile, he argued (not for the first time), and her doctor was in court if the judge was willing to hear him. The judge was; but the doctor could not be found. Sir Frank, seeing the opportunity to give his client the moral high ground as well as the victory, stood and said that whatever the judge decided, 'far from doing anything to deter your Lordship, I would encourage your Lordship to take that course'. As such, Frank would always be able to say that it was 'by our kindness and at our intercession' that Lina was allowed to serve her term as a first-class misdemeanant. The men, once again, were not so fortunate, but at least were not condemned to hard labour.

Mabel, who, as soon as the judge had spoken, tearfully asked for permission to see her mother, was heard to observe, 'This has broken my heart' as she left the courtroom, oblivious to all warnings of danger from the press of the crowd that had gathered in the narrow corridors to hear the sentencing.

The outcome of the trial was met with almost universal press approval. Lina was castigated as having demonstrated 'vindictive spite of the most rancorous kind'.[4] The *Star* branded it 'the vilest, most vindictive, most malodorous case on record'. Never before, it said, has there been such a case 'in which the sewer of a sordid human heart has been so widely opened'. Lina's punishment, which was 'to live in the solitary of her own soul, a prey to the furies of her foiled passions' for the next eight months, was well deserved.[5] There was satisfaction in the manner in which Justice Hawkins had condemned her conduct 'as severely as if he had been addressing a washerwoman in the dock' and some approbation that in passing an 'unvindictive' sentence he had 'shown one of the best aspects of justice'.[6] Factions of the more radical press found his leniency disappointing. *Truth* went so far as to suggest that as a first-class misdemeanant, Lina would hardly suffer more than from 'a period of confinement in her own apartments', further expressing the opinion that any negative effect on her reputation 'hardly applies' in her case.[7]

Given that Lina instigated both the gathering and publication of the libels, their objections have foundation. As a first-class misdemeanant, she could wear her own clothes, purchase her own food and some liquor from outside the prison. She was allowed furniture, books and newspapers, to have a relative visit twice a week and a solicitor as often as required. By comparison, the men, though not condemned to hard labour, would still work a gruelling ten-hour day at something of 'a manufacturing or industrial nature', have a plank bed to sleep on and have to earn a mattress through good behaviour; just as they had to earn other perks such as 'approved reading material'. They were allowed no visitors and no letters for the first three months and then had to earn one twenty-minute visit and the sending and receiving of one letter every three months thereafter.[8] Though the motivation behind the system was that 'such prisoners [convicted of criminal offences] may have the advantage of the incentives to industry and good conduct', critics found the imbalance between Lina's incarceration and that of Aylott and Cockerton unjust; though perhaps the sight of Justice Hawkins racing round to the Home Office the following morning might have appeased them somewhat. His purpose was to let the Home Secretary know that his order that Lina be imprisoned in the first-class was only meant as a temporary measure – an act of humanity driven by her ill health, which, on her improvement, should be rescinded and the rest of her sentence undertaken at Wormwood Scrubs where she would be treated with equal severity to the men. The Home Secretary replied that he could not increase sentence but only mitigate or pardon. This did not stop Justice Hawkins instructing the Old Bailey registrar to write the following week to press the point again. Statements were taken from Lina's doctor and Dr Scott as to her state of health and a suggestion put forward that though they could not change her sentence for the worse, perhaps Justice Hawkins' intention might be most nearly carried out if Lina remained in the first-class but the warders at Holloway were instructed to 'not be too easy in granting the privileges they had the power to grant'.[9] There is no evidence that this suggestion was ever put into practice.

Neither is there extant evidence to substantiate other stories that appeared in the press during Lina's incarceration – that Frank applied to the Home Secretary to be able to visit her in prison, or that the Home Secretary had been petitioned for Lina's early release on the ground of her ill health – both of which would have been the subject of a Home Office file. Yet if Frank had desired to see Lina, it further suggests his continued affection towards her, rather than his seeking an opportunity to gloat. For though Lina had made herself his sworn enemy, Frank never berated her for her actions beyond describing her to Santayana as possibly 'insane'. It was left to Alys to voice the family's relief that Lina had been imprisoned, and express fear that on her release she would be so full of hatred she might 'try to shoot him';[10] and to Santayana to brand her a 'wicked and vindictive' woman, adding that he had 'never heard of such characters in life or in fiction'.[11] Frank had always considered Mabel the guiltier of the two, for raising the whole spectre of Roberts in the first place. Lina, he thought, was 'a weak, kind-hearted woman' who, though 'by instinct a blackmailer and a preyer on men', probably never 'fully realized what she was doing'. Mabel 'did know the truth, and therefore knew that her allegations were false'.[12] By implication, then, were Lina's not?

This is impossible to determine. The libels stated that Frank had forced himself on the younger men; Frank had denied it. But equally conceivable is the prospect that some kind of homosexual activity had taken place consensually. The men might have had very different social standings, but were not dissimilar in age. On Jubilee Day 1887, Frank and Cockerton were both approaching their twenty-second birthdays, Aylott his nineteenth and Kast his seventeenth. In addition, Aylott's confessed freedom with his employer, along with Frank's 'democratic' upbringing which allowed him to associate with servants on equal terms, suggests the possibility of an easy crossing of the usual master/servant line. That Frank's two summers 'indulging in wild follies' when he was in his early twenties might have involved consensual sexual activity with willing members of his crew is not impossible. 'Soldiers, sailors, convicts, and in fact members of all communities deprived of intercourse with women' knew this to be true, just as did the Greek philosophers and every public schoolboy, argued Bernard Shaw in a letter to the editor of *Truth* after the Cleveland Street scandal, and, if 'freely consented to and desired by both', was a matter that concerned them and them alone. But his was a lone voice, as demonstrated by the fact that his letter was never published.[13] The question of whether the men were willing participants could never be raised while the practice itself was illegal, but it is beyond doubt that there was greater currency in the idea that they were not. Blackmail was an integral part of the sodomite's world. The threat of exposure to extort money was termed 'the common bounce' and the 'bouncer' considered a serious potential threat to a man's reputation.[14] In Frank's case, there had been no attempt at blackmail in the common way. Was this because the men had nothing to blackmail him with, or because Frank had already proved himself immune to manipulation?[15] Unlike other men in his position, Frank was not afraid to defend himself in public because he gave no credence to the stigma society attached to court actions. He put his faith in the legal system to face down any slur on his character. In the face of Lina's most devastating attack, said Santayana, he showed 'a most admirable courage'.[16]

But what had Lina really hoped to gain from her ill-advised, desperate move? She claimed she hoped to influence the Lords of Appeal, and most definitely, they did see the documents and did read them. The Lord Chancellor referred to them when passing judgment on the appeal as 'a gross and scandalous contempt' concerning which, if it had not already been dealt with in the criminal court, it would have been his duty to summon the authors himself and 'in the absence of some explanation or excuse to move that they should be committed to prison'.[17] But what if the criminal court had found in Lina's favour? How could the Lords have upheld the appeal court judgment if prior homosexual behaviour had been proved? A conviction for sodomy was one of the few things that would have entitled Mabel to an absolute divorce.[18] If this was Lina's real hope it was wild indeed. Such a petition had never been brought before the divorce court.

Mabel and Lina would not be the last to feel Frank's inflexibility and be pushed to extreme measures in the face of it, but in their case, the task proved greater than their strength. Lina emerged from prison a broken and defeated woman. After serving a little over six of her eight-month sentence, she was released from Holloway on 15 July 1897. Mabel arrived at the prison in a private carriage just before 10 a.m. accompanied by a lady's maid, a female friend and Lina's solicitor. She reportedly looked 'very pretty in a charming summer toilette of pink and white'; her mother, however, appeared 'anything but well' having 'visibly aged'. The pair had a 'most affecting meeting' before driving off, followed by a four-wheeler heavily laden with Lina's belongings. Lina told a reporter she had been treated with 'the utmost consideration' and 'favouritism' by her custodians, which she believed to be the result of pity.[19] The following Monday, she returned home to Bray, where she was presented with a 'handsome bouquet' by the small group of friends and sympathisers who came out to meet her.[20] As if to underline, for the last time, the difference between her treatment and Cockerton and Aylott's, the men's release was not reported.[21]

The day after Lina was freed, the House of Lords appeal judges finally delivered their verdict. After much debate, their lordships were as divided as were the appeal court judges before them. For those Lords eager for reform, it felt like an opportunity to look forward instead of back; to acknowledge the previous forty years' great social changes in, as Lord Hobhouse put it, employing 'a wider and more reasonable criterion' for judging a case. But the Lords against reform argued that widening the sphere within which a marriage might be deemed impossible would unsettle the law and throw it into hopeless confusion. In the end, the lords favoured looking back and upheld the appeal court decision by five votes to four.[22]

'It was a small margin to lose by,' said a philosophical Frank.[23] After eight years of grief from the Scotts he was considerably poorer, his eventual union with Mary looked increasingly less likely, but otherwise he was more or less unchanged; unless it be that he 'so completely outgrew Hellenism … that he readily denied that [it] had ever amused him'.[24] And if he had, who could blame him? The sordid use Lina had made of his relations with men was a world away from the love and brotherhood he had espoused at Oxford. On one level, Frank considered himself victorious: the Scotts never gave him any more trouble of 'that sort' again.[25] Yet he was still tied to Mabel in law. And the verdict of the lords of appeal would have longer-lasting and wider ramifications than merely prolonging his own personal marital difficulties. In upholding the clearest and most unambiguous definition of legal cruelty ever made, *Russell* v. *Russell* [2] became a case of legal significance for the next seventy years; a measure by which to judge cruelty until it was dropped as a ground for divorce in 1969 in favour of the more innocuous 'unreasonable behaviour'.[26]

18

Mrs Somerville

'South London Councillors, where have you been?'
'We've all been to Windsor to see the Queen.'
'Councillors, Councillors, did you all pair?'
'We all took our missuses.' (Earl Russell: 'Mine wasn't there.')
South London Chronicle, 17 July 1897

The Scotts may have been silenced by Lina's incarceration, but still the echoes of their accusations reverberated around Frank. His venture into politics provoked such quips as the above and mooted questions about his suitability in the light of his all-too-public private life. After Lina's indictment at Bow Street, the *Chronicle* had also dared to say 'at least one or two plain words' about Frank's affairs, suggesting that even if he were innocent, he must be 'utterly devoid of judgment or perspicuity' for ever involving himself with the Scotts; 'and yet he has been chosen to voice the opinion of Newington on the Council'.[1] Perhaps this was only to be expected from a Tory paper, but theirs was not the only doubtful voice; and not all were concerned with Frank's marital affairs.

West Newington – which Frank loved for being 'very sympathetic and very progressive'[2] – was a radical ward that had balked at the prospect of an aristocratic representative when his name was first proposed, but hoped Frank would give 'good and faithful service' to party and community.[3] Frank, no doubt, would say he had. Certainly, he was very active, putting a significant amount of energy into the half-dozen committees on which he sat, particularly favouring Asylums and Highways. But Frank was not by nature a follower and his party should have been warned of things to come when he announced during his very first speech that 'little dissentions upon various subjects were a sign that men thought for themselves'.[4] Frank had never done anything simply because it was expected, and had 'an odd incapacity for realizing an opponent's point of view', making his career thornier than it need have been.[5] Some of his views were in line with his party's – he spoke in favour, for example, of removing the House of Lords' power of veto over Commons legislation, which, he said, made 'a fraud and a farce' of popular government[6] – but in voting at the LCC his 'opponents' were not always on the other side of the political divide, and this became a huge (and, to Frank, inexplicable) annoyance. When, for example, the licences of the Empire and Palace Theatres came up for renewal in October 1895, Frank called restrictions on them 'merely irritating without being effective' and not 'in accordance with the general sense of the community' and voted with the conservative Moderates in favour of, among other things, lifting the ban on alcohol consumption on the premises.[7] The Moderates were outvoted, but Frank was still the object of an angry letter in the liberal *South London Press* which expressed the opinion that his actions went against the endeavours of his own constituents who sought to rid their brothers and sisters of alcohol's 'evil temptation'.[8]

It had never been intended that the LCC be as subject to party politics as was Parliament, but inevitably, as competition to dominate the council grew, increased pressure was applied to members to follow party lines. In the Asylums committee this was not too problematic. Its duty was to house, clean and clothe the city's insane. In Frank's time, it ran five asylums housing 2,400 lunatics, later adding a sixth. Frank sat on all their subcommittees and was chairman at Hanwell for three years. Perhaps his commitment stemmed from family concerns about insanity.[9] Either way, he found the job rewarding and took a pragmatic approach to difficult tasks – such as reading inmates' letters to see if they were coherent enough to be sent to relatives, or making decisions as to their discharge – demonstrating a great deal of tolerance and kindness towards them.

More controversial was his work for Highways, especially as regards the council's gradual takeover of the city's tramways. When Frank became chairman, they were already two years into negotiations with the North Metropolitan Tramways Company (NMT) for the running of trams north of the river. The proposal was that NMT would lease the whole system from the council and run it on their behalf for a fourteen-year period. The Progressives proposed accepting this only on the condition that the company committed to a ten-hour working day and six-day week. Labour representatives wanted this reduced still further to an eight-hour day. The company said its workforce (who only averaged a 5.5-day week anyway) objected to either restriction as both would prevent them making up time taken off for holidays. Frank voted with the Moderates to accept an unconditional lease, and after they won he was summoned to West Newington to explain himself. He had thought, he said, when he was elected, he would have 'a reasonable independence in his action', and as chairman had not thought it good practice to go against the draft agreement given the lengthy negotiations.[10] Further, he had been shown a memo signed by 75 per cent of NMT workers stating that they were content with their current hours and wages. He was therefore convinced his action was right. His constituency would continue to think otherwise.

When the council subsequently took over the whole of the south system and Frank's committee proposed connecting the two over London's landmark bridges, there were further vociferous objections due mostly to aesthetics from (as Frank saw it) the 'non-tramway-using public' who argued over such matters as whether the tramline should run down one side of Westminster bridge, the centre, or not at all.[11] Frank stood his ground – his position was on the side of progress which he considered beneficial to his south-of-the-river constituency – and came under increasing attack from his own party for his independence in handling the matter. Complaints were voiced that he did not attend Vestry meetings, which would have enabled him 'to better understand Newington's requirements',[12] and on 10 October 1897 it was announced that he would not stand for re-election in the constituency in March 1898. Frank publicly claimed he had been squeezed out by the secretary of the Liberal Association who wanted the seat for himself. Privately, he told Santayana that his constituents would not have him 'partly because I voted against 8 hours for tramway men, partly because they think my morals not up to the Wandsworth standard!'[13] His recent address to the Newington Reform Club on the subject 'What is Morality?' was doubtless a factor. Frank had defined morality as nothing more than 'the course of conduct which tends to the ultimate happiness of the individual and of the society' and condemned Christianity as outdated, divorce by consent and nudity in art as perfectly moral and showed 'a healthy contempt' for the monastic life, which he dismissed as 'an attempt to escape moral damage by shirking the battle of life'. 'All this,' said the *South London Press*, 'was very unorthodox.'[14]

February 1898, then, saw Frank fighting for Hammersmith alongside Sir Robert Garnett Head. It was a hard-fought battle but the odds were against them and the Moderate candidates won with a comfortable 12 per cent majority. Frank, however, was returned to the council as an Alderman – though not without the loss of his treasured chairmanship of Highways, which he took very badly.[15]

Despite the loss, the Hammersmith election would remain memorable. Since the libel trial, Frank had been growing increasingly personally dissatisfied. Amberley Cottage had been rebuilt after the fire, but had become 'distasteful' to him, despite its new mod-cons of 'steam radiators and a telephone!'[16] The river had lost its appeal and TH was out of bounds due to extensive building work which he complained 'crawls on'. In addition, the Scotts continued to pester him to pay Mabel's £1,500 legal bill accumulated during the Lords appeal, and all attempts to secure evidence of adultery on Mabel's part had proved futile. Frank was tired of the whole business. The tone of his letters to Santayana became decidedly subdued: 'I am neither well nor content nor happy,' he wrote in November 1897. Santayana worried that Frank might be sinking into depression. Though in his next letter, of May 1898, Frank denied he was 'especially unhappy', he considered it was 'chiefly due to the opiate of work'. He revealed that Mary had moved into a flat in Battersea (but did not say why) and was undeniably despondent: 'When one has no home and no home life, one does get bored,' he wrote; the only consolation being friendships formed during his Hammersmith campaign, particularly those of George Somerville and his wife, Mollie.

The Somervilles were both older: Frank was then thirty-two, George forty-seven and Mollie about forty.[17] Their backgrounds were vastly different: George was the son of a Glasgow cotton merchant and Mollie the daughter of a master shoemaker from Ireland. Despite this, they had much in common. George was an electrical engineer and a Liberal. He had long been involved in the burgeoning telephone industry, moving with Mollie from Aberdeen to Manchester in 1891 to become district manager of the New Telephone Company. By spring 1896, they had moved to London, where George became secretary to the newly established UK Telephone Defence Association, a short-lived organisation established to improve 'the wretched telephone system and ... upset the present oppressive monopoly, which is the worst obstacle in the path of progress'.[18] Frank's former partner, James Swinburne, was also a member and with its progressive aims and Frank's long interest in telegraphy the organisation gave George and Frank considerable common ground.

The Somervilles received Frank at their four-storey Georgian town house at 35 Shepherd's Bush Road, and Frank invited Mollie and George to Amberley Cottage where he introduced them to Mary. With George and Mollie lived their two young sons, John Alec, seven, George junior, six, and Mollie's sixteen-year-old son, Stanley, from her former marriage to Dundonian stockbroker's clerk James Watson. Mollie was described by an associate as a 'bright and exceptionally clever woman' with a 'striking personality'.[19] In Manchester, she had written a bold and heartfelt column for Dublin-based periodical *Today's Woman*, which contained society news but also highlighted poor working conditions for women in Manchester's factories and mills and the plight of its workhouse consignees. She criticised the do-gooder lady visitors to the workhouse who often did more harm than good – their victims 'crushed by the invectives hurled at them ... [and] rendered hopeless and helpless by the overpowering goodness of woman, who, as a rule, never felt a tithe of the struggle these poor creatures fight against'. She praised the Guardians of Stockport Workhouse who 'are so friendly with the paupers ... [talking] to them ... about their health, families, hopes of getting out, etc.' She wrote with sympathy and benevolence of living conditions in women's lodging houses in the poorer parts of the city, with humour of her attempts to 'stir up' the ladies of the Heaton Chapel Literary and Philosophical Society whose 'great want of energy or something else' allowed them to be dominated by their male counterparts, and with enthusiasm of her experiences canvassing for the Liberals in the 1895 General Election.[20] On her move to London, she became a prominent member of the Pioneer Club and threw her not inconsiderable energy into a number of local opportunities then opening up for women. She became a manager for the London School Board overseeing the running of three schools in the Shepherd's Bush area and got elected to the Fulham Board of Guardians, where she was active on a number of committees responsible for the housing and healthcare of the region's poor. In July 1897, she became secretary of the Hammersmith Women's Liberal Association (HWLA) and in the same month co-founded the Metropolitan Association of Women in Council, which sought to educate women and secure them equal rights with men. At their first meeting, Elizabeth Wolstenholme Elmy spoke on the subject of women's suffrage. This same political zeal Mollie threw behind Frank's campaign for the Hammersmith seat. She was considered 'a person of importance in the constituency' and she and Frank 'seemed to take to each other at first sight'.[21]

Slowly, over the next year, George faded into the background as Mollie's political activities aligned with Frank's. In May 1898, she proposed the vote of thanks for Frank's speech to the HWLA on 'women taking their proper place in the affairs of the nation' in which he advocated equal rights and female self-reliance.[22] In June, they both attended a meeting of the British Women's Temperance Association to discuss the use of lady missionaries to attend women summoned to the West London Police Court. As Frank was not himself a West London councillor and later clearly stated that it had been Mollie who had involved him in the campaign for women's rights, it seems likely that she engaged his services for both these events. She also visited Amberley Cottage without George, but with 'Miss A' – a friend from the Pioneer Club – who, Frank said, played 'the most sympathetic gooseberry' as he and Mollie became closer.[23] Then, in summer 1898, Mollie first met Santayana. He described her as 'a fat, florid, coarse Irishwoman of forty, with black curls, friendly manners and emotional opinions: a political agitator and reformer'. Quickly, she revealed her aspirations to him:

> She took me aside at once and began to lament that Russell should be attached to that dreadful dull stupid girl [Mary Morris]. He must be rescued ... I didn't think he wished to be...[24]

It seems he was wrong. In spring 1899, Mollie had a relapse of a former heart condition. Frank offered her Amberley Cottage for her convalescence. 'A hopeless invalid', she took the house for the good of her health.[25] Her children accompanied her. George wrote to her there and visited often. Frank, it seems, did likewise. Friends also visited and were entertained by Frank and Mollie as a couple; the writer, illustrator and women's suffrage campaigner Laurence Housman was among their guests that April. Then on 5 July, after a three-month stay, the children were unexpectedly returned to their father. Mollie and Frank had 'slipped away silently' the day before on the evening train to Southampton, from where they took a night boat to Le Havre to board the French steamship *La Bretagne* bound for New York.[26] Their plan was to put into practice the 'desperate expedient' Frank had considered for himself and Mary some five years previously.

They journeyed first to Chicago to consult a lawyer as to the current state of Illinois's divorce laws. To their disappointment, they found that pressure from the anti-divorce lobby in response to an increase in migratory divorces had led to a general tightening of laws in the east, and Illinois now required a year's residency before the filing of a divorce petition was permitted. It had also legislated against connivance, which meant that Frank and Mabel's agreeing to live apart precluded his divorcing her there. The lawyer suggested they try Arizona or North Dakota, but their laws also required a year's residency which Frank was keen to avoid. He and Mollie headed out further west and, after a tour of the Grand Canyon, where Mollie proved her convalescence complete by undertaking a long trail on horseback and camping under the stars, they arrived in Nevada in late August. There, Carson City lawyer Edward D. Vanderlieth confirmed that a six-month residency would qualify them under Nevada law to apply for absolute divorces from their English spouses on any one of seven grounds – impotency, adultery, one years' wilful desertion, a felony conviction, habitual drunkenness, extreme cruelty, or neglect – without any stipulation as to collusion or connivance.[27] Their plan looked achievable at last. They settled in Glenbrook on the east shore of Lake Tahoe, sixteen miles south-west of Carson City.

Glenbrook called itself a town but had only one small hotel, a half-dozen houses, and a population of no more than sixty. It had been an important timber provider for the Comstock silver mine in the Virginia mountains, but by this time the sawmill was closed and the sleepy settlement so quiet that the hotel manager expressed himself surprised at their intended stay. Yet where better to hideout and wait for the requisite time to pass than one of the smallest towns in the least populous state of the union? The scenery was breathtaking: 'No words are too strong to express the crystal purity of its waters', the mountains towering 2,000–4,000 feet above the lake and the purity of the air which 'rivals that of the water'. True, the overall effect was compromised by the extent to which the mountains had been 'skinned of trees by avaricious lumber men', but the prospect of a long sojourn on the banks of the largest alpine lake in North America to secure their freedom was compelling.[28] They put up at the hotel and began searching for a home.

It didn't take long to find 'a tumble-down, untidy but prettily situated' wooden house, set back a hundred yards or so from the lake within a six-acre field, surrounded by apple and plum trees and boasting a 'comfortable' veranda with steps down to a long wooden path that finished at the lake.[29] Inside, the furnishings were austere but greatly enhanced by Mollie's liberal application of floral fabrics and the large open fireplaces. Frank kept up his business affairs at a writing table at one end of the house while Mollie lounged at the other with her books and mandolin, her habitual cigarette hanging precariously from her mouth. In mid-September, Mollie's eldest son, Stanley, joined them from England. Two Chinese servants were brought in from the hotel, which had closed for the winter, and when Mollie rescued a wild kitten abandoned by its mother after Frank shot the rest of her brood, the makeshift family was complete.

The 'Russells' befriended the 'genial and good-natured' townsfolk, proving they were not 'haughty Britishers' by quickly adapting to

Glenbrook life; though they revealed neither their status nor purpose in being there.[30] They embraced the simple life: Mollie built a wigwam by the lake and sat smoking, painted up like a Native American; Stanley built a raft and paddled about the bay. They did not mind the approaching winter, which drove many residents to warmer climes. They played chess in the evenings or socialised with the remaining townsfolk, introducing them to the traditional bonfire on Guy Fawkes' night. For Thanksgiving there was a shooting party and, as winter deepened, there were dances, surprise parties and snowfalls.

Spring saw the return of the residents, but also brought the Russells' stay to an end. In April, they gave up their house and travelled forty miles to Douglas County where on the 14th, in a Genoa courthouse the size of a small village schoolroom, before an audience of six, Judge Mack took only a few minutes to award Frank a divorce from Mabel on the single ground of her desertion, and Mollie a divorce from George on the ground of his cruelty. The following day, the Russells went north to Reno and booked into the Riverside Hotel under the name 'JF Russell and party'. There, on 15 April 1900, Frank and Mollie were married by Judge Benjamin Franklin Curler with Stanley and the hotel's clerk as witnesses.

There is no evidence that George Somerville was cruel. Mollie had never attempted to separate from him in the UK and the Nevada divorce went undefended – either because George chose not to fight, fully cognisant of the scheme, or failed to do so, blissfully unaware. By Nevada law, if a marital crime was committed outside the state (or country) the only means by which it was necessary to advise the defendant of the pending suit if they could not be personally notified was by publishing a notice in 'a weekly newspaper printed in or nearest to the county in which the suit was pending, for three months in succession'.[31] Mollie may have written to George; Frank certainly wrote to Mabel *and* published the required notices in the *Genoa Courier* between 9 March and 13 April. He omitted his title, to avoid drawing wider press attention – even the judge who married them had been unaware of Frank's status – but otherwise covered all bases (or at least appeared to). It was not until Frank himself made the following announcement in the *Times* on 18 April 1900 that the whole scheme was exposed:

RUSSELL – COOKE – On the 15th inst., at Reno, U.S.A., by the Judge, John Francis Stanley, Earl Russell, to Mollie, daughter of the late George Cooke, of Cumbernauld.

Mabel, by contrast, knew everything. Frank later freely admitted that she had been told before he and Mollie left for America. Further, that he had deposited £5,000 in a bank account for her sole use should she act suitably surprised when she heard the news and then sued for a UK divorce on the grounds of his adultery and 'technical bigamy'. By the time she was called upon, Mabel was well equipped to give a star turn. While Frank had been planning his and Mollie's American flit, she had made her idle stage threats real by accepting the lead role in the musical comedy *A Runaway Girl* with George Edwardes' touring company. She made her debut in Plymouth on 13 March 1899, singing with a 'sweet voice' to 'warm applause' and (said *Era*) 'may do well ... when she becomes more conversant with the details of make-up and stage deportment'.[32] Initially, she found the schedule gruelling and was often too unwell to perform, but by April 1900, success in the provinces had earned her a London debut singing the highly patriotic 'Bravo, Volunteers!' to a tune of her own composition in variety performances at the Tivoli Theatre and Canterbury Music Hall. Her performance was 'very popular', though the *Post* suggested this perhaps had more to do with the Union Jack she dramatically pulled from her bosom at the end of the last chorus than the quality of her singing. Still, she was on form for her crucial off-stage performance. Frank had insisted she receive the news in public to avoid the suggestion of collusion. On 19 April 1900, therefore, she made herself conspicuous at the Tivoli and was reportedly in high spirits when she left to lunch with her mother, returning later in a distressed state and thrusting into the manager's hand a newspaper containing Frank's notice. She feigned such upset at the 'terrible blow', which was 'such a dreadful addition' to all her troubles, that she was 'nearly prostrate' and had to be excused that evening's performance. Lina emphasised their shock by publicly stating that for the whole of the previous year, they had heard nothing of Frank.[33]

On both sides of the Atlantic the press went into overdrive. Was it a hoax? Was this new marriage legal? Was the divorce? Had Frank become a naturalised American to secure his freedom? What would that mean to his peerage? How could there be two living Countess Russells at once? In some English papers the 'lax' and 'loosely administered' American laws were scorned in equal and opposite measure to the praise given Frank in others for his courage in defying their English counterparts. But more than anything, the papers wanted to know, who was this Mrs Somerville who quickly became known in the UK as the 'American Countess'?

The answers were not always complimentary. The American press described Mollie as unprepossessing, being 'short, stout' with 'ruddy complexion'.[34] She had 'coarse, sharp cut features' and was no spring-chicken with a son of twenty-three. She would make 'a mighty poor clinging vine to almost any massive oak', commented the *San Francisco Call*, presumably casting Frank as the oak.[35] Mollie was not impressed. Stanley was not yet twenty and the implication that she was old enough to have a twenty-three-year-old son when she took a husband of thirty-four irritated her. Frank, meanwhile, remained nonchalant as pressmen hounded them from Reno to Denver and back to Chicago. Independently, he took a little detour to Kokomo, Illinois, to indulge his latest passion and purchase a brand-new 8hp Haynes-Apperson motor car to replace his miserably underpowered and unreliable 2.5hp Benz back home. By the time they boarded the SS *Ivernia* in New York bound for Liverpool, the British newspapers had delved into Mollie's past and published her history, embellished in places by various obliging neighbours.

Mollie hailed from County Galway, the youngest daughter of Irish Protestants George Cooke and his wife Mary (*née* Mitchell). Little is known of the Cooke family, but they appear to have owned some land from which George received an annuity. George himself was described as a man of 'superior stamp', a master bootmaker of 'considerable ability'. He moved with his family from Ireland to Scotland sometime around 1881, living both in Glasgow and Cumbernauld, Stirling, where he was described as reserved but amiable and esteemed.[36] It was suggested that his move to Scotland had been necessitated by reduced circumstances resulting from a boycott, but it is equally possible that the family followed or accompanied Mollie, who had by then fallen in love with her first husband, James Watson. Watson, twenty-six, had travelled the other way – from Scotland to Dublin – in 1874 to study at an agricultural college. Family tradition suggests he subsequently found employment with the Cooke family, where he met Mollie. The couple decamped to Scotland and married at Glasgow United Presbyterian Church on 28 February 1881. Stanley was born on 3 April the same year.

Stanley's presence at Frank and Mollie's wedding heightened press interest in Watson, who was described by the *Aberdeen Press* as 'a dreamy sort of individual' whom Mollie divorced on account of neglect. He had joined a 'peculiar sect' in Glasgow and would return from meetings 'idle and absorbed', refusing to work, thereby allowing family funds to run short.[37] This rather incredible story is for the most part substantiated by Mollie's deposition given in support of her divorce plea in December 1889, from which it further transpired that in September 1884, Watson abandoned her to join a spiritualist community in the US – *Shalam*, in New Mexico. At first Watson made half-hearted requests for Mollie to join him, but the community's austerity did not appeal to her and Watson sent no money to facilitate the move. So, Mollie moved to Aberdeen, took in a lodger and worked at a 'scientific dressmaking agency' to make ends meet. In December 1888, she sued for divorce on the single ground of wilful and malicious desertion exceeding four years, which was all she required for an absolute divorce by Scottish law. The uncontested divorce was granted on 28 May 1889 and Mollie given sole custody of Stanley. Watson was ordered to pay £15 p.a. plus 5 per cent interest in alimony for their son, which doubtless Mollie never received. Within a month, he had remarried in Chicago, and within two, Mollie married her lodger, George Somerville. Their first child was already on the way.

The *Aberdeen Press* reported that Mollie had shared Watson's interest in spiritualism; Mollie's amenable neighbour told its correspondent that she had known Mollie as a 'highly sensitised medium', an expert at table-rapping, who held 'intimate communications' with the spirit world.[38] Mollie's own later writing confirms this interest and also the inheritance of the gift of second-sight from her grandmother. Whether, however, there was any truth in the 'amusing stories' her neighbour told of Mollie and George's courtship – how she would appear to him wings spread in 'spiritualistic fashion' – is another matter. Nevertheless, unlike the American papers, the

Scottish press concluded that Mollie was a strong and ambitious woman, of 'considerable energy, able to push her way successfully, both with and without a husband', who would 'conduct herself with no small amount of grace and dignity' in her new position.[39]

In England, Frank's family and friends were less enthusiastic. Aunt Maude declared herself 'horrified' and John J. Withers 'furious' that Frank potentially left himself open to prosecution for bigamy.[40] To Frank, however, one divorce was morally as good as another, 'otherwise you confound legal subtleties as to domicile with ethics'. It was all really rather straightforward: he had not seduced an innocent nor broken up a happy home and, corseted by the 'Ecclesiastically ridden' English law, they had invoked the only laws available 'to sanction the course which commends itself to our consciences and morals: and at last I obtain domestic felicity and a home and happiness'. The fact that Alys and Bertrand failed to acknowledge them on their return upset him. He had supported Bertrand's choice of Alys – neither questioning her suitability nor prior conduct – and felt he had earned his brother's support in return. He told Bertrand, 'Your happiness was what I cared for – why now should you be indifferent to mine? ... I don't often appeal for sympathy, but I care for yours, and frankly, I do not understand your attitude.'[41]

Bertrand, however, was put out at not having been told anything of the scheme until his assistance was required. Frank had written from America informing Bertrand that he had sent Mabel's notification of proceedings to his house, 'Millhanger' in Fernhurst, Sussex. Mabel had never lived there or even visited, and by April 1900 the property was empty. Any letters were automatically redirected to Bertrand by the local postmaster, and no doubt Frank expected Bertrand to intercept his to Mabel, so that she could claim ignorance of the affair. Neither did Frank take into account how Bertrand and Alys might feel about his treatment of Mary, whom they had gone out of their way to befriend for his sake. They also doubted the permanence of Frank's affections for Mollie, and Bertrand wrote to tell him so. Frank accepted their feelings regarding Mary but denied his 'affection, respect and admiration' for her had diminished. He had simply come to realise that he did not feel for her 'that enduring passion and satisfying companionship which should exist towards one's wife'. Perhaps he should have realised it sooner, but having done so he could not have stayed with her even if he had not left with Mollie. He knew he had not taken the easiest path but was convinced of its moral correctness:

> I foresaw that I should probably lose the friendship of you and others who knew of [Mary], and that I should lose respectability for which I had acquired a dangerous liking: not to mention the break of habit and the pain to [Mary] which has caused me intense sorrow, especially as she was in no way to blame.

He expressed regret that Bertrand did not 'appreciate' Mollie, but chose to consider Bertrand's invitation that did not include her 'an inadvertence' rather than a serious suggestion.[42]

Bertrand would in time accept Mollie as he had Mary, but would never appreciate her as Frank would have liked. He admitted she was strong-willed and referred to her on one occasion as 'sensible and superior', but otherwise never said anything complimentary about her in public or private.[43] Of Mary, there is little more to say. Like Kate Williams, she very quickly dropped out of the picture. Also like Kate, she remained unmarried and childless, living on 'private means' for the rest of her life – whether at Frank's expense or through legacies from her own family is unclear. She moved from Sussex to Kent before retiring to Battisford, Suffolk, where she died on 4 May 1956, three weeks before her eighty-fifth birthday, leaving the princely sum of £98 to a niece.

Frank and Mollie, meanwhile, set up home at Amberley Cottage with Stanley. They swapped Frank's bachelor pad in Temple Gardens for more suitable rooms at 3 Raymond Buildings, Gray's Inn. On 30 May 1900, George Somerville filed for divorce, accusing Mollie of adultery and bigamy and citing Frank as co-respondent. Frank's carefully worded answer was that he 'denies adultery' and 'does not admit the bigamy'.[44] The case came to court on 11 December, went undefended and was swiftly resolved in George's favour. Frank was ordered to pay costs of £145 and damages of £1,500, of which £1,250 was to go into settlement for the Somerville children. George was given full custody. Mollie would never see her youngest child again – George jnr died of TB aged twenty. Neither would she see John Alec until 1928, when the daughter-in-law she knew nothing about wrote to tell her of the birth of a granddaughter, Mary. It was, said Santayana, a sacrifice of which she never complained.

On 26 June 1900, Mabel Edith also filed for divorce, accusing Frank of bigamy and adultery with Mollie. A deposition was obtained from George Cheek, the Riverside Hotel clerk who had witnessed the wedding. Frank filed no answer. The case came before Sir John Gorell Barnes on Thursday 28 March 1901. This time, Mabel had the stage to herself and the veteran divorce court barrister Mr Inderwick in her corner. The proceedings were so swift that news reports contained no extraneous detail. The only new information concerned the intentionally misdirected notice from America, which Mabel confirmed she never received. Inderwick had little to do except declare that there was nothing from the previous trials that prevented the judge from awarding the decree on the proof of the Reno marriage on the understanding that the English court did not recognise the American's jurisdiction to grant Frank his divorce. A decree *nisi* was awarded with costs.

In the meantime, Frank retook his seat at the LCC the week after the *Ivernia* docked as if nothing had happened and Mollie settled into the life of a countess, indulging her social, political and literary tastes by founding a London club.

'The Pharos' opened on 8 November 1900 at 21 King William Street, Charing Cross; it was one of a number of 'cock-and-hen' clubs where 'literary and artistic people and social workers' of both sexes, 'in sympathy with progressive thought', could meet, play low-stakes card games, eat 'dubious dinners', hear lectures and engage in 'advanced discussions'.[45]

Frank became its chairman and a trustee. Early on, Jepson recorded a 'terrifying struggle between two advanced groups of ladies and their weak-witted male dependents' for authority, after which it settled down under the Russells' management and attracted a vast membership from among London's intelligentsia.[46] On 14 April 1901, it moved to larger premises at 3 Henrietta Street, Covent Garden, where some 200 people reportedly gathered to hear recitations by stage actresses Janet Achurch and Beatrice Lamb and hear musical pieces performed by musical director Edmund Rickett and others.

Notable members of the Pharos included G. K. and Cecil Chesterton and their old friend E. C. Bentley, who wrote for the *Daily News* and ensured that its goings-on were constantly in the public eye. Its inclusivity, Bentley wrote, was reflected in its 'heterogenous' décor: there were Indian carpets, an odd assortment of comfortable armchairs and sofas, firm tables and others that were not to be trusted with afternoon tea. On some walls hung original Rembrandt etchings, on others a 'terrible series of drawings' depicting moral lessons; on yet another, a rogue's gallery of revolutionaries.[47] Its members included 'vegetarians, garden-settlers, free lovers, actors out of engagements, journalists and authors … artists, fortune-tellers, spiritualists, founders of new religions and many people of unknown and mysterious professions'.[48] The journalist W. R. Titterton remembered it as being distinctly bohemian, a place where 'everybody was in earnest, and everybody larked'.[49] In 1901, the club put on Bernard Shaw's new play, *The Admirable Bashful*, and in October 1902, it played host to two high-ranking Boers in London to promote General Viljoen's memoirs of the war. The club itself had no political affiliation – though at one time there were rumours that Russians could be found plotting revolution in its back drawing-room – and its members in general were 'all in revolt against something'. Lectures included such diverse topics as 'Labour Politics' by Keir Hardy, 'Japanese Love Songs' by Frank's old university friend Osman Edwards, the 'Land Question' by Hilaire Belloc, and others on Thomas Hardy, trade unionism, Welsh folklore, and vivisection. Its weekly debates were 'notable' and Frank and Mollie's sharp-witted friend Amy Otter gained some notoriety at them by proving herself as magnificent a debater as she was a dedicated and uncompromising shop inspector at the LCC.

For a time, Frank's association with the club revealed him at his most genial and light-hearted and its membership soared to 400. But it was not to last. Titterton, Chesterton and others left when, in an attempt to raise its tone and reputation, 'Lord Russell's friends spoiled it by upholstering the furniture and raising the subscription', introducing a chef to replace the women's notoriously awful dinners.[50] Subscriptions doubled from a guinea to two, the literati didn't pay, and the atmosphere of the club eventually died completely when Frank sued twenty of its members in disgust. A very public slanging match ensued with writer Bart Kennedy over whether Frank's legal right to drag them through the courts was 'necessarily an equitable right'.[51] By December 1905, the club's doors closed and it went into receivership.

For that first year, however, following their return from America, the Pharos and the LCC were sufficient to lull the Russells into a false sense of security as regards their as-yet-unresolved marital affairs. Their social circle accepted them as they were and Mollie confidently appeared on the 1901 census as 'Mollie Russell', Frank's lawful wife. Stanley had become Frank's private secretary and was listed likewise as his stepson. But their situation reflected growing international concerns over the mockery migratory divorces were making of national divorce laws. Questions were being asked that required answers. Was it legally or morally right that a person of means could travel abroad and set up temporary residence in another country to secure a divorce that would not be legal in his own? Frank and Mollie's return to England had brought the matter to a head with a concrete example of the problems that needed addressing. For here was a member of the nobility, living openly with a woman he called his wife, having been denied a divorce by the highest court in the land from his first wife, still living, who had successfully obtained a decree *nisi* against him on the grounds of adultery and bigamy. Could this be allowed to stand?

By English law, the intervening period between the decrees *nisi* and *absolute* is specifically designed to allow the proctor – the monarch's representative in the divorce court – time to scrutinise its legality. His intervention is usually triggered by the attorney general in cases of doubt. Frank's status and his and Mollie's apparent flouting of the law probably made a proctor's investigation inevitable; though, interestingly, he did not similarly investigate George Somerville's divorce from Mollie. Frank claimed he was singled out because his face did not fit; because he was 'an unbeliever and a radical'.[52] Other members of his family held a different view. They believed Frank's divorce was challenged by direct order of King Edward VII, who, having ascended to the throne in January that year, was keen to throw off the playboy image he had earned as Prince of Wales and 'strengthen his own reputation for morality'.[53] Once again, Frank's all-too-public private life put him in the firing line, while (to quote Frank) 'another nobleman who had done exactly the same thing was not prosecuted because he was a favourite at Court'.[54] The upshot was that in May 1901, the king's proctor, Hamilton Cuffe, 5th Earl of Desart – who was then also director of public prosecutions – sent his assistant, William Brown, to Nevada. Brown went to see the Douglas County clerk to procure evidence of Frank's divorce and spoke to Judge Curler who performed the wedding ceremony. Judge Curler must have been shocked to learn who the English bridegroom really was. He immediately lent his support to the proctor and agreed to return with Brown to England. He gave a full deposition at Bow Street on 14 June 1901, alongside DI Stephen Gummer of Scotland Yard who verified Frank's handwriting in the Riverside Hotel register against various other sworn documents. A warrant was secured for Frank's arrest, which DI Gummer served on him at Waterloo station on Monday 17 June, as he alighted from a train. 'For me?' exclaimed Frank, who was taken straight to Bow Street where he was charged by the magistrate in his private rooms and bailed for £1,000 plus two sureties of £500 provided by friends from the NLC.[55]

Frank described the arrest as 'almost an impertinence'.[56] After a year undisturbed, he believed himself safe from prosecution; guilty perhaps of a marital offence, but certainly nothing criminal. Yet on Saturday 22 June 1901, he appeared again before the magistrate to hear Mr H. F. Bodkin put the prosecution's case. Judge Curler was called and swore not only that Frank's Nevada divorce was illegal in the UK but that it was invalid in America: there should have been forty days between the last published notice of proceedings and his case being heard. Frank's feelings can well be imagined as he heard the 'odious' and 'unspeakable' Curler make this pronouncement. There was nothing in the wording of the Nevada law to suggest that Curler was right, but no means by which Frank was immediately able to prove it.[57] His barrister, Willie Matthews, argued for delay: the 'exceptional expedition' with which the case had been brought 'did not find his client in a state of preparedness'. A trip to America was required to secure material necessary for his defence. But the magistrate would not oblige him. Further testimony regarding the 'Millhanger' letter and confirming Mollie's presence at Amberley Cottage provided evidence enough to proceed and Frank was duly indicted and committed for trial at the Old Bailey.

19

A Jury of His Peers

English law, if not ostensibly designed to confuse, still does so by its many circumlocutions and extensive use of jargon, the untangling of which requires a certain Stanley-like pernicketiness. American laws – still comparatively untested at the time of these events and open to interpretation – were often simpler. Frank's experiences had interested him in both. For someone in his position, the law might have been a natural career choice after university had he completed his degree. His sending down, however, had diverted his course and found him at the end of the century hurtling towards the trial by his peers described in the preface of this book. Yet his interaction with lawyers proved influential and in 1899 – before his American sojourn – the thirty-three-year-old Frank was duly admitted at Gray's Inn. There he studied under Ernest Cockle, whose knowledge of English law was considered vast and who later became a valuable member of the attorney general's office. It took time for Frank to get to grips with the Roman Law required for his first exams, but Cockle finally instilled in him an appreciation for the *ratio decidendi* – the rationale on which a law is based – and after six years' hard study, Frank was finally called to the Bar on 17 May 1905; though not before feeling the full weight of the law on his own account. To Bow Street, then, we return (with a certain amount of very un-Stanley-like trepidation at the legal entanglements before us) and to Frank's committal to the Old Bailey.

Its first immediate effect was that Frank's barrister, Willie Matthews, appeared before the Old Bailey's recorder the Monday following to beg him to see what the magistrate had not: that gathering material for Frank's defence from America would take time and a delay was therefore necessary for justice to be done. The request was denied. On the recorder's advice, the grand jury returned a true bill on the Tuesday declaring that there was sufficient evidence to justify Frank's prosecution. The Lord Chancellor, Lord Halsbury, was then contacted and asked how he wished to proceed. As bigamy was a felony, a long-protected quirk in English law made it Frank's 'privilege' to be tried by his equals. The so-called 'privilege' of peers' had been introduced by the Normans and vociferously defended by the barons who fought to have it laid down in the Magna Carta. After much debate between crown and nobility as to the crimes it should cover and for whom, an Act of 1557 formalised it into a system still recognisable in 1901. As such, it was not so much a 'privilege' in the sense of a choice, but the relic of a time when the nobility could not conceive fair judgment from anyone from a lower caste. Thereafter, it was defended simply because it was the peers' right to do so. As such, Frank's trial would take place in the House of Lords whether he liked it or not. The only question was, how?

Letters flew between the PM, the palace, parliament and the Old Bailey, resulting in Edward VII appointing Halsbury Lord High Steward for the duration, with the specific task of overseeing and trying the case on his behalf. A writ of *certiorari* was issued to officially remove jurisdiction from the Old Bailey to the House. On Thursday, Halsbury proposed the appointment of a select committee to consider how best to proceed to a 'speedy trial'. Among those chosen were some familiar names: Sir Henry James, by then Baron James of Hereford, who had represented Frank against Mabel in 1895; Lord Lindley, one of the appeal court judges; and Sir Henry Hawkins, who had imprisoned Lady Scott in 1897 and since 1898 had sat in the Lords as Baron Brampton. There were also three lords of appeal from the 1896 hearing, along with eight others of high standing including the Lords Privy Seal, Great Chamberlain and Chief Justice.

With many of their lordships not having been born let alone present at the time they last hosted a trial, their first task was to study procedure. Between the sixteenth and eighteenth centuries, there had been trials by peers every ten or twenty years, but in the nineteenth, there had been only that of Lord Cardigan, who on 16 February 1841 was prosecuted for duelling. That trial had been staged in Westminster Hall in front of 120 peers, each with eight tickets at their disposal for the admission of friends. It had been a much-anticipated early Victorian medieval-style pageant.[1] But at the dawn of the modern age, there was no appetite for replicating such ostentation over the mere difference between a peer and his wife. The committee, however, were determined to be guided by tradition and, ignoring public opinion, quickly announced that the trial would be held on Thursday 18 July 1901 at 11 a.m. – less than three weeks hence – in the magnificent Royal Gallery.

The announcement brought Willie Matthews to the House, to appeal again for delay. The Lords were as unobliging as the recorder. The Lord Chief Justice said Frank should have anticipated a criminal charge as soon as Mabel was awarded her decree *nisi* in March and begun his enquiries then. Halsbury added that he had 'never seen the like before where the merest suggestion that there *may* be witnesses ... was presented as an application for postponement' without affidavits, rebuffing Matthews' further claim that there was no time to secure affidavits with the comment, 'Is there not a telegraph?' The argument was sealed by the attorney general pointing out that if they delayed, they might lose their star witness: Judge Curler was expected back in America at the beginning of August. Matthews' suggestion that justice should take precedence over the prosecution's convenience fell on deaf ears.[2]

The preparation necessary for the trial was on a par with that of any great state occasion and was undertaken under the watchful eye of the press with 'all those grand old solemnities which make the British aristocracy the contempt – and the secret envy – of the world'.[3] A request was sent to the palace for guards to attend the trial and for sufficient police to keep the approaches to the House clear. The committee drew up and circulated the rules of engagement. Those lords attending had to maintain both their seats and silence throughout. Any concerns they might have during the proceedings were to be retained until they had withdrawn after all the evidence had been heard. All were to be attired in parliamentary robes – all, that is, except Frank, who was to be denied the honour. The office of works embarked on converting the Royal Gallery into a courtroom, the smaller Queen's Robing Room into a ladies' retiring room and 'the small office at the bottom of the stairs' into a consulting room for counsel. An announcement was made in the House that tickets for spectator's seats would be issued by the Lord Great Chamberlain's office on a first-come-first-served basis at a rate of one per peer with eighty reserved for peeresses and forty for the eldest sons of peers. In the same manner, tickets for a further 200 seats beyond the bar would be distributed to 'strangers' and another hundred to members of the Commons; though this last was abandoned after the speaker insisted that MPs should not be allocated tickets, but allowed to turn up on the day as they saw fit and enter the Gallery via the Norman Porch where a messenger would be posted to control numbers, confirm identity and let them pass. The clamour for tickets on the day of distribution caused mayhem in Westminster's Old Palace Yard; and afterwards, reports were made of tickets being sold to the highest bidder, with one correspondent claiming to know of a peer's son who declined to let his go for less than £60. On the day itself, the MPs under their own loose arrangement came and went throughout the proceedings to such an extent that it was claimed many more than 100 witnessed at least some of the trial.

As details of the forthcoming event were published, the press voiced its disapproval; and none more loudly than the radical *Daily News*. 'A more absurd procedure than this trial by the Peers cannot be imagined,' its correspondent wrote. Across the UK, the privilege was condemned 'a relic of feudalism' of questionable taste and wisdom in a democratic age. 'In the eyes of the law all men are equal,' said the *Bolton Evening News*, 'and a peer should not be entitled to any exceptional procedure.' Distinguished peeresses secured their places 'just as they would book a box for a farewell performance of some great singer'. Many hoped and predicted that this would be the Lords' swansong, declaring that the average Englishman could not help but 'share the feelings of amusement with which all nations of an equal degree of civilization are regarding this absurdity'. The whole business was considered 'a national joke' – and not a cheap one at that. Who, asked *The Globe*, is to pay for it should Frank be acquitted? It was a widespread concern – not only for the expense of fitting out the Royal Gallery, but the hidden cost of the necessary suspension of other courts to enable ten high court judges to be present to advise on critical points of law; to say nothing of the expense of bringing Judge Curler over from America and housing him here for the best part of two months. 'Apparently the charges are borne by the Lord Chamberlain,' reported the *Daily News*, 'who afterwards sells the upholstery for what it is worth.' The point was raised in the Commons by Irish Nationalist John Gordon Swift MacNeill, who challenged the First Commissioner of Works to publish an estimate of costs for the Royal Gallery conversion – a cost that was later determined to be in the region of £300 to £400, though newspapers wildly guessed that if hidden costs were included, the sum was nearer £2,000–5,000.[4] Such was the common man's disapproval that, on the day of the trial, Swift MacNeill was given leave to introduce a bill to abolish peers' privileges completely; though it would take another forty-seven years for this to happen.[5] Such also was the outspokenness of the press that the irreverent *Sporting Times* got away with pronouncing that even 'Russell the Reckless' would have wanted to get the trial over and done with before the grouse-shooting season started had he been 'any sort of a sports man, instead of an ass'.[6]

Meanwhile, the old-world ceremonies continued and on the day before the trial, the King held an investiture at Marlborough House, in which the officials of Parliament and Crown – the Gentlemen Usher of the Black Rod and Norroy King of Arms – were summoned into the presence of the Lord Chamberlain. They were presented with a white staff and given directions to deliver it to Halsbury as a symbol of his authority over the trial in the King's absence.

The morning of the trial dawned. Had he been able, Frank would have forgone his 'privilege', considering it nothing of the kind, and ventured instead to the Old Bailey where, ironically, he thought he would have got a fairer hearing. The Lords being the highest court in the land, he could not appeal its verdict, nor evade its sentence by claiming duty to the monarch.[7] Whatever their lordships decided, Frank would have to accept. In no time at all, the medieval pageant was underway and Frank brought to the critical point at which he was asked how he wished to plead.

Before he could open his mouth to speak, his counsel, Mr Robson, was on his feet: 'May it please your Lordships, I have, on behalf of the defendant, before he pleads to this indictment, to move that the indictment be quashed on the ground that it discloses no offence according to the true construction of the Statute under which it is framed.'

This, then, was to be Frank's defence. There would be no challenge of Judge Curler's erroneous assertion and no claim of inconsistency that Frank's American divorce was considered illegal in England, but his

American marriage perfectly legitimate. The only person to raise this question was a grand juror at the Old Bailey who was told by the judge, 'You may take it that [the marriage is legal] for the purpose of today at any rate.'[8] Instead, Robson chose to challenge the indictment on the legal principle of *lex loci* – that is, the principle by which a crime can only be prosecuted in the country in which it is committed. In 1901, there were three exceptions to this rule: murder, the manufacture and employment of explosives, and bigamy; for which the maximum sentence was seven years' penal servitude. This last exception, Robson would claim, was untested and the Act that formalised it worded in such a way as to render Frank's indictment null and void.

As Robson launched into his long-winded explanation, the general expression of the peers changed from 'alertness and humour by distinct gradations to one of obvious perplexity, and then of profound boredom'. Many must have felt that the spirit of *Jarndyce* v. *Jarndyce* had leapt from the pages of *Bleak House* to settle over the stiflingly hot courtroom in which they were all trapped. Only Frank, it was said, remained cool and avidly attentive as he watched the peers struggle to make sense of Robson's distinction between the words 'elsewhere' and 'anywhere'.

Robson's point, in essence, was this. The wording of the legislation concerning bigamy read:

> Whosoever, being married, shall marry any other person during the life of the former husband or wife, whether the second marriage shall have taken place in England or Ireland or elsewhere, shall be guilty of felony, and be convicted thereof...[9]

If *elsewhere* meant *anywhere*, then the inclusion of 'in England or Ireland' was redundant. Therefore, *elsewhere* must not have been intended to mean *anywhere* when the statute was written, but rather, 'elsewhere within the King's dominion' – for example, Scotland. Frank's crime having been committed outside that dominion, he could not be charged.

Halsbury could barely believe his ears. 'That is the extent to which your argument goes?' he asked. Yes, replied Robson, before continuing at great length – and then being followed by his junior, Mr Avory – on the same point for a further three-quarters of an hour; the transcription filled fourteen typed pages.

In his argument, Robson drew attention to the wording of other statutes, starting first with murder committed by an English citizen abroad which came under the jurisdiction of the English court with the very specific instruction 'whether within the Queen's dominion or without'.[10] He drew other examples from colonial statutes with similar pernicketiness, then strengthened his argument with judgments on other *prima facie* cases. In an 1860 case concerning the purchase and sale of slaves in Brazil, for example, the judge had dismissed the case on the ground that there was 'a rule that legislation *prima facie* is limited to that which is within the jurisdiction of the legislating body', which Brazil was not.[11] Frank's case, Robson argued, was also a first impression and therefore could not be tried in an English court until 'some legal enactment or some traditional body of law forbidding the act' had established a precedent.

Frank thought it a brave attempt argued with 'great skill'.[12] The Lord Chancellor dismissed it out of hand. The discussion which had continued at 'inordinate length' was really 'too plain for argument'. It was not even necessary to call for the opinion of the attorney general. Frank was asked again for his plea. In a clear voice he replied, 'Under the advice of counsel I plead guilty.'

There was no great expression of sensation in the Royal Gallery as there might have been in the Old Bailey – the peers and their guests were only just rousing themselves from their heat- and tedium-induced stupor, and the MPs were positioned so far to the back of the court that they could barely hear what was being said and were only just catching on that, beyond sentencing, the trial was effectively over. Robson immediately launched into his speech in mitigation. Though ignorance of the law was no defence, he explained how Frank's interpretation of the 'not very stringent laws' of Nevada had led him to conclude that his period of residency was sufficient for his divorce to be legal, missing the point that those laws had been framed to service a population of newcomers seeking permanent or long-term residency. He tried the Lord Chancellor's patience by referring to the legal advice Frank had taken in America, concerning which they had failed to produce affidavits, before moving on to the safer ground of the degrees of bigamy as it was perceived by the English court. Frank had not duped an innocent into a marriage, ignorant of the existence of his first wife. No one, in fact, could be ignorant of his situation, his story having been reported so widely across the globe. Mollie had been a willing participant and Mabel could hardly be said to have been hurt by Frank's actions given her own prior behaviour.

Frank's whole pitiful story was relayed in detail. The opinions of the judges from the previous trials were re-quoted, and Mabel's groundless accusations deplored once again. Frank's vindication had been won only at the cost of being 'forbidden the hope of a home' which he could not help craving. Robson called on the 'just and wise discretion' of their lordships to hand down a lenient sentence. He asked them to hear Frank speak in his own defence.

'It was not until the Earl himself addressed his peers that one woke up to the real object of the trial,' said the *Western Morning News*. It was universally regarded as a manly speech, spoken clearly and confidently. Frank's sincerity was never in doubt as he spoke of his 'reluctance and distaste' at having to plead guilty to such a crime committed not in any 'spirit of bravado or … defiance' but through his mistaken interpretation of the law, for which he had the profoundest respect. His sense of fairness was applauded as he took the blame solely on his own shoulders, praising the efforts of his counsel and clearing them of any suspicion of wrongdoing or poor advice. The touch of pathos, as he recalled his misfortunes of the previous twelve years and spoke of Mollie, who had consented to be his wife, was surprising but not overdone. There was a general muttering of approval as Frank surrendered himself to their lordships' judgment in a manner that would often be recalled as his reputation as a skilled orator grew.

The Lord Chancellor then commanded Black Rod to remove the prisoner and the peers to remove themselves to the upper chamber to consider their verdict. In accordance with tradition, the lords spiritual were excused the burden of having to pass sentence on a fellow human being and allowed to leave the court. In the chamber, Halsbury reminded the peers that they were now free to pass comment as they saw fit, before speaking on his own part of the 'terrible catastrophe' and 'almost intolerable provocation' that had led Frank to this end. No one, he said, doubted the misery of his domestic situation; and yet, there was the question of example. Halsbury did not believe that any lawyer ever told Frank his second marriage would be supported by English law, and others must be prevented from following suit. The gravity of Frank's offence was lessened by Mollie's complicity, but his defiance of the law must be addressed. He therefore suggested that the sentence should be three months' imprisonment as a criminal in the first division. He invited the assembly to comment, but all remained mute. After only twelve minutes' deliberation, the peers returned to the Royal Gallery to hand down sentence.

Frank was brought forward and bowed to their lordships. Starting with the most junior, the peers spoke in turn with their right hand on their breast declaring 'upon their honour' Frank's guilt. Halsbury then addressed the court with great solemnity of the pain it caused them all that 'a great historic name should be degraded by such a conviction'. His sympathies seemed to be with Frank as the 'intolerable provocation' he spoke of in the chamber now became the 'extreme torture' that had provoked him to act unadvisedly.

Frank received his sentence and was led away, Lyulph Stanley shaking his hand as he passed and Mollie falling in behind as he neared the Norman Porch. A proclamation was read dissolving the court. Halsbury broke the white rod over his knee to symbolise the end of his stewardship (though rather unheroically; to the amusement of many, he almost toppled back into his chair as the staff resisted his best efforts). The whole trial had lasted less than two hours; rather an anti-climax after the weeks of build-up in the press.

Frank was removed to Holloway spitting with anger and indignation. His speech was not the one he would have chosen. He would have liked to have said he'd had no choice but to act as he did to get rid of the 'horrible woman' to whom he was tied; that Mabel had known all about it; that his actions had hurt no one; that his being picked out for prosecution was unfair; and that the peers had acted like sheep in not challenging his sentence. Later, when Lord Monkswell called the sentence severe, Frank chastised him for not speaking up at the time. Sympathy after the event did him even less good than Halsbury's on the day, and for the first few weeks of his incarceration, he paced his cell like a tiger, 'raging with fury and with a thwarted and impotent sense of kicking against the pricks', convinced that had he been plain John Russell, tried at the Old Bailey, he would have been sentenced to a token single day's imprisonment.[13] This was a rather bold assertion. Though the *Proceedings of the Old Bailey* clearly show there was no such thing as an average sentence for bigamy – the scope for wrongdoing being vast – there are recognisable patterns in sentencing which strongly suggest that Frank's apparent flouting of the law and his claiming ignorance of wrongdoing worked against him as much as Mollie's complicity and Mabel's behaviour (abhorred but not criminal) worked in his favour and, everything considered, his sentence was regarded as fair.[14]

After the event, Frank described his incarceration in Holloway as 'restful and agreeable' once he had calmed down and squeezed out of the system a few extra perks. He exercised with fellow first-division prisoners and enjoyed 'ample' meals brought in from outside and served by 'magnificent attendants in the King's uniform'. He read the complete works of Shakespeare – twice – and refamiliarized himself with his Bible, agnostic though he was by then.[15] At the same time, he caused the Home Office continuous irritation. First, there was a petition for his release submitted by Frank himself only nine days into his imprisonment. It contained all his previous objections substantiated by a letter from Nevada attorney William Vanderlieth, citing cases that demonstrated Judge Curler's error and crying 'shame' at the English legal system. Then there were claims that Frank's health and business interests were suffering and that Mollie's fragile heart would not take the strain, but none of these were sufficient reasons for an early release. Then followed a petition to remove the grille between him and Mollie in the visitors' room, which made their time together 'difficult and irksome', affected his 'health and spirits' and strained his weak eyes. It was supported by a marvellous letter from Mollie, simply signed 'Mollie Russell' which threw the department into chaos as to how they should address her in their reply: 'Countess Russell' was clearly wrong, 'Mrs Russell' implied recognition of the marriage, and 'Mollie' was far too informal. If they dared to continue to call her 'Mrs Somerville', no doubt she would voice her indignation to the press. After a flurry of memos, they decided not to reply at all and instead allow the removal of the grille.[16]

Other petitions for Frank's early release followed. The first, from Henry Labouchere, cited Frank's public service record and unfair treatment and boasted a host of diverse signatories – the artist Philip Burne-Jones, author Joseph Conrad, publisher William Heinemann, a war correspondent, the Lord Mayor of Dublin and at least two MPs. A second, containing ninety-six signatures from various members of the professional class (and claiming also to have been signed by Judge Curler himself; though curiously this page had gone missing), recalled Frank's extreme provocation and ignorance of wrongdoing. A further twenty-three signatures were later added, including those of a number of churchmen (of various denominations), two jewellers, an innkeeper, a draper and several of Frank's cousins. A third petition was really just a letter sent in ahead of the collection of signatures asking if the Home Secretary would receive a third appeal. It was probably very sensible: he remained unyielding.

Then there was a request that Frank should be allowed to see his own doctor. Frank had befriended Dr Scott, the Holloway physician who had obstructed the questioning of Kast during the libel trial, to the extent that they were often to be found in each other's company and would 'make the prison ring with shouts of laughter'[17] but there was no comfort like seeing your own medical man. Permission was granted and the result, unsurprisingly, was another petition. Frank's health, which had once been described as inconveniently and disadvantageously strong, was now (apparently) threatening to break down. The immovable Home Secretary demanded a second opinion and Frank, as a result, stayed put. Subsequent letters from Mollie were ignored through embarrassment, confusion and irritation.

Meanwhile, on the outside, various government departments argued over the spoils of the trial. Within hours of its completion, the First Commissioner of Works received a letter from the Lord Great Chamberlain claiming the furniture and fittings as a privilege of his office. What he intended to do with them he did not say, but apparently a precedent had been set with previous trials that he was keen to continue. The commissioner was astonished: 'I cannot think that this contention is seriously put forward – in the year 1901!' he exclaimed. It was an 'absurd and antediluvian system' which he wished to upset. The King had disallowed perquisites for the forthcoming coronation, and he didn't see why this should be any different. Unfortunately, the Lord Great Chamberlain didn't agree and another flurry of letters and memos ensued, which continued almost as long as Frank's incarceration and ended with his acceptance of three 'ordinary (worn) chairs – not the gorgeous arm-chairs' which were all the first commissioner would begrudgingly concede.[18]

As regards family, with Lady Stanley's death in 1895 and Lady John's in 1898, it fell to subsequent generations to comment on Frank's fate. This time the Stanleys came to the fore, differing in their views as might be expected. Lyulph made a very public display of support at the trial, Maude wrote to say Frank got what he deserved, Algernon dissociated himself from the couple considering them 'not really married' and Blanche told friends the whole thing 'haunts' her, while her eldest daughter (also Blanche) wrote to Frank that his sentence had been given 'of necessity, but with regret' and that all her sympathies were with him.[19] Edward VII's involvement is impossible to prove. Mollie's lack of prosecution for the same crime might suggest Frank's scapegoating, but might equally be the result of a general reluctance to prosecute female bigamists. The fact that Frank was officially pardoned for his crime the year after Edward's death might also seem suspicious, were it not for certain family connections. By 1911, when Frank received his pardon, the Home Secretary responsible for securing it was one Winston Churchill, by then the son-in-law of Frank's cousin Blanche who had written to him in prison extending him her sympathies. Either way, the 'desperate expedient', trial and conviction achieved the desired ends. On 24 June 1901, the day before the true bill was returned against Frank at the Old Bailey, George Somerville was granted his decree *absolute* and on 28 October, eleven days after Frank's release from Holloway, Mabel got hers. It was a fact that did not escape notice.

The sharp-eyed Georgina Weldon – the cause of the passing of the 1884 Matrimonial Causes Act, who had spent the intervening years badgering the Home Office over various litigations – wrote to Frank in the wake of his trial, claiming he need have looked no further than one of her own cases to find his defence; that he was guilty of nothing more than gammoning Nevada State and could not have been found guilty of bigamy in England 'if you did not want to be'. The whole spectacle was 'a trick for *your* advantage' she told him, and his three-month imprisonment and the £30,000 it had cost him in fees over twelve years the necessary price of his freedom.[20] Her observations are easy to dismiss from a legal perspective, but in essence, she is not wrong.[21] Frank did need the divorce court to condemn him a bigamist to give Mabel her second marital crime. His gamble was that the criminal court would turn a blind eye. Either way, it is fair to say that Frank put his freedom to better use than Mabel. At 10 a.m. on Thursday 31 October 1901 at Holborn Register Office, Frank married Mollie to the authorities' satisfaction, witnessed by her son, Stanley, solicitors Doulton and Withers, and their good friend from the Pharos club, Amy Otter. Frank wore his habitual frock coat, accessorised with buttonhole and top hat, and Mollie, a neat travelling dress. It was a ceremony without occasion: a formality in Frank's eyes.

Mabel, meanwhile, believed that in summer 1902, on the fashionable reaches of the Thames, she had caught the eye of royalty. On 19 December, she married Prince Athrobald Stuart de Modena in a private ceremony at Southsea Register Office only to discover that he was not the thirty-one-year-old heir to the Austrian Emperor's mighty fortune, but the considerably less exotic William Brown, a twenty-six-year-old footman who had charmed his way into polite society, married Mabel and then (presumably thinking better of it) fled to Madeira. On his return in April 1903, he gave himself up and appeared at Portsmouth police court charged with giving false information on the marriage register. The fraudster smiled and laughed his way through the proceedings and Lina, who still made good press, was quoted word for word in the *Standard*, describing how she and Mabel had been taken in and eventually disabused of their error rather ignominiously by the secretary of London's fashionable Empress Club. Brown was indicted, remanded in custody and charged three months later at Winchester assizes. He pleaded guilty and was sentenced to time already served. After a brief and almost unbelievable reconciliation, Mabel found herself back in the divorce courts, claiming cruelty and adultery. The case went undefended and the last that was heard of Brown was when he appeared on a debtor's charge in January 1904 in Toronto, Canada, for which he blamed Mabel's non-payment of £3,000 she had promised him to collude in the divorce.

It was, too, the last that was heard of Mabel, who quietly retired with Lina to Bray, where (if Frank is to be believed) she 'continued to live off men' and died of consumption – 'the normal end to a life of that kind' – on 29 September 1908 at the tender age of thirty-nine.[22] A year later, Lina followed.

20

The Fox without a Tail

Frank had not been idle during his incarceration. On Thursday 17 October 1901, when he emerged through the portal of Holloway Prison, he carried with him a manuscript of *Lay Sermons* written within. He did not see, he later said, why John Bunyan should be the only man to write a book in prison and, finding himself with time on his hands, had taken the opportunity to develop some ideas he had long held. It was not, however, in the spirit of Bunyan that he sat down to write – 'mine own self to gratify' – but rather as an avowed agnostic to preach to those 'revolted by dogma' that a high degree of religious feeling and irreproachable moral code needn't depend on orthodoxy.[1] The resultant twenty-two sermons, provocatively addressed from Holloway Prison, were reminiscent of his juvenile religious discussions with Lionel Johnson and published within weeks of Johnson's sudden and tragic death. Johnson had moved to London after Oxford, been a founder member of the Rhymer's Club, had two volumes of poems published and numerous criticisms, but his health had been poor and the familial gout from which he suffered, assisted by the alcohol he had used since Oxford to overcome chronic insomnia, had done its worst, leaving both hands and feet painfully crippled and affecting his heart. He died of a stroke on 3 October 1902, having fallen in a pub four days earlier and hit his head, knocking himself unconscious. Collections of his poems and criticisms appeared continuously during the first twenty years of the twentieth century and today Johnson still holds a place as an important if somewhat overshadowed member of the decadence movement.

Frank's *Lay Sermons*, by comparison, were considered 'not profound, nor very brilliantly written' but 'direct, lucid, pointed, and sincere'.[2] They offered the reader advice on personal conduct and their children's education, warned against succumbing to the sins of personal vengeance or lust and praised the value of supplication in prayer and living in sympathy and tolerance with mankind. Given his history, said Santayana, they could easily have been dismissed as 'cant and hypocrisy', yet here was Frank 'blurting out his sincerest convictions, like any poor man ranting in Hyde Park', asking – or rather, demanding – to be taken seriously.[3] Even so, their publication was considered somehow regrettable. It was audacious for a childless man to recommend an upbringing remarkably reminiscent of his own and dangerous for a member of the nobility to credit Walt Whitman's understanding of God over that of the Established Church. Public perception of agnosticism as akin to atheism rendered his preaching confusing and some of his questions appeared to seek moral justification for his own behaviour. In one example, he asked whether a man long married, on realising what he felt for his wife was 'mere companionship', ought not to tell her:

> ... would he be right to stifle his passion for another woman and save the pain and scandal for his wife and children: or is he in doing so false to the highest and truest instincts of nature, and preparing a life for himself in which, day by day, he must wither by killing the imperious God-given desire for the fullest of life, and act a living lie in continuing to live with an unloved mate?[4]

In all bar the legal bond, this described perfectly his predicament with Mary and Mollie. Consciously or otherwise, he had chosen this watershed moment in his life to address the 'curiously distorted view' the world had of him as philanderer, sodomite and bigamist by publicly espousing his self-determined egocentric morals; seeking the world's acceptance while refusing to court its approval. The net result was that Frank's beliefs were judged as being 'in a transition state'. It was deemed a pity he did not wait until they were 'fully formed' before publishing.[5]

There was nothing half-baked, however, about his opinions on English divorce law and, in a bid to turn the catastrophe of his early adult years into something meaningful, his next act was to take on the upholders of its injustices in their bastion of class and creed: the House of Lords.

Frank was not the first to attempt divorce law reform. In 1892, William Hunter, MP for Aberdeen, had presented a private member's bill in the Commons to bring English law in line with that north of the border. Scottish law treated men and women equally as regards offence and relief and had since 1573 allowed divorce for desertion as well as adultery. Hunter argued the inequality of the English law was immoral.[6] His speech was heard by a half-empty house with some sympathy but also resentment that a Scottish member should attempt to reform English law. The bill stalled after a scathing attack from the attorney general. In the ten years between this and Frank's first attempt, there were no other official challenges.

On 1 May 1902, in his first major speech in the Lords, Frank introduced his own divorce bill, well aware that his far-reaching proposal would neither be welcomed nor encouraged. He did not, however, anticipate its contemptuous reception. He had resisted proposing reform while still extricating himself from Mabel, aware that such an action might be misconstrued as not entirely disinterested. That settled, he now considered that time served at his majesty's pleasure exonerated him and he would no longer (as Frank himself put it) be taken for the fox who had lost his tail.[7] He was wrong.

The bill was not so much an amendment as a complete rewriting of the Matrimonial Causes Act. Its proposals, though familiar today, were considered radical bordering on revolutionary.[8] In an eighty-minute speech, Frank told his fellow peers that his bill had not been hastily prepared, but drafted over three years after eight spent considering the question. Apparently unconcerned about offending the lords spiritual, he told them that the root of the problem was the failure of the 1857 Act to separate the actions of the civil court from those of the Ecclesiastical Court before it. It had been rushed through Parliament to no one's satisfaction. He now proposed a detached common-sense approach befitting the modern age. Marriage was a civil contract: so should divorce be. Accordingly, he proposed that in addition to adultery there should be five further individual grounds that would qualify *either* a husband or wife for a full divorce: cruelty, three years' penal servitude, incurable lunacy, three years' living apart, or one year if both parties agreed. Also, that a wife should be able to sue a co-respondent for damages as a husband then could; that judicial separation and restitution of conjugal rights be abolished; that county courts be given jurisdiction over cases of those with an income of £500 p.a. or less; and that the time between the decrees *nisi* and *absolute* should be reduced to one month if there was no appeal.

Other clauses dealt with procedural changes to liberate civil courts from the last vestiges of ecclesiastical law and addressed marriage law in general. The only aspects of the 1857 Act that remained untouched were those providing for nullity suits and settlement of property.

Frank's justification for such widespread reform hinged on three guiding principles: morality, conformity and equality. He condemned the 1857 Act as an uncomfortable compromise between differing interpretations of Christ's teaching on the sanctity of marriage and its indissolubility. He endeavoured to prove how un-radical his proposals actually were by quoting people he regarded as more palatable and influential – Gladstone, for example, who had said during the 1857 debate that a husband's adulterous practices were actively endorsed and a wife's unchastity condoned by inequality. Frank argued that as the law stood, if *both* parties committed adultery, they were condemned to remain married despite their being no clearer indication that the marriage bond was broken.

On the immorality of judicial separation, Frank quoted Palmerston's view that it tempted both parties to form 'undesirable' connections. To this he added his own opinion that judicial separation was an 'illusory remedy ... wholly inapplicable to the nature of the offence' which condemned innocent parties to live 'a mutilated life, without a home, a spouse, or a family, or the chance of obtaining any'. In 1857, the Bishop of Exeter had described it as a remnant of Rome – Frank questioned whether it should be allowed to remain in a Protestant country. As the abandoned spouse was often the wife, he asked their lordships to consider the hardship and wretchedness she suffered in being denied the opportunity to remarry, to take a new husband to protect her. It was their duty, he argued, to offer her protection in law who had no means of protecting herself. To not do so was to be 'cold, unfeeling, barbarous'. In allowing a full divorce for cruelty or wilful desertion – or desertion by other means, such as a long-term imprisonment or permanent confinement in an insane asylum – his bill would right these wrongs and bring English divorce laws in line with those in other Christian countries. It was 'ridiculous' to determinedly ignore the example set by Scotland's more liberal laws. She was not overrun with divorce suits, as many feared England would be if the laws were relaxed; neither were Scots considered more immoral. Frank asked only for conformity of laws within our own union.

In other clauses, however, he was undeniably asking for much more than conformity. By proposing divorce by mutual consent, he was introducing the concept of no-blame divorce for the first time. People made mistakes, he argued, and should be allowed to correct them. Further, extending jurisdiction to county courts would facilitate divorce for huge swathes of the population catered for only in theory by the 1857 Act.[9] For Frank, equality meant more than between the sexes; the law should be democratic across the classes. Yet with the cost of the average undefended case being £50 to £150, increasing exponentially for defended cases, nine-tenths of the population were effectively excluded; especially when the expense of having to travel to London, bring witnesses and provide them with board and lodgings was considered.

Frank's speech was greeted with stony silence. Halsbury's face 'betokened storm ... [His wrath] growing on him, whether he would or not' as Frank spoke 'without apparent embarrassment' and Mollie looked on from the Peeress's Gallery. When he stood to make his customary response, the 'bellicose little Lord Chancellor did not mince his words'.[10] He first announced his regret that such a bill had been introduced. It practically sought 'the abolition of the institution of marriage'. The clause advocating divorce by mutual consent was an 'outrage' on their House and an 'insult' to them personally. As such, he declined to discuss 'a great many of the other topics which might fairly be the subject of discussion' and moved not that the second reading of the bill should be postponed for a period of months, as was the polite manner in which unwanted bills were shelved, but for its immediate rejection; in this he received unanimous consent.

It was certain, said the *Leeds Mercury*, 'that there was no other peer who would have ventured to present such a bill ... with such comparative unconcern'. It was not a compliment. The *Manchester Courier* agreed that Frank deserved his dressing down. Even the radical *Daily News*, then populated with friends from the Pharos, said that Frank had gone too far. Treating marriage so lightly was 'to strike a deadly blow at national morals'.

Divorce, at present, 'is associated with shame and exposure'. To relieve it of such would make it popular.

Frank, however, was undeterred. He immediately retaliated in a debate at the Pharos, denouncing Halsbury's response as an attempt to abolish free speech and deliberately misrepresent his bill. Then on 15 December, he presided over the first meeting of his rather cumbersomely named Society for Promoting Reforms in the Marriage and Divorce Laws of England. The meeting was well attended and it was quickly agreed that the society take up Frank's proposals. Such reform, Frank told the assembly, would end such practices as 'mug hunting' among the lower classes, where a wife provoked her husband into cruelty in front of a witness and then took him to a local court to secure a separation and maintenance order before setting up in sin with another man at his expense.[11] It would end the habit among the wealthy of employing keyhole detectives, bribing servants and publishing their shameful evidence. There would be no more adultery, and morality would improve in general. They were high ideals valiantly presented, said the *Daily News*, but still frightening to contemplate.

Emboldened by the society's support, in a move described by cultural historian Samuel Hynes as admirable for its courage, Frank returned to the House the following year, defying the lords spiritual and the Lord Chancellor with a second draft.[12] It was not dissimilar to the first, with the exception that he had removed divorce by mutual consent. Again, Frank made a long speech, opening with the jibe that his previous attempt – 'reasonable, temperate, logical, and respectful to this House' – would have been successful had it not been for Halsbury's 'remarkable observations', 'apparent fury' and 'lack of courtesy in debate'. He therefore hoped that, having removed the offending clause, he could expect the Lord Chancellor's support.

This time, Frank did not rely on speeches made in the 1857 debate, but went back to the Reformation and a document entitled the *Reformatio Legum Ecclesiasticarum*, prepared in 1552 to define Henry VIII's overhaul of ecclesiastical laws. Frank claimed it would have become law under Edward VI but for his untimely death and the reinstatement of a papist regime under Queen Mary. In dealing with marital crimes, it would have abolished judicial separation and allowed divorce for desertion and what it called 'mortal enmities'. It had been prepared by 'divines and lawyers of the highest authority' and was acceptable to the Church.[13] Frank's new proposal sought only to bring into law that which Queen Mary refused. By granting divorce for three years' separation, he denied that he sought to abolish the institution of marriage, but simply to terminate marriages which had already ceased to be in everything but the legal tie. He reinforced his argument with passages from the 'vast mass of correspondence' he had received in the previous year from ordinary folk let down by the law, and submitted to the House that his revised bill was 'an honest attempt to remedy an intolerable state of things' for the good of morality. He begged the House to consider that every judicial separation threw upon the world two potential adulterers, cautioning them that 'it is easy to legislate for human nature, but it is less easy to control it after your legislation'. In an impassioned plea, he asked:

> Is there no one in this House who feels that this state of things needs a remedy? Are your Lordships satisfied, because in your individual cases the law may not bear hardly upon you, to leave such a blot upon the social legislation of this country? The proposals which I have put before you, and I say this unhesitatingly, make for the increase of social purity ... make marriage a more real thing than it is as present, and ... adultery looked upon, as it is not often looked upon now, as a disgraceful, a discreditable, and an unnecessary crime.

The noble lords received the challenge as they had the rest of the speech: by 'straining their ingenuity in devising attitudes and expressions to convey their frigid displeasure'. Halsbury sat unmoved, with 'eyes fixed in a faraway meditative gaze at the ceiling'. All eyes avoided Mollie, who again boldly took her seat in the Peeress's Gallery; and as Frank retook his own on the 'radical' side of the House, 'cheery-faced, boyish, and self-possessed', he smiled down at a subdued but impenitent Lord Chancellor.[14]

'I do not propose to repeat what I said [last year],' Halsbury began, 'but I adhere to every word.' Frank did not appear to him 'to understand the gravity of what he is doing' in proposing a bill which dismissed all the wisdom of the legislature passed down to the present time. He denied his prior language was too strong and repeated his assertion that Frank's bill was an insult to their Christian assembly. He called once again for its rejection on the basis that it was 'only in the nature of a protest by himself'. A second reading was once again unanimously denied.

The difficulty was that there was no appetite for reform of such a highly contentious cross-party issue in either House. Divorce, it was argued, affected a very small percentage of the population yet still threatened to challenge the moral foundation of society. The kind of transparency that Frank espoused was too much for the Edwardians, who clung to Victorian values in a desperate bid to resist inevitable change. As the renowned stage actress Mrs Patrick Campbell so aptly put it, you can do what you like in the bedroom, as long as you don't bring it out into the street and frighten the horses. Frank had already been perceived as doing just that through the courts.[15] Now he was seen as attempting it again in the Lords. A less conceited man might have stuck the remnants of his tail between his legs, hung his head and walked away, but Frank had the reform bit between his teeth and was determined not to be thwarted, believing wholeheartedly that he had morality if not God on his side. For a while his was a lone voice, but slowly (and somewhat less confrontationally) others began to take up the cause.

In 1904, a young graduate of Lincoln's Inn asked John J. Withers to introduce him to Frank. His name was Edmund Sydney Pollock Haynes. He would, in due course, become well known as E. S. P. Haynes, a writer, lawyer and legal critic with much to say on the subject. He quickly joined Frank's society, became his secretary in 1905 and in 1906 was instrumental in its amalgamation with the recently formed Divorce Law Reform Association. The new society – the Divorce Law Reform Union (DLRU) – secured the support of many 'persons of position', quickly boasting over 300 members with one single objective: to press for a Royal Commission to investigate options for reform. The suggestion that Frank take the helm, however, was dispatched by several influential members who refused to remain in a society led by a convicted bigamist. With his name considered prejudicial to the cause, Frank was asked to take a back seat, and the businessman W. Ramsay Fairfax took over, eventually being replaced by Sir Arthur Conan Doyle.

None of this prevented Frank continuing his personal campaign. On 1 August 1905 he was back in the Lords proposing a *third* amendment to the law, this time 'very considerably modified … in deference to the feelings of the House'.[16] His new bill proposed only one alteration: divorce for desertion – not after three years to conform with Scotland, but after two – the qualifying period for a judicial separation under English law. He recommended it by referring them to an article from the *Times*, which, he quipped, could 'not be accused of being a revolutionary newspaper'. Commenting on a case in which a husband was found to have unlawfully (albeit kindly) abducted and imprisoned his wife at home after she failed to comply with his restitution order, the *Times* asked why, if her living apart from him were condoned by the court, he should not 'in common justice' be completely free of her and able to marry again: 'Freedom is a very fine thing, but let it not be one-sided.'[17]

Frank's change of tack appealed directly to their lordships' gentlemanly sympathies and pocketbooks. He toned down his previous rhetoric, acknowledging that it was the government's responsibility to suggest reform in line with public opinion and advising the House that his purpose in bringing this bill was simply to give their lordships the opportunity to consider 'whether any remedy is needed' and what that remedy might be. Perhaps less wisely, he also told them that he did this as a free-thinker resentful of Church control over the State. Nevertheless, he sought to assure Halsbury that he was not 'thirsting to avail' himself but rather to use his personal experiences to do 'all I can to prevent other people undergoing unnecessary suffering'. He thereby successfully avoided Halsbury's wrath if failing to soften his resolve. The usual niceties restored, the second reading of the bill was politely deferred for three months.

By this time, it was no longer idle to suggest that public opinion was swinging towards reform. Influential names were gradually being added to the cause, and none more so than the president of the divorce division himself, Sir John Gorell Barnes. In April 1906, in his summing up of *Dodd* v. *Dodd*, Gorell Barnes made a damning indictment of the whole system as being 'full of inconsistencies, anomalies, and inequalities almost amounting to absurdities'. He further suggested that any reform that did not abolish judicial separation, place the sexes on an equal footing and permit divorce for offences that 'render future cohabitation impractical' would be inadequate; like Frank, he felt that such reform would 'largely tend to greater propriety'.[18]

Armed with Gorell Barnes' comments and Haynes' speech writing skills, Frank returned to the Lords for one final appeal on 22 July 1908.[19] By this time, Frank's association with the DLRU had convinced him that the only way forward was for a Royal Commission; and by rights, it was his to argue for. The last commission on the subject had been sanctioned by his grandfather, Lord John, and resulted in the passing of the 1857 Act. Now Frank told the House that the Liberal government ought to have taken up the cause after their landslide victory in 1906. He called their lordship's attention to it because the government had not. He considered the situation critical when some 7,000 separation and maintenance orders were issued each year and when a man in Gorell Barnes' position felt it necessary to make so 'explicit and clear a statement' against the existing laws.[20]

His argument could no longer be denied. Even in his negative response, the Lord Bishop of Bristol went so far as to say that a Royal Commission 'which will tend rather to stringency than leniency' was necessary. Lord Loreburn, who had succeeded Halsbury as Lord Chancellor, continued his predecessor's condemnation of Frank's reforms and a second reading of the bill was overwhelmingly defeated, but it no longer signified. Gorell Barnes had accepted a peerage in January 1909, giving him a voice in legal reforms. In July he secured a Royal Commission in exchange for dropping a motion for county court jurisdiction over divorces for the poor. In October 1909, it was announced that Lord Gorell himself would be its chairman.[21]

Far from advocating stringency, the commission's majority report came down in favour of reform. The commission heard evidence from a vast array of witnesses between February and December 1910 from all churches, from legal professionals (including Frank), the press, police, medical officials, and other activists. Its report was published two years later in November 1912. On three points they unanimously agreed: local court provision for the poor, equality of the sexes in offence and relief, and a form of censorship to preserve morality, such as giving a judge discretion to close the court during part of a case or restrict reporting, with pictorial representations absolutely prohibited. On extending the grounds for divorce they were generally in favour, but not unanimously. Their recommendations echoed all those voiced by Frank in 1902 – divorce for cruelty, three years' wilful desertion, incurable insanity and imprisonment under commuted death sentence – further extending them to include habitual drunkenness after three years' failure to reform. The leniency of their recommendations led to criticisms from the minority that in providing means for the dissolution of more or less any marriage that had broken down, whether irretrievably or not, they were in all but name offering divorce by mutual consent without any religious principle underpinning their policy; this argument was strengthened by the majority report's unfortunate reference to the 'reasonable meaning' of the expression 'for better, for worse' which was picked up by critics and used against them.[22]

The publication of the commission's report coincided with a flurry of books on the subject, including Frank's aptly titled *Divorce* (1912) in which he reiterated the position he had unswervingly held for the previous ten years. In its preface he was unrestrained, unequivocally stating that his purpose in regaling the reader with a brief history of the ecclesiastical basis for divorce was to demonstrate that 'many features of the present law, some merely quaint, others undesirable and oppressive, would never have been introduced by a sane politician or jurist into a code of divorce written upon a blank page' and making no apology for the 'occasional strong expressions of dissent from the idea that people living in the twentieth century are still to be subject to ecclesiastical tyranny'.[23] *Divorce* was advertised in the *Globe* as 'the best book on the most important subject of the day', highlighting Frank's 'unusual general ability, legal training and personal experience' which uniquely positioned him to give a 'lucid explanation' of the law's anomalies.[24] It was generally well received in the radical press – the *Guardian* praising it as a welcome follow-up to Frank's 'serious and minute study' of the subject demonstrated in his 'four carefully drafted bills', and the *Observer* applauding its low-cost accessibility (it retailed at 2s 6d as compared to 7s 6d for Kitchin's *History of Divorce* published the same year).[25] Even the *Daily News*, which had balked at his reform proposals in 1902, expressed the opinion that Frank's views were 'not very terrible and are well worth consideration' – at least as far as equality, insanity and imprisonment were concerned.

The chief practical interest in *Divorce* was the county court proposal; the most questionable was divorce by mutual consent.[26] On this, Frank was frightening the horses again; not this time by raising the ugly spectre of homosexuality but by lifting the veil on heterosexual promiscuity. Adultery was rife in smart society, he wrote, but couples came to private arrangements so the public never heard of them. Among the working classes, the situation was the same, but their actions were hidden from scrutiny by their inability to afford court fees. If one faced up to the reality that judicially separated couples would not remain celibate, then every order let loose four potential adulterers. Further, knowing that any prospective legislation was wholly in the hands of men, he attempted to scare his readers into backing reform by drawing their attention to the potential dangers of the current situation. As the law stood, a judicially separated wife could set up in an adulterous relationship with another man and her husband would be unable to divorce her, having already been found guilty of a marital crime himself. Another wife could effectively hold her husband to ransom by acknowledging his aggravated adultery but refusing to sue him for anything more than judicial separation, thereby vindictively binding him to her for life. These unscrupulous wives needed legislating against, he suggested, and his proposal for abolishing judicial separation and widening the grounds for divorce would solve the problem. His argument was absolutely factually correct, but not everyone was persuaded. The conservative press ignored the book completely.

It should not be assumed that reform swiftly followed; in fact, quite the opposite. Whatever justifications there were, divorce remained a hugely controversial issue with many opponents. The Church exerted its influence in the Lords through the bishops, and the press were not impartial. The *Times* summarised both the majority and minority commission reports for their readers, but also printed the latter in full and distributed it as a free supplement to all its readers. Meanwhile, in the Commons, despite their huge majority, the Liberal government delayed. The issue was inextricably linked with others culminating at the same time: 'contraception threatened the family and the birth rate, divorce threatened the Church and the stability of society, suffrage threatened political balances, and so even the most moderate move toward liberation seemed a rush towards chaos'.[27] In novels and plays, unhappy marriages were remedied by free love or divorce or both.[28] Freedom of choice became the battle cry of the new century, and the fact that Frank's book challenged polite society to acknowledge what went on behind closed doors and highlighted the comparatively liberal divorce laws across Europe did nothing to calm anxieties. It was of no concern to the British government that Belgium offered divorce for 'unwavering and legal expression of parties that their common life is insupportable', or that in France 'continued refusal' was sufficient, or in Germany, 'insuperable aversion'. Variances with British colonies cut as little ice as those with Scotland. Criticisms and arguments over the majority commission report gave the government reasons aplenty for procrastination. Very soon, the Great War gave them another.

All the recommendations Frank made in 1902 eventually became law, but regrettably he did not live to see it. After the war, reform came slowly and painfully. It took the exertions of another peer, Viscount Buckmaster, to bring anything like a workable solution – though his suggestion of divorce after five years' separation was still too radical for the House in 1918.[29] In the end, reform was piecemeal. By the terms of the 1920 Administration of Justice Act, poor persons' and undefended cases could be heard at some Assizes. By the mid-1930s nearly half of all divorce petitions were heard locally. Despite the leniency of the Royal Commission report, the only amendment instigated by the 1923 Matrimonial Causes Act was to place men and women on equal footing as regards divorce for adultery. Societies continued to apply pressure though differed in their goals, with Frank switching allegiance from the cautious DLRU who refused to back divorce by mutual consent to become a vice-president of the Marriage Law Reform League. A certain amount of press control was exerted by the Regulation of Reports Act 1926, in the interest of public morals. E. S. P. Haynes and many others continued to write on the subject, including Bertrand Russell in *Marriage and Morals* (1929). Yet it was not until 1937 that the subtle manoeuvrings and compromises of Alan Herbert MP saw grounds for divorce widened to include three years' wilful desertion, cruelty, and incurable insanity of five years' duration. The compromise 'in true support of marriage' was that a couple must have been married for three years before a petition could be filed. The inclusion of insanity effectively introduced the first no-blame divorce; mutual consent would finally be legislated in 1969 for marriages that had 'irretrievably broken down'. Today, mutual consent after two years living apart is sufficient. The interval between decrees *nisi* and *absolute* was reduced from six months to six weeks in 1946. Within 100 years of the first Matrimonial Causes Act, over 90 per cent of all petitions went undefended. Within three years of the 1969 Act, the number of divorces per annum exceeded 100,000 for the first time. Arguments as to the morality of divorce and its impact on society continue to rage.

21

Great Reform Acts

Divorce reform was not the only cause Frank took on during this period. Finding himself at last with a stable, supportive home life and free of the burden and distraction of costly lawsuits, the first ten years of his and Mollie's marriage were immensely productive. The causes he chose were as diverse as they were ambitious, but if they had a common element it was that each raised the hackles of his deeply embedded sense of injustice and involved an underdog for whom Frank became a self-appointed spokesman. His commitment once given never wavered.

His next campaign had its foundations in the exclusive gentleman's world of motoring where underdogs might be considered scarce. In 1899, Frank had spent £20 on life membership of the fledgling Automobile Club of Great Britain and Northern Ireland (AC), then in its third year and eight away from receiving its royal charter to become the renowned RAC. The AC was 'the arbiter of automobilism in all its aspects' and Frank, at one time or another, sat on all its committees.[1] It provided a clubhouse for its members where a gentleman could relax without 'company manners' (ladies were permitted between 3 p.m. and 6 p.m. and confined to the General Reception Room). It protected members' and trade interests, organised runs, hill climbs and rallies. AC road maps and route planners pinpointed automobile-friendly hotels, opening up the countryside as never before. By so doing, it quickly attracted negative attention. Woodrow Wilson once said that nothing spread socialistic feeling in America faster than the motor car; Piers Brendon, the RAC's biographer, said the same applied to England, where the motor car 'brazenly, noisily and intrusively brought class-distinction to [the commoner's] door'.[2] Very soon, the automobilist became, in Frank's words, an 'object of hatred', living in 'an atmosphere of persecution'[3] – the pestilent Toad of Kenneth Graeme's *Wind in the Willows* (1908), hurtling down country lanes, driving other users off the road.

Self-defence, then, became a requisite part of automobilism. From as early as 1898, the AC found itself defending members against police speed traps. Benignly, it discouraged 'scorchers', clocked at dizzying speeds of over 20 mph when the limit on open roads was 14 mph, with the threat of expulsion for 'ungentlemanly' or 'unsportsmanlike' driving 'prejudicial to the interests of automobilism'.[4] But as technology advanced, a growing number of second-hand cars were bought by middle-class motorists outside club control. The AC sought to bring them under its influence (without relinquishing its exclusivity) by founding the Motor Union (MU) in 1901, open to anyone, affiliated to the AC, but denied many of its privileges. It became the uneasy alliance that gave Frank his underdog.

In 1902, Parliament suggested registering motor cars to ease policing of speeding motorists. John Scott Montagu MP – later 2nd Baron Montagu of Beaulieu – the AC's spokesman in the Commons – backed the idea, recommending that the club accept it in exchange for an abolition of speed limits, which had become nonsensical and were largely ignored. There was resistance to the proposal, with some thinking Montagu offered too great a concession. Frank led the revolt. Why should a man have to go about in a 'disfigured' vehicle, 'labelled wherever he goes' when it had not yet been proved that the police were unable to identify offenders without them? All motorists were 'well known by sight', he argued. Further, speed alone was not an accurate measure of 'furious' driving. Frank favoured driver examinations over registration, which branded them all potential lawbreakers and regarded Montagu's position as tantamount to 'a desire to ram the Bill down our throats, and burke all public discussion of its merits'. It would get them no concessions at all, but surrender their power, which, he argued, was then on a par with the Jockey Club's.[5]

In at least one respect, Frank was right: there were no concessions. The Motor Car Act passed easily in September 1903, becoming law on 1 January 1904. It legislated a three-year trial of registration (awarded by local councils at the cost of £1), compulsory driving licences and a 20 mph speed limit, with the facility for local governments to apply for 10 mph limits in certain designated areas. Frank immediately advocated a campaign of resistance. This 'monstrous piece of legislation' should be 'fought by every means possible' he argued in the AC's journal. The AC and MU should punish members who brought motoring into disrepute and appeal every case of apparent prejudiced conviction, applying continuous pressure on MPs and peers until the act be repealed or amended. In a further article for *Autocar*, he nitpicked at the difficulty of keeping the registration plate clean on dirty or dusty roads, and condemned the policy for taking the police 'from their business of repressing crime to swell the county funds by fines for speed in the open country, precisely where no member of the public is endangered'. He used his new legal skills to highlight loopholes in the law that a motorist could use to escape conviction if caught.[6]

The MU (on whose committees Frank also sat) immediately began a plan of campaign to discredit 'pointless' speed checks on safe, straight stretches of country roads. But the AC executive resisted. It had already rejected Frank's proposal that they publish a 'trap map' and establish a code of private signals by which drivers could alert each other to their presence. Through grassroots support, Frank was voted onto the Executive and Publications Committee in January 1904 where he continued to agitate. The Publications Committee met 'in secret' and had 'great power' in editing the mouthpiece of the organisation.[7] Frank secured Edgar Jepson the job of editor. Jepson quickly found himself plunged into 'a world of feuds, intrigues, and jealousies'.[8] In March, Frank travelled to Winchester with Mollie and MU secretary Rees Jeffreys to gather evidence against the city's application for a reduced speed limit within its boundaries.

It is somehow ironic that Frank's beloved Winchester was the first city to apply for the 10 mph restriction, but the anti-lobby was well prepared and the application duly denied. It is doubly ironic that during this expedition Frank was caught speeding and fined £5 plus costs, despite Mollie giving evidence against the 'wobbly and nervous' cyclist who testified to Frank's alleged 20 mph, and Jeffreys' swearing that Frank's Napier could never achieve the 40 mph another witness claimed he had been doing.[9] Still more ironic was the fact that Frank had been caught out by witness recognition of his highly distinctive registration plate: A1.

Ever the pragmatist, when Frank realised that registration was inevitable, he had used his position at the LCC to secure A1. There is an apocryphal tale that Frank secured it by queuing all night outside LCC offices to be first in line when registration began – or that his driver or butler did. Bertrand much later revealed that Frank told him he had simply awarded it to himself. Either way, A1, in suggesting itself as England's first number plate, cemented Frank's motoring credentials.[10] It also caused him no end of bother. Over the next two years, he was caught by Surrey police (renowned for their extreme vigilance) no less than four times. Each time, true to his word, Frank appealed, arguing finicky points of law. On each occasion he lost. His fines increased from £5 to £15. Eventually magistrates threatened to suspend his licence if he persisted in breaking the law. He gained what was to him another undeserved reputation as a 'hooligan driver' singled out for persecution for the active campaign he had waged against Surrey police. In irritation, he sold both car and plate in 1906 to the LCC chairman, Evan Spicer.[11]

Frank's campaign against the police began after he was called to the Bar in May 1905. He found himself handling a large number of briefs for motoring offenders. Some came through the MU; others through the Automobile Association (AA), established by AC dissidents in 1905 with one single agenda: to fight police harassment. Frank immediately joined. The AA planted scouts on roads to warn drivers of speed traps and threw their resources behind member prosecutions. In one significant case, Frank defended a scout prosecuted for perjury. The prosecution accused the scout of lying on behalf of another speeding AA member, saying he had not even witnessed the offence; Frank accused the police of vindictiveness because they knew the man was a scout. The scout was acquitted and Frank rewarded with committee positions and by being asked to draw up club rules. Within a year, their membership had mushroomed from 300 to 3,000, equalling that of the AC and advancing on the 5,000-strong MU.

A common enemy, however, did not heal organisational differences. The AC continued to resist MU demands for equal privileges. When in 1907 the MU began to employ their own AA-style anti-police tactics, the AC, on the cusp of receiving its royal charter, severed all links with them. Angered by their attitude, Frank sided with the MU, resigning his position on the AC executive. At the same time, he accused the AA of becoming 'cautious and respectable' as their numbers swelled. They 'waxed fat and rich', he said, refusing any longer to fight.[12] Seeing no other reason for their existence, Frank resigned his membership. By 1910, the MU was absorbed into the AA and Frank's involvement with the AC no longer extended outside the clubhouse. The 'monstrous' Motor Car Act would stay on the statute books until 1930, when Frank would somewhat unexpectedly get another shot at it.

In the meantime, the law was proving a 'jealous mistress'.[13] Frank did not have the patience necessary to charm his chambers clerk into giving him choice briefs and became somewhat pigeonholed. To underline the point, in 1906 he was approached by James Timewell of the Police and Public Vigilance Society to act for them at the forthcoming Royal Commission inquiry into the duties of the Metropolitan Police. The commission's remit was to investigate accusations of bribery and undue force by officers in cases of drunkenness, disorder and solicitation. It examined nineteen cases, twelve of which came from Timewell. Proceedings ran along the lines of a law court with witnesses allowed counsel. Frank represented all twelve of Timewell's clients and later claimed that it was largely as a result of his cross-examination of policemen that some level of police wrongdoing was proved in half their cases – in one instance, of such severity that a man's urethra was ruptured after he was kicked in the groin by a constable.[14] Nevertheless, the *Times* had 'no hesitation' in reporting that the Metropolitan Police on the whole 'discharge their duties with honesty, discretion and efficiency', and by the time the commission reported, Frank's 'jealous mistress' was taking a back seat to other potentially more rewarding diversions. He and Mollie had taken an apartment at 57 Gordon Square, in the heart of the Bedford Russells' Bloomsbury, and Frank's association with the MU had provided a lucrative business opportunity. After splitting with the RAC in 1907, it had started its own insurance company with Frank as a director. The company was 'extremely successful' under the chairmanship of Lionel Rothschild and the combination of its success and some bad luck with his estates encouraged Frank to broaden his business interests.[15]

As the eldest son, Frank's inheritance had been principally property. He had inherited Ravenscroft and his grandfather's estates in Ireland – 3,265 acres surrounding the beautiful Gothic Ardsallagh House in Navan, County Meath, and 1,107 acres in County Louth, generating an approximate revenue of £4,500 p.a. The house was let to a Mrs Johnston when in May 1903 it was significantly damaged by fire; eight rooms in one wing were almost completely destroyed. The repairs cost Frank £2,300 and a year in court trying to get the Northern Insurance Company to cover his claim. At arbitration, the decision went in his favour, but only to the tune of £1,705 (the arbitrator expressing the opinion that the work could have been done cheaper). It was followed by a further claim from Mrs Johnston of £150 for repairs done during her tenancy which, after much squabbling, Frank was ordered to pay with costs. Whether through necessity or aggravation, Frank sold the property in November 1903 for £31,800, retaining only the land in County Louth.[16] The liquidation of his assets allowed him to speculate further in business.

He took offices at 6 Bond Court, Walbrook, to mark his conversion from law to business and, at first, invested in other insurance companies. At least two became insolvent while he was director, involving him in 'very heavy loss'.[17] A change of direction as chairman of the National Radium Trust, established in 1910 to mine radium and other radioactive substances to supply the medical profession, ended with the company being dissolved in 1912. If it appears his judgement as a 'city gent' was questionable, he was certainly not alone. Historian David Cannadine suggests not only that it was common practice for patricians to invest in business or take 'ornamental' directorates at this time but that their subsequent success or failure was largely pot luck.[18] Association with mining companies was very popular, and in 1911 Frank was awarded a directorate of the Globe & Phoenix Gold Mining Company of Rhodesia with an annual salary of £2,000. But by far his most successful ventures at this time were in motoring. When Humber went public in 1909, Frank became its chairman. It made the national press when he took receipt of a 28hp limousine in 1912, and by 1913 the company was one of the largest UK car manufacturers, second only to Wolseley. For Frank, it resulted in multiple enjoyable trips to the plant in Coventry, a lifelong commitment to Humber cars (including having a 15.9 tourer made especially for him in 1919) and a long association in which he spent at least fifteen years as either chairman or deputy. Only his association with Plenty's of Newbury lasted longer.

The upshot of all of this was that there was money to spend on Telegraph House. As often as business allowed, Frank would be found directing various improvements to the estate while Mollie tended the garden. By the time Santayana visited in August 1909, a large extension had been built and a square tower with windows on all sides. Frank's avenue of copper beeches planted along the drive more than ten years previously were starting to look established and the stables had been converted to garages. A tennis court had been laid, 220 acres of land acquired, and a further exchange of land agreed with his neighbour at Up Park. A private road had been built to ease access from the main road in the valley below, and a second was planned to extend across the estate to the newly acquired Kill Devil Copse. Slowly, TH was becoming the country estate Frank had always coveted. He and Mollie invited friends down from London for bridge and whist parties and, as the prime organiser of the annual South Harting Hill Climb, Frank made the expansive grounds available to competitors – Mollie handing out prizes in the judges' tent while their staff served afternoon tea. Yet, even without such renovations and entertainments, TH under Frank was never quiet. A disgruntled Santayana reported there being 'seven dogs, one cat, and three automobiles, a pumping-engine for water, another for electric light, and a general restlessness in the house'.[19]

The machinery was inevitable. Frank spent his life 'inextricably entangled in motor cars and electrical gadgets'.[20] The dogs were Maltese terriers bred by the housekeeper, Miss Young. Both Frank and Mollie adored them. Whenever they were away from TH, Frank would have Miss Young keep an account of their daily doings. Frank was also responsible for the restlessness. Domestic fulfilment had not blunted the corners of his fastidiousness. The adjectives Santayana once applied to his interactions with Mabel were equally relevant to Mollie. Frank was 'excessively virtuous and incredibly tyrannical' and in their 'intimate relations he was exacting and annoying'.[21] He still had the childlike tantrums that caused his father so much grief and alienated Jowett. The servants often bore the brunt. He gave Miss Young notice 'once a month for several years', accusing her of thinking 'that she owned the place', becoming 'rather unmeasured in her speech, and so inattentive to her duties'.[22] The comments say more about Frank than Miss Young, who lasted many years at TH, was as devoted to Frank as Mollie and had the strength of character to resist his outbursts. Both women knew how to handle him – apparently through a combination of mothering and diplomacy. Mollie genuinely loved him, understood he must be master in his own home yet was never as subservient as her predecessor. In addition, her outside interests afforded them both a degree of independence.

Mollie was grounded. When she became a countess, she did not relinquish her previous causes; neither did she make excessive use of her title. In public and private she always signed herself 'Mollie Russell'. An interview with the *Dundee Courier* in 1904 demonstrates her attitude. Comparing American women with English, she said Americans were over-protected and 'wanting in that self-reliance which is the glory of British women, and the best hope for our freedom'. The American 'rocks as she reads', waiting for her husband to come out of the smoking or billiard room where she is not allowed, 'looking bored, until bedtime comes'. British women would never stand for that; and though American women may be 'for a time the most amusing', the British woman 'wears best ...

she acts, and takes what she wants, and her men respect her for her capability'.[23]

While Frank was otherwise employed, therefore, Mollie was to be found opening bazaars for the Social Democratic Federation and demanding her right to a place in the press gallery of the Commons. She defended female workers' rights, bemoaning their disqualification from careers in medicine, journalism and the law and their lower wages in factories. From here it was a very short step to women's suffrage. Mollie was an 'interested participator' in the discussion following Christabel Pankhurst's speech in Covent Garden in November 1906, afterwards completely converting Frank to the cause.[24] After the collapse of the Pharos, she and Frank started another club in Queen's Square, with a distinctly feminist agenda. There, Mollie spoke on the 'Proper Place for Man', quipping that as men were often heard to declare themselves the best cooks, dressmakers and managers of hotels, they should swap occupations.[25] Later, she would challenge them to give women the authority to govern at home while they occupied themselves with 'Imperial things': 'Let them go on worrying themselves about their Dreadnoughts, but let us have care of the children, so that we can make them physically fit to man them,' she cried. She threw down the gauntlet to prime minister Herbert Asquith to give women more than just a 'vague promise' of the vote.[26]

Asquith would not, as his well-documented battles with the suffragettes testify. Frank and Mollie both disapproved of later suffragette tactics, but both conceded that when the Pankhursts relocated from Manchester to London in 1906, they put women's suffrage on the agenda. Together, they attended the famous spectacle at Bow Street in 1908 when Christabel Pankhurst subpoenaed Herbert Gladstone and Lloyd-George. They spoke out about force-feeding and the atrocious conditions of imprisoned suffragettes, arguing that as political prisoners, they should be sentenced in the first division. But they also both strongly believed in democracy, and when Mrs Despard broke away from the Women's Social and Political Union (WSPU), accusing it of becoming a dictatorship under the Pankhursts, and formed the Women's Freedom League (WFL) in February 1908, Mollie went with her. The WFL espoused 'vigorous agitation' in the form of 'public meetings, demonstrations, debates, distribution of literature, newspaper correspondence, and deputations to public representatives'. It welcomed women of all political persuasions and overtly stated that 'all members must approve, though they need not actively participate in militant actions'.[27] Their version of militancy involved picketing Downing Street and the Commons. They did not disrupt political meetings, assault ministers or (as Mollie so eloquently put it) 'chase Mr Asquith at golf'.[28] Mollie was as active within the organisation as it was possible to be, drawing the line only at actions that threatened imprisonment. By January 1909, she took a seat on three committees: Press, Socials and National Executive. She organised 'At Homes' from the Queen's Square Club, wrote leaflets and became a director of WFL journal *The Vote*. In February 1909, when Miss Muriel Matters famously flew over Parliament in a hot air balloon scattering leaflets on the crowds below, Mollie was on the ground handing out more of the same. But more importantly, with Frank having helped her get over her fear of public speaking, Mollie took to the stage for the WFL and organised public speaking classes from 57 Gordon Square. Fliers show that Mollie's was a veritable UK tour, with speeches as far afield as Tunbridge Wells, Pontypridd and Glasgow. In July, she led a demonstration in Trafalgar Square.

Her speeches were full of wit and fervour, her quick retorts entertaining and her commitment undeniable. She told her Cheltenham audience that 'Votes for Women' was inscribed on her heart and mind and that she would continue to work for it until Asquith had them likewise. 'Don't be afraid of what men will say,' she told them, 'but get as much money as you can out of them.' She challenged women to suffer for the cause; and when a man stood up and shouted, 'I say no!' Mollie retorted, 'There are none of you men capable of doing it.'[29] In London, before the Men's League for Women's Suffrage she turned the tables on female anti-suffragists, keeping the audience laughing with 'a running fire of raillery'.[30]

Frank, meanwhile, found himself addressing both the Men's League and the WFL no less than fifteen times throughout 1908–9 and on numerous occasions thereafter, proving when bombarded with 'many disagreeable home truths' as to the shortcomings of the Liberal government (to which he listened with 'utmost good humour and sympathy') that he was 'a man first and a Liberal second'.[31] He represented suffragists appearing at the police courts and turned down a brief for a Lords judgment against the suffragettes. Nowhere were the Russells more in accord than on this political platform. The same cannot be said for the diverse membership of the WFL. In July 1909, there were differences over the level and nature of militant action carried out by some of its members, and when the Militant Sub-committee was called to task, it transpired that they had no minutes of their meetings to demonstrate which were approved and which not. Mollie proposed that actions resulting in arrest should be temporarily halted; others argued they should continue their assault on the Commons and to make speeches at the gates. It appears there were further differences behind the scenes. Mollie had come to believe that the general public had been made sufficiently aware of their campaign, and that they should shift emphasis away from overt displays of defiance towards consistent petitioning of MPs and peers to monopolise on ground already made. The WSPU, in vowing to fight any party who refused to put women's suffrage on their agenda, had made it impossible for the government to shift its position even if they felt inclined. The WFL should now work to steel the government to do what was necessary. She felt they were in danger of losing public support if they continued to support militancy. Others disagreed, and soon after, Mollie resigned from the National Executive, or was pushed; the last mention of her was on 25 July 1910:

> It was agreed that it would be better to ask the Head of the Propaganda Dept: not to ~~let~~ invite Countess Russell [to] speak on our platform again.[32]

This was disastrous for Mollie and would unwittingly be compounded by Frank's invitation to his friend from the Reform Club – a certain Mr H. G. Wells – to join them at TH for the Easter weekend, 1911. For the invitation would once again set in motion the turbulent tides of Frank's love life with an enticement to Wells that would have dire and unforeseen consequences for his hosts: 'Elizabeth will very likely be coming down by the same train,' Frank wrote, 'but without her German Garden.'[33]

22

Twin Souls

Who, then, was 'Elizabeth'?

It was the question fans and critics alike had wanted answering since the publication of a unique little book called *Elizabeth and Her German Garden* in September 1898, which had been a surprise hit for its anonymous first-time author, achieving twenty-one reprints in its first eight months and sparking such a trend that (as one critic put it) swathes of 'tiresome women' started 'smirking coyly about their gardens as if they were having a remarkably satisfying affair with their delphiniums'.[1] Reviewers found it difficult to classify. It was not a gardening book since it contained no tips of any value to the average grower (yet Mollie would say she started gardening 'after reading with admiration how Elizabeth mastered hers' and that she had planned the gardens of TH in accordance with its schemes[2]). Neither was it a novel, as the absence of plot line and character arcs testify. Rather, it was a witty account in journal form of a novice's attempt to create an unconventional garden around her husband's seventeenth-century *schloss* in Pomerania, strictly in accordance with her own tastes and ignoring all practical considerations. It opens quite simply, 'I love my garden' and after a brief description goes on to record the author's rapturous arrival in a 'world of dandelions and delights'; to tell how she absorbed herself completely in horticulture, forgetting all wifely and motherly duties until her husband – the 'Man of Wrath' – objected. Thereafter, Elizabeth's gardening highs and lows are described alongside the various doings of her family and the comings and goings of uninvited guests, about whom she declares, 'I know little and care less'.[3] Her caustic pen blithely satirised those around her, drawing comparisons with Jane Austen.

The book's expression of independence tapped into the struggle of the 'new woman' for autonomy, quite apart from offering an insider's view of another culture at a time when all things German held a conspicuous attraction. It was an instant hit, but not without critics; the harshest was Arthur Quiller-Couch who wrote in *The Speaker* that though the book's sentimentality 'demands a certain amiability of nature, a certain gentleness of disposition towards its surroundings', Elizabeth revealed in her writing that 'she was not only selfish, but quite inhumanly so', her mind of that order 'which finds a smart self-satisfaction in proclaiming how thoroughly it is dominated by self'.[4] Clearly 'Elizabeth' – whoever she was – repelled those who distrusted 'clever' women. But for those who were 'tantalised by delightful little descriptions of the neighbours, who are never allowed to appear for more than about half a page and are "got rid of after a due administration of tea and things you are sorry afterwards that you said"', there was plenty more to come.[5] A sequel, *Solitary Summer*, appeared in 1899, followed by a novel, *The Benefactress*, in 1901 and then three more publications between 1904 and 1907, by which time 'Elizabeth's' true identity – the secret of which had proved an effective (if unintentional) marketing ploy – was well known.

She was the Countess von Arnim, the daughter of English merchant Henry Beauchamp and his Australian wife, Louey, who was not an 'Elizabeth' at all, but had in fact been christened Mary Annette in 1866 and who, in 1889, had been wooed by the recently widowed Count Henning August von Arnim-Schlagenthin, fifteen years her senior. They had married in 1891 and had five children in ten years – Evi, Liebet, Beatrix, Felicitas and Henning Bernd. Since the publication of *German Garden*, she had moved freely through London's literary circles, which, like so many overlapping spheres on a Venn diagram, eventually brought her into contact with Frank and Mollie. She was known to novelist Marie Belloc Lowndes, with whom Frank had been friends since 1894 and who recalled that, when in London, Elizabeth was often the guest of Frank's aunt, Maude Stanley.[6] Elizabeth was also on intimate terms with Frank's erstwhile would-be guardian Thomas Cobden-Sanderson ('Cobbie') and was well-known to Frank's cousin, Lady Agnes Grove. In 1907, she had been introduced to H. G. Wells, who knew Frank through the NLC and Reform Club. Then, in 1909, she had accepted an invitation to TH, initiating what Mollie described as a 'delightful friendship' based on their mutual love of gardening.[7] By the time Frank issued his invitation to Wells in March 1911, Elizabeth was widowed, had relocated to London, was building a mountain chalet in Switzerland and had for several months been corresponding with Wells in admiration of his most recent work *The New Machiavelli*. Frank's invitation marked the beginning of Elizabeth and Wells' relationship.[8]

So much for 'Elizabeth' the entity; as a person, she was more enigmatic still. Mrs Belloc Lowndes confessed to being greatly puzzled by her. She was 'extremely modest, in fact absurdly modest' about her writing, yet beneath this Marie saw 'a malicious, even a cruel, side in what appeared a guileless nature'.[9] It sometimes revealed itself in her writing. In *The Caravaners* (1909), for example, Elizabeth exposed the chief protagonist – another German – to such 'perpetual ridicule' that critics opined she must have written it 'in a temper with some original', demonstrating an 'elfish malice' which if not so comic would be bitter.[10] Such comments reveal one aspect of a complex personality variously described as fun-loving, self-effacing, quick-witted, musical, dynamic and kind. To her father, she was 'a rare and fascinating combination of dove and serpent'.[11]

In this, as in almost every other respect, she differed 'grotesquely' from the straightforward and outspoken Mollie.[12] In appearance, neither was considered a beauty, though there was much to admire about Elizabeth. She was 'a small, exquisitely made woman, with charming, irregular features', 'rather prominent merciless pale blue eyes' and an 'unusually individual' and 'demurely drawling' voice. Described as 'a very bright and original little lady' with a bewitching personality, she 'bubbled over with humour' and was 'shrewd, wise and witty'.[13] Mollie, by this time, had grown 'fat and florid': 'She toddled about in her loose tea-gowns with her little pack of white lap-dogs about her feet' and was not considered a social success.[14] Neither woman was sentimental – Mollie hated 'any demonstration of affection in public' and Elizabeth had a 'horror of anything approaching it'.[15] At root Mollie was a 'good soul' with 'a natural motherly kindness' while Elizabeth, though kind to friends, was known for her detachment. According to daughter Liebet, who wrote Elizabeth's biography under the pen name Leslie de Charms, her mother's 'self-evident truth' that 'happiness is practically synonymous with independence ... would call for continual defence against a stubbornly opposing world'.[16] For her children it was sometimes especially hard. Her interest in them as they grew beyond dependence would 'increase or diminish according to her estimate, just or mistaken', of their having developed into 'worth-while individuals'.[17] Diminutive she may have been, but a pushover she was not. Mollie was proud of their friendship – at least until Elizabeth became a rival for Frank's affections.

In the months following Mollie's departure from the WFL, the Russells had been growing apart. Frank's business interests often kept him in London while Mollie retreated to TH where she embraced her aspirations to write. A hut was built for her to work in near a rose garden in the grounds of TH and an 'open-air retreat about a quarter of a mile from the house' where in fine weather she would sleep out.[18] As Frank disliked insects and enjoyed neither eating nor sleeping outdoors, both became places of solitude. When she was in London, there were arguments and Frank's secrecy drove a wedge between them. Early in 1910, he somewhat suspiciously removed his office from their Gordon Square home without her knowledge, having first got her out of the way. Her subsequent demand for an explanation was summarily dismissed: 'He called me *woman* and roared silence.' It caused friction between them that spilled over into what should have been a pleasurable excursion to Egypt, during which Frank cursed Mollie for being a 'sulky insolent brute' and she hardened her heart towards him – his 'arrogant manner' making 'my whole soul rise in rebellion'. After several days a 'patched up state of affairs' existed between them and for the rest of the excursion Frank is hardly mentioned in Mollie's diary; she describes their travels and conversations with friends but little more.[19]

Then, in 1911, Bertrand revealed his own long-standing marital difficulties with Alys. It had been ten years since he had concluded that he no longer loved her, corresponding with (but never directly attributed to) his falling in love in 1901 with Evelyn, the wife of Alfred North Whitehead, with whom he would collaborate on the three-volume *Principia Mathematica* (1910–13). According to Bertrand's biographer Ray Monk, Bertrand became so absorbed with Evelyn that he barely noticed the distress it caused Alys. For a year he tried to disguise his feelings, even after Alys voiced 'the ridiculous delusion that thee no longer cared for me', only eventually confessing the truth after a direct confrontation in June 1902. Thereafter, he convinced himself that the transference of his affections was somehow Alys's fault. Over the next eight years, as their relationship continued on what Monk called 'its grim and joyless descent into sham and melancholy', Bertrand came to pity Alys but resented the increasing effort needed to tolerate her, devising a *modus vivendi* in which he never so much as looked at her 'so that I avoid the pain of her insincere expression and the petty irritation of her awkwardness of movement'. Such was her sorrow that by the time Alys developed a breast tumour in 1907 it was her 'blissful hope' that it would be cancerous and that death would release her. Her 'crushing disappointment' when it transpired that the only thing eating away at her was an 'awful craving hunger for Bertie's love' makes for particularly painful reading.[20] But it was not until Bertrand met and fell hopelessly and obsessively in love with Lady Ottoline – the 'tall and striking aristocratic' wife of Phillip Morrell, an old Oxford friend of Alys's brother Logan, 'with an extravagant taste in clothes and finery, and a reputation for independence and unconventionality' – that the pair would be forced to confront the situation. Bertrand spent the very same weekend that Frank and Mollie were entertaining Elizabeth and Wells making love to Ottoline in what he described as 'an absolute revelation to me of the possibilities of happiness and of love'.[21] It did not mark the total transference of Ottoline's affections to Bertrand, but did result in Bertrand's separation from Alys on terms agreed in a few months of 'messy and ill-tempered negotiations' led by Logan.

When Frank heard the news, he wrote to Bertrand, 'People of good manners can often manage to get on in the same house, once they have agreed to differ.' He hoped it would be the case for them.[22] Clearly Frank was unaware how far apart they had grown. A week later, he confided to Bertrand that he had 'been having his own domestic upheavals', but that Mollie had persuaded him 'to do everything decently and without fuss'.[23] Perhaps, then, Frank's poorly timed suggestion went beyond mere brotherly advice.

The subsequent publishing of Mollie's first book, *Five Women and a Caravan* (1911), recounting the adventures of a group of friends on a touring holiday in the south of England, does little to dispel the idea of their growing disconnection. *Five Women* is a personal account written in story form, an oddly imbalanced book in which the unnamed narrator becomes so involved in commanding her little troupe that she neglects to write home to her 'owner' but never wastes an opportunity to preach women's rights to her naïve companions or any and all of the locals they meet on their travels.

On retiring from the WFL, Mollie had said that she could do as much for the cause by 'writing and proselytising' and this appears to be the book's *raison d'être*, hiding, as one critic put it, behind 'a peaceful green cover' where 'one does not look for a suffragist tract'.[24] It divided critics, with some complimenting the manner in which Mollie gave 'pointed and well-fashioned expression to her own pronounced views' while others deplored her 'torrential tirades'.[25] The conversion of her caravan into a 'mission van' was more often than not determined to have spoiled 'a very delightful story, for the Countess writes smartly and brightly', yet seemingly without humour.[26] In writing, Mollie lost the wit so readily conveyed in her speeches, yet was not dissatisfied with the result. 'Frank is trying to keep me in my proper place,' she wrote to Bertrand, 'in case of pride's direst punishment, but I just hand him a batch of selected reviews & extinguish him.'[27] Neither did she object to obvious comparisons with Elizabeth, despite being found wanting. In directly referencing Elizabeth in three different places in the book, Mollie appeared rather to invite it. Perhaps she wouldn't have had she heard Elizabeth's supposed comment to Wells after their weekend visit in 1911 – that Frank was 'an attractive misunderstood man who needed only an able wife to be reinstated socially'.[28]

Frank was clearly unhappy. Early in 1912, he confided to Bertrand that he was contemplating a family of illegitimate children. He was by this time forty-seven and Mollie in her early fifties. Since 1910 they had lived as 'brother and sister' and Frank, whose natural state was 'polygamous without being inconstant', was clearly being unfaithful; however, the prospective mother of his unorthodox family went unnamed.[29] Bertrand, who had never particularly warmed to Mollie, suggested that perhaps it would be better if Frank divorce her and remarry if his desire for children was so strong. 'Poor man,' he concluded, 'he is full of unsatisfied domesticity.'[30]

During the Easter vacation, Bertrand witnessed the couple's interactions on a motoring tour of the West Country.[31] He found Frank 'in a state of nerves, rather tense, easily losing his temper with servants or people on the road' at whom he swore 'with a concentrated passionate fury' when they wouldn't get out of his way. Yet Bertrand developed a new appreciation of Frank during this excursion. Having recently allowed his own 'mad dogs' an airing on a solitary trip to Dorset,[32] he observed,

> I have only quite lately begun to know and understand my brother. I find him full of a rather fine courage, so successful that I had never suspected its existence. His life is tragic, because he has great ability and energy which finds no outlet.

Frank was 'fussy and complaining' with the waiters, but 'mixed it with so many jokes and so much bonhomie that the waiter couldn't help laughing … My imagination is living his life very actively', Bertrand wrote, expressing more affection for Frank as his closest living relative to Ottoline than to anyone before or since. About Mollie, he was less forgiving, choosing to relay Frank's ribbing of her for being 'much-married'. He found it amusing that when Mollie had said she'd never been widowed and never wanted to be, Frank had quipped, 'No my dear, you never gave them time', and took exception to Mollie's assurances that women were just as sexual as men, dismissing it as her own projected propensity. Clearly, Mollie had been seeking companionship elsewhere, but denied being unfaithful as Bertrand here implies:

> My brother and his wife jointly assured me, with some earnestness, that she is not *au mieux* with R. J. Campbell. If she ever was, it has certainly been over a long time.

A Nonconformist minister, Fabian and active member of the ILP, Reginald Campbell was a political acquaintance with whom the Russells were on friendly terms. He was their guest at TH alongside Santayana and John Sargeaunt the following year, during which time Mollie also befriended Cambridge anthropology professor A. C. Haddon, a delightful yet shy man. Mollie urged patience with Haddon, asking Bertrand to 'be nice to him for my sake',[33] and Frank stayed oftener at his club, indulging in meaningless infidelities and gambling increasing amounts of his dwindling income at bridge, with higher stakes than the Pharos would ever have allowed. That year, they also holidayed separately: Frank with William, Viscount Pirrie and his wife Margaret for three weeks on their 'scrumptious' yacht, and Mollie on a slow motoring tour with one of her caravanning friends.

At the same time, Elizabeth and Wells were becoming fractious – a fact for which each blamed the other. According to Wells, Elizabeth ruined their affair by wanting more than 'fun and fellowship'. She became resentful of his family and began to 'demand depth of feeling'. In her jealousy, she 'was comic and malicious and unendurable', teasing him and inventing nicknames for his wife. When she heard that Wells was seeing someone else in London, she called him 'half a lover', and as there was 'no way of disputing it', they parted.[34] To Elizabeth, it was Wells who was doing all the chasing and she who refused him. 'There is nothing, I suppose, so disconcerting as being stalked when you don't want to be,' she declared in her comic autobiography *All the Dogs of My Life* (1936), before describing 'the lovely morning he went away' and the relief in liberation after having been 'groping around so long among unshared emotions – which is even worse, I think, than groping among shared ones'.[35] Elizabeth had a propensity to present herself as the victim of uninvited and unwelcome courtships. From *Dogs* comes the story of Henning's pursuit of her around Europe in 1889 and subsequent proposal on the steps of the Duomo in Florence with the words, 'All girls like love. It is very agreeable. You will like it too. You shall marry me, and see.' And the tale of how her traitorous dog, Coco, seemed 'to recognise a suitor directly he set eyes on him ... marking him down for immediate attention and encouragement', enthusiastically welcoming Frank on his arrival at her Swiss chalet on the fateful occasion when they crossed the line between friends and lovers – Frank who 'hadn't been invited, but, on some pretext which I afterwards perceived to be thin, just came' (which blatantly wasn't the case).[36]

This manner of writing enabled Elizabeth to maintain an authorial detachment and convey an impression humorous and simplified, with truth in essence but not always in fact. It makes it impossible to unpick a chain of events with any certainty, which was no doubt its intention.[37] From Elizabeth's journal, however, comes the suggestion that as regards Wells, she *had* encouraged him – at least with the prospect of romantic friendship – and had invited him to her chalet in November 1912, but when he 'didn't want to come enough' had bowed out of the affair with the sentiment, 'Alas for the end of what was going to be so lovely.'[38] Wells, who would not accept her refusal, sent 'a stream of reproachful letters' before appearing on her doorstep 'determined to get a hearing'.[39] There were 'horrid talks' and a reconciliation of sorts. But when in 1913 Wells became involved with Rebecca West there were afternoons of 'quarrelling & cursing each other' as Wells refused to see why he could not make love to both women simultaneously, and journal entries such as 'G unendurable' and 'a devil in G of cruelty and horridness' which repelled Elizabeth. When he left the chalet on 5 November 1913, she wrote, 'G's departure out of my life! Thank God – Restored to Freedom'; when West fell pregnant it marked the 'End of G'.

Elizabeth's new-found freedom was quickly impinged upon by Frank. Contact had been maintained over the previous two years with several visits to TH (with and without Wells), an invitation for Frank to attend a soirée at Elizabeth's London apartment and several lunches with Mollie, the last being on 16 December 1913. On 27 December, Frank arrived at the chalet, invited as he was to spend Christmas with Elizabeth and her guests. Two things are unclear: who decided Mollie would not join them and Elizabeth's intentions towards Frank. In any case, within days, formal references to 'Russell' in her journal gave way to the more familiar 'Francis'. By 2 January 1914 – a month after the 'End of G' – the start of their intimacy is marked with the entry: 'Took lugs & went out with Francis alone down to Darnona. He left after tea to all our sorrow.' Two days later, back at the Reform Club, Frank poured out the emotions she had excited in him in a letter addressed to 'My adored and adorable one', in which he asked why, after an intimate evening together, she did not 'fly into my arms that I might add that hug & kiss to my other memories?' before confessing,

> I love you, I love you, I love you – it rings in my ears, it throbs in my veins, it makes music of life & work, it uplifts, thrills and enchants me.

Elizabeth, it seems, had requested they take it slowly, but Frank could not: 'I pretend that I will take from now till June considering, weighing, thinking. It is a lie & a mere pretence.' He confessed he had secretly admired her for two years and could not contain himself longer: 'I knew the die was cast when I accepted your invitation – & therefore I hesitated and trembled to accept. I knew I could not be near you so long without showing you my heart, & I knew we were twin souls.' His love was 'no idle sport, no casual aside, but an upheaval, a bursting, a flow of red hot lava'. He asked if she wanted to be so loved: 'For I cannot play – I am in earnest & it hurts – but with what sweet pain.' If she did not feel the same, 'it makes no great difference ... But you do love me darling don't you – or you will. Tell me you do – I am hungry for love.' He asked her to read Browning's poem *Cristina*, before directly asking whether she could love him 'without stint or limit, afterthought or forethought, dearly tenderly and passionately' as he loved her. Ordinarily, he confessed, he hid his feelings because they scared him, but 'from now to June – languishing – I shall live for you, think of you, work & play for you, that I may come to you a free clean man fit to offer love to so dear a mate'.[40]

Everything Elizabeth needed to know about Frank was in this letter. Later, she would profess (and Bertrand would believe her) that she only accepted Frank's advances because she believed him safely married – a curiously similar claim to her protestation that she encouraged Wells hoping only for romantic friendship. Frank's letter belies that assertion. If nothing else, the reference to *Cristina*, a poem she must have known, made his feelings and intentions clear:

> She should never have looked at me
> If she meant I should not love her!
> There are plenty — men, you call such,
> I suppose — she may discover
> All her soul to, if she pleases,
> And yet leave much as she found them:
> But I'm not so, and she knew it
> When she fixed me, glancing round them.

The change she had brought about would be to his 'triumph' if she felt the same (to 'walk the earth in rapture' having discovered God's greatest secret in the binding of two souls in love); to his 'undoing' if she did not – 'This world's use will have ended'. The only question was, how would Elizabeth respond?

Her reply has not survived, but her reaction to receiving Frank's letter gives more than fair indication: 'Got a wonderful letter from Francis. Wondered if it wouldn't shine through me visibly and give me away.' On 8 January, she replied. Her letter filled Frank with 'unspeakable joy':

> I nearly swooned with joy gratitude & thankfulness to Heaven that had given me such a love when I read & kissed again & again your dear words. Darling, darling, darling I am a young man today my heart a flutter with the spring, my head in the stars and my proud foot and glowing eye challenging the world with my happiness. Crowned with your love, dearest of women, of what am I not capable!

There were hesitations on her part, but he swiftly dispatched them. Her admission that she felt shy with him was gainsaid: 'I am large – simple – natural – once I am in your heart & mind there can be nothing but love between us.' Her fear of the force of passion awakened was echoed: 'I know, I too am terrified of love – exquisite pain and exquisite pleasure.' But his assurance that 'love shall flower naturally – I am always yours to do with as you will' was contradicted by the declaration that 'not for the whole world would I be at peace again'.[41] For here was Frank in turmoil not felt since his affair with Agnes Tobin twenty years earlier, and nothing would stem its tide. Where Agnes had fled, Elizabeth was swept along. Alone now on her snow-clad mountain, she 'meant to work but thought of F. and happiness instead'.

A month of 'perfect weather' and 'perfect sunshine' followed until Frank's return on 6 February spelled 'perfect sunshine inside as well as out'. After three days he left with the blessing, 'God keep you, my Heavenly Love'. With his departure, the weather broke, giving way to fierce gales and greyness. Little else is recorded in Elizabeth's journal until 23 February when she wrote, 'Got letter from F. that he is getting divorced from Mollie.' Then, in an entry for the 25th, 'Francis left Mollie.'

Did she guess he would take this step so soon? Probably not. But Frank did not have the temperament that would allow him to linger in a loveless marriage as Bertrand had done, fearful of the harm to his reputation; and Elizabeth was, after all, a free woman. Why should they wait? With Elizabeth suddenly uncharacteristically subservient, desiring 'to serve, to obey, to stand with bowed head and hands folded, to be, as it were, the handmaid of the lord',[42] he forged ahead, writing Mollie a starkly contrasting note from the RAC:

Dear Mollie,
I told you on Tuesday night that I could not live with you any longer and I left on Wednesday. Since you asked to have it in writing I now confirm it that I have left you for good.

Yours, F.

Refusing to believe he was in earnest, Mollie responded with haughty wit: 'I really look upon your action in leaving as a form of self-denial, for you left Ash Wednesday, the beginning of Lent. I would really advise you to try a milder form of abstinence – like the boy who determined to give up soap.' But Frank was adamant: 'I have no quarrel with you and bear you no ill-will but it would be impossible [to continue living with you].'[43]

'What folly,' protested Santayana when Mollie confided in him, falling into sympathy with her as he had once done with Mary when Mollie was the offender, 'after having found a remote refuge and domestic peace with this good woman, and tested the union for so many years, that he should now drive her away, and not only launch upon a new and dangerous voyage, but destroy his home port?'[44] Bertrand's reaction was the complete opposite: 'I said I was glad, and he seemed relieved.' Frank had been afraid his brother would be shocked, but instead, Bertrand, feeling 'sudden affection' for Frank, took the opportunity to confide that he too had given Alys grounds for divorce.[45] Mollie, meanwhile, throughout this whole episode, had retained her attachment to TH and consoled herself for Frank's shortcomings as a husband with whiskey and water and in writing a second novel, *An Excellent Mystery* (1912). Sadly, it was nothing of the kind, but a wandering and sorrowful reflection on her early life in Ireland and her first marriage and divorce. Praised at the time for highlighting the inequities of English divorce laws compared to Scotland's, its value today lies chiefly in its autobiographical content thinly disguised as fiction and in the poignancy of her naming characters after the children she had left behind for the man who would shortly abandon her. In less than a year, the fact that she had dedicated the book to Frank would no doubt stick in her craw as much as would the bitter irony of having written in *Five Women* of her joy when Elizabeth had come to see her garden 'and whispered to it softly how much she loved it' once she had become her rival.[46] Mollie's publisher went bankrupt and her book sold very few copies. There were no comparisons with Elizabeth this time and Mollie's appeal dwindled. A third manuscript, *The Love Child*, never saw the light of day. But would Elizabeth eclipse her as a wife so easily?

Within a week of his confession, Frank was back with Elizabeth in Switzerland. He had flu, but they lay in the sun together and were happy. On the same 'dull, sad, empty day' when he left, Mollie filed a petition for restitution of conjugal rights. Frank returned to London to find himself 'tormented by talk' as rumour of their separation circulated. Elizabeth followed on 22 March and they dined together every day in private, her identity as his new paramour a closely guarded secret. On 31 March, she left London for a prearranged trip to Italy wearing a ring Frank had given her to seal their engagement. He wrote her 'dear' letters, but also complained of 'being worried by well-meaning friends'. Towards the end of May, in an ultimate gesture of intimacy, Frank sent Elizabeth his bundle of Lionel Johnson's letters written from Winchester College nearly thirty years previously. She stayed in all day to read them. By the end of the month they were both back at the chalet, where for nearly two weeks nothing was written in Elizabeth's journal save the single word 'Francis'.

Though Elizabeth's second daughter, Liebet, described Frank's presence as importunate, there is nothing in Elizabeth's journal at this time to suggest that she was unhappy to fall in with Frank's every whim. His domineering manner she even described as restful to begin with. It seemed that nothing could mar their happiness. Not even the escapades of Elizabeth's youngest daughter, Felicitas, who had been caught stealing money at school in Lausanne and removed to a new, stricter establishment in Marburg, central Germany. The atmosphere in the house was 'particularly untroubled and harmonious' for guests who arrived shortly after.[47] No one would have guessed anything unsavoury had happened.

On 13 July 1914, Mollie's petition for restitution came before the court and the judge ordered Frank's return within a fortnight. The letters quoted above and printed in the papers were written, according to Santayana, with that in mind – the tone of them 'put on for effect'. Really, he said, 'they are flinging things at each other's heads'. It was a factor keeping him in Paris: he wanted to keep out of the fray as the Russells' battle threatened to rival the gathering storms of war.[48] The petition, of course, was necessary to give Mollie desertion as a ground for divorce (the second ground eventually engineered by Frank with an unknown obliging woman at the Hotel Great Central on Marylebone Road on 20 February 1915), but Frank was finding that he could not simply demand Mollie's compliance when divorce was neither in her best interests, nor what she necessarily wanted. As Europe's nations were drawn into conflict by prior treaty obligations, Frank found himself fighting Mollie for the termination of their own contract as she refused to file a petition for separation. Meanwhile, in Switzerland, Elizabeth read in the London papers of the Austrian ultimatum to Serbia and, much to the amusement of her English guests, ordered extra provisions. It all seemed so unnecessary on such a beautiful day on their isolated mountain: 'The world looked so reassuring, the valley so shining and placid, the chalet so gaily THERE ... and we sitting in front of it lavishly nourished.'[49] But the pending war was undeniable, and, quite apart from any political or military manoeuvrings, Austria's ultimatum sent shock waves through European stock markets. In panic, exchanges closed their doors. With the first of a succession of war declarations on 28 July, New York wavered and the prospect of a crash in London became real. Like so many others, Frank's investments suffered and he found himself facing a financial crisis of his own. By 31 July, when the London Exchange closed for the first time in its history, he was 'racked with neuralgia & all raw nerves from worry'. He confided his troubles to Aunt Maude but could not bring himself to ask her for a loan. Elizabeth, who had applied to the Deutsche Bank in Berlin to have her own funds transferred to accounts in England and Sierre, wrote offering assistance. Frank gratefully accepted and described the sudden change of atmosphere in London as the prospect of being dragged into a European war superseded any potential civil conflict with Ireland:

> The state of things is awful tonight: people failing right & left. New anxieties and terrors every hour – Russia mobilising, Germany a martial law etc. ... Never in our lifetime has there been anything like this crisis – people are actually buying flour tonight – it all seems quite without reason – unworthy of any civilisation – I am as much amazed as horrified. Everyone goes about feeling dazed & helpless – the less thinking ones with a sorry laugh! God help us.[50]

Santayana left Paris for London. He had intended only to do some shopping and see a few friends and then return, but would find himself in England for the duration. On 1 August, with no good news from the Deutsche Bank, Elizabeth considered trying to get to England to retrieve funds, but when the stationmaster at Sierre told her to expect the journey to take ten days, she changed her mind and returned home. With each successive day came new declarations of war between Germany, Russia and France. The Swiss government began to move troops to their borders, fearing their neutrality might be threatened. Sierre was overrun with soldiers, the gendarme oversaw trading, hotels closed and there were rumours of lawlessness. By the time Germany entered Belgium, ignoring the British ultimatum to respect her neutrality, Elizabeth began to fear being caught on the wrong side. Her loyalty was to England, but her nationality and name were German. She made plans to leave the chalet. An 'inexpressible dreariness ... a horribly oppressive Sunday feeling' had settled over it, but she could not depart without money. Finally, on 20 August she heard from the bank that she would be able to retrieve 5,000 francs in another four days. On 28 August, armed with passports her brother, Dr Stanley Beauchamp, had borrowed from an obliging patient, Elizabeth, Evi and Liebet left the chalet. Her son 'H. B.' was already at school in England. Beatrix and Felicitas were left behind in Germany. The party travelled by train under the assumed name of Arnold, via Bern, Geneva, Lyon and Paris, arriving at Le Havre on 1 September in time to board the overcrowded night steamer – the two girls chastised to remain silent throughout the voyage for fear their German accents would give them away. On their safe arrival in England they were sent to family and the 'fearfully happy' Elizabeth went on to London alone.

To mark her safe return and the start of their new life together, Elizabeth dined on 3 September with Frank at Gordon Square. The following day he motored her to Richmond Park, and on the 5th to the home of her sister Charlotte, who lived not 20 miles from Telegraph House. With increased togetherness came Elizabeth's first taste of Frank's temper when he was 'much upset' by disruption of their plans to meet a few days later in Battersea Park, but it was followed by a 'lovely day with Francis among beeches and bracken. Too perfect for words.' By the end of the month, Elizabeth had been granted British citizenship and the couple celebrated with a trip to the Peak District, where once again Frank could not help losing his temper and becoming 'tyrannical' at plans upset by bad weather and poor service. Elizabeth recorded it a 'pity' he spent three full days being 'rather dreadful and tiresome'. It made her doubt their future happiness, and on their return she wrote to him about the 'hopelessness of marriage'. An apologetic Frank responded with a gift of apples, flowers and a pheasant, and visited a few days later armed with more flowers and full of 'dear sweetness'. It did the trick. For the rest of the year he was on his best behaviour and remained in favour. In October, when Cobbie was 'very extreme and unfair about F', Elizabeth resented it; and when Frank brought news of Mollie's 'vindictiveness and dishonesty' in continuing to refuse to divorce him, she 'felt downcast & disinclined to face a future of separation and loneliness'.

The battle that had been raging all this time with Mollie was over money. Mollie had no choice but to accept Frank was leaving, but was not going to let him go without a decent settlement. The fight was bitter, but in the end worth it. On 14 September 1914, Frank set up the Mollie, Countess Russell Trust, putting in £3,000 of Plenty & Son debentures, various gold mining shares and, after November 1914, an increasing investment in the war loan. John J. Withers was made sole trustee and its primary consideration was that Mollie should receive a life annuity of £600; the remainder was to be reinvested or go to Frank.[51] With business concluded and Mollie satisfied, she filed a petition for divorce on 20 November 1914.

December, then, was pleasurable, despite the war. Elizabeth had taken a flat in Albemarle Court and a cottage in Radlett and saw Frank often, dividing her time between London, Hertfordshire and Sussex. Days were spent together walking and talking, and evenings with Frank reading Browning aloud or explaining elemental chemistry 'in the clearest cleverest way'. When he was gone, she missed him. Frank wrote addressing her 'My perfect one, my beloved Theo, my heart's delight, my joy!'[52] On the 18th she noted, 'Watched for him all morning with nose against window pane. Queer!' They spent Christmas at Charlotte's, where occasional disagreements were brushed aside, and then travelled to Radlett to see in the New Year alone – Elizabeth without her children for the first time. 'What happiness I've had this whole year because of him,' she wrote in her journal as 1914 drew to a close. 'It has been the happiest year of my life.'

23

Conscientious Objections

Much, then, was expected of 1915. Elizabeth worked and walked at Radlett and took trips to London when she felt solitary. Frank visited often, taught her to drive and in the evenings read her French literature, Shakespeare, Hardy's poems and Elizabeth Browning's sonnets. When he was attentive and made her laugh, he was 'dear & perfect'; when he was 'boyish' it was 'as I love him to be'. But Elizabeth struggled with his capricious moods. On 20 January, they had their first major falling-out after Frank returned from a business meeting in a 'tiresome, absorbed mood which gradually chilled me'. They argued, and Frank left the following morning with a 'thick cloud' between them. The subsequent 'silence & loneliness' of Radlett rendered Elizabeth 'extremely miserable'. She was unable to work and Frank's 'exhortations' that she let it go didn't help. On his next visit, they were 'placid & content – but there wasn't the customary glory & light about it'. It marked the start of a pattern that was to emerge over the coming year as their differences began to show. An 'imperfect understanding' at the beginning of April 'led to words' which Elizabeth 'took much to heart. So foolish!' A 'not very satisfactory' evening later in the month meant she 'did not sleep an *instant* all night – but not a single one!' And in May, after she turned up unannounced at TH, where Frank was entertaining friends – despite knowing how averse he was to anything unexpected – she was left to reflect that, though he had seemed pleased, the surprise had been ruined by her fear of his anticipated reaction. To her, they were 'losing heavenly happinesses' as a consequence; to Frank, this was life settling into its normal course. How could their love ever live up to its promise if these differences went unresolved?[1]

It was a question their friends could easily have answered, though doubtless to neither's satisfaction. Santayana, indeed, had tried, likening Frank to Henry VIII in desiring 'to *marry* all his lady-loves; but that only made him wish later to cut their heads off'. He suggested with

Frank's 'fixed habits' he would be difficult to live with and was quickly proved right.[2] On 5 June, Frank confessed to Elizabeth that, despite promising not to, he had been playing bridge until the early hours and had lost £30 to £40. Elizabeth was 'greatly disappointed' and 'full of doubts about the future if I were ever to marry him'. It was bad timing. They were just then off to TH, where Elizabeth was to meet Bertrand for the first time.

Elizabeth liked Bertrand instantly; he reminded her 'so very much of H. G.' Bertrand showed more reserve, writing to Ottoline that Elizabeth seemed 'rather given to flattery' and, though he found her 'agreeable' in the moment, on reflection concluded, 'I don't much like her for the same reasons as made me dislike her in her books.' He didn't say what those reasons were, but did think she would keep Frank in order.[3] If only she could! The visit was followed by a week in Kings Langley, where she and Frank had taken a 'nest'. There were moments of pleasure, but also episodes when Frank's temper got the better of him. A punctured tyre on their second morning led to Elizabeth being 'ordered about & scolded as though I were a chauffeur'. Rain put a damper on things again. Elizabeth's mind turned to Wells and on a 'sudden impulse' she telephoned and went to see him while Frank was engaged elsewhere, 'thirsting to hear him on the war'. Thereafter, back at the nest, Frank's chemistry readings lost their appeal. '*Gott strafe* (God's punishment),' she wrote in response to Kipling, which she described as 'very grievous to my soul'. To compound matters, Frank was increasingly distracted and inattentive. After visiting Elizabeth on 25 June, she recorded that when he left, for the first time since they had been together, 'it never occurred to him to kiss me. Funny.'

Perhaps, then, it was a good thing that Frank was shortly to depart for Rhodesia on business. Their last evening together on 3 July was filled with 'happiness & sorrow mixed'. This time, Frank did kiss his 'little love', but his excitement at his forthcoming adventure was unmistakable. Elizabeth conveyed her own feelings with a line from Horace transcribed in the front of her journal: '*Quid desiderio sitpudor aut modus?*' – 'What limit, or restraint, should we show' – the line continues – 'at the loss of so dear a life?'[4] Perhaps she thought he might never return. Fear of U-boats had already seen Frank's companion bow out. And two months was such a long time to be apart – '[Frank] hopes to be back in September, if not torpedoed,' Bertrand told Ottoline.[5]

The purpose of the trip was to inspect the gold mines of the Globe and Phoenix Mining Company (G&P). Frank's association with G&P had been lucrative, but not easy. He had become chairman early in 1914 after a period of infighting between shareholders and directors over salaries. The position embroiled him in two further lawsuits. The first was a private suit against Kendrick Murray, Secretary of the Chamber of Commerce, whom Frank sued for slander after Murray reportedly told a potential business associate in the very public RAC lounge that Frank had been bankrupted three times and was not therefore 'a safe pair of hands'. The judge believed Murray's claim, that it was a general conversation about *a* Russell and that Frank was not identified as *the* Russell concerned, and found in Murray's favour. Frank still insisted on it being stated in open court 'that there was not the slightest foundation for the words alleged to have been uttered'.[6]

Then followed the epic battle between G&P and the Amalgamated Properties of Rhodesia (APR) over claims that G&P had extracted £400,000 of gold without paying APR the half share to which they were legally entitled. Frank's inspection of the mine was to secure evidence to the contrary and select credible witnesses for the forthcoming action. The case came to court on 26 October 1915. After 143 days in Chancery, during which expert engineers and geologists gave lengthy and complex explanations of the formation and mining of ore reefs in support of G&P, and barristers on both sides exchanged 'frequent outbursts of temper and recrimination', the judge found in their favour, dismissing the case with costs.[7] Frank was praised for having admirably steered a difficult course; especially after seeing off an appeal by APR and the recovery of £76,837 in costs. A subsequent unsuccessful Lords appeal by APR which ended on 8 April 1919 further cemented Frank's reputation. And when another company he helmed – the Olympic Fire and General Assurance Company – ran into difficulties the following year, Frank convinced shareholders not to vote for liquidation – a result which 'really amounted to a vote of confidence in his lordship'.[8] In business, it would seem, Frank had at last found a use for his powers of persuasion. Pity then that within days of this compliment he should take the unprecedented step of calling an extraordinary meeting of G&P's shareholders to accuse two of its directors of conspiring in its takeover. The assembly declared it 'scandalous' to have brought such baseless charges against 'two gentlemen whose integrity and honesty were unquestioned', and Frank was forced to resign.[9] The grounds for his accusation were never revealed.

While Frank was in Rhodesia, Mollie's decree *nisi* was granted on 13 July 1915, raising the very real prospect of his remarriage. His bride-to-be wavered. Though she felt 'a great waif & widow & forlornness' without him, released from the magnetism of Frank's insistent personality his faults could be considered more objectively. Elizabeth doubted his capacity to overcome them. On the other hand, their marriage would rescue her from a German connection which was becoming increasingly distasteful. In London she had been asked outright if she had a husband somewhere in Germany fighting against the Allies, and in Sussex, walking across the meadows one day, some children had wondered if she were a spy! When Bertrand and Cobbie came to stay at the beginning of September, she confided her misgivings to them both. Bertrand immediately conveyed them to Ottoline, relaying Elizabeth's confession that Frank's sudden and early proposal 'took her breath away, and rather flattered her ... she drifted, said nothing definite, but allowed him tacitly to assume everything' and now the 'inexorable moment' when she would have to decide was upon her:

Her objections to him are the following:

(a) He sleeps with 7 dogs on his bed. She couldn't sleep and write in such circumstances.

(b) He reads Kipling aloud.

(c) He loves Telegraph House, which is hideous.

Bertrand immediately saw that these reasons were 'all three well chosen to appeal to me' and suspected that Elizabeth had 'set herself the task of getting me to be not against her if she breaks with [Frank]. But it is an impossible task. I am too fond of my brother, and shall mind his suffering too much, to forgive her inwardly even if she has a perfectly good case.'[10]

Cobbie, who did not have the same loyalty to Frank, recorded in his journal that Elizabeth, who 'loves to be loved', was gradually 'being absorbed into the system of [Frank's] devotion – I might perhaps more accurately say, into the atmosphere of his egotism'. She might be happy there, he observed, 'but it will be an atmosphere of his creation, and her own liberty will be lost'.[11]

Frank returned on 15 September oblivious to everything and Elizabeth recorded 'Great & infinite bliss to be together again'. She was 'heavenly happy' during a long weekend at TH. But by the following weekend, Frank had become 'tiresome & worrying' again and things were 'strained and wretched' between them. Elizabeth determined 'to go away for a long time'. Within a day 'wisdom prevailed' and it 'gnawed away at my heart' that Frank stayed away, even though she'd asked him to. Then, at the beginning of November, Frank disappeared for four days without a hint as to his whereabouts. Elizabeth's frantic telegrams to the Reform Club and his office went unanswered. On his reappearance, she was astonished to find him oblivious, 'not a bit realizing what it had cost me'. As 1915 drew to a close she measured the contrast between this year and the last. Frank's inability to remain 'dear & sweet' and her sensitivity to his increasingly frequent tantrums and recriminations had taken her by surprise. An 'extraordinarily happy' Christmas with Bertrand at TH was afterwards ruined by Frank's moods, which Elizabeth attributed to an excess of mince pies and port! Yet still she clung to the hope that all would be well. The closing remark in her journal was that it had been a year with 'many happinesses in it, all, I think, owing to my dear F. (Also pains).'

The paramount struggle for 1916 – for Frank and Elizabeth and the world at large – was liberty. Santayana had already observed early in 1912 that Frank's attempts to combine individual liberty with democracy (when they are '*really incompatible*') had been detrimental to his relationships *and* his career.[12] That December, Frank had surrendered some political autonomy by declaring himself a Fabian – his first formal allegiance since his LCC days. Only a handful of nobles espoused socialism and Frank was the first peer to join the Fabian ranks. The press, who readily acknowledged his long-standing support for schemes that improved the lot of the working class, declared themselves unsurprised – 'Only the timid', they said, saw it as portending 'the end of all things'.[13] The socialist paper

Justice rather blandly suggested that Frank 'may possibly make Socialism more commendable to his peers' though doubted whether 'more than a few would be "saved"'.[14] Yet the move led to much speculation as to Frank's political future. Having already fervently supported the curbing of the Lords' powers with the 1911 Parliament Bill, Frank could now take further steps towards its annihilation as a recognised representative of the Labour Party in the Lords – their first – but the *Daily Herald* – the mouthpiece of the Labour Party – tended to think he would continue as always to take 'an independent line on social questions'; and almost immediately, Frank did just that.[15]

On 31 January 1913, Frank spoke in the Lords against the 'absolute and dangerous immunity' of trade unions, but claimed he did so as 'a candid friend' of Labour and 'an admirer of the work that trade unions have done'.[16] It was a significant speech that set his position in relation to Labour for the next dozen years. As a 'candid' friend he recognised he would become 'that generally unpopular person' who stood apart and pronounced judgement from the side-lines. His autonomy, then, was not completely surrendered; but he had good reason. Union disputes had escalated to some 857 in 1912, involving 1.2 million workers and a loss of 40 million working days, and had become more militant. Syndicalism was on the rise and, it was feared, sought to 'seize control of the means of production and distribution by revolutionary means, and impose a form of communism on the country'.[17] Frank abhorred this trend just as he had the militancy of the suffragettes, writing in the *Syndicalist*, 'A mob of riotous workmen intent upon doing physical injury to any workman who is not a unionist, or intent upon wrecking other people's property ... however much justice there may be in [their] demands ... [does] as much harm to their cause as the Government that has to use bayonets against them does to the cause of law and order.'[18] He wished to see the working man fairly rewarded for his labours, but not by revolution.

Frank had joined the Fabians – the oldest of the socialist organisations – in order to promote a policy of nationalisation, but would not yet commit himself to Labour, who rejected syndicalism but actively sought to irrevocably intertwine its fortunes with those of the unions while generally downplaying socialism for fear of alienating prospective voters in the middle ground. Labour was then still finding its feet as a force in politics. It was only just beginning to organise under Ramsay MacDonald's chairmanship and the Parliamentary Labour Party (PLP) struggled to look anywhere near ready for office. Labour was also tied into an uneasy agreement with the Liberals not to compete against each other at elections, and hesitated and disagreed over supporting more radical policies, such as women's suffrage, for fear of overstraining Liberal condescension. This was crucial for Frank who rather took the opposite position, declaring himself 'unafraid' of the term socialism. He set out with his usual zeal to disseminate his vision of a socialistic society, speaking on a number of platforms throughout 1913 and 1914. Not by revolution but by 'restraint, discipline, and education' could the working classes' lot be improved, and 'the first great step was the abolition of the ownership of land' and the 'reorganisation of industry' to produce shorter hours and better working conditions.[19] Many Tory papers were sceptical, pointing out that Frank was still himself a landowner (albeit of a very small portion), but he was absolutely sincere in what he said and considered his own aloofness as merely enabling him to say what Labour then could not, and to continue to fight causes that were not yet high on Labour's agenda.

One such cause was mental health. As a long-standing supporter of the campaign to improve the understanding and treatment of lunacy, Frank was actively involved with the Medico-Legal Society, becoming its president for the year 1912–13. On 22 July 1914, Frank presented a bill in the Lords drafted by the Society, the BMA and the Medico-Psychological Association advocating and seeking to facilitate early treatment for the poor.[20] It was overrun by the advent of war, but would be a cause he would never abandon.

With war came more pressing issues, not only in terms of how it should be fought but whether it should be fought at all. Bertrand considered the war unjust and joined the anti-war Union of Democratic Control (UDC).[21] He tried to convince Frank to do likewise. Frank sympathised but ultimately thought, once begun, the war had to be seen through. He had a patriotic pride in the manner in which Britain fought Prussian tyranny. He also thought Bertrand went 'too far' in expressing provocative anti-war views. After reading Bertrand's 1915 article 'An Appeal to Intellectuals', in which he likened the warring factions to two dogs fighting in the street and dismissed moral reprobation as nothing more than the embodiment of hatred and hatred the mechanical product of biological instinct, Frank wrote expressing his doubt that even he 'would not, at any rate to some extent, in common with the rest of us, shrink from a German and all that he represents, after this war'. An Allied victory was of 'enormous importance' – or at very least the overthrow of the Kaiser in favour of a German republic – and Frank wished Bertrand had expressed himself a little differently because his comments jarred, much as would those of an advocate of the Christ myth theory if in 'contemplating a Christian martyr burnt at the stake, [he] were to spend the time in pointing out that there never was an historical Jesus'.[22]

January 1916, however, saw the brothers united at last over conscription. Bertrand instantly declared it 'a wholly evil thing' and a 'cruel plot' against organised labour and the rising influence of trade unions.[23] In the Lords, Frank took a similar position, though tempered to suit that august assembly. As one of only two peers to speak against the first round of conscription, he questioned whether anyone had 'considered with a broad view the distribution of the man power in this country between industry and fighting', suggesting that as a nation of great industrial and financial prosperity, Britain would better serve the Allied cause by keeping its commerce intact than sending all its workers to the front. He also declared an 'instinctive abhorrence' to making men fight against their will and argued the idealistic perspective that compulsion lessened Britain's glory as the only Allied nation to have thus far raised an army solely of volunteers.[24] He had become acutely aware of the tension between individual liberty and the requirements of state since the outbreak of war, and after the passing of the 1914 Defence of the Realm Act (DORA) had set himself the task of policing its boundaries and resisting any additional legislation that infringed upon what might be considered reasonable. Conscription was a step too far. As he wrote in the *New Statesman* on 22 January 1916, 'The nation coerced, dragooned, and regimented is a nation infected with the Prussian spirit; it is no longer that free England of whose traditions we are proud.'[25] When, only four months later, conscription was extended to married men, he reminded the House that the Prime Minister had assured the nation when the first Military Service Bill became law that it would not set a precedent for general compulsion, and yet there they were. Already the consequences of compelling men to do that which they were determined not to was being felt and Frank inevitably found himself speaking out on behalf of conscientious objectors.

It was not that he necessarily shared their views – he certainly did not agree with the 'absolutists' who preferred to go to jail than assist the war effort in any way – but he respected their right to hold their position unmolested. Public opinion labelled them 'shirkers' and the local tribunals set up under military control to determine the validity of their claims for exemption subjected them to aggressive questioning, often attempting to browbeat them into changing their position and handing down unequal verdicts. Temporary exemptions were conditional on the claimant undertaking non-combative duties behind the lines. Permanent exemptions were almost never awarded. Often the right to appeal was withheld. Those who were denied exemption were interned in army detention barracks and subjected to violent and degrading treatment in an attempt to break their will. It was an unprecedented situation that divided opinion. In the first Lords debate on the subject, Frank defended COs, saying, with some irony, that he understood 'people of inflexible determination' and agreed 'that all persons of strong opinions are a nuisance. It is very tiresome when people will not think the same as you do, and still more tiresome when they will not do what you tell them to' but, he reasoned, the majority of COs were 'men of the highest character and principles' and did not deserve to be treated 'in a way in which any noble Lord individually would be ashamed to treat a fellow creature'.[26]

Thereafter, Frank spoke whenever the subject arose. He abhorred the cavalier attitude of the tribunals. He defended those who were not members of pacifist churches such as the Quakers or Christadelphians, arguing that it was not only the religious who possessed a conscience. He regretted that COs were sent to the front to become a centre of disaffection harmful to morale, and questioned why the government could not devise a means of dealing with them not designed to immediately rouse their objections: there was plenty of necessary road-building or factory work to be done. After the government established domestic farming programmes and suchlike as an alternative to non-combatant service, Frank continued to draw attention to the brutal treatment of absolutists who refused even that – though he considered them 'wrong-headed and obstinate'. On 4 July 1916, he raised the case of C. H. Norman, a member of the No-Conscription Fellowship, sentenced to two years' detention at Wandsworth Barracks, shocking the House with extracts from Norman's diary describing treatment that today would be considered torture. The commandant at Wandsworth, he said, endorsed such treatments; and Brigadier-General Childs was personally responsible 'that [such] brutality in a subordinate is excused or winked at'. Then, after expressing his own certainty that their lordships would deprecate any such attempts to terrorise men into making them act against their consciences, he moved 'that in the opinion of this House it is undesirable to subject military prisoners to punishments not authorised by law' – a resolution phrased in such a way that none could vote against it – and was 'jolly as a boy' to have won 'a little triumph' for the cause.[27] Thereafter, he continued in a similar vein in opposition to the deportation of Russian refugees who refused to enrol in the British Army, to the prohibition of pacifist meetings under DORA, and in defence of British subjects interned without charge.

Meanwhile, on his personal domestic front, Mollie's decree *absolute* had been issued on 24 January, and several days later Frank wrote to Bertrand that 'with such stealth you probably did not observe it' he had become a free man and had immediately surrendered that liberty to 'the finest, most wonderful and most loving woman in the world, who also has the courage to marry me'. Her sister approved, he said, and he would 'do all in my power to ensure peace and great happiness for the tail end of my life'.[28]

Frank and Elizabeth's wedding was a private affair, witnessed only by Charlotte and Bertrand beneath a blanket of thick yellow fog on a rainy Friday, 11 February 1916 at the Register Office on Henrietta Street. Charlotte might have approved, but Elizabeth's mother, who had been kept in the dark, was 'incredulous' and Frank's Aunt Agatha, who had had so much to do with the fallout of his first marriage, though unsurprised, found it 'nonetheless painful' both for its potential failure and for the 'not so pleasant' stories she had heard about Elizabeth.[29] Cobbie – despite his earlier doubts – said he could 'not do otherwise than rejoice at the sight of so much happiness'.[30]

Frank immediately set about introducing Elizabeth around, resulting in friendships with three of his oldest friends and their wives: Edgar and Frieda Jepson, Harry and Winifred Marillier, and St George and Edith Fox-Pitt. He took Elizabeth to dine at the RAC, and introduced her to the Pirries, John Sargeaunt and Amy Otter (whom Elizabeth found 'very overwhelming and efficient'). In April they visited Winchester and she met Revd Dickins ('who clearly thought that as I had married F. I must be improper'). They motored on into the West Country, and on their way back called in on St George's sister, Lady Agnes Grove. Then, in June, Santayana was invited to TH and afterwards said of Elizabeth that though she was rather pretty, amusing and cleverer than her predecessors, she had 'no *fond*, no heart, and I hardly think the union (and hence my acquaintance with her) will be very long-lived'. He gave the marriage no more than a year or two – 'like the war'.[31]

And what of Mollie, who had been forced to stand aside to accommodate this unpromising union? Santayana saw her only once after she and Frank separated, bumping into her quite by chance on the seafront at Brighton, surrounded by 'a bevy of little white dogs ... richly draped in furs, and rounder than ever'. She invited him to her lodgings where he found her happily ensconced with 'easy-going' friends, surrounded by 'card-tables, glasses and bottles ... so much in her element'. She appeared happy, but was she *happier*? Santayana concluded not – 'her pride had been wounded' and she had made 'great sacrifices' to be with Frank; but she had a fixed income and could grow old in peace.[32] She retired to a rented house in West Hampstead and eventually to a 'flatlet' in Holland Park. Her health continued to be fragile but, she told her son ahead of their 1928 reunion, 'I have great optimism and my Irish humour is still strong'.[33] It would sustain her for many years, and the terms of her departure from Frank's life would keep her in his story yet.

Her replacement, meanwhile, was struggling. As Cobbie had predicted, the world that Elizabeth married into was of Frank's making. With the exception of her family, the friends they saw were largely his, as was the routine they followed. Though he gave her Mollie's hut at TH to work in, there was little time to write in it. What with redecorations at Gordon Square, Bertrand's lectures and Frank's speeches in the Lords, dinners at the RAC or with friends, Elizabeth was kept busy running around after her new husband in support of him as his wife. In sharp contrast were the many evenings Frank would suddenly announce he was dining at his club alone, often not reappearing until the early hours of the morning. These evenings Elizabeth spent at Gordon Square, reflecting on the disappointment of her married life and her sheer bewilderment at Frank's sudden fits of temper. 'I find it shattering, the insecurity of it, the jumpiness,' she wrote on 17 April, only two months into their marriage. She told herself that before they were married he 'never once in all the two years showed this temper', which, though not strictly true, expresses the extent of her dismay – as do her frequent complaints of the 'horrid scolding of Miss Young' whenever they returned to TH, where Frank was 'especially intolerable and quarrelsome'; the 'rude & disgusting' behaviour that she told him she wouldn't tolerate; the tempers which 'I can't go on every day recording'; the petting of the dogs 'and I left out in the cold'. It was becoming 'an impossible life if one is to remain sane' and her wretchedness became a common feature of her journal, as did their arguments 'about my faults & his virtues'.

Miss Young appears never to have objected to her treatment, writing to Bertrand on Frank's death of her 'treasured memories' of 'the many years, so happily spent at Telegraph House' and how she would miss writing to and receiving letters from Frank, which she occasionally did right up to his death.[34] Elizabeth, on the other hand, objected very much and her various reactions only seemed to make matters worse. On several occasions when she was 'goaded to impatience' an argument escalated 'with the usual hopeless results'. When she tried to humour him with her 'funny little activities' he was not to be so cajoled. In desperation, she determined to 'sedulously cultivate not caring' and by mid-August, with everything else having failed, resorted to 'absolute passivity'. It appeared to do the trick – at least there was calm – but ultimately this was not the way to deal with Frank. It simply gave him more licence to project his own behaviour onto her.

What could account for it? Was this just Frank in his uncompensated state, unchanged since 1890 when Mabel Edith fled back to her mother after only three months of marriage? Or was there something else? It has been suggested that shortly after their marriage a horrified Elizabeth discovered a secret cocaine addiction. This is based on a single journal entry concerning a cocaine-based prescription and another reporting Frank's objection to Elizabeth being in his office. Without further evidence, it is impossible to assess how long Frank took such medication. Cocaine was not then a freely available recreational drug. Its illicit use was very much limited to Soho and the West End and the 'leisured class that regards itself as Bohemian' – the so-called 'smart set' in which Frank had no part.[35] Much more likely is that his addiction was to gambling, and his drug of choice bridge. The fact that he was temperamentally worse away from London and the manner and speed in which he would abandon Elizabeth on their return both point to this. 'He can't for a day not go away to his bridge,' she recorded on 16 June.

In the midst of all this, on 4 June 1916, Elizabeth heard that her youngest daughter, Felicitas, was dead. News from Germany was slow and it took two weeks for her to learn that the cause was pneumonia. Frank was sweet and kind for a couple of days, then reverted to type. A remorseful Elizabeth reflected on the fact that Felicitas had died miles away from home 'without her mummy & only sixteen'. Days before her first meeting with Santayana, Elizabeth recorded that she had got down to the 'very dregs of hopeless misery'. By the end of July, after many more 'horrid scenes' with Frank, she concluded, 'Life not worth living.' She wrote to Liebet in America that for her own sanity she needed a break and was secretly planning to join her there when H. B. was safely installed at Eton that September. She was 'practically in prison' at TH, she wrote; every request to go out was met with 'bad blood'.[36] And when Santayana visited again in August, he found 'the moral atmosphere already very heavily charged with matrimonial thunder, and the lady so largely took me into her confidence, when by rights I am *his* friend, that my position became a delicate and almost a false one'.[37] On 26 September – after only six months of marriage – while Frank was in London, Elizabeth motored to Charlotte's from where she caught a train to Liverpool and made good her escape on the *Adriatic* to New York. She was greeted by Liebet and the pair travelled to San Ysidro, California, where on 1 November she wrote to tell Frank of her whereabouts.

Between her leaving and this letter there was minimal contact. The note Elizabeth had left telling Frank she was leaving (but not where she was going) had provoked a response 'crying out very pitifully why had I used him so'. Since then, only one letter had reached her and it spoke 'not a word except of business'. Frank did look for her and appears to have asked friends to help. On 7 October, Agnes Grove tried to find her, but of course she was already too late. A letter from Bertrand, written on 5 October and arriving with Elizabeth on the 31st, revealed that Frank had shown him her departing letter. Bertrand described it as full of hatred. Elizabeth responded that the 'great complication in my misery is that I love him ... for all the dear things he is right at the back'. She would give the whole world to 'run straight back to him & get into his lap & stay there *tight* forever. And that *is* what I would do if I had the faintest hope of it's being understood ... It would be the sweetest thing,' she said, 'but oh Bertie, how can he ever really change himself?' She asked Bertrand to make Frank see what she had failed to: that his moods had ruined everything. Echoing Mabel's plea so many years earlier that Lina be allowed to live with them for her protection, Elizabeth insisted that if she returned 'it would be *vital* that G.S. [Gordon Square] should be where [Bertrand's] headquarters are' and in a second letter explained that all she wanted was that home should be 'a place of affection, a place of contentment ... I *can't* live in an atmosphere of qualms.'[38]

To what extent Bertrand intervened is unclear, but on 22 November he wrote to Ottoline, 'My brother has had a friendly letter from Elizabeth and is very happy — I do hope she will come back. He is really very devoted to her.'[39] On 21 December, Frank started for the US, arriving in California on 5 January 1917. There he stayed with Elizabeth and Liebet for two months. Liebet – who was no fan of Frank's – later recorded that he arrived 'with hardly any warning ... jauntily, and quite sure of a welcome' and proceeded to ruin their enjoyment by ordering everything with 'a heavy hand'. She watched incredulously as her mother 'bowed to it all, ever anxious to assuage, to pour balm, to agree to the most outrageous demands'.[40] But Elizabeth was happy. In March, she accompanied Frank back to New York, where she stayed until she heard he had safely disembarked at Liverpool. In America, she completed a novel and saw Liebet married before eventually following Frank in the summer. Back at TH on 15 August, she wrote to Liebet that she was 'in a bath of love, as I told you I would be'; that Frank (who appears in the letters as 'Dad') 'envelopes me to the exclusion of the world – but it is very sweet and presently there'll be a few peep-holes I expect when he has got over the first fine careless rapture ... I regard my visit to America as the best thing in every way I ever did.' It certainly appeared to have effected a change. The following week, H. B. was amazed 'at the flow of billing and cooing that goes on'. Frank remained 'a mass of dimples – they've never disappeared once yet even for a moment' and Elizabeth felt 'very smug and spoilt'.[41] Throughout September, things continued in a similar vein. When Santayana visited later that month, he reported that the couple were having a second honeymoon: an 'embarrassing and not very agreeable sight for the by-stander'.[42] In London, too, Elizabeth got her wish. Bertrand had moved into Gordon Square the previous summer, though more for pecuniary reasons than her gratification. Nonetheless, Elizabeth found herself 'greatly amused and entertained' by the brothers, describing her *ménage* as one of 'volcanic interest':

> My two men continue to afford much excitement and variety in the *ménage* – Bertie is the most charming queer creature – elf-like, imp-like, a Christ and a devil, angelically saint-like and thoroughly malignant – the weirdest of human beings – and Dad you know...[43]

Meanwhile, it was not Frank's political activities that dominated the Russell household for once, but Bertrand's. Since March 1916, he had been actively involved with the No-Conscription Fellowship (NCF), an organisation that was largely made up of absolutists against alternative service. As a forty-three-year-old married man, Bertrand fell outside the conscription parameters but was eager to be involved. He spoke at the NCF conference in April, wrote a weekly column in its journal *Tribunal*, pamphlets, articles and letters to the press and generally agitated to try to provoke his arrest for the publicity it would draw to the campaign. In May 1916, when the circulation of one of his pamphlets led to the prosecution of several NCF members under DORA, Bertrand wrote to the *Times* revealing his authorship. Within a fortnight he was summoned. His case was heard at the Mansion House on 5 June and he was fined £100 plus costs. When his appeal was subsequently rejected, he refused to pay, hoping again to provoke arrest. Instead, bailiffs were sent to seize his books and furniture. At auction, his non-NCF friends bought them back to prevent his imprisonment, but they could not prevent further ramifications. In July 1916, the Home Office refused Bertrand the necessary passport for a lecturing obligation at Harvard and he was sacked by Trinity College. Undeterred, he went on a 'stop-the-war' tour of South Wales and was exhilarated by the reaction he received. Frank cautioned him not to get carried away. Beware popular audiences, he advised: 'The average [member] is a fool that any able man who can talk can sway him for a time' and the heady effect of this adulation 'a little like taking to drink'. He was concerned that Bertrand would regret acting in such a manner as to effectively cut himself off from academic life and suggested, 'What the world wants of first class intellects like yours is not action – for which the ordinary politician or demagogue is good enough – but thought, a much more rare quality ... you are *wasting* yourself.'[44]

Still undeterred, Bertrand resolved to travel to Haverhill, Suffolk, to inspect one of the CO work-camps. The Home Office, fearing he intended to incite the COs to down tools, responded rashly by pressuring the War Office to ban him from designated 'prohibited areas'. These were mostly coastal regions and the prohibition intended to stop spies passing information to Germany. In Bertrand's case, it was a knee-jerk reaction that would cause the government much embarrassment. Bertrand toyed with them by getting others to read his lectures in banned areas. Behind the scenes, George Cockerill, Director of Special Intelligence at the War Office, effectively asked Bertrand to behave himself so they could lift the ban. Bertrand refused to stop publicly advocating pacifism. He continued his column for *Tribunal* and covertly authored the absolutist plea *I Appeal unto Caesar*.[45] But by September 1917, he had become disillusioned by infighting within the NCF and had determined to return to philosophy. He accepted a commission from an American publisher for the book that would become *Roads to Freedom*, planned a lecture series on mathematical logic to be delivered that winter and began winding down his NCF activities. To assist and encourage him, Frank took it upon himself (with early signs of success) to lobby George Cockerill to lift the ban.

Unfortunate, then, that Bertrand was talked into writing one last article for the *Tribunal* for their first edition of 1918, and that in that piece, which appealed for early peace negotiations with Germany, he should write, 'The American garrison which will by that time be occupying England and France, whether or not they will prove efficient against the Germans, will no doubt be capable of intimidating strikers, an occupation to which the American Army is accustomed when at home.'[46] All Frank's good work was undone – and worse. George Cockerill immediately withdrew from discussions and on 9 February Bertrand was summoned to Bow Street charged with making statements 'likely to prejudice His Majesty's relations with the United States of America'. He was sentenced to six months' imprisonment in the second division, commuted to six months in the first on appeal.

Thus, on 1 May, the Gordon Square *ménage* was relieved of its 'queer creature' who was removed to Brixton and Elizabeth was left alone again with Frank. Bertrand would be sorely missed, but his incarceration introduced the Russells to a new cast of characters: Dorothy Wrinch, a mathematics student who had come to Gordon Square for weekly tuition sessions with Bertrand after his sacking from Trinity; Gladys Rinder, a prominent member of the NCF; and, of course, Bertrand's love interests: Ottoline, who had long since ceased to be a sexual partner but remained a confidant, and her replacement, the 'young and strikingly attractive aristocratic actress' Lady Constance Malleson, more commonly known by her stage name, Colette.[47] Collectively, they would become Bertrand's regular visitors and correspondents during his jail term, directed by Frank, whose position and personal experience of prison ideally qualified him for the job of Bertrand's right-hand man. From the moment Bertrand crossed the threshold, Frank took over all personal, financial and business matters for his brother. Elizabeth furnished his room and Frank saw to it that various perks were added to the concessions already allowed prisoners in the first division. He used his 'devastating charm' to see to it that Bertrand was granted permission to review books and send out approved manuscripts, that his light could stay on until 10 p.m. and that visitors could bring flowers. Three visitors were permitted in any one weekly visit: Frank or Elizabeth with two others from a list of priority and compatibility drawn up by Bertrand beforehand.[48] To get round the restriction of a single weekly outward letter – usually to Frank – Bertrand included messages for Frank to pass on, which read like 'messages of a medium trying to get through things from another world'.[49] There were love letters to Colette written in French and disguised to look like the products of his research and others to colleagues and friends hidden inside the uncut pages of books, such that his correspondence became substantial. In return, Frank and Elizabeth wrote him joint letters which amply reflect their respective personalities: Frank's contributions were businesslike, keeping Bertrand appraised of actions taken on his behalf and war news; Elizabeth's contained things she thought he would *really* want to know – chiefly about Colette. The two women had become firm friends and often visited together, though Colette never on the same week as Ottoline.

The flow of information into and out of Brixton reveals much, not only about Bertrand but also Frank and Elizabeth, filling a gap left in their story by the absence of Elizabeth's journal for 1917. Clearly her confidence that she and Frank had weathered their personal storm was premature. A comment from Bertrand in a letter to Ottoline of 16 June is very telling: 'I must explain about money,' he wrote. 'My brother's quarrels with his wife may require me at any moment to take her side, and perhaps leave him. If I leave him, I starve.'[50] Elizabeth's confidences had finally won him over. Colette, too, must have been in the know – another of Bertrand's letters to her reveals that Elizabeth was considering a second flight: 'I do *hope* she won't leave my brother before I come out, but if she does, she must always keep in touch with me – she will always have my affection.'[51] This change of attitude, brought about by his stay at Gordon Square and Elizabeth's attentiveness during his incarceration, was expressed simultaneously with praise of Frank to Gladys Rinder for his having done 'masses of business for me, all with wonderful success'.[52] From this point forward, Bertrand considered his allegiance split, despite the certain knowledge that his intimacy with Elizabeth would not be well received: his brother's jealousy, he said, was 'quite oriental'.[53]

Frank, meanwhile, continued to campaign on Bertrand's behalf. He negotiated with Bertrand's publisher, Stanley Unwin, who agreed to take *Roads to Freedom* for UK publication. Further, on 22 July, Frank was able to tell Bertrand that Cockerill had agreed to lift his ban, and, four days later, that he had seen the Home Secretary, Sir George Cave, and 'am authorised to say you shall have 6 weeks remission'.[54] Though Bertrand's much later recollection – that Cave was Frank's fag at Winchester and therefore bound to do his bidding – proved incorrect,[55] Frank used all his influence to try to secure an August release. In the end, Bertrand was released on 14 September; but not back into the Gordon Square *ménage*. Perhaps sensing a growing allegiance between his brother and wife, Frank had told Bertrand he was no longer welcome. They did, however, all celebrate the Armistice together and also Christmas, which was notable for having 'no quarrels'. It would not last.

24

Paradise Lost

'F. did something wrong.'[1]

On 15 January 1919, Elizabeth took a phone call for Frank at Gordon Square that he said had not come through to his club because he could not tell business associates he played bridge in the afternoons. But Elizabeth knew he was not at his club that afternoon; ergo, 'he was doing something wrong'. Two days later he lunched with a lady called Ruth Anderson and the following day refused to stay at home with a sick Elizabeth but 'rushed off in his car' to show it to Ruth and 'came in most reluctantly after 5 on my insisting'.[2] Coincidence? Perhaps, though Elizabeth would later come to suspect an affair *and* had already told Santayana that Frank was sleeping with Frieda Jepson. Santayana was not convinced: 'Elizabeth ought to have known; but she was beginning at that time to hate her husband, and hatred is a great deceiver.'[3] On 1 February, she told Liebet that Frank was going to sack his secretary having engaged another 'for carrying on purposes', describing him as 'an elderly roysterer' who, despite repeated adulteries, 'goes on being fond of me – or behaves like it'. Then, on 24 March, believing conclusively 'F's renewed adultery', Elizabeth left Gordon Square for good. A note told Frank of her discovery but, again, not where she was going. She took refuge with her brother and wrote to Liebet that Frank's behaviour 'made it impossible for a decent woman to stay' but that she did not feel as wretched as last time, knowing now 'how utterly *bad* he is'.[4]

Frank's immediate reaction to this second flight is recorded only by others. Elizabeth imagined him happily 'plotting how to punish me'. She took a flat at 2 Whitehall Court where Bertrand visited her. Bertrand, by contrast, thought Frank took it surprisingly well. On 12 April he told Ottoline that Frank 'pretends to be heart-broken but isn't. He is friendly to me, and glad I should see Elizabeth. She is hurt that he takes her going so quietly.' In his role as go-between, Bertrand expected both to quarrel with him but found Elizabeth the more exacting – though she 'cheered up' when Frank instructed his lawyer to tell hers that he was 'contemplating suicide'![5] Yet as all prospects of a reconciliation evaporated, so too did Frank's equanimity. Over the Easter weekend, while Frank was absent, Elizabeth went to Gordon Square to remove most of her furniture. The following week she sent removers – Shoolbred's – to clear out her belongings from TH. Frank hurried round to their warehouse to inspect the items taken, afterwards writing angrily to Bertrand that he belittled his grievances and was failing to use his influence to 'persuade' Elizabeth to return. He demanded Bertrand cut off communication with her as Elizabeth's brother had with him. Bertrand expressed surprise that Frank should not want Elizabeth to see 'the only person at all likely to soften her towards you' and claimed Elizabeth had been 'exceedingly inclined towards a reconciliation' until she received Frank's writ.[6]

The writ was for an action in the King's Bench which began on 8 July against Shoolbred's for trespass and the unlawful removal of items from TH.[7] Expressing Frank's hurt and frustration, it was perceived as the action of an impuissant man who, having lost his wife, was reduced to nitpicking over a handful of possessions: five books, five cushions, some flexible wire and light bulbs that he'd bought, a tea-table, chessboard, hammock and tennis balls that were gifts from Elizabeth and some furniture which Elizabeth had paid for in lieu of a verbal agreement to share the cost of improvements at TH. Under oath, Frank was forced to admit that the cushions, though disappeared from TH, had not actually been seen at Shoolbred's; likewise the light bulbs, which had been in Elizabeth's cupboard and, he assumed, taken with it. In Elizabeth's defence Sir Edward Marshall Hall showed as much zeal as he had in Lina's libel trial. He revelled in Frank's admission that he had no objection to Elizabeth taking items of 'personal affection' if done in accordance with 'the terms that I offered' (which were extensive) and Frank's description of the 'many months of secret preparation, plotting and spying' that had led to his wife 'furtively' leaving the house. With righteous indignation Frank confessed that his reasons for exerting his 'strict legal rights' were that Elizabeth had concealed her address, abandoned her position as his wife and 'browbeat and terrorised' his servants in the removal of her belongings. Elizabeth's contrasting witty turn magnified Frank's unreasonableness. She recounted how she had previously said to him, 'What a good thing this is my tea-table ... How angry you would be at all these stains on it if it were yours' and claimed she would never had given him the hammock as it 'would not have held him'. It was strictly for her use and that of 'small visitors'. The upshot was that the judge agreed with Marshall Hall that Frank had 'lost his head' over the matter. Frank left the courtroom with a lantern, three books, the chess-set and tennis balls, but poorer for the costs.

After the trial, Elizabeth wrote to Bertrand of her much-anticipated return to Switzerland. He replied saying how 'hateful' it was to think of her so 'tormented and battered'. He hoped she had now 'done with F': 'You have won your liberty, which is worth a price' and now 'can build up friendships with people who will appreciate you without wanting to destroy you'.[8]

He hoped being back at the chalet would be healing. It proved to be. Very soon Elizabeth was hard at work on her next book.

Frank, meanwhile, had not completely 'lost his head', but was deep into a project very close to his heart. Three days before Elizabeth's flight in March, he had written to Stanley Unwin proposing the volume of Lionel Johnson's adolescent letters. Unwin immediately accepted, no doubt keen to capitalise on the publication of two volumes of Lionel's poems that appeared in 1915–16. Frank's reasons for publishing are unclear – unless the idea presented itself through his dealings with Unwin on Bertrand's behalf the previous year – but his candid introduction described the letters as having been his 'salvation in many a dark hour'. They were the product of a man for whom he retained a 'passionate devotion and admiration' and must have been a welcome distraction from the situation with Elizabeth.[9] Having declined to do extensive notes, he had the manuscript submitted by 6 May and published by September. The poignancy of the letters was not lost on critics – one of whom wrote that 'a far-wandered spirit … beat its wings against the mortal bars in the prison-breast' of the 'ardent, lonely' young Johnson[10] – but exception was taken to Frank's criticisms of Lionel's parents as 'narrow-minded and prejudiced Anglicans' who had provided an 'arid' home life for their son; indeed, the *Spectator* concluded that the anonymous editor's information must have been slight as the material did not 'eke out the malice'.[11] It was a public condemnation repeated privately by Lionel's sister, Isabella, who threatened legal action to have the book withdrawn. Frank was unapologetic. These things were always 'painful, surprising and unbelievable' to families, he responded, but that was no reason not to say them. Isabella's reaction only confirmed his judgement.[12] The book remained unchanged.

Back in Switzerland, Elizabeth finished *In the Mountains* in February 1920 and saw it published in August. Written in journal form, it opens with the anonymous narrator crawling up the mountain 'like a sick ant … too tired even to be able to thank God that I had got home' after five years' absence, never dreaming 'I would come back to it alone'. 'How rich I was in love; now how poor, how stripped of all I had' after the 'dreadful betrayal of trust that is the blackest wretchedness of all.'[13] The book has been interpreted as Elizabeth's reflection on masculine destruction as embodied both by Frank and the Great War versus the feminine healing powers of nature, empathy and forgiveness.[14] After a dark beginning, its message is hopeful. Yet Frank continued to haunt its author. Back in England with Charlotte on 23 May, Elizabeth 'looked through field glasses at the Awful Back of TH' and exclaimed, 'oh the horror!'[15] Frank wrote her 'horrible insulting' letters, supposedly dictating them to his secretary and sending copies to her friends. Bertrand told Ottoline the letters went into 'the most intimate details' and that Frank was proud of them.[16] It was Frank's tendency, Bertrand later observed, to become 'cruel and unscrupulous' when he lost anyone's love and his heart was wounded.[17]

Elizabeth, meanwhile, accused Frank of infidelity with Ruth Anderson – a fact he expressly denied, describing Ruth as 'virginal and Churchy to a degree' and therefore 'kind'.[18] She continued to see Bertrand, Santayana, the Marilliers and Fox-Pitts. It was all maddening for Frank, but whether sufficiently so as to make him write and circulate a 'rather clumsy parody' of *In the Mountains* as Wells claimed, or highlight 'every familiar reference to faithless wives' in it and post 'the resulting dossier' to Elizabeth as Frank Swinnerton professed, is unclear. And though the end product undoubtedly suggested the fact, there is a certain poetic licence in the further suggestion that Frank thereby directly triggered Elizabeth's ultimate revenge: her 'intolerably cruel' novel, *Vera*.[19] Begun two months before *In the Mountains* was released, *Vera* gave Elizabeth 'much trouble'. She wrestled with it throughout January and February, completed it in March and saw it published by Macmillan on 13 September 1921, eventually satisfied it was her best work.

According to Santayana, Elizabeth did not set out to write about Frank, but as the theme was 'her own domestic tragedy' the male protagonist became increasingly like him as the story progressed.[20] Key elements of the plot do not relate directly to them and the setting is sufficiently disguised as to not perfectly describe recognisable locations, but inevitably, if not intentionally, the characters took on attributes that Santayana deemed 'photographic'. Into the young heroine, Lucy, Elizabeth poured her retrospective feelings regarding Frank's courtship and in the comic tyrant, Wemyss, magnified his faults. Lucy hangs on Wemyss's every word. He becomes her 'tower of rock and refuge', first in the role of 'near male relative' and afterwards as lover. An initially 'horrified' Lucy is 'engulfed' in kisses, 'swallowed up' in Wemyss's 'victory', the 'great, glorious, central blaze' of a love she gradually returns, won over by his 'simple, adoring letters'. When they are apart, she has 'misgivings', but Wemyss forges ahead with wedding plans, oblivious to her feelings, determined to possess his 'little love'. Once married, his boyishness gives way to childish tantrums, his high spirits become demanding and exhausting, he is hurt by any slip in Lucy's undivided attention and sulks or becomes fault-finding in the highest degree. Lucy always somehow manages to say or do the wrong thing and soon learns that 'a doubt in her mind was best kept there'. Wemyss makes impossible and contradictory demands of servants, releases unbridled rage one minute and is playful the next. In one cringeworthy passage he asks Lucy, 'Who's my duddely-umpty little girl?' as he bounces her up and down like an infant. His odiousness is inescapable. 'When we relish the defects of the hero in *Vera*,' Swinnerton wrote, 'we are as it were hand in glove with the author, who, perceiving our enjoyment, will playfully decorate her accurate observation with newly invented absurdities of the most scathing – and, to the victim, infuriating – order.'[21]

Though today von Arnim scholars read more into *Vera* than a straightforward dissection of Elizabeth's relationship with Frank, and her most recent biographer generously suggests that Wemyss is 'an amalgam of the many objectionable male characteristics [Elizabeth] had encountered',[22] there is no doubt contemporaries interpreted it as being meant for Frank, the seamless blurring of fact and fiction tarring him with a warped and heavily laden brush. Santayana suggested it was written with 'the spite of a hunted animal' and its publication in Frank's lifetime truly cruel.[23] In due course, it resulted in Bertrand advising his children, 'Do not marry a novelist' and caused his future wife, Edith, to reflect that Elizabeth had a 'sweet-sour flavour' which might be considered 'corrosive'. Colette said that Bertrand 'never quite forgave' her for it.[24] And Frank? He did what he always did: in furious indignation he turned to the law.

On 5 October 1921, Vandercom & Co. wrote to Elizabeth's publisher that Frank's being so 'insultingly caricatured and brought into contempt' was a 'covert and scurrilous attack' on his character. They demanded *Vera*'s withdrawal as a 'serious and damaging' libel.[25] MacMillan denied that Wemyss was anything other than fictitious. A gleeful Elizabeth wrote to Liebet that Frank's action 'put the cap on his own head!' It would also heighten interest in a book that otherwise 'simmers: more discussed and less bought' than any of Elizabeth's others.[26] Frank backed down but did not do so willingly. The pair continued to badmouth each other. When Bertrand married Dorothy Wrinch's friend Dora Black in September 1921, Frank's speech included reference to 'that wife who libels me'.[27] Subsequently he apparently made the absurd suggestion that Elizabeth's relationship with Cobbie, then eighty-one, was more than platonic. In return, Elizabeth claimed Dorothy was now her 'illegitimate' replacement. Elizabeth's continued contact with Bertrand and Santayana earned them both accusations of disloyalty.

In this frame of mind, Frank sat down to write *My Life and Adventures*, published in March 1923. On the whole, the book was well received. The *Mail* commented that, 'steering clear both of apology and boastfulness', Frank had produced 'a very human document'. The *Sketch* quoted extensively from it, praising its 'considerable humour'. The *Guardian* took the opportunity to suggest that it demonstrated the wisdom that earls should 'live like earls and not like electricians' and the *TLS* said it showed Frank for what he was: a 'conscientious rebel'. Others praised Frank's candour, suggesting that, though he could not be mistaken for a modest man, he was at least intense and sincere. All agreed it was entertaining. Jepson said it brought back 'so vividly' the old days which 'had grown dim'.[28] Nobody mentioned its omissions. Bertrand, for example, disappears from the book after childhood to re-emerge at the end only to substantiate Frank's reflective comments on religion and science. Frank's friendship with Santayana is reduced to 'an acquaintance of long standing'.[29] Elizabeth is completely shunned. There is not one word or line in reference to her. It reads as if she never existed. Instead, Mollie is honoured with a photograph entitled 'The Countess Russell' and the statement, 'Though I have been married often – too often, Lord Halsbury thought – I have really only had one wife.'

In the wake of *Vera*, Frank chose the moral high ground, claiming his reticence was to prevent 'those who still live' being 'embarrassed or wounded by such frankness'. Yet his closing 'Au Revoir' to his readers and the allusion in his final paragraph to further life experiences 'both sad and joyful' which 'if it were desired, I should like to be permitted to dwell upon' left Elizabeth in trepidation of a second volume.[30] Wisely she kept her disparaging portrayal of him in *Dogs* until after his death. Santayana, by contrast, honestly conveyed to Frank his disappointment in the diminution of their friendship, but not before feeling Frank's continued displeasure when his suggestion that he visit TH as usual that summer was greeted with a lukewarm 'Do as you like'. Only now that Elizabeth had put a barrier between them did Frank confess to ever feeling 'attached' to Santayana when it carried with it the accusation of betrayal. Santayana went to TH, was 'largely ignored', had half expected to see Mollie reinstated but was taken instead to visit a widow whom he assumed was 'the star now in the ascendant'.[31] It was the last time the friends would meet.

As for Elizabeth, she found relief in her escape but never stopped lamenting her folly in involving herself with Frank. Though she concluded she needed the war and a second husband to 'really grow up', a 'dark shadow' periodically cast itself over her journal long after Frank's death.[32] On 6 February 1939 she wrote,

> 25 years ago today F. arrived at the chalet early a.m. where Teppi and I were alone. The blue drawing-room. My doubts and misgiving. His overwhelmingness. Teppi's enthusiasm – '*Dieses Auge*', etc. Ah, if only I had steered clear of that devil then! It was a Friday.[33]

She would always view Frank in this way and their relationship as 'a great love and a great betrayal'. Frank would too, but the betrayal, of course, was not his but hers. In a last letter to Santayana – a letter that to some extent lessened the bitterness of their last meeting – Frank confessed,

> ... when Elizabeth left me I went completely dead and have never come alive again. She never realised how I worshipped and loved her, and how I idealised what is in essence a worthless character, and her light-hearted cruelty killed something in me which has never revived ... I ascribe my bad heart entirely to the year's anguish I suffered after she left me and her betrayal with a kiss of Judas.[34]

The tragedy of Frank's life might be said to lie in his inability to realise the home life he craved with the woman he professed to love the best. His health began to deteriorate: he developed angina. Once again, personal happiness became dependent on the opiate of work and the empty vices into which he sank. To compound matters, from 1921 his business and gambling practices resulted in the very real threat of bankruptcy. Frank left Gordon Square for a less prestigious apartment in Bayswater and Mollie was forced to accept a reduction in her annuity of £200. TH went into the Mollie, Countess Russell Trust and Withers took over its legal administration, promptly raising a £4,200 mortgage against it and buying its furniture and effects for £1,000. Both were rented back to Frank for £800 p.a. In 1922, Frank borrowed £2,000 from Bertrand and the following year, he sold the remainder of his

Irish land. By July 1924, he could no longer pay his rent. He moved out of TH into the neighbouring gardener's cottage. For three years, Frank was reduced to the position of caretaker while his beloved TH sat empty. Timely investment in a Bolivian tin mine in 1926 enabled the mortgage to be settled, but Withers still advocated selling. Frank could not bring himself to, but to all intents and purposes his estate was lost.

In December 1926 Bertrand offered to take TH, thinking it answered all their needs. He and Dora were looking to start an experimental school and needed premises.[35] TH provided the perfect location. Frank readily agreed. He suggested that for £600 p.a., it could be taken out of trust and leased to Bertrand directly. Withers vetoed the suggestion. What if Mollie outlived Frank? TH was still needed to secure her annuity. In the end it was decided that Bertrand would let house and furnishings from the trust for ten years at £400 p.a. to exactly cover Mollie's claim. Frank would vacate the cottage and move temporarily into premises nearby. Quickly, however, he demonstrated a reluctance to go by pressing Bertrand to buy the gardener's cottage with 7 acres from the trust to fund the building of a house for himself somewhere else on the estate. A concerned Dora went to see Frank and found him 'difficult and queer and, I think, rather ill'. His close presence, she feared, would 'cast a gloom' over their enterprise.[36] They delayed, concentrating instead on converting TH into Beacon Hill School, and Frank finally departed for a smaller property, Dyke House, in Methwold, Suffolk. He was not happy about it, and expressed as much over the next four years in a campaign of 'small annoyances'.

Early arguments concerned furnishings and effects. Frank drew up a list of items he could not take with him or would have no use for. Certain furnishings were included in the lease, but other items he pressed Bertrand to buy – everything from tools to pot-plants, garden furniture and a host of sundry items, including a telescope and hammock (reminiscent of, but presumably not, Elizabeth's). He behaved like a 'common swindler' in Bertrand's view, and when Dora dared to suggest that the contents included in the lease were overvalued, Frank declared he 'couldn't communicate' with her. Bertrand refused to mediate: 'I hate quarrelling with my brother far more than you realize,' he wrote to Dora from the safety of Cornwall.[37] He directed her to his solicitor, Crompton Llewellyn Davies, younger brother of Frank's old Oxford friend Maurice. Crompton suggested a new agreement, whereby they would take TH unfurnished for £200. Withers seemed amenable, but 'will Frank be willing to give up the pleasure of cutting off his nose to spite your face?' Crompton asked Bertrand.[38] Apparently not. Frank's refusal to compromise or renegotiate was 'really maddening' and culminated a year later in Frank's 'favourite form of amusement': a threatened lawsuit. Keen to avoid the scandal and expense, Bertrand yielded 'not to justice but to blackmail'. Dora wished to proceed, but Bertrand's nerves were 'not sufficiently tough' to take on Frank in the high court.[39] When Frank subsequently settled for a very reasonable £61, Bertrand was astounded: 'What a funny fellow my brother is ... I can only think he desired the sensation of successful bullying and having acquired that, was comparatively indifferent to the cash.'[40] It was not the end of the matter. There were further disagreements over water and electricity supplies and wear-and-tear to the furniture. Legal action was threatened over the telescope, which was returned 'damaged' (Frank suspected schoolchildren had interfered with it and demanded £6 compensation). Bertrand would have readily paid 'a lump sum to secure immunity from irritation' but doubted whether they would ever be able to anticipate 'all the different ways in which my brother could annoy me and rule them all out'.[41]

These issues seemed petty, but were in fact an expression of something much deeper. For though Frank had scorned his rank, title and Russell ancestry, for all his rebellion, he had made Telegraph House his earldom. Aware of the folly of attachment to 'external things' and the apparent inconsistency with his politics, he had become in his personal habits 'as conservative as any fellow Wykehamist could be', detesting change in his surroundings to such an extent that 'I once went so far as to tell the House of Lords that I believed I was the only real Tory in it'.[42] In the last decade of his life, he became an increasingly frequent sight in the Lords, surrounded by other noblemen all equally attached to their country estates. Frank's was of his own making: his first true home since Ravenscroft. Thirty years earlier he had proudly fenced it in and given it the acronym TH to juxtapose PL and all it stood for. No doubt he had at one time envisaged passing it on to a son of his own. It had been logical to give it up to his younger brother, but his being compelled to do marked it as a failure. Bertrand said, 'He hated it, and ever after bore me a grudge for inhabiting his paradise.'[43] It was an issue they never completely resolved.

25

A Labouring Lord

In October 1930, Bertrand wrote, 'When the present government falls, or India becomes free (whichever may happen first), I suspect that [Frank] will begin worrying us again about furniture, house-painting, fences, etc.'[1] He supposed the lull in Frank's aggravations was due to his being occupied elsewhere. Much had changed in the dozen years since the end of the war, both in the political landscape and Frank's contribution to it. The Labour Party had proved itself as part of the wartime coalition and the Liberals all but nailed their own coffin. When Labour took office on their own account, briefly in 1924 and again in 1929, Frank at last took his place within Labour's ranks; however, it was not a straightforward transition. Frank might have been Labour's 'candid friend' since 1913, but the single Labour peer listed in the *Constitutional Yearbook* for 1920 was probably not him but the Earl of Kimberley who afterwards became a Labour county councillor. By 1930, Labour still only boasted seventeen peers. Doubtless Frank was among them. But his prior misdemeanours, prolonged independence, continued outspokenness and radical causes hindered his advancement and have effectively wiped him from the pages of Labour's history.[2]

One place in which Frank's radicalism was plainly exhibited was in his 1922 article 'The Difficulties of Bishops' for the Rational Press Association annual. In it, he made a scathing attack on the influence of the Established Church both in the divorce court and in state schools. Another, was in his far more politically damaging association with the British Society for the Study of Sex Psychology (BSSSP), to which he had by then been introduced by Laurence Housman.[3]

The BSSSP had been founded in 1913 'to advance a particularly radical agenda in the field of sex reform' based on the work of writers such as Edward Carpenter and Havelock Ellis.[4] At its meetings controversial issues such as the evils of prostitution, sexual ignorance, disease, homosexuality and 'aberrations of various kinds' were discussed. It was a small but serious society, attracting educationalists, feminists, Malthusians, doctors, lawyers, writers, Fabians, divorce law reformers and advocates of free love. For Frank, membership was a natural adjunct to that of the Medico-Legal Society. The BSSSP confronted socially unacceptable sexual matters with 'insistent investigation' and 'suspension of judgment' – though its members were aware that, from the outside, the 'discussing of intimate and unsavoury sex matters before a public audience of both sexes' no doubt looked salacious.[5] Given Frank's history, one might assume he attended meetings unabashed, but it appears not to have always been the case. When Housman was timetabled to speak on 'exhibitionism' in May 1921, he mildly advised Frank not to come, 'as I may shock you and make your legs blush – or whatever is the most Victorian part of you which succumbs to maiden modesty when "things are said"'.[6] By December 1922, Housman was under the impression Frank had 'shaken the dust of the B.S.S.P. [*sic*] off your feet forever, because it outraged your Victorian modesty!' But in February 1923, Frank paid his dues and in November donated a typewriter and suggested further that, as there was to be a paper on contraception that month, Dr Marie Stopes should be invited to attend.[7]

Marie Stopes had approached Frank in August 1921 after she heard of his 'most cogent arguments against the enforced provision of further canon-fodder and Empire-builders' to the Medico-Legal Society.[8] She offered him the vice-presidency of her new Society for Constructive Birth Control (CBC). He accepted 'with pleasure if you think it won't do you harm', adding, 'I am told to my amusement that I have an entirely undeserved reputation as a profligate roué and it might be said I was controlling my own lapses.'[9] His self-effacing caution proved correct. Marie was forced to withdraw his name after two of her most useful supporters threatened to resign if Frank took the position. 'Aren't people funny,' he wrote in response to her regretful communication, but agreed to give the CBC his wholehearted support anyway, even proposing the vice-presidency to Bertrand at Marie's request. It was the start of a long association which developed into friendship. Frank gave Marie legal advice during her highly publicised libel litigation against Dr Halliday Sutherland for his scathing attack on her promotion of the 'rubber check pessary', and empathised with her 'sense of injury and injustice' when she lost.[10] He advised her to dismiss the judge's accusations of obscenity in her writing. Every social reformer got accused of blasphemy or obscenity, he wrote; it was 'a sort of antiquated earth-work behind which the old guard of reaction entrench themselves'.[11] Interestingly, though, he also suggested she didn't appeal, feeling the odds were stacked against her. She ignored him and won, only to see the verdict overturned in the Lords.

In overtly supporting the CBC, Frank attended meetings, delivered occasional lectures and led discussions. He wrote letters to the *Daily Herald* correcting their misconceptions about Marie's clinic and publicly defended her book *Contraception* (1923), calling it 'a serious attempt to deal with an important subject' which had seen her 'singled out for prosecution'.[12] He even accosted the Director of Public Prosecutions, Sir Archibald Bodkin – renowned for upholding the obscenity laws – but failed to secure approval for Marie's contraceptive propaganda. At the same time, he could be found in the Lords seeking reform of outdated and little-used blasphemy laws and remained outspoken on divorce reform on the three-year run-up to the controversial 1923 Matrimonial Causes Act. Little wonder, then, that when Labour formed a minority government in January 1924, Frank was overlooked.

Historian Martin Pugh has commented that because the first Labour government was largely ineffectual, it is difficult now to comprehend the 'shock waves' their election sent through British society.[13] In the Lords, in June 1923, concern over the growth of socialism had led the Conservative Lord Birkenhead to question the effect it would have on their House. How would it look and act under Labour? Would they find themselves void of constitutional power? There were real fears that socialism would tend towards Bolshevism. As one of the few Labour supporters in the House, it fell to Frank to respond. His continued assertion that nationalism was the socialist ideal did not allay fears; neither did their lordships welcome his distinction between Labour and the Liberals, whom he accused of passing just enough ameliorative legislation to prevent revolution but no more.[14] Ironically, it was also uncomfortable for senior members of the PLP. Though Labour campaigned on a socialist agenda, Ramsay MacDonald was perfectly clear that the primary purpose of his first government would be to gain public trust, not to implement a radical agenda. Frank was dismissed as a loose cannon with a personal history unfitting him for office. Instead, when the time came, MacDonald approached members of other parties to fill key offices. Some crossed the floor: Lord Haldane (Liberal) became Lord Chancellor and joint leader of the Labour Party in the Lords with former Conservative Lord Parmoor. Others did not: Lord Chelmsford remained Conservative, only accepting the post of First Lord of the Admiralty on the understanding that any disagreements with government policy would swiftly lead to his resignation. Frank was naturally aggrieved. During a debate of the joint leaders' statement of government policy he made his feelings plain, stating that though Labour was fortunate to have such a large reservoir of talent from other parties, he hoped it would not be 'at the expense of principle'. The government, he said, spoke with 'such gentle voices' and such low tones as to be 'almost inaudible'. It did not so much represent a child in swaddling clothes as a child 'changed at birth'. Frank had not even been invited to PLP meetings, despite arguing his thirty-five years in the Lords (seven as a Labour Party member) made him more 'parliamentary' than most. He vowed to keep 'a wary and suspicious eye' on their new recruits.[15]

The speech was widely reported. On reading it, a gleeful Elizabeth wrote to Liebet, 'I expect they couldn't stand the idea of his horrid past, his regrettable present, & his certainly disastrous future.'[16] Others were more sympathetic. Housman wrote, 'I thought you were going to be Lord Chancellor or something … but I read between the lines that you and Ramsay don't love each other.' Still, Housman added, on hearing that Frank's very public objection had at least secured him access to PLP meetings, 'perhaps your smile & sleek voice will do the rest'.[17] There was too little time to tell. The government collapsed in the December.

The story of Labour's second government was very different. In the intervening years Frank had remained vocal on issues of personal importance, but also proved his worth to the PLP. A major gain from the 1924 government had been his appointment to its Royal Commission on Lunacy, which, after two years gathering evidence, called for an emphasis shift from detention to prevention and care. Its report came after the Labour government had fallen, but had party backing and the support of a number of influential medical societies. Frank pressed Baldwin's Conservative government to act on its findings, describing it as a pleasure to be able to address their lordships for once on a 'non-controversial subject'.[18] Frank further demonstrated party loyalty on 14 July 1926 when he made a scathing attack on Conservative peers for obstructing free speech with their early closure of the previous week's debate on the Coal Mines Bill while Labour peers were still speaking. The parliamentary peers did not concur with Frank's point of view, but by his action were at least forced to hear out what the peers had originally intended to say. Though few in number, the huddle of Labour peers – Frank among them – were exerting their new-found authority as representatives of what had become the main opposition party, stubbornly resisting Lords reforms that Frank described as a 'Greek gift' from the Tories intended to put them in a permanent minority in the House.[19] Throughout this period, Frank's reputation as a skilled orator grew – and not only within his own party. After a very considered speech in which he suggested he might support the 1927 Liquor (Popular Control) Bill – at least in principle – Lord Birkenhead described Frank as 'a most persuasive and acceptable advocate of any cause which he undertakes in this House'.[20] In 1928, he was chosen to sit on a select committee for railway reform and throughout that year had been 'practically' leader of the opposition in the House, taking up the slack for an ageing Lord Parmoor.[21] As a mark of his final acceptance by Labour, on their re-election in June 1929, Frank was chosen against custom to offer the address in reply to the King's Speech.

Such acceptance also led at last to a minor government position. On 11 June 1929, Frank was appointed parliamentary secretary to the Minister of Transport, Herbert Morrison. It was not the acknowledgement he would have liked for his previous five years' exertions – Frank told Bertrand he had hoped to be made Lord President of the Council or Leader of the Lords, but both positions went to Parmoor. A 'very complimentary and apologetic' MacDonald convinced Frank transport was where he belonged.[22] His qualifications were self-evident and reform of the 1903 Motor Car Act long overdue. A royal commission had been appointed in 1905, but had failed to provide real impetus. So much needed to be done that it was difficult to know where to start. Several piecemeal reforms had been attempted, one by Frank himself. In July 1925, he introduced a bill to make third-party motor insurance compulsory. The bill largely failed on being considered a fringe issue: 70 per cent of motorists took cover voluntarily and priority concerns were over increased traffic volume and road deaths, usually involving pedestrians. No amount of Frank's exasperation that their lordships always 'run off upon the question of reckless driving' when anything motor-related was discussed would dissuade them from the realities of 1.8 million vehicles on increasingly inadequate roads and over 6,000 fatalities.[23] Baldwin's Conservative government had introduced a bill in 1928 but, as Frank later quipped, had not the courage to see it through, sending the matter instead to another commission.

As such, when the second Labour government took office in June 1929, the issue landed in Frank's lap. Principally drafted by Morrison and Frank, the Road Traffic Bill reflected the findings of the commission and the RAC and AA's general positions and, in addition to introducing widespread regulations for public service vehicles, brought into law several policies Frank had espoused for twenty-seven years. It must have been of great satisfaction to him to introduce into the Lords a bill that would abolish the speed limit for light passenger vehicles. The 20 mph limit was anachronistic, he told the assembly, and it would be unwise to replace it within another law that would 'not be enforced by public opinion'. Psychologically, the effect of a fixed speed limit had been 'thoroughly bad'. The public had been 'hypnotised' by it. In truth, there was 'no such thing as a limit of speed which is reasonable at all times and in all places'. It diverted attention from what really mattered: dangerous driving. A 'reasonable driver' apprehends dangers and adjusts his speed accordingly. The Safety-First Association had concluded that 64 per cent of accidents were not the motorist's fault (in the Commons, Morrison blamed 'reckless walkers'), so the bill sought to bring *unreasonable* drivers to task by increasing penalties for dangerous driving (to include fines, prison sentences and disqualification) and introducing the lesser classification of careless driving and penalties for drunk driving. It did not propose driving tests which, they were satisfied, had 'absolutely no value', but health checks would be obligatory before licences were granted and a Highway Code introduced which could be used as evidence in a law court. Frank recommended the bill to the House as a 'bold attempt' to deal with the thorniest motoring issues of the day and looked forward with 'great apprehension' to the amendments he foresaw being proposed at committee stage.[24]

Well he might. The bill took seven months to pass through Parliament, the speed limit issue was hard-fought on both sides and the final Road Traffic Act, which was given royal assent in August 1930, comprised 123 sections over 114 pages. In total, fifteen pages of amendments were adopted. For successfully piloting it through the House, Frank was widely complimented. Lord Cecil, Marquis of Salisbury, who had been Conservative PM at the time of Frank's bigamy trial, praised his 'conciliatory disposition' over the handling of amendments. Earl Beauchamp (Liberal) said it was a long time since such a complicated bill had been so well conducted and Frank's good temper over it 'an example' to them all. ('Hear, hear.') Earl Howe (Conservative) expressed 'nothing but admiration' for Frank – despite his 'half-baked' compulsory third-party insurance making its way into the act. 'Unkind,' cried Frank. It had in fact, been 'cooked several times' as the quantity of amendments testified![25] Neither would it turn out to be the Act's most controversial aspect. As might well have been predicted by a modern reader, the number of fatalities increased and after only four years, with 7,343 deaths on the roads, the 30 mph speed limit we now have in built-up areas was introduced along with compulsory driving tests.

Nevertheless, Frank was at last proving himself a dependable party man. He was also suddenly in a position to enact another pet project. He introduced the Mental Treatment Bill into the House on 19 November 1929. It got royal assent in July 1930 and marked a significant shift towards psychiatric care by extending voluntary admission to all approved mental health premises, introducing temporary admission into psychiatric institutions for 'curable' patients who were unwilling to go into mental hospitals ('asylums' no longer) and empowering local authorities to open outpatient clinics.

Such increased parliamentary commitments naturally left Frank less time and energy to pursue his controversial outside interests. Though young compared to Parmoor, Frank was still sixty-four. His letter to Marie Stopes of 19 November 1929 shows he was feeling the effect of his increased workload. It was kind of her to invite him for Christmas, he wrote, but 'I am so tired now and I expect to be so much more tired by then that I was contemplating going to bed for a week'.[26] He missed several of her lectures, but sent Amy Otter and his secretary of four years, Lela South, instead. Within a fortnight of his letter, demands on his time increased still further when a 'studious country clergyman' spotted that the Labour government had one more under-secretary sitting in the Commons than regulations allowed, and Frank, in what Lord Gorell termed 'a beneficial by-product of inadvertence', was duly promoted to Under-secretary of State for India under William Wedgewood Benn.[27]

Though the 11th Duke of Devonshire (then still in short trousers) would later quip that 'no one who hasn't been a Parliamentary Under Secretary of State has any conception of how unimportant a Parliamentary Under Secretary of State is', the fact that Frank had been given the India office was testament to growing confidence in him. A pity, then, that he should almost immediately open his mouth and put his foot in it by categorically stating, contrary to the government's position, that Indian independence was 'at this moment impossible', calling such resolutions 'foolish' and likening its advocates to a child that must 'learn to walk before it can run'. The comments were published worldwide. They were true but too candid, said the *Scotsman*. Frank defended them by claiming both that they had been taken out of context and that his speech had been hurriedly prepared after two days spent nursing his favourite dog, 'Sweetbriar', who died the following day: 'one of the saddest blows of my life'. But pro-independence activist Pandit Nehru countered that in his 'distressed state of mind' Frank had 'blurted out the unvarnished truth' of the government's position. The *New Leader* called for Frank's resignation, branding his comments 'singularly gauche and ill-considered'.[28] But he had become too valuable to let go. Labour needed representation in the Lords and it was scant. As such, Frank stayed put and was called upon to present many bills in the Lords throughout 1930 that were not his by dint of government office: the

Workman's Compensation Bill, the Unemployment Insurance Bill (Nos 3 & 4), the Coal Mines Bill and the Marriages Provisional Order Bill. He also sat on the Lords' Special Orders Committee for the 1930–31 session and worked hard to redeem himself with Indian nationalists, who reportedly came to recognise him as a 'real friend' of Indian political advancement who distinguished himself at the first Round Table Conference, November 1930 to January 1931.

Small wonder, then, that Frank genially referred to himself as the 'maid of all work' for the cabinet.[29] Had he been ten or twenty years younger, had he still had Mollie's support or succeeded with Elizabeth, he might have accomplished much. As it was, the workload took its toll.

After the conference, Frank took a much-needed break on the Riviera, accompanied by his secretary, Lela South. On 2 March, Amy Otter and a female companion joined them at Toulon, from where Frank was due to depart the next day. He was recovering from flu and told assembled friends he would not make it beyond Marseille and would have to be cremated there. He said it with a smile and they all thought he was joking. Yet, on 3 March, in his rooms at Marseille's Hotel Noailles, Frank suffered a fatal angina attack. He was found on the bathroom floor, where he had died alone.

Bertrand was stunned. He hadn't known of Frank's condition. He arrived in Marseille to find Amy holding the fort and Lela 'completely collapsed, part of the time sick, and the rest of the time in a dead faint'.[30] In bitterness and grief he wrote to Ottoline that the ladies had left Frank to go to luncheon, knowing he might die at any moment: 'They both think they were devoted to him.' Bertrand felt Frank's loss more deeply than he should ever have expected. Frank had died stoically, he wrote; 'a man of fine courage, which never faltered either in misfortune or in the face of death'.[31] Yet, he was still the brother with 'hair-shirt' qualities. In death, he looked 'more than life-size and terribly cruel, like some heathen deity to whom human sacrifices are offered'.[32] In life, he had been 'rather a ruffian';[33] the brother who had bullied him as a child and written in the wake of Elizabeth's departure, 'You know that you have never been loyal to me yet in any crisis of my life' and meant it.[34] As such, when Frank's will was read and it transpired he had left him nothing, Bertrand took it as an expression of Frank's continued resentment.

Echoing his father's unorthodox decision all those years previously, Frank left everything to a person whose loyalty and dependability he had never had cause to question: Amy Elizabeth Otter. To her, Frank entrusted his entire legacy – a fact she had not known until Bertrand informed her. Lela had typed Frank's will, but the name of the beneficiary had been left blank for Frank to fill in by hand. It must have been galling for Bertrand. Quite apart from the long-term financial implications, it meant he had to consult Amy on every aspect of the funeral arrangements. It was regrettable, said Amy, but she accepted the responsibility and in a businesslike fashion continued supporting Lela, who was 'really trying to take hold of herself', and decided in favour of a secular ceremony without flowers or the wearing of mourning, both of which she was certain Frank would dislike.[35]

Frank was cremated 'quietly and reverentially' on 6 March in the presence of the British Consul and one staff. His final trip across the Channel on the 23rd was in the embassy bag. His chauffeur from Dyke House drove Amy to the Foreign Office to collect his ashes and deliver them to TH, where on 30 March a simple ceremony was led by Frank's replacement at the India Office, Lord Snell. Frank's ashes were scattered in 'a sanctuary surrounded by shrubs' in the grounds.[36] In his address, Lord Snell described Frank's 'genius for friendship': 'There was nothing remote or austere in his nature, nor was there anything cheap or shallow in his geniality. He met men on equal terms ... had a gift for exposition and a controversial capacity ... He held and fought for unpopular views, but he never thought of taking refuge in any obscurity of phrase or misleading euphemism...'[37] Beatrice Webb wrote to Bertrand praising Frank's capacity to 'subordinate his personality' to the job in hand and of his 'strange relationship' with Herbert Morrison (given their respective ranks and upbringings).[38] Morrison himself wrote saying he found Frank, 'as everyone did, a very loveable and interesting man' who had an 'acute understanding' of the psychology of that 'somewhat difficult assembly' the House of Lords, where Frank's 'persuasive elegance', 'growing popularity', ability and geniality were praised.[39] In a most touching tribute, Russell Wakefield, Bishop of Birmingham, wrote, 'He deserved a happy life and if people only took the trouble to understand him he *gave* happiness ... [he was] *most* loving and lovable' and 'almost over tender' if 'sometimes over hasty in judgment'.[40] Collectively, the tributes show another side to Frank often obscured by his coarser qualities.

Friends brought the news of Frank's death to Elizabeth. Some congratulated her. On 9 March she wrote in her diary how happy she was at her 'blessed release from a wicked cruel man'. When Bertrand wrote to inform her that everything (including her old love letters) had been left to Amy, she wrote, 'These post-mortem vengeances! How very characteristic.' It was 'odious' to have her 'private letters handed over to such a person' – 'one of his women'.[41] In fact, they could not have been safer. It was natural for Elizabeth to assume that Amy was Frank's last fling, but from their respective reactions to his death and Frank's penchant for secretaries, one might consider Lela the more likely candidate. Amy was a sworn spinster, had her own residence at 2 Hyde Park Mansions (which she shared with her mother until 1923) and had, since 1907, been an inspector for the Ministry of Health's Lymph Establishment. Frank never spoke of her as anything other than 'a very good specimen of a Civil Servant'.[42] She, in turn – clearly and undeniably devoted to him – protected his privacy by destroying the vast majority of his personal papers – Elizabeth's letters included. She was fair and amicable in her dealings with Bertrand over Frank's estate, valued at £10,130 but still cash-poor. When creditors threatened its bankruptcy, Bertrand lent her £3,500 to prevent it, on the understanding that TH and Amy's reversion on the war loan would come to him on her death. Withers continued to irritate over finicky details of the Mollie, Countess Russell Trust and Amy risked his wrath by gifting books from Frank's library to friends she thought should have them. For four tedious years the monumental mess of Frank's financial affairs dragged on, until, on 22 February 1935, riddled with cancer and knowing she had only days to live, Amy put her affairs in order and sent her goodbyes to Bertrand. Her dying wish was that her ashes be scattered where Frank's had been at TH.

On 12 April 1932, Bertrand officially took Frank's position in the House of Lords. He would barely use it or his title. In 1937, he sold TH for £5,468. That too was a sadder parting than he had anticipated. After forty years' association, TH 'represented continuity'.[43] He continued to correspond with Elizabeth infrequently until her death in 1941. His financial obligation to Mollie, though reduced by the sale of TH, continued until her death in 1942 at the (approximate) age of eighty.

EPILOGUE

Song of Myself

During the research and writing of this biography, I was asked many times who Frank Russell was. The easiest answer became its title – he was Bertrand's brother – but it was hardly complete. My hope was that having got to the end of his story and recounted so many things others said about him, the definitive answer would come from Frank himself. Unfortunate, then, that he restricted self-reflection in his memoirs to the simple statement that one can never really 'know thyself', excellent precept though it might be:

> ... even if one tries to put away that self-deception to which we are all prone and to stand dispassionately with a cool and critical eye outside one's self, how impossible that knowledge is to attain.

Much less do we know the inner life of others:

> Only Omniscience could have such knowledge, and all that we can do is to avoid the crude, harsh and stupid judgments pronounced by those who think the Universe can be weighed in their shallow brainpans.[1]

I wonder what he would have thought of the judgments pronounced about him by others in these pages – my own included.

Fortunately, in his last letter to Santayana written a fortnight before his death, Frank was more forthcoming. In it, he admitted the extent to which the 'real part' of him found no expression: 'My very extensive external activities are to me of the nature of Maya or illusion. They interest me, they are my job, and I do them, but they are not part of my real life.' After all his 'adventures' and at the point at which he had finally been (as Santayana put it) 'rehabilitated officially', his achievements – the things by which society measured his success – were the least significant. The truest part of him was still that which in adolescence had connected with Lionel Johnson. 'To all intimate friends,' Frank wrote, 'I have always admitted [Lionel] was my dearest friend and the greatest influence in my life.' Santayana, who afterwards based the character of a wayward sea captain in his 1935 novel *The Last Puritan* on the young Frank, approved. It meant his old friend's early transcendentalism was alive and well, even if buried so deep under the detritus of his transgressions that 'his wives, I expect, never understood it was there'. But Santayana also perceived that it had made Frank reckless. Everything was 'a desperate and worthless gamble ... Any lust, any convenience, any enterprise, any stale moral or political nostrum would do to play with: the point was to dream your dream out, and to have your way in it.'[2]

Frank's friendship with Lionel set him on a path that ended with one of the two greatest shocks of his life: his sending down from Oxford. Quite apart from how it was twisted in the divorce court, Frank believed, 'My rage and mortification at being so wronged produced a bitterness and permanently injured my character.' His youthful 'eager passions to serve and help humanity' were blocked; his 'urgent desire to live and experience' was never to be channelled into 'the wish of my schooldays', engendered by Lionel and their self-styled religion, 'to be a consoler and a helper to the poor'.[3] His 'spiritual idealism', however, remained recognisable in him throughout his life. On his death, Bishop Wakefield had written that Frank '*was* a religious man', though unorthodox, who had developed, as had Lionel, 'a curious and quite beautiful drawing towards Roman Catholic views'.[4] Yet it is idle to suggest that had he not been sent down Frank might have been spared so disastrous a marriage as that with Mabel Edith or the other great shock of his life – Elizabeth's departure – which robbed him of what he took to have been a second great connection. To suggest as much absolves him his share of the responsibility for his misfortunes and neglects the fact that by the time he was sent down, his impatience 'at the mere suggestion of any yoke upon my neck or check upon my freedom' was already established. If not *this* Mabel Edith or *this* Elizabeth, there would have been others – male or female – whom Frank would have perceived as restricting his freedom and fought as vociferously. The child was father to the man and left the impression, often repeated, that he was better with men than women; better still with animals, machinery and places that did not answer back. He was not an evil man. Neither by modern standards was he 'wicked'. Throughout his life, his strong identification with his youthful self, misunderstood, persecuted and wronged, led him to seek reforms that benefited many an underdog, but also made him 'suspect the satisfied', 'distrust the majority', impatient with acquiescence and unsuccessful in love – as rebellious and aloof as his most beloved friend in his own way – 'at peace with myself if not the world',[5] clinging to the words of their prophet-poet,

Trippers and askers surround me,
People I meet, the effect upon me of my early life or the ward and city I live
    in, or the nation,
The latest dates, discoveries, inventions, societies, authors old and new,
My dinner, dress, associates, looks, compliments, dues,

The real or fancied indifference of some man or woman I love,
The sickness of one of my folks or myself, or ill-doing or loss or lack of
   money, or depressions or exaltations,
Battles, the horrors of fratricidal war, the fever of doubtful news, the fitful
   events;
These things come to me days and nights and go from me again,
But they are not Me myself.

Apart from the pulling and hauling stands what I am,
Stands amused, complacent, compassioning, idle, unitary,
Looks down, is erect, or bends an arm on an impalpable certain rest,
Looking with side-curved head curious what will come next,
Both in and out of the game and watching and wondering at it.[6]

Notes

Texts referenced extensively have been abbreviated as follows: *My Life and Adventures – Life*; Bertrand's two-volume autobiography – *ABR1–2* and his *Amberley Papers – AP1–2*; Santayana's *Persons & Places – PP* and *Marginalia – M2*; volumes of Bertrand's letters, *SLBR1–2* and Santayana's, *LGS1–3*. Otherwise, the Russell brothers appear as FR and BR throughout. Other Russells are referenced as LdJR – Lord John Russell; LJR – Lady John, LAR – Lady Agatha Russell; RR – Rollo; MER – Mabel Edith; MR – Mollie; AR – Alys; and DR – Dora. For continuity, I have applied this to the ladies' correspondence written before their respective marriages. Being known to the world by her pen-name, 'Elizabeth' remains as such. Amberley is A; Kate – KA. Lady Henrietta Stanley becomes LHS; Maude – MS; and Lyulph – LS. Lady Scott is LSS. Regular correspondent Ottoline Morrell – OM – is the only non-family member's name abbreviated. Where multiple texts by the same author have been used, abbreviated titles or acronyms follow the author's surname. An acronym or abbreviation followed by a date refers to a periodical. Keys can be found in the bibliography beginning on page 335.

Introduction

1. Shikibu, Murasaki, *The Tale of Genji* (London: George Allen & Unwin, 1935), p. 628.
2. Cocks, p. 119.
3. Jack Badley to Maurice Davies, 1 Nov. 1923, in private collection.
4. Bartrip, p. 102.
5. 'I have a very short memory, except for such things as I absorb and recast in my own mind; so that I am a good observer and critic, but a bad historian: let the reader of this book take warning' (*PP*, p. 190).

1. Origins and Inheritance

1. When Lord John became a hereditary peer in 1861, he passed the lesser title bestowed on him – Viscount Amberley of Amberley, Gloucestershire – to his eldest son.
2. DR, p. 278–9.
3. MS to Lady Georgiana Peel, 19 Aug 1865, RA1:421.079808.
4. Cannadine, *AA*, p. 1.
5. Lowndes, p. 41.
6. *Life*, pp. 8–9.
7. *ABR1*, p. 35.
8. Adelaide, Lady Ribblesdale, was widowed by Thomas Lister, 2nd Baron Ribblesdale, in 1832. Their daughters, Adelaide, Isabel and Elizabeth – all under the age of five when Ribblesdale died – were brought up by their mother and Lord John.
9. McCarthy, pp. 67–73.
10. *Life*, p. 11.
11. Mitford, *LA*, p. xxii.
12. *Life*, p. 56.
13. Mitford, *SA*, p. 44.
14. Roberts, p. 2.
15. Hawkins, p. 124.
16. *AP1*, pp. 282–3.
17. *Life*, p. 50.

2. A Limb of Satan

1. McCarthy, p. 165.
2. *AP1*, p. 385.
3. *ibid.*, p. 392.
4. Surely this is *Mrs Beeton's Book of Household Management*, first published in book form in 1861.
5. KA to Georgy Russell, 24 Oct. 1865, *AP1*, pp. 414–15.
6. *AP1*, p. 372.
7. *AP2*, p. 305. Collier's pamphlet *Punishment in Education* (1872) condemned the whole system of punishment and reward as immoral.
8. *Life*, p. 21.
9. LdJR to A, 1 Nov. 1867, *AP2*, p. 95.
10. 'Granny to Frank', RA1:731.005307.
11. *AP2*, p. 83.
12. *ibid.*, p. 88.
13. Rachel Lucretia Russell, born 2 Mar. 1868, was named for the Quaker and women's rights activist Lucretia Mott, whom the Amberleys met on their 1867 tour of the US.
14. LdJR to A, 25 June 1868, *AP2*, p. 120.
15. *Medical Times*, 8 Aug. 1868.
16. *Exeter & Plymouth Gazette*, 14 Aug. 1868.

17. *Times*, 30 Nov. 1868.
18. The couple met in France, married in a Muslim ceremony in 1862 in Algeria, then again in Constantinople. Their marriage was kept secret for fear of Lord Stanley's disapproval. A third marriage took place after Stanley's death, in England. None of these marriages appear to have been legal – Fabia reportedly had a husband still living in Spain (Mitford, *SA*, pp. xiii–xiv).
19. Sanderson to KA, Sep 1865, *AP1*, 411. Thomas James Sanderson was at this time a down-at-heel and dissatisfied barrister. In 1882, he married Annie, daughter of reformer Richard Cobden, and took her name to become Thomas Cobden-Sanderson. In 1884 he started Doves Press.
20. *Life*, p. 4.
21. *ibid.*, p. 13.
22. *PP*, p. 296.
23. *Life*, pp. 22–3.
24. KA to MS, 1 Apr. 1869, DSA:175/2.
25. Herford, pp. 96–97.
26. LHS to KA, 15 Apr. 1871, *AP2*, p. 400.
27. KA to Miss Hentze, 8 Oct. 1871, *ibid.*, pp. 415–16.
28. Alexander Campbell Fraser was a philosophy professor at Edinburgh University. Amberley lived with his family during the academic year 1860–1. They remained lifelong friends.
29. *AP2*, pp. 507–8.
30. KA to MS, 4 Aug. 1872, DSA:175/2.
31. *AP2*, pp. 511–12.
32. *ibid.*, pp. 516.
33. LJR to A, 28 May 1873, *ibid.*, pp. 542–3.
34. *ABR1*, p. 26. Author's emphasis.
35. Unsourced fact revealed by Bertrand in *ABR1*, p. 17.
36. *AP2*, p. 571.
37. LJR to A, 28 Mar. 1875, *Life*, p. 28.
38. *Life*, p. 29.
39. Spalding was allowed to retain the salary Amberley had settled on him and retired to the south of France, where he died on 31 Oct. 1877 (*Nature*, vol. 17 (8 Nov 1877), pp. 35–6).
40. *Life*, p. 30.

3. Natural Freedom and Frankness

1. KA to MS, 15 Jan. 1868, DSA:175/2.
2. *Life*, p. 33.
3. MS.5725, MS.6222–3.
4. *Life*, p. 33.
5. *ibid.*
6. *ibid.*, pp. 33–5.
7. *ibid.*, pp. 51.
8. Jackson, p. 62. Annabel was the daughter of Scottish MP Mountstuart Grant-Duff and a frequent visitor to PL during Frank's youth.
9. Wood, p. 15. Diana and Flora were the daughters of Lord Arthur Russell, Lord John's nephew by older brother, George.

10. *Life*, p. 38.
11. *ibid.*, p. 41.
12. Victoria to LJR, 30 May 1878, MacCarthy, p. 253.
13. RA1:731.080044, p. 152.
14. *Life*, p. 51.
15. M2, pp. 213–14.
16. GBS to FR, 11 Apr. 1923, *ABR2*, p. 172.

4. Manners Makyth Man

1. *Life*, p. 91.
2. Thucydides 1.22.
3. GBS to FR, 11 Apr. 1923, *ABR2*, p. 172.
4. *Life*, p. 91.
5. Santayana, *Notebook IV*, p. 68.
6. *Life*, p. 73.
7. *ibid*, p. 60.
8. *ibid*, p. 76.
9. *ibid*, p. 75.
10. E17/32; 'Mrs Richardson: An Appreciation' in *Wykehamist*, no. 440 (Dec. 1909), pp. 367–8.
11. Mansfield, p. 18.
12. *Life*, pp. 65–6.
13. All definitions taken from Stevens.
14. So-called because historically the boys would take classes in the cool cloisters in summer to avoid the oppressive heat of school.
15. In the original rule, it applied to walking between school and chapel, and school and cathedral, and was still enforced in Frank's day.
16. The Tunding Row, 1872, broke out after a boy refused to sit the notions exam and was 'savagely' thrashed by the senior commoner prefect. The facts became public, there were letters to the *Times* and an inquisition. Afterwards, under the 'new regime' a tunding was limited to a dozen strokes. By 1920, it was replaced with a beating on the bottom of no more than ten strokes.
17. A true Wykehamist never used a definite article in introducing a familiar place, but did sometimes pluralise it, i.e. *Hills* for the nearby St Catherine's Hill, used by the boys for recreation (Stevens, p. xvi).
18. *Life*, p. 63.
19. RA1:731.080042, pp. 21–2. A *mill* was a fight.
20. ibid., p. 13, p. 82.
21. *Wykehamist*, no. 173 (Feb. 1883), p. 122.
22. *Life*, p. 345.
23. RA1:731.080042, pp. 6–11. The *Moabites* were boys in Moberly's House and *lobster* meant to cry (probably from the Hampshire word 'lowster' meaning to make any unpleasant noise).
24. *Wykehamist*, no. 171 (Nov. 1882), p. 109. Winchester College Football (or simply *our game*) is unlike regular football. Designed to be played in a confined space surrounded by a net, it is a fast-paced, high-scoring game in which the ball is kicked but not dribbled and not touched except to save a goal or kick-off after one. Towards the end of short-half, the best players from competing teams

were picked for *fifteens* and *sixes*, named for the number of players. A *hot* was the equivalent of a rugby scrum, played whenever the ball went out.

25. RA1:731.080042, p. 15. *Infra-dig*: scornful, from Latin *infra dignitatem* – beneath dignity.
26. To *quill* was to curry favour; to be *quilled* therefore, to be pleased.
27. RA1:731.080043, p. 186. Lionel Johnson went up to Winchester in short-half 1880 and was therefore a new college man at the time of this entry. When a pupil *gets books*, they are top of their class and moved up to the next division.

5. A Spiritual Rebel

1. *Life*, p. 90.
2. Waugh, p. 91; Fisher, p. 37.
3. *Life*, p. 90.
4. *Wykehamist*, no. 396 (Oct. 1902), p. 456.
5. *PP*, p. 300.
6. FR, 'Introduction' in Johnson, pp. 10–11.
7. *Life*, p. 93.
8. *ibid.*, p. 94.
9. RA1:731.080043, pp. 9–28.
10. *ibid.*, pp. 37–40.
11. Johnson's letters in this volume were written to Frank, Charles Sayle, whom Frank would meet at Oxford, and Jack Badley, who was at Cambridge and previously known to Sayle at Rugby.
12. Pittock, pp. 5–6.
13. Johnson, p. 15.
14. *PP*, p. 300.
15. Johnson, pp. 18–19.
16. *ibid.*, p. 21.
17. RA1:731.080043, pp. 83–5.
18. Johnson, p. 33.
19. *ibid.*, pp. 34–6.
20. RA1:731.080043, pp. 90–102.
21. *ibid.*, pp. 105–111.
22. Johnson, pp. 49–50.
23. RA1:731.080043, p. 118.
24. FR, editor's note in Johnson, p. 50.
25. *Life*, p. 104.

6. The White Flower of a Blameless Life

1. RA1:731.080043, pp. 43–47.
2. *Life*, p. 95.
3. Symonds, R., p. 24.
4. Jepson, *MV*, pp. 95–6.
5. *Life*, p. 106.
6. *ibid.* pp. 100–104.

7. In 1881, Wilde sent a complimentary copy of *Poems* to the Union. It was returned after an undergraduate – Oliver Elton (later a prominent literary scholar and critic) – made an impassioned speech against accepting it; not because the poems were thin ('and they are thin') or because they were immoral ('and they are immoral') but because he felt they plagiarised Shakespeare, Byron, Swinburne and others (Newbolt, p. 96). In 1884, the Librarian considered buying a copy, but the proposition when put to the vote lost by 132 to 139 (*WMN*, 25 Feb. 1884). Frank recorded the event as 'very amusing', but not whether or which way he voted (RA1:731.080044, p. 125).
8. *OT*, 24 Nov. 1883.
9. RA1:731.080043, p. 77.
10. *Life*, p. 104.
11. RA1:731.080043, p. 57.
12. *ibid.*, p. 86.
13. RA1:731.080044, p. 149.
14. RA1:731.080043, p. 46.
15. RA1:731.080042, p. 157.
16. Maurice Davies, quoted in Hobson & Ginsberg, p. 21.
17. Ellman, p. 538.
18. Recorded in Benson diaries, vol. 175, f. 39. Eton College holds no record of Ion having been sent down.
19. Jepson, *MV*, pp. 105–6.
20. Though formally sent down, Ion was invited to return in 1888 as a student at Charsley's Hall – an establishment licensed by the university to take men who had dropped out or been rejected by their college. He never took up his place. By 1895 he had retired to Buenos Aires to become a sheep farmer. Numerous 'wives' subsequently appeared on the scene, but no evidence that he actually married any of them. He ended his days in Fort Augustus, Scotland, where he died of heart failure aged fifty.
21. RA1:731.080043, p. 82, p. 94.
22. *ibid.*, p. 94.
23. *ibid.*, p. 130.
24. Sayle Diaries, 24 Nov. 1893, MS Add.8501, p. 19.
25. RA1:731.080043, pp. 137–141.
26. Johnson, pp. 50–2.
27. RA1:731.080044, pp. 122–152.
28. *ibid.*, pp. 155–60.
29. *ibid.*, pp. 158–63.
30. Fletcher, p. xxii.
31. Kempis, p. 29.
32. Johnson, pp. 75–6.
33. Oates, p. 238.
34. RA1:731.080044, p. 163.
35. *ibid.*, p. 129.
36. *ibid.*, pp. 163–4.
37. *ibid.*, p. 176.
38. Johnson, p. 105.
39. Johnson to Sayle, 31 May 1884, MS Add.8548.

40. RA1:731.080044, p. 180.
41. *ibid.*, pp. 199–210; Johnson, p. 124.
42. RA1:731.080044, p. 221.
43. *ibid.*, pp. 224–8.
44. Johnson, pp. 130–2.
45. Johnson, p. 74. This letter is erroneously dated April 1884. Lionel visited Frank in Oxford in April 1885.
46. *Life*, pp. 107–8.

7. A Very Improper Friend

1. *M2*, pp. 217–8.
2. *PP*, p. 309.
3. Santayana, *Notebook IV*, p. 29.
4. Dowling, pp. xiv–xv. *Paiderastia*: the love of boys.
5. Jowett to Lady A [Airlie or Abercrombie], 27 July 1884, Abbott, vol. 2, pp. 269–270.
6. For full discussion of evidence concerning this event, see Inman; for further questioning of its interpretation, see Shuter.
7. Abbott, vol. 1, p. 204.
8. Jowett to LHS, 07 Dec 1891, IF6/61.
9. *PP*, p. 309.
10. Santayana, *Notebook IV*, pp. 29–38.
11. Until the 1861 Offences Against the Person Act, sodomy was a hanging offence. This Act made actual sodomy a misdemeanour, punishable by penal servitude for life or no less than ten years, and attempted sodomy or indecent assault, by either penal servitude for three to ten years or imprisonment for two years with or without hard labour (s.61–3). The 'Labouchere amendment' (Criminal Law Amendment Act, 1885, Part 1, s.11) was proposed and passed on the ground that the 1861 Act failed to punish same sex activity in the home – indecent assault being largely a public crime – and widened the net to include gross indecency to capture those 'filthy practices' between men in private that largely went unpunished (Mead & Bodkin, p. 69).
12. Chandos, p. 301.
13. William Alger, *The Friendships of Women* (1868) quoted in Oulton, p. 39.
14. Cocks, p. 5.
15. If this is true, he apparently did not feel the same about his Winchester diaries, which he not only kept but quoted from in *Life*.
16. Mary's handwriting is identified by letters to Santayana; the timing of the transcription dated by her well-documented presence in Frank's life.
17. Johnson to FR, 15 May 1885, MS Add.8548.
18. *Life*, p. 108.
19. Johnson to FR, 21 May 1885, T2/F7.
20. RA1:731.080044, p. 132.
21. Jowett to FR, undated, RA1:732.80060.
22. Recollections of Newbolt in Benson Diaries, vol. 175, ff. 39–40.
23. Johnson to Sayle, 31 May 1885, MS Add.8548.
24. Johnson to FR, 21 July 1885, T2/F7.
25. Johnson to Sayle, 31 May 1885, MS Add.8548.

26. Johnson to FR, 30 May 1885, T2/F7.
27. Johnson to Sayle, 31 May 1885, MS Add.8548.
28. Johnson to Sayle, 14 July 1885, T2/F7.
29. Jowett to John Ffolliott, 5 July 1885, IV/A8/24.
30. Johnson to Badley, 19 July 1885, T2/F7.
31. Johnson to FR, 5 Aug. 1885; 21 July 1885, *ibid.*
32. FR to Richardson, 24 July 1885, E17/3.
33. Prior to this, there is not a single mention of Frank in any of Sayle's meticulously kept diaries; neither are any subsequent meetings recorded (MS Add.8507).
34. Sayle, p. vii.
35. Symonds to Sayle, 19 Nov. 1885, Symonds, p. 94. Symonds had also been Jowett's pupil and famously confronted him with what he came to regard as the damaging effect of placing 'the most electrical literature in the world' in the hands of young men with homosexual tendencies 'pregnant with the stuff that damns him' (p. 347).
36. Sayle Diaries, 21 Jan. 1887, MS Add.8501.
37. Benson Diaries, vol. 175, ff. 35–36, ff. 39–40.
38. *Life*, p. 108.
39. Jowett to FR, 17 May 1886, RA1:732.80057.
40. Jowett to FR, 21 May 1886, RA1:732.80058.
41. Johnson to FR, 5 Aug. 1885, T2/F7.

8. A Series of Adventures

1. Add MS 81690, f. 8.
2. *Life*, pp. 111–12.
3. Add.MS 81690, f.10.
4. FR to Richardson, 1 Sep. 1885, E17/3.
5. *Life*, p. 118.
6. *New North West*, Montana, 11 Dec. 1885.
7. *Life*, p. 120.
8. *PP*, p. 291.
9. *ibid.*, pp. 291–2.
10. Reflections on Frank's US tour taken from *Life*, pp. 117–138 and letters to Sarah Richardson, E17/3.
11. *Salt Lake Tribune*, 1 Jan.; *Oakland Tribune*, 16 Jan. 1886.
12. Much would be made of this incident in Frank's later court battles, with the implication that Frank's intentions towards Quai Paak were improper. Frank would assert that he did not know why Paak had been sent home – he was not consulted and never asked. Lady Stanley reportedly gave the boy some money and sent him back to California. Last known whereabouts of Quai Paak: he sailed from California on SS *Belgic* on 29 Mar. 1890 bound for Hong Kong.
13. Dyer to Richardson, 11 May 1886, E17/3.
14. Dodgson to Johnson, 21 Aug. 1886, Add MS 46363.
15. *Life*, p. 140.
16. McCormick, p. 20.
17. *PP*, p. 145.

18. *ibid.*, p. 134.
19. FR to Santayana, 12 & 19 Aug. 1894, MS-3699; *PP*, pp. 292–5.
20. McCormick, p. 119.
21. *PP*, p. 294.
22. Santayana to Henry Ward Abbott, 23 Apr. 1887, *LGS1*, pp. 62–3.
23. *PP*, p. 297.
24. Santayana to Abbott, 20 May 1887, *LGS1*, p. 76.
25. *ibid.*, 27 May 1887, pp. 77–8. 'Country matters' implying sex (Hamlet, III. ii.102–110).
26. Santayana's only comment on his sexuality was in February 1929, in conversation with his personal assistant, Daniel Cory. Santayana referred to A. E. Housman as 'what people nowadays call "homosexual"', adding, 'I think I must have been that way in my Harvard days – although I was unconscious of it at the time'; his knowledge of such things being 'indirect' (Cory, p. 40). McCormick, writing at a time when salacious speculation was rife, concluded that this was an evasion – particularly in relation to Frank – but there is no evidence of any sexual relationship between them, or indeed between Santayana and anyone else.
27. Account of this tour taken from Jepson, *MV*, pp. 125–155 and *Life*, pp. 143–155.
28. The nature of extant records makes an assessment of Frank's income an educated guess. Bertrand talked of receiving £20,000 when he came of age (*ABR1*, p. 82), but as Frank's entitlement was to property, the same cannot be inferred for him. Santayana suggests £15,000 with no basis for the suggestion (McCormick, p. 76). Perhaps closer to the mark was Jepson's assertion that at the time of their Mediterranean tour, Frank's income was £5,000 p.a.; a figure Frank disputed in 1894 as being nearer £3,500 yielded from his inherited Irish estates (J77/534/16305).
29. *PP*, p. 315.

9. Material for Incandescence

1. Page inserted into Sarah Richardson's notebook, E17/4. In November 1889, Major-General Sir Claude Arthur Bray was Mrs Dick's guest and meeting Frank for the first time.
2. Johnson to Santayana, 2 Aug. 1888, *PP*, p. 303.
3. Dodgson to Johnson, 4 Sep. 1886, Add MS 46363.
4. *Life*, p. 310.
5. Arapostathis & Gooday, pp. 81–3.
6. Dodgson to Johnson, 11 Jan. 1889, Add MS 46363.
7. Lady Scott was known as and signed herself both 'Lina' and 'Lena'. As 'Lina' was her preferred spelling, I have kept to this throughout, except when directly quoting a source using the variant.
8. Frank's recollections taken from *Life*, pp. 156–60.
9. Margaret Richardson's Diary, 29 June 1889, E17/7.
10. Dodgson to Johnson, 2 Aug. & 31 Dec. 1889, Add Ms 46363.
11. BR, *CP1*, pp. 48–51.
12. FR to MER, 5 Oct. 1889, HAR07025.
13. MER to FR, 4 Aug. 1889, *ibid.*

14. MER to FR, 6 & 10 Aug. & 18 Sep. 1889, *ibid.*
15. In 1886, Giddy, then twenty-one, married Arthur Edward Saunders Sebright, twenty-six, son of 8th baronet Sebright of Besford, Worcester. She afterwards sued for annulment saying she was induced to take part in the ceremony 'by fraud and duress'. The marriage had not been consummated and the judge believed Giddy's protestations of coercion and found in her favour (J77/359/0862).
16. FR to Villiers, 26 Dec. 1889, *MP*, 26 Nov. 1896.
17. The day before the marriage, Claude Edward snr created a trust fund for his eldest son providing him the annuity. On his death, he also directed that Claude's share of his inheritance be paid into the fund to be held in trust for his children, effectively bypassing him in all but the annuity. No such provision was made for his younger son, Bertie, who received a lump sum in excess of £25,000.
18. J 77/167/4109.
19. J 77/167/4128.
20. Breach of promise actions were open to both sexes but largely intended to protect women from seduction or abandonment by an unscrupulous fiancé. Popular in the first half of the nineteenth century, juries awarded ever increasing damages for the 'moral injury' inflicted by a broken engagement and any material consequences, i.e., the birth of an illegitimate child. Towards the end of the century, there were growing concerns that many actions were being brought 'by women manifestly wanting money from men whom they cannot possibly want as husbands'; the threat of public scandal being used as blackmail (*Times*, 15 Feb. 1878). By the time Lina brought her case against Captain Spicer, public opinion would therefore have been against her in every respect.
21. Frank's reflections on the week before the wedding taken from RA1:731.080044, pp. 90–116.
22. The visit was arranged by the Stanleys, principally for appearance's sake. Frank wrote to Mabel from Oxford: 'It *is* dull here! The Master hasn't another soul in the house, and spends his time sleeping or working. But even that is not so dull as when he walks me round the quad for half hours at a time, 2 miles an hour, and never opens his mouth the whole time' (4 Aug. 1889, HAR07025).
23. *PP*, p. 318.

10. To Love, Honour and Obey

1. LSS to FR, 13 Feb. 1890, HAR07025.
2. *Life*, p. 156. This connection between Mabel and William George Robert, 4th Earl Craven is mentioned nowhere else. If not true, it's an incredible statement for Frank to have made, even though Craven was then deceased. The lack of any press corroboration suggests, if there was a connection, it didn't get very far.
3. LSS to FR, 13 Feb. 1890, HAR07025.
4. *PP*, p. 667. This passage was removed from the original published version for fear of offending any living descendants. Kate and Ellen Williams make an appearance under the pseudonyms 'Emma' and 'Jennie Billings'.
5. RA1:731.080044, p. 105.
6. *Times*, 8 Dec 1911.

7. Juxton, p. 15.
8. LSS to FR, 22 & 25 Feb. 1890, HAR07025.
9. Evidence given in *Russell v. Russell, LES*, 4 Dec. 1891.
10. RA1:731.080044, p. 109. Mabel's fear was not uncommon. Steinbach points out that, while not universal, many young Victorian women found themselves caught between an ignorance of sex that was held as an 'aspect of respectability and a point of pride', a fear of conception and childbirth and the myth that women were 'passionless' leaving them woefully unprepared for a full and rewarding married life (pp. 241–3).
11. Edward's father had left £30,000 in his will to be divided equally between Edward and his mother. His engagement to Mabel was announced in the *Post*, 11 Jan. 1888, three weeks before her nineteenth birthday. Four months later, it was announced that the wedding was off. No reason was given (*YH*, 17 May 1888).
12. *Married Love* (1918) was considered both scandalous and liberating in equal measure, but its necessity amply demonstrated by the 230,000 copies sold within its first five years. Cutting through the 'muffled confusion of individual gossip' which 'disturbs a silence, shamefaced or foul' Stopes spoke directly to young couples in unambiguous language with the object of increasing the joys of marriage and showing how much sorrow could be avoided through awareness of each other's needs and desires (pp. 14–17). Frank later became a staunch supporter of Stopes' campaign for birth control.
13. Opening Speech for the Defence, *MP*, 1 Dec. 1891; MER to FR, 9 May 1890, HAR07025.
14. All subsequent letters between family members from 8 May 1890 to 2 Nov. 1891 taken from HAR07025 unless otherwise specified.
15. FR to Alfred Percy Doulton, 8 Jun. 1890, *MP*, 5 Dec. 1891.
16. BR, *CP1*, p. 52.
17. FR to Santayana, 9 Oct. 1890, MS-3699.
18. Lady Cardigan to MER, 21 Nov. 1890, HAR07025.
19. Petition, J77/461/4047.
20. *Russell v. Russell* [2]. Court of Appeal, Probate Division ([1895] P 315), p. 322.
21. Particulars of Petitioner, J77/461/4047.
22. Frank was against this attempt, thinking it would weaken their case if they did not answer the accusation in court (FR to Doulton, 25 Jan. 1890, RA1:733.128514).
23. Leslie Roberts to Doulton, 4 Feb. 1891, RA1:733.005732.
24. FR to Doulton, 5 May 1891, RA1:733.128514.
25. FR to Santayana, 7 Jan. 1891, MS-3699.
26. FR to LJR, [?] May 1891, HL/PO/JU/4/3/467, p. 422; FR to LAR, 28 June 1891, *ibid.*, p. 425.

11. In the High Court of Justice

1. The 1873 Supreme Court of Judicature Act reorganised the eight pre-existing English courts into one new Supreme Court, which was itself split into the High Court of Justice and the Court of Appeal. The High Court was organised into three divisions: Queen's Bench; Chancery; and Probate, Divorce and Admiralty (now the Family Division).

2. *Life*, p. 166.
3. Walker-Smith, pp. 6–10.
4. Queen's Counsel (QC) denotes a senior advocate appointed by the monarch to be one of her 'learned counsel'. Appointed annually, they make up approximately 8 per cent of barristers. When the tradition began in the late sixteenth century, silk was a rare commodity and they alone were allowed to wear it, to distinguish them from their junior counterparts. Hence to be made QC is to 'take silk' and QCs are known colloquially as *silks* (Rita Patra, 'Taking Silk', *Patra* (29 Oct. 2013) <https://blog.patra.com/2013/10/29/taking-silk/> accessed 16 Jan. 2020).
5. O'Brien, pp. 77–100.
6. William Snowdon Robson first represented Frank at Hampton Petty Sessions in 1889, when Frank's neighbour Mr. H. E. Tatham, sued for damage to two islands he owned in the middle of the Thames at Hampton, which he said had been damaged by a huge wave kicked up by the 'excessive and very dangerous speed' Frank was navigating his steam launch along the river. Despite a stout defence, Frank lost and was fined 30s plus costs. Frank, of course, appealed, but lost again. Robson later held the offices of Solicitor General (1905–8), Attorney General (1908–10) and was made Lord of Appeal in Ordinary and a life peer in 1910.
7. The description of the trial is based on three major sources. Where possible, testimony is taken from extracts in *Appeal Cases and Writs of Error* [1897], HL/PO/JU/4/3/467. Further quoted testimony and descriptions of the scene in court are taken from the following periodicals, 1–5 Dec. 1891: *BNL*, *LES*, *MP*, *PMG*, *RN*, *SDG*, *Star*, *Times*. The *Star* more than any other paper gave details of the costumes and attitudes of key players. Letters read out in court were sometimes only mentioned in passing in the press – their content is taken from HAR07025 and referenced accordingly.
8. The only newspaper article about Frank at this time was the report in *Le Figaro* mentioned in chapter 10. Lina had claimed there was another in a London newspaper on 7 March 1891 with the dubious headline 'Earl Russell's Moral Rottenness' but failed to produce it. Doulton's searches at the time and my own now also failed to turn up the article. Doulton's conclusion was that it had been 'concocted' and heavily hinted that either Lina or Mabel were responsible (Doulton to LSS, 22 May 1891, HAR07026).
9. Eliza Ann Vale to MER, Nov. 1890, HAR07025.
10. LSS to Doulton, 2 Dec. 1891, HAR07025.
11. *Life*, p. 165.
12. *ibid.*, p. 166.
13. *ibid.*, pp. 159–60.

12. The Cachet of the Court

1. FR to Santayana, 19 Dec. 1891, MS-3699.
2. 'The Bright Side of the Russell Case', *PMG*, 5 Dec. 1891, p. 1.
3. Cocks, p. 78.
4. *MP*, 5 Dec. 1891.
5. 'The Cachet of the Court', *Vanity Fair*, no. 1207/XLVI (19 Dec. 1891), p. 483. Mrs Grundy was originally a character who never appeared but

was alluded to as a figure of disapproval in Thomas Morton's play *Speed the Plough* (1798). She represented a puritanical, priggish person and is referenced perpetually throughout the Victorian era. *In camerâ*, from Latin, *in a chamber*, means in private.

6. *MP*, 5 Dec. 1891. Author's emphasis.
7. 'What We Think', *Star*, 5 Dec. 1891, p. 1. This was a leader in the *Star* separate from the main report of the case and presumably not therefore part of the 'representative' cuttings Frank sent Santayana.
8. *ibid.*
9. *DC*, 5 Dec. 1891, p. 5. This belief is not recorded or evidenced anywhere else.
10. *The Dwarf*, vol. II/52 (8 Dec. 1891), p. 5.
11. *LES*, 5 Dec. 1891.
12. FR to Santayana, 19 Dec. 1891, MS-3699.
13. Sometime after Isaac's death in 1898, the family moved to Chiswick. Kate never married, but lived with her sisters, Ellen (also a spinster), Maude and Maude's husband, John, until she died of natural causes on 4 August 1944, aged seventy-seven.
14. RR to MER, 18 Oct. 1890, HAR07025.
15. *SDG*, 5 Dec. 1891.
16. 'Mud Shovelling by Machinery', *SJG*, 5 Dec. 1891, p. 3.
17. 'The *Chronicle* says...', *PMG*, 5 Dec. 1891, p. 6.
18. 'The Earl Russell Matrimonial Case', *YP*, 5 Dec. 1891, p. 2.
19. 'Lady Russell: A Sweet Beauty', 5 Dec. 1891, p. 5.
20. 'Crushed Lives: Lady Scott's Letter to the Dwarf', *Dwarf*, vol. II/52 (8 Dec. 1891), p. 15.
21. *Truth*, 10 Dec. 1891. Additional facts included an action Lina brought against her brother, William Burney, for annoyance, after he turned up drunk on her doorstep in 1885 and created a disturbance in an attempt to secure money; and her condemning of Lord James Douglas to Holloway in 1888 for breaking a restriction order previously placed on him when his unwanted attentions towards Mabel became a nuisance.
22. *Globe*, 5 Dec. 1891, 4; *SDG*, 5 Dec. 1891.
23. 'The *Liverpool Post* says...', *PMG*, 5 Dec. 1891, p. 6.
24. *Star*, 5 Dec. 1891, p. 1.
25. Butler, Josephine, 'Reversing the Russell Case', *Star* (8 Dec. 1891), p. 3. In 1885, Butler campaigned with W. T. Stead against child prostitution, which resulted in the series of articles for which Stead is best known – *The Maiden Tribute of Babylon* – and to the passing of Henry Labouchere's Criminal Law Amendment Act, 1885, which, among other things, raised the age of consent for girls from thirteen to sixteen.
26. 'The Russell Case: An Interview with Lady Russell', *Hawk*, 8 Dec. 1891, p. 561.
27. *M2*, p. 219; McCormick, p. 77.
28. Recalled by Santayana, *PP*, p. 484.
29. *Hawk*, 8 Dec. 1891, pp. 561–2.
30. LS to Jowett, 30 Sep. 1891, IIC/C1/158.
31. Jowett to LHS, 7 Dec. 1891, I/F6/61.
32. 'A Glimpse at Lord Russell's "Past Life"', *Vanity Fair*, no. 1206/XLVI (12 Dec. 1891), pp. 462–3.

33. Cocks, p. 4.
34. Frank quoted from this sketch extensively in *Life* without acknowledging it was written by a friend (pp. 109–10). Though the author was never identified, the style of writing and whimsical attitude make Edgar Jepson the most likely candidate. Jepson was then living in London, carving out a career as a writer and hanging out with the poets of the Rhymer's Club. He wrote articles for several papers, as was then common practice for budding writers. He was editor of *Vanity Fair* for a short time in the early twentieth century (*MV*, pp. 208–88; *ME*, pp. 106–12).
35. Lina wrote to Frank in late November 1891, 'you <u>know</u> I love you both' (HAR07026); and in Frank's short diary of Jan.–Feb. 1890, Lina is frequently referred to as 'darling Bo', where Mabel is simply 'Mabel' (RA1:731.080044).
36. FR to Santayana, 14 Mar. 1892, MS-3699.
37. MER to FR, [?] January 1892, HAR07026.

13. Conjugal Rights and Wrongs

1. Hansard, vol. 1, c. 171. For more on this see chapter 20.
2. GBS to FR, 11 Apr. 1892, Shaw, p. 336.
3. FR to GBS, 16 Apr. 1892, Add MS 50512.
4. Cretney, pp. 143–5. The amendment removed the necessity for a two-year interval between petitions; the two weeks was established by standard practice.
5. All letters between family members from 8 Mar. 1892 to 10 Apr. 1895 taken from HAR07026 unless otherwise specified.
6. FR to Santayana, 17 July 1892, MS-3699.
7. 'Amateurs at the Royalty', *Era*, 16 Apr. 1892, p. 9.
8. *MP*, 28 July 1892.
9. *SJG*, 28 July 1892.
10. B 12/3 [551].
11. Evidence given in *Russell v. Russell* [2], *LES*, 6 & 10 Apr. 1895.
12. FR to Santayana, 2 Jan. 1896, MS-3699.
13. *PP*, p. 470. Mary appears under the pseudonym 'Martha Turner'.
14. 'The Orphanage', *East and West*, Easter 1886; Sister Rachel, All Hallows Convent, emails to the author, 24 & 25 Jul. 2017.
15. *SLBR1*, p. 61.
16. *PP*, p. 470.
17. *Life*, p. 186.
18. *SBS*, 29 Apr. 1893.
19. FR to Santayana, 17 Jul. 1892, MS-3699.
20. *National Review*, no.120 (Feb. 1893), pp. 764–6.
21. *Smart Society*, vol. 1/19 (15 Feb. 1893), p. 5.
22. *GH*, 2 & 19 Aug., 1893; *SDT*, 17 Aug. 1893.
23. *DDE*, 12 June 1893.
24. *ABR1*, p. 38.
25. Monk, p. 73.
26. *PP*, p. 477.

27. BR to AR, 8 Mar. 1894, *SLBR1*, pp. 60–1.
28. Answer of Respondent, J77/534/16305.
29. *Life*, p. 188.
30. *ibid.*, p. 180.
31. Usborne, pp. 47–8.
32. *M2*, p. 220.
33. Meynell, Francis, 'A. T. and A. M.' in Tobin, p. xiii.
34. *PP*, p. 472. Agnes appears under the pseudonym 'Veronica'.
35. FR to Santayana, 27 Jan. 1895, MS-3699.
36. *PP*, p. 473.
37. *Life*, p. 182.
38. 'on the knees of the Gods' (Homer, Il. & Od.). FR to Santayana, 12 Aug. 1895, MS-3699.
39. Monk, p. 87.
40. FR to BR, 12 Jun 1900, RA1:730.46888.
41. Series of letters between BR and AR, 13–21 Oct. 1894, RA1:710.55091–103; RA3:434.123621–29.
42. FR to BR, 23 Oct. 1894, RA1:730.46881.
43. FR to Santayana, 19 Oct. 1894 & 27 Jan. 1895, MS-3699.
44. Morris to Santayana, 29 Jan. 1895, *ibid.*
45. FR to Santayana, 5 Mar. & 10 Apr. 1895, *ibid.*

14. In the High Court of Justice, Again

1. 'Bench and Bar', *Vanity Fair*, 5 Dec. 1891, p. 442.
2. *Saffron Waldon Weekly*, 29 Oct. 1897; *APJ*, 26 Jul. 1907.
3. Philips, p. 205.
4. Balfour-Browne, p. 84.
5. Smalley & Escott, p. 129; O'Brien, p. 257.
6. Philips, p. 222.
7. Smalley & Escott, pp. 128–129.
8. Kingston, p. 152.
9. Philips, p. 222.
10. *MEN*, 22 Nov. 1897.
11. The majority of testimony taken from extracts in *Appeal Cases and Writs of Error* [1897], HL/PO/JU/4/3/467. Further quoted testimony and description of the scene in court from the following periodicals, 6–10 and 24–27 Apr. 1895: *LES, MP, Star, Telegraph, Times*.
12. Affidavit of Dr Matthew Henry Gardiner, 23 Nov. 1894, J77/534/16305.
13. Answer to interrogatories, 8 Dec. 1894, *ibid.*
14. Deposition of Dowager Countess Russell, 16 Dec. 1894, *ibid.*
15. Deposition of Lady Mary Agatha Russell, *ibid.*
16. *Star*, 9 Apr. 1895, quoting from 'The Litany', *Book of Common Prayer*.
17. *London Figaro*, 25 Oct. 1894. In response, Mabel's solicitor sued for contempt of court and attempted to get the editor committed to Holloway, but the Judge was 'not inclined to inflict an extreme penalty because the newspapers of this country were generally very well conducted'. He fined Hunter £50 plus costs (*MP*, 13 Nov. 1895).
18. LHS to Lord Stanley, 10 Mar. 1852, Mitford, *SA*, p. 58.

19. Nevill, p. 193.
20. Dickinson was a distant cousin through Lina's mother, Cecilia Caroline Searle.
21. FR to Santayana, 10 Apr. 1895, MS-3699.
22. *ibid.*
23. FR to Santayana, 27 Apr. 1895, MS-3699.
24. Holmes, p. 153.

15. Will No One Rid Me of This Pestilent Wife?

1. In a small concession to Suffragists, the Local Government Act allowed property-owning women not only to vote for the first time (at this level only) but also to stand for election to Parish and District councils (but not County Councils). Women were also allowed to stand for the newly reformed Boards of Guardians of the Poor Law Union and to act on School Boards.
2. Frank to Alys, 28 Nov. 1894, RA3:434.123694.
3. *LM*, 25 Dec. 1894.
4. FR to Santayana, 5 Mar. 1895, MS-3699.
5. *St Stephen's Review*, 16 Apr. 1892. The series of three articles which ran from 12 to 26 Mar. 1892 under the title 'Varsity Socialists' had painted a none too flattering picture of the socialist movement in Oxford during Frank's time there. In response to Frank's letter it substantiated its report by commenting that Frank had been introduced to the Socialist League by Ion Thynne with a subscription of 5s. Given Frank's reaction to Morris's speech at the Russell Club in 1883, it is possible his enrolment had been one of Ion's pranks.
6. οὐκέτι transliterates as 'ouketi', meaning no longer or no more. It appears most often in Greek New Testament verses relating to marriage: 'So they are no longer two but one flesh. What therefore God has joined together let no man separate' (Matthew 19:6).
7. Background information taken from Neil-Tomlinson, pp. 109–128.
8. *Life*, p. 314.
9. *ibid.*, pp. 315–6.
10. *ibid.*, p. 291.
11. FR to Johnson, 24 Aug. 1895, WICC195.
12. *LES* & *MP*, 29 Apr. 1895.
13. Reply to Alimony Answer, 3 Aug. 1894, J77/534/16305.
14. Law Times, pp. 295–7.
15. *ibid.*, pp. 297–303.
16. Biggs, p. 42; Holmes, p. 155.
17. Petitioner's Costs, 2 Dec. 1895, J77/534/16305.
18. *Lords Journals*, 27 Mar. 1895.
19. *LES*, 26 Nov. 1896.
20. FR to Santayana, 2 Jan. 1896, MS-3699.
21. BR to AR, 18 Oct. 1894, RA1:710.55101.
22. Doulton to Santayana, 3 Dec. 1895, MS-3699.
23. *Times* and *LES*, 24 Nov. 1896.

24. *MP*, 12 Oct. 1896.

25. *SWE*, 25 Nov. 1896.

26. *LES*, 24 Nov. 1896.

27. Santayana to Boylston Adams Beal, 10 Oct. 1896, *LGS1*, p. 168.

28. FR to Santayana, 9 Feb. 1896, MS-3699.

29. *ibid.*

30. Roberts claimed damages in respect of three libels: the *Hawk* interview and Mabel's two letters dated 13 & 29 Dec. 1892 in which she had threatened to go to the press.

31. Roberts' apology was not cheap. The following January, friends at Cambridge opened an expenses fund to help him recoup some of the £800 it had cost him to clear his name. The list of subscribers, who between them raised £300 net, is a veritable who's who of the educational elite both within Cambridge and without, all eager to lay down their guineas in sympathy with the horrible position in which Roberts found himself. Bertrand put down £10 – one of only a handful of people to be quite so generous (EFB/5/2).

32. Santayana to Guy Murchie, 12 Aug. 1896, *LGS1*, p. 161.

33. *LES*, 16 Nov. 1894.

34. *Life*, p. 262.

35. Newnham College Register. Given the High Church status of All Hallows in Norfolk where Mary was schooled, this explanation is credible, but extensive research by the Sisters at Carshalton has drawn a blank; the most likely inference being that this was an expedient to avoid questions being asked of Mary's early departure from Cambridge.

36. *LES*, 24 Nov. 1896.

37. *Life*, p. 207.

38. *M2*, p. 221.

39. Deposition of Ellis Eyton Baines, 9 Oct. 1896, CRIM 1/46/4.

40. *Life*, p. 207.

41. Ida Augusta Franklin (née Burney) was indeed Lina's sister. She had married her first husband at seventeen and been divorced by him in 1878. In 1880, aged twenty-five, she married Charles Harris Franklin. A masseur in 1896, by 1891, she claimed to be a nurse and single, calling herself 'Ida Marchand'. In 1901, she passed as a widow. In 1906, Franklin entered the workhouse, while all trace of Ida is lost.

42. Depositions of Edward Wallet & Arthur Carrez, 10 Oct. 1896, CRIM 1/46/4.

43. *Times*, 7 Jun. 1920.

44. Matthews' mother was the New York stage actress Lizzie Weston; his stepfather the comic actor Charles James Matthews. 'Willie', as he was affectionately known on the circuit, took his stepfather's name and was called to the Bar in 1872.

45. Marjoribanks, pp. 90–1.

46. Santayana to Beal, 10 Oct. 1896, Santayana, *LGS1*, p. 169; *HT*, 10 Oct. 1896.

47. Deposition of Detective Inspector Alfred Leach, 10 Oct. 1896, CRIM 1/46/4.

48. Deposition of Detective Sergeant Arthur Hailstone, 10 Oct. 1896, *ibid.*

49. Morton, James, 'Bowing Out of Justice' and 'Kings of the court', *The Law Society Gazette*, 9 Sep. 2005 & 23 Feb. 2007.
50. *LES*, 13 Oct. 1896.
51. *MP & LES*, 13 Oct. 1896.
52. Lambert was a director of Humber (1888) and the Great Horseless Carriage Co. (1896). How he came to pay Lina's bail is unknown. In 1899, he resigned his various directorships after being tried at the Old Bailey for fraud. He was acquitted, but declared bankrupt the following year.
53. FR to Santayana, 14 Oct. 1896, MS-3699.
54. *ibid.*, 11 Nov. 1896.

16. Hell Hath No Fury

1. The London street 'Old Bailey' follows the line of the old fortified city wall. It housed the Lord Mayor's session house which was subsequently nicknamed 'Old Bailey' for its location. It was renamed 'Central Criminal Court' in 1832 after its jurisdiction was widened to cover areas outside the city. The current building was opened in 1907.
2. Testimony, descriptions of the scene in court and content of Frank's letters to Lina taken from the following periodicals, 24 Nov.–15 Dec. 1896: *LES*, *MP*, *NOW*, *SJG*, *SWE*, *Star*, *Telegraph*, *Times*.
3. Birrell, p. 56.
4. *Kitson v. Playfair* [1896].
5. Marjoribanks, p. 37.
6. *ibid.*, p. 105.
7. Philips, p. 167.
8. Cocks, p. 79.
9. Kast's date of birth was 17 July 1870, making him in fact sixteen when he was employed by Frank. It is not clear whether Kast purposely implied he was a minor when the offence took place or whether his age was misreported in the press. The protection of minors had been a moral issue of some weight since 1885 (see Chapter 12, fn.25).
10. Nowhere is the Victorian attitude towards homosexuality made clearer than in the wording of this Act, where sodomy is grouped with bestiality. Clause 61 reads: 'Whoever shall be convicted of the abominable crime of Buggery, committed either with Mankind or with any Animal, shall be liable at the Discretion of the Court, to be kept in Penal Servitude for Life or for any Term not less than Ten Years.'
11. CRIM 1/46/4.
12. This letter appeared in the *Star* and *LES* with slightly varying transcription – 'your daughters' (plural) in the *Star* and 'our chances of happiness' in the *Standard*. It was considerably précised in the *Post* and *Telegraph* but both papers agreed that 'invitation' was correct, where the *Star* and *Standard* both had 'concession'.
13. *ST*, 5 Dec. 1896.
14. *OBS*, 2 Feb. 1890.
15. RA1:731.080044, pp. 90–117.
16. Conversation between Ronald Clarke and John G. Slater, relayed to the author by Slater. At the time, it was unclear to Slater whether Clarke was

in possession of evidence beyond that cited here, or whether he was being provocative and using his friend as a sounding board for his thoughts, as was his wont.

17. AR to M. Carey Thomas, 11 Jan. 1897, RA3:434.122429.
18. *PP*, pp. 317–8.
19. CRIM 1/46/4.
20. This seems a weak point for both Frank and the defence. Frank was forced to admit that both entries were made on 11 July 1887, but not called to account for it. Later in the case, the defence would make little of the fact that this admission shows that the logbook was not kept up on a daily basis as Frank claimed, even if it did not prove he had doctored it long after the event.
21. *Life*, p. 208.
22. FR to Santayana, 9 Feb. 1896, MS-3699.
23. *PP*, p. 310.
24. *R. v. Scott & others*: Copy Evidence of Mrs Sarah Richardson, E17/12.
25. CRIM 1/46/4.
26. *Life*, p. 208.
27. AR to Thomas, 11 Jan. 1897, RA3:434.122429.

17. The Protestations of Lady Scott

1. Testimony and descriptions of the scene in court taken from the following periodicals, 4–9 Jan. 1897: *LES, MP, NOW, PMG, SJG, SWE, Star, Telegraph, Times*.
2. CRIM 1/46/4.
3. Santayana, on first hearing that Frank was considering purchasing the monastery (*after* he'd received the letter from Doulton), expressed surprise at the plan, sufficient to provoke the response from Frank: 'I know no reason why you should not associate me with Sicily – I am very familiar with Naples and very fond of the whole of that southern part' (FR to Santayana, 9 Feb. 1896, MS-3699). Frank had visited Naples on his Mediterranean tour, but had made no further reference to it, and apparently, no further visit between these dates.
4. *Truth*, 14 Jan. 1897.
5. *Star*, 9 Jan. 1897.
6. *SWE & LDN*, 9 Jan. 1897.
7. *Truth*, 14 Jan. 1897.
8. The earning of perks was regulated by a strict point system. Calculation suggests it would take a minimum of three months to accumulate sufficient points to earn additional visits and letters (Standing Order 203: System of Progressive Stages, 13 Jul 1892, HO 144/270/A58558).
9. HO 144/270/A58558.
10. AR to Thomas, 11 Jan. 1897, RA3:434.122429.
11. Santayana to Susan Sturgis de Sastre, 14 Jan. 1897, *LGS1*, p. 182.
12. *Life*, p. 160.
13. On 26 Nov. 1889, George Bernard Shaw wrote this letter to the editor of *Truth* in protest against the increased tendency to prosecute consenting adults for homosexual practices since the Labouchere amendment, thereby

using the law as 'the instrument of God's vengeance', for which he saw no justification. The letter has been described as 'one of the most explicitly pro-homosexual documents of the Victorian era' though there is some debate over whether it was actually sent (Kaye, pp. 222–6).

14. Cocks, p. 121.
15. Frank had proved this when, in 1892, he volunteered to give evidence in the 'Oxford Blackmail Scandal' exposed by *Truth*, in which several aristocrats had been bribed with fabricated sexually explicit letters. Frank was among the blackmailer's targets, but had refused to comply. Instead, the gentleman concerned had been summoned by Frank and Lina and 'given a good talking to' ('The Lord, the Law-Tutor, the Lady, and the Love Letter' in *Truth*, 24 Dec. 1891; *LES*, 2 Mar. 1892).
16. Santayana to Sturgis de Sastre, 14 Jan. 1897, *LGS1*, p. 182.
17. Mews, p. 123.
18. The other individual grounds being rape or bestiality; each so rarely proved as to be irrelevant (MacQueen, p. 150).
19. *RN*, 18 Jul. 1897.
20. *RM*, 20 Jul. 1897.
21. Indeed, due to lack of extant records, it is not even clear whether the men served their full sentences. After their release, Cockerton continued to live in West Ham, a marine engineer, until his death in 1916; and Aylott returned to his prior employment in Algiers, where he married and fathered a daughter. After returning to England, he settled in Essex, became a salesman and fathered four more children. He died in 1948 aged seventy-nine.
22. Mews, p. 122.
23. *Life*, p. 219.
24. Santayana, *Notebook IV*, p. 25. In this notebook, used to jot down ideas for his memoirs, Santayana had originally described Frank's Hellenism as 'dilettante'. Concerning his denial that it ever amused him, he initially wrote that he 'actually forgot' it did. Both of these he corrected in favour of the passage quoted above.
25. *Life*, p. 209.
26. Divorce Reform Act 1969, s.2.

18. Mrs Somerville

1. *SLC*, 24 Oct. 1896.
2. *Life*, p. 221.
3. *SLP*, 13 Apr. 1895.
4. *ibid.*, 27 Apr. 1895.
5. Haynes in *Saturday Review*, 14 Mar. 1931, p. 369.
6. *SLP*, 27 Apr. 1895.
7. *MP*, 26 Oct. 1895.
8. *SLP*, 30 Nov. 1895.
9. See Chapter 3 for histories of Willy and Agatha Russell.
10. *Life*, p. 232.
11. *ibid.*, p. 225.
12. *SLP*, 21 Aug. 1897.

13. FR to Santayana, 28 Nov. 1897, MS-3699.
14. *SLP*, 8 Jun. 1895.
15. The Progressives had eight Aldermanic seats to fill in 1898; the Moderates, two. Each Alderman served for six years, giving continuity to the work of the council, which could otherwise, in theory, be completely re-elected every three years. Candidates were voted in by elected party members on the LCC. Despite receiving the support of his fellow Progressive councillors, Frank felt himself 'debarred' from the Highways committee as punishment for his tramways voting the previous year. At the first council meeting after the election, he put forward a motion that he should replace one of the other newly appointed committee members. The move was considered 'unfortunate and unseemly' and the motion rejected out of hand (*Globe*, 22 Mar. 1898).
16. FR to Santayana, 28 Nov. 1897, MS-3699.
17. Mollie's exact age is unknown. Her family hailed from County Galway where records of her birth and baptism were destroyed in a church fire (MR to John Alec Somerville, 16 Feb. 1929, in private collection).
18. Science Notes, *PMG*, 24 Feb. 1896.
19. *APJ*, 24 Apr. 1900.
20. 'Notes from Manchester', *Today's Woman*, 30 Mar., 13 Apr. & 18 May 1895.
21. *Life*, p. 233.
22. *WLO*, 20 May 1898.
23. *Life*, p. 233.
24. *PP*, p. 476.
25. *Life*, p. 237.
26. *ibid.*, p. 234.
27. Gillespie, Sec. 23, p. 97. These laws were laid down in 1861 on the creation of Nevada state and were relaxed still further in the 1930s to allow divorce after only six weeks' residency, giving Reno its sin-city reputation and leading to the coining of the term 'renovation' to describe the act of getting a Reno-style migratory divorce (Harmon, p. 50).
28. *Life*, p. 242.
29. *ibid.*, pp. 242–4.
30. *ibid.*, p. 257.
31. Dept. Commerce & Labor, p. 305.
32. *Era*, 18 Mar. 1899.
33. *LDN*, 19 Apr. 1900.
34. *Daily Gazette and Bulletin* (Williamsport, PA), 25 Apr. 1900.
35. *San Francisco Call*, 19 Apr. 1900.
36. *Falkirk Herald*, 25 Apr. 1900.
37. *APJ*, 24 Apr. 1900.
38. *ibid.*
39. *ibid.*, 24 & 25 Apr. 1900.
40. AR to BR, 1 May 1900, RA3:434.123757.
41. FR to BR, 12 June 1900, RA1:730.46888.
42. FR to BR, 19 June 1900, RA1:730.46889.
43. BR to OM, 12 Apr. 1912, RA3:69.18506.
44. Answer of co-respondent, J77/693/1073.
45. *LDN*, 22 Apr. 1903; Jepson, *ME*, pp. 78–9.

46. Jepson, *ME*, p. 88.
47. *LDN*, 22 Apr. 1903.
48. 'Cock-and-Hen Clubs of Soho: Freaks at the Pharos', *ST*, 5 Mar. 1921, p. 5.
49. 'The Truth About Bohemian London', *Sphere*, 10 Jan. 1925, p. 46.
50. Titterton, pp. 31–2; Chesterton, p. 38.
51. *LDN*, 10 & 12 Aug. 1904.
52. *Life*, p. 283.
53. Conrad Sebastian Robert, 5th Earl Russell, in Holmes, p. 159. Mrs Belloc Lowndes also said that Countess Airlie (Blanche Stanley, as was) confided to her that she had heard the same story at court (Lowndes, p. 44).
54. *Life*, p. 283. The identity of this nobleman remains a mystery.
55. CRIM 1/67/4; *SJG*, 18 June 1901.
56. *Life*, p. 280.
57. The wording of the original law simply specifies that if the defendant fails to appear after the publishing of the notice in the local paper for three months in succession, *or* after 30 days personal service of summons, 'the evidence may be heard, and the cause decided, at that term' (Gillespie, Sec. 23, p. 97). The statute remained unchanged in 1900 (Dept. Commerce & Labor, p. 305).

19. A Jury of His Peers

1. Public opinion went against Cardigan when he got off on a technicality. The prosecution proved that he *had* fired on his opponent, Captain Tuckett, but could not prove beyond doubt that this was the same 'Harvey Garnet Phipps Tuckett' named in the indictment. The peers unanimously acquitted him and the whole sordid mess was over in a day; though not without the *Times* alleging high-level complicity in the leaving open of the loophole that allowed him to get off scot-free (*Times*, 17 & 18 Feb. 1841).
2. *LDN*, 5 July 1901.
3. Details of preparations for the trial, press reaction and atmosphere on the day – in this chapter and the preface – taken from the following periodicals 5–19 July 1901: *APJ*, *BEN*, *BNL*, *Globe*, *DM*, *SJG*, *LDN*, *MP*, *Telegraph*, *Times*, *WMN*, *WT*, *YEP*. Details of the trial itself from 'Proceedings of the Trial of Earl Russell', HL/PO/DC/CP/33/6.
4. Hansard, vol. 97, cc. 593–4; vol. 97, c. 838. Figures from the *Sunderland Daily Echo* and *Western Times*, 19 July 1901 represent the extremes of figures suggested by the press.
5. The Lords chose to abolish their own privilege before it was imposed on them, inserting a clause into the Criminal Justice Act, 1948 which was accepted by the Commons.
6. *ST*, 13 July 1901.
7. The substantive 'privilege of peerage', by which a peer found guilty of a first felonious offence (other than treason or murder) could avoid his punishment by claiming that he needed to remain accessible to the sovereign at all times, was abolished in 1841 after Lord Cardigan threatened to claim it had he been found guilty.
8. *Times*, 26 June 1901.
9. Offences Against the Person Act, 1861, s. 57.

10. *ibid.*, s. 9.
11. *Santos v. Illidge* [1860].
12. *Life*, p. 281.
13. *ibid.*, p. 287.
14. The *Times* in particular voiced the opinion that 'the sentence did fit the crime and was no more or less than would have been metered out to a common offender at the Assizes' (19 July 1901).
15. *Life*, pp. 286–7.
16. HO 144/951/A62795.
17. *Life*, p. 287.
18. WORKS 11/96.
19. Lowndes, p. 46; Blanche Hozier to FR, 19 July 1901, RA1:732.80073.
20. Georgina Weldon to FR, 19 Oct. 1901, RA1:732.80076. For an account of the Weldons' story, see chapter 13. Frank himself estimated the financial cost of his legal battles with Mabel (*Life*, p. 290). He also pointed out that it would have been cheaper to pay Mabel the £1,000 p.a. she had originally asked for on their separation, but her accusations of immorality made it imperative he defend his name through the courts.
21. In *Rivière v. Weldon* [1880] Georgina was found guilty of libelling a man whose second and third marriages made under false names – on English and foreign soil – were declared illegal and therefore not bigamous. Her suggestion that Frank could have used this defence is wrong: he had not married under an assumed name, only concealed his title.
22. *Life*, p. 290.

20. The Fox without a Tail

1. FR, *LS*, v–vii.
2. *TLS*, 7 Nov. 1902, p. 336.
3. *PP*, p. 475.
4. FR, *LS*, p. 25.
5. *LDN*, 28 Nov. 1902.
6. Hansard, vol. 3, cc. 1437–49.
7. 'If you had not yourself lost your tail, my friend, you would not thus counsel us' (Townsend, George Flyer, *Three Hundred Aesop's Fables* (London: Routledge, 1871), p. 43).
8. Hansard, vol. 107, cc. 389–409.
9. The 1857 Act enabled the divorce court to sit outside London and poor people to sue *in forma pauperis* but 'the former provision was never acted on, the latter remained ineffective' (McGregor, p. 18).
10. *PMG, MC & LM*, 2 May 1902.
11. Piecemeal legislation between 1878 and 1902 impowered magistrates to award separation and maintenance orders to wives whose husbands were cruel or habitually drunk, who deserted or were imprisoned for terms greater than two months. Relief was often inadequate – a husband paid no more than £2 a week until 1949 – but orders were popular and claims for relief flooded in. In the ten years between 1897 and 1906, over 87,000 orders were granted (McGregor, pp. 23–4).

12. Hansard, vol. 124, cc. 202–13.
13. 400 years later, the Church would dissociate itself from the *Reformatio Legum*, calling it the 'work of extremists'. This argument, dismissed by social scientist O. R. McGregor as historically inaccurate political expediency, demonstrates the extent to which the Church argued for the indissolubility of marriage well into the twentieth century (McGregor, pp. 8–9).
14. *MC & YP*, 3 June 1903.
15. 'Mrs Pat' had been a darling of the stage since her performance in Pinero's 'woman with a past' play *The Second Mrs Tanqueray* (1893). Her comment in response to hearing of a homosexual affair between two actors has been quoted as epitomizing the attitude of Edwardian England to sex (Hynes, p. 186) and was linked to Frank's escapades in the title of Holmes' article.
16. Hansard, vol. 150, cc. 1064–1071.
17. *Times*, 20 Mar. 1891, concerning *R. v. Jackson* [1891].
18. *Dodd v. Dodd* [1906] P 189, p. 207.
19. Hansard, vol. 193, cc. 4–13.
20. At the turn of the century, the number of petitions for divorce was still low – approximately 800 p.a. – with a further eighty petitions for judicial separation. There were nearly ten times as many maintenance orders (McGregor, pp. 24, 36).
21. Interestingly (and for once rather modestly), Frank credited Lord Gorell with bringing about the Royal Commission; Haynes credited Frank. More recently, historians such as Stephen Cretney have concurred with Frank while acknowledging Haynes' perception of Frank as a pioneer in the field (Cretney, pp. 205–9), securing Frank's place in the history of divorce law reform overlooked by earlier writers such as Stone and Phillips.
22. Cd.6478, p. 100; 'Such a construction of the solemn oath of fidelity ... is absolutely barred by the concluding words "until death do us part"' (Bosanquet, p. 452).
23. FR, *D*, pp. v–vi.
24. *Globe*, 20 Nov. 1912.
25. *MG*, 13 June 1912; *OBS*, 25 Feb. 1912. *Divorce* was clearly aimed at those Frank thought would most benefit from reform – the educated middle and lower classes. Kitchin offered a more studious, in-depth and closely referenced account of divorce law in Britain, the USA, British Colonies and Europe, aimed at a more intellectual readership.
26. *LDN*, 24 Apr. 1912.
27. Hynes, p. 211.
28. Examples include Arnold Bennett's *Whom God Hath Joined* (1906), Bernard Shaw's *Getting Married* (1908), Wells' *Ann Veronica* (1909), and Hall Caine's *The Woman Thou Gavest Me* (1913). Caine used *Divorce* in writing his hugely popular novel, but the compliment was not returned: Frank criticised the novel for its protagonist's 'furtive and discreditable adultery' which he considered immoral on the ground that 'dishonesty and deceit cannot be good for the soul or the character' (RA1:732.080115–6).
29. Hansard, vol. 1, cc. 1184–1231.

21. Great Reform Acts

1. Brendon, p. 10.
2. *ibid.*, p. 76.
3. *Life*, p. 295.
4. Brendon, p. 58.
5. *AC Journal*, 19 Dec. 1902, p. 400; 12 & 19 Mar., 14 & 21 May 1903, pp. 278, 294, 518, 545.
6. FR, 'An Analysis of the New Act' in *Autocar*, no. 412/XI (12 Sep. 1903), pp. 338–340.
7. *Life*, p. 293.
8. Jepson, *ME*, p. 91.
9. HC, 30 Apr. 1904.
10. It is possible that A1, though the first plate issued in London, was not actually the first in England. All plates were then issued by councils. Orme-Bannister claims Somerset, Buckinghamshire & Hastings all started issuing registrations in November 1903, a month earlier than London (pp. 244–5).
11. With hindsight, this might have been Frank's worst financial decision. In 1959 the plate sold for £2,500. Ironically, in the 1920s, Frank led a public outcry against the Roads Act which tied number plates to their original vehicle. The Ministry of Transport unofficially rescinded the order in 1921 and then officially in 1985 when the DVLA 'coincidently' expressed an interest in selling 'Cherished Numbers' (Orme-Bannister, p. 244). The current whereabouts of A1 is unknown but rumour has it that at one time the Brunei Prince Jefri Bolkiah had A1 and 1A on a pair of white Bentley Azures. A1's potential value continues to excite speculation, F1 having sold in 2008 for £440,625 and '1' for a cool £7.2m (*Mail on Sunday*, 14 May 2016).
12. *Life*, p. 295.
13. *ibid.*, p. 307.
14. The constable concerned, PC Ashford, was subsequently tried at the Old Bailey for actual bodily harm and sentence to nine months' hard labour (t19081020-49).
15. *Life*, p. 317.
16. *Irish Independent*, 13 Apr. 1904; *BNL*, 11 May 1904; *DDE*, 27 Apr. 1906.
17. *Life*, p. 317.
18. Cannadine notes that by 1896, some 167 peers were company directors (a quarter of the entire nobility); by 1910, the figure was 232 (*DFBA*, p. 407).
19. Santayana to Sturgis de Sastre, *LGS1*, p. 406.
20. 'Colette', quoted in Clark, p. 343.
21. PP, pp. 317–8.
22. *Life*, p. 270.
23. DC, 12 Apr. 1904.
24. LDN, 2 Nov. 1906.
25. LES, 6 May 1907.
26. CO, 2 July 1909; LDN, 4 Dec. 1908.
27. 2WFL/4/1/a.
28. CO, 7 July 1909.
29. *Cheltenham Looker-on*, 3 Apr. 1909.
30. WF, 22 July 1909.

31. *ibid.*, 6 Feb. 1908.
32. 2WFL/1/01, p. 228. Correction in original document.
33. FR to Wells, 11 Apr. 1911, RA3:484.120802

22. Twin Souls

1. This was Rebecca West, writing long after she became the cause of friction between Elizabeth and Wells (*New Statesman*, 15 Oct. 1921).
2. MR, *FWC*, p. 91.
3. Elizabeth, *EGG*, pp. 3–8, p. 57.
4. 'Another View of Elizabeth' in *The Speaker*, 1 Apr. 1899, pp. 371–2.
5. *The Spectator*, 8 Oct. 1898, quoting *EGG*, p. 47.
6. Marie Adelaide Belloc was the sister of Hilaire Belloc. Frank befriended her in 1894 through Bertrand. Her memoirs, *The Merry Wives of Westminster* (1946), describe her connection with the Stanley family and her association with Elizabeth. According to Jepson, Mrs Belloc Lowndes (as she became in 1896) 'knew everyone and went everywhere' and blended a pained expression with a 'mischievous glee' in the stories she told of her acquaintances (*MV*, p. 121).
7. Holmes, M., p. 5.
8. I use the term 'relationship' advisedly. Wells' own account of their affair – 'The Episode of Little e' in *Wells in Love* (1984) – unequivocally states his successful seduction. Walker has found much to criticise in the account, taking David C. Smith's comment – that much of Wells' fiction of 1912–22 included autobiographical reworkings of his own failures and frustrations – as also applying to his pursuit of Elizabeth (Walker, *AAV*, p. 58). Others take Wells' comments at face value. The success or not of his seduction has little bearing on the part Elizabeth played in Frank's life.
9. Lowndes, p. 70.
10. Precis of reviews in Charms, p. 128.
11. Charms, p. 92.
12. Lowndes opined, 'Each of the women he married, almost grotesquely different the one from the other, was entirely unsuited to be, in any sense of the word, his wife' (p. 45).
13. Wells, p. 87; Lowndes, p. 69.
14. *PP*, p. 478.
15. MR, *FWC*, p. 200; Charms, p. 78.
16. *PP*, p. 476; Charms, p. 89.
17. Charms, p. 112.
18. *Life*, p. 268.
19. Mollie's diary, 1910, in private collection.
20. Monk, pp. 151–192.
21. *ibid.*, p. 214.
22. FR to BR, 6 June 1911, RA1:730.119592.
23. BR to OM, 13 June 1911, RA3:69.17189.
24. King, Richard, 'With Silent Friends' in *The Tatler*, 19 July 1911, p. 74.
25. *PMG*, 18 Aug.; *LDN*, 29 Aug. 1911.
26. *YP*, 26 July 1911.
27. MR to BR, 24 July 1911, RA1:710.55322.
28. Wells, p. 91.

29. FR to Elizabeth, 4 Jan. 1914, ER1735; *PP*, p. 477.
30. BR to OM, 24 Jan. 1912, RA3:69.17413.
31. Bertrand's observations in letters to OM, 5–12 Apr. 1912, RA3:69.17507–9 & 18506.
32. In March 1912, Bertrand confessed to Ottoline the violence of his suppressed emotions: 'It doesn't do for me to relax too much – the forces inside are too wild … some of them are mad dogs and are not safe to leave at large' (Monk, pp. 256–7).
33. MR to BR, 5 June 1913, RA1:710.55324.
34. Wells, pp. 90–1.
35. Elizabeth, *Dogs*, pp. 94–5.
36. *ibid.*, pp. 20, 94, 113.
37. Juliane Römhild considers *Dogs* 'less an attempt at telling "how it really was" than a fantasy of how things should have been, using a simple yet sophisticated construct to detract the reader from too close an examination of the author herself'. As such, it 'relies on atmosphere and mood to convey a life story noticeably bare of biographical facts' (pp. 139–40).
38. All references to Elizabeth's journal come from transcripts ER99 (1913) and ER100 (1914).
39. Charms, p. 146.
39. Wells appears in Elizabeth's journal throughout their intimacy as 'G'. It appears to have been her habit to choose a distinct name for her intimates: all her children had pet names and Frank would soon appear as 'Francis'; she was the only person never to call him Frank.
40. FR to Elizabeth, 4 Jan. 1914, ER1735.
41. FR to Elizabeth, 11 Jan. 1914, ER1736.
42. Elizabeth, *Dogs*, p. 119.
43. *Times*, 14 July 1914.
44. *PP*, p. 480.
45. BR to OM, 28 Feb. 2014, RA3:69.18147.
46. MR, *FWC*, p. 93.
47. Charms, p. 160.
48. Santayana to Charles Augustus Strong, 17 July 1914, *LGS2*, p. 186.
49. Elizabeth's recollections quoted in Walker, pp. 170–1.
50. FR to Elizabeth, 31 July 1914, ER1737.
51. Deed of Trust, 2 Nov. 1929, supplemental to Indenture dated 14 Sep. 1914, in private collection.
52. FR to Elizabeth, 12 Dec. 1914, ER1741. By 'Theo' Frank implies Θεός or God.

23. Conscientious Objections

1. All references to Elizabeth's journal in this chapter come from transcripts ER101 (1915) and ER102 (1916).
2. *PP*, p. 482.
3. BR to OM, 7 June 1915, RA3:69.18458.
4. Horace, *The Odes*, 1:24.
5. BR to OM, 30 May 1915, RA3:69.18456.
6. *Times*, 18 June 1914.

7. *DDE*, 25 Nov. 1916.
8. *Globe*, 10 Feb. 1920.
9. *YEP*, 16 Feb. 1920.
10. BR to OM, 9 Sep. 1915, RA3:69.18494.
11. Cobden-Sanderson, pp. 278–9.
12. Santayana to FR, 2 Jan. 1912, *LGS2*, p. 66.
13. *Millom Gazette*, 31 Jan. 1913.
14. *Justice*, 21 Dec. 1912.
15. *DH*, 9 Dec. 1912.
16. Hansard, vol. 13, cc. 408–12.
17. Heffer, p. 672.
18. FR, 'Lord Russell Protests' in *The Syndicalist*, vol. 1/3 (Mar–Apr 1912), p. 3.
19. *Cambridge Independent Press*, 2 May 1913; *SDT*, 4 Oct. 1913; *HT*, 30 Jan. 1914.
20. *Hansard*, vol. 17, cc. 89–92.
21. Officially established in September 1914, the UDC campaigned for greater parliamentary control of foreign policy and against the imposing of punitive measures, humiliations or annexations on the defeated nation after the war. Bertrand was one of its early members.
22. Frank to Bertrand, 11 Nov. 1915, RA1:730.46902.
23. Monk, p. 448; *Labour Leader*, 6 Jan. 1916.
24. Hansard, vol. 20, cc. 971–1016.
25. Quoted in Haynes, *DL*, p. 25.
26. Hansard, vol. 21, cc. 919–22.
27. *Ibid.*, vol. 22, cc. 521–46; ER102, p. 23; *Life*, p. 328.
28. FR to BR, RA1:730.46903.
29. LAR to BR, 17 Feb. 1916, RA1:736.100280.
30. Cobden-Sanderson, p. 286.
31. Santayana to Sturgis de Sastre, 22 June; to Strong, 1 July 1916, *LGS2*, pp. 249–250.
32. *PP*, pp. 480–1.
33. MR to John Alec Somerville, 12 Feb. 1928, in private collection.
34. Anne Young to BR, 5 Mar. 1931, RA1:735.70957.
35. *Evening News*, 13 June 1916; Berridge, Virginia, 'The Origins of the English Drug "Scene"' in *Medical History*, vol. 32 (1988), pp. 51–64.
36. Charms, p. 181.
37. Santayana to Strong, 27 Aug. 1916, *LGS2*, p. 251.
38. Elizabeth to BR, 30 Oct. & 3 Nov. 1916, RA3:69.18620.
39. BR to OM, 22 Nov. 1916, RA3:69.18622.
40. Charms, pp. 190–1.
41. *ibid.*, pp. 195–6.
42. Santayana to Sturgis de Sastre, 10 Oct. 1917, *LGS2*, p. 291.
43. Charms, p. 196.
44. FR to BR, 16 & 30 Jul. 1916, RA1:730.46907–8.
45. *I Appeal unto Caesar* was published in August 1917 and accredited to Margaret Hobhouse, the socially more acceptable sister of Beatrice Webb, to influence Liberal circles. In four months, it was reprinted four times, selling 18,000 copies (Clark, p. 331).

46. BR, 'The German Peace Offer' in *The Tribunal*, vol. 90 (3 Jan. 1918), p. 1.
47. Monk, p. 477. Colette was the daughter of Hugh, 5th Earl Annesley and his wife Priscilla. She had married fellow actor Miles Malleson in 1915 and met Bertrand through the NCF in 1916. Their affair lasted until 1920 and their friendship for life.
48. Clark, p. 343; FR to BR, 31 May 1918, RA1:730.46916.
49. Elizabeth to BR, 22 June 1918, RA1:730.46920.
50. BR to OM, 16 June 1918, RA3:69.18678.
51. BR to Colette, 31 July 1918, RA3:596.116363.
52. BR to Rinder, 17 June 1918, RA3:596.19326.
53. BR to OM, 1 Aug. 1918, RA3:69.18683.
54. FR to BR, 26 June 1918, RA1:730.46929.
55. Several versions of this recollection exist. Clark quoted Bertrand as saying this about Cave; Monk said he incorrectly applied it to Cockerill on a BBC interview in 1946. Both are inaccurate as neither Cave nor Cockerill were Wykehamists, but it is not unreasonable to assume that there were others in government known to Frank who were.

24. Paradise Lost

1. ER104, p. 1.
2. Ruth Anderson appears in Elizabeth's diary (summer, 1918) as an associate of Frank's. She remains a rather shadowy figure, described by Bertrand as being one of a 'rum party' of three females staying at TH in October 1919. She apparently worked at *Vogue*, 'is proud of having claustrophobia, and talks without ceasing'. Bertrand also said it was one of the others whom Frank then found 'attractive'; Bertrand thought them all 'silly and dull' (BR to Colette, 11 Oct. 1919, RA3:596.19570).
3. *PP*, p. 300.
4. Letters to Liebet, ER665; ER668.
5. BR to OM, 12 & 17 Apr. 1919, RA3:69.18751, 18736. There is no suggestion Frank's threat was at all serious.
6. BR to FR, 19 May 1919, RA1:730.46935.
7. Taken from typescript of *Russell v. Shoolbreds, Ltd.*, 8–10 July 1919, ER7.
8. BR to Elizabeth, [?] July 1919, RA3:102.54220.
9. FR, 'Introduction' in Johnson, pp. 9–13.
10. *YP*, 26 Nov. 1919.
11. *Spectator*, 10 Jan. 1920, p. 19.
12. FR to Unwin, 13 Oct. 1919, RA3:70.48725.
13. Elizabeth, *ITM*, pp. 3, 25.
14. Römhild, chapter 4.
15. ER105, p. 6.
16. BR to OM, 17 Nov. 1920, RA3:369.18785.
17. *ABR1*, p. 26.
18. FR to BR, 8 Jan. 1921, RA1:730.46939.
19. Wells, p. 91; Swinnerton, *FIF*, p. 57; *ABR2*, p. 153.
20. *PP*, p. 484.

21. Swinnerton, *FIF*, p. 53.
22. Walker, p. 248.
23. *PP*, p. 484.
24. *ABR2*, p. 154; ER to Colette (notes), RA3:967.310924; Colette to ER, 17 Mar. 1971, RA3:967.310923.
25. ER1772.
26. Elizabeth to Katherine Mansfield, 7 Nov. 1921, ER1482.
27. Elizabeth to Mansfield, 27 Sep. 1921, ER1480.
28. Jepson to FR, 2 Mar. 1923, RA1:732.80106.
29. *Life*, p. 120.
30. *ibid.*, pp. 344–8.
31. *PP*, p. 518; Santayana to Strong, 29 Sep. 1923, *LGS3*, pp. 152–3.
32. Elizabeth, *Dogs*, p. 119; Charms, p. 336.
33. Charms, p. 385. '*Dieses Auge*' – those eyes. Teppi was governess to the von Arnim children who afterwards stayed on as companion to Elizabeth.
34. *PP*, p. 307.
35. Information taken from Turcon unless specified.
36. DR to BR, 20 June 1927, RA2:710.103976.
37. BR to DR, 23 Aug. 1927, RA2:760.133921
38. Davies to BR, 14 Sep. 1927, RA2:760.133007.
39. BR to Davies, 6 Dec. 1928, RA2:760.133105.
40. BR to Davies, 15 Dec. 1928, RA2:760.133112.
41. BR to Davies, 14 Oct. 1930, RA2:760.133253.
42. *Life*, p. 345.
43. *ABR2*, p. 153.

25. A Labouring Lord

1. BR to Davies, 14 Oct. 1930, RA2:760.133253.
2. Frank officially joined the Labour Party after the 1918 Constitution introduced individual membership, but was probably counted among the sixty-seven peers listed in the 1920 yearbook as having no formal political allegiance. As a hereditary peer he had no obligation to be anything else. Frank gets no mention in the *Dictionary of Labour Biography* (2018) or either Thorpe or Pugh.
3. Earl Russell, 'The Difficulties of Bishops' in *The R. P. A. Annual* (1922), pp. 25–31. The RPA was dedicated to publishing books and pamphlets on science and critiquing organised religion. Frank was an honorary associate from 1927 to 1931.
4. Hall, L., p. 665.
5. *ibid.*, p. 671.
6. Housman to Frank, 6 May 1921, RA1:732.080194.
7. Housman to Frank, 13 Dec. 1922, RA1:732.080198; FR to Secretary of BSSSP, MS-00518:10.5.
8. Hall, R., p. 195.
9. FR to Stopes, 10 Aug. 1921, Add MS 58556.

10. The pessary was a small barrier device of Marie's design that fitted around the cervix. It eventually fell out of use as the larger diaphragm or 'Dutch cap' was regarded as easier to use.
11. FR to Stopes, 1 Mar. 1923, Add MS 58556.
12. *DH*, 17 May 1923.
13. Pugh, p. 172.
14. Hansard, vol. 54, c. 520.
15. *ibid.*, vol. 56, cc. 136–8.
16. ER761.
17. Housman to FR, 4 Apr. 1924, RA1:732.080202.
18. Hansard, vol. 66, cc. 232–48.
19. *ibid.*, vol. 72, cc. 644–54. See also vol. 67, cc. 956–65.
20. *ibid.*, vol. 68, c. 256. Frank wanted an end to tied pubs and was generally pro-temperance though not in favour of total prohibition.
21. BR to FR, 14 June 1929, RA1:730.46961. Parmoor was then in his late seventies; Haldane had died in 1928.
22. *ibid.*
23. Hansard, vol. 64, cc. 687–711.
24. *ibid.*, vol. 75, cc. 931–994.
25. *ibid.*; *MG*, 5 Feb. 1930.
26. FR to Stopes, 19 Nov. 1929, Add MS 58556.
27. *Times*, 5 Mar. 1931; Hansard, vol. 75, c. 924.
28. *Lancashire Daily Post*, 6 Jan.; *MG*, 9 Jan.; *New Leader*, 10 Jan. 1930.
29. *Times*, 5 Mar. 1931.
30. BR to Buckland, 8 Mar. 1931, RA1:735.70906.
31. BR to Mr Watts, 10 Mar. 1931, RA1:735.70988.
32. BR to OM, 9 Mar. 1931, *SLBR2*, pp. 300–1.
33. BR to OM, 12 Oct. 1931, *ibid.*, p. 302.
34. FR to BR, 15 Sep. 1920, RA1:730.46938.
35. Otter to BR, 11 Mar. 1931, RA1:735.70935.
36. *MG*, 31 Mar. 1931.
37. Add MS 58556.
38. Webb to BR, 26 Mar. 1931, RA1:735.71038.
39. Morrison to BR, 5 Mar. 1931, RA1:735.70980; Hansard, vol. 80, c. 301; vol. 80, c. 381.
40. Wakefield to BR, 7 Mar. 1931, RA1:735.70990.
41. Walker, p. 351; Charms, p. 330.
42. FR to Stopes, 25 Jan. 1922, Add MS 58556.
43. *ABR2*, p. 278.

Epilogue: Song of Myself

1. *Life*, p. 344.
2. *PP*, pp. 307–8.
3. *Life*, pp. 344–5.
4. Wakefield to BR, 7 Mar 1931, RA1:735.70990.
5. *Life*, p. 345.
6. Whitman, Walt, 'Song of Myself', v.4 in *Leaves of Grass* (Philadelphia: Rees Walsh & Co., 1882), pp. 31–2.

Bibliography

Archival Material

The British Library
Correspondence of Oscar Wilde & others, Add MS 81690
Correspondence with G. B. Shaw, Add MS 50512
Johnson–Dodgson Correspondence, Add MS 46363
Stopes Papers, Add MS 58556

Cambridge University
Manuscripts and Archives: Diaries of Charles Sayle, MS Add.8508–10; Letters to Charles Sayle, MS Add.8548
King's College: The Turin Papers, Roberts' Expenses Fund, EFB/5/2
Pepys Library, Magdalene College: Diaries of Arthur Christopher Benson, v.175

Cheshire Archives
Stanley Family Collection, DSA 99, 175/1, 175/2

Columbia University, NY, Rare Book & Manuscript Library
George Santayana Collection: *Autobiography (Notebook IV)*

Huntington Library, CA
Elizabeth Mary Russell, Countess Russell Papers, transcripts of diaries, ER98–103, correspondence, ER1735–1742

London Metropolitan Archives
Fulham Board of Guardians signed minutes, FBG/035
School Board for London register of staff, SBL/1515

London School of Economics Archives
Women's Freedom League constitution, 2WFL/4/1/a
Women's Freedom League minutes of National Executive, 2WFL/1/01

Loras College, IA
Raymond Roseliep Papers, T2/F7

McMaster University, Ontario, Canada, William Ready Division
Bertrand Russell Archives (RC0096), extensive correspondence prefix RA1-RA3;
    Frank Russell diaries, RA1:731.080042–4

The National Archives
Central Criminal Court depositions, CRIM 1/46/4, 1/67/4; court book, CRIM
    6/19
Divorce and Matrimonial Causes files:
Russell v. Russell: J77/461/4047 [1891]; J77/534/16305 [1895]; J77/695/1144
    [1901].
Scott v. Scott: J77/112/415 [1871]; J77/167/4109 [1876]; J77/167/4128 [1876];
    J77/280/8243 [1883]
Scott v. Sebright: J77/359/0862 [1886]
Somerville v. Somerville & Russell: J77/693/1073 [1901]
High Court of Justice in Bankruptcy register of petitions, B 11/9 [1892]; register
    of receiving orders, B 12/3 [1891–2]
Home Office files, HO 144/270/A58558, 144/951/A62795
Lord Chancellor's Office registered file, LCO 2/173
Office of Works & Successors file, WORKS 11/96

The National Archives of Scotland
Divorce and Matrimonial Causes file, *Watson v. Watson*: CS46/1889/7/31 [1889]

Oxford University
Balliol College Archives: Jowett Papers, IF6/61, IIC/C1/158, IV/A8/24

Parliamentary Archives
House of Lords Appeal Cases and Writs of Error [1897], HL/PO/JU/4/3/467
House of Lords Journals [1895], HL/PO/JO2/127
Records of the Trial of Earl Russell, HL/PO/DC/CP/33/6

Royal Bank of Scotland Archives
Child & Co. ledger pages, CH/203/190

University of Texas, Harry Ransom Centre
George Santayana Collection: MS–3699
British Sexology Society Records: MS-00518

Wellcome Library Collections, Archives and Manuscripts
Manor House Asylum casebooks, MS.5725, MS.6222–3

Winchester College Archives
George and Sarah Richardson Collection, E17/3–12
Letters to Lionel Johnson, WICC195

Published Material

Abbott, Evelyn, *The Life and Letters of Benjamin Jowett* (London: John Murray, 1897)

Adams, H. C., *Wykehamica* (Winchester, J. Wells, 1878)

Arapostathis, Stathis & Gooday, Graeme, *Patently Contestable* (Cambridge, MA: MIT Press, 2013)

Arnim, Elizabeth von, *Elizabeth and Her German Garden* (London: MacMillan, 1898)

Arnim, Elizabeth von, *All the Dogs of My Life* (London: Virago, 1995)

Badley, John Haden, *Memories and Reflections* (London: George Allen & Unwin, 1955)

Balfour-Browne, John Hutton, *Forty Years at the Bar* (London: Herbert Jenkins, 1916)

Bartrip, Peter, 'A Talent to Alienate: the 2nd Earl (Frank) Russell (1865–1931)' in *Russell*, vol. 32 (2012), pp. 101–126

Biggs, John M., *The Concept of Matrimonial Cruelty* (London: Althone Press, 1962)

Birrell, Augustine, *Sir Frank Lockwood: A Biographical Sketch* (London: Smith Elder, 1898)

Bosanquet, Helen, 'English Divorce Law and the Report of the Royal Commission', *International Journal of Ethics*, vol. 23 (July 1913), pp. 443–455

Brake, Laurel & Demoor, Marysa (eds), *Dictionary of Nineteenth-Century Journalism in Great Britain and Ireland* (London: Academia Press and The British Library, 2009)

Brendon, Piers, *The Motoring Century: The Story of the Royal Automobile Club* (London: Bloomsbury, 1997)

Brockliss, Laurence, *The University of Oxford: A History* (Oxford: Oxford University Press, 2016)

Cannadine, David, *Aspects of Aristocracy* (London: Penguin, 1994)

Cannadine, David, *The Decline and Fall of the British Aristocracy* (New York: Vintage, 1999)

Chandos, John, *Boys Together: English Public Schools 1800–1864* (New Haven, CT: Yale University Press, 1984)

Charms, Leslie de, *Elizabeth of the German Garden* (London: William Heinemann, 1958)

Chesterton, Mrs Cecil, *The Chestertons* (London: Chapman & Hall, 1941)

Clark, Ronald, *The Life of Bertrand Russell* (London: Jonathan Cape and Weidenfeld & Nicholson, 1975)

Clarke, Sir Edward, *The Story of My Life* (London: John Murray, 1918)

Cocks, H. G., *Nameless Offences: Homosexual Desire in the 19th Century* (London: I. B. Tauris, 2010)

Collier, W. F., *Punishments in Education* (London: Longmans Green, 1872)

Cobden-Sanderson, Richard, *The Journals of Thomas Cobden-Sanderson* (London: Richard Cobden-Sanderson, 1926)

Cory, Daniel, *Santayana: The Later Years* (New York: George Brazillier, 1963)

Cretney, Stephen Michael, *Family Law in the Twentieth Century: A History* (Oxford: Oxford University Press, 2003)

Department of Commerce and Labor, *Special Reports: Marriage and Divorce 1867–1906. Part 1: Summary, Laws, Foreign Statistics* (Washington: Government Printing Office, 1909)

D. G., *The Royal Courts of Justice: Illustrated Handbook* (London: D. G., 1883)

Dowling, Linda, *Hellenism and Homosexuality in Victorian Oxford* (New York & London: Cornell University Press, 1994)

Ellman, Richard, *Oscar Wilde* (London: Penguin, 1987)

Fisher, H. A. L., *An Unfinished Autobiography* (Oxford: Oxford University Press, 1940)

Fletcher, Iain, 'Introduction' in *The Complete Poems of Lionel Johnson* (London: Unicorn Press, 1953)

Foster, Joseph, *Oxford Men* (Oxford: James Parker, 1893)

Freeth, F. A., 'James Swinburne, 1858–1958' in *Biographical Memoirs of the Fellows of the Royal Society*, vol. 5 (1960), pp. 253–268

Gillespie, William Martin, *Laws and Territories of Nevada* (San Francisco: Valentine, 1862)

Green, Sarah, 'The Undeveloped Body of Lionel Johnson' in *Notes and Queries*, June 2016, pp. 281–283

Hall, Lesley, '"Disinterested Enthusiasm for Sexual Misconduct": The British Society for the Study of Sex Psychology, 1913–47' in *Journal of Contemporary History*, vol. 30/4 (Oct. 1995), pp. 665–688

Hall, Ruth, *Marie Stopes: A Biography* (London: André Deutsch, 1977)

Harmon, Mella Rothwell, 'Getting Renovated: Reno Divorces in the 1930s' in *Nevada Historical Society Quarterly*, vol. 2/1 (Spring 1999), pp. 46–68

Hawkins, Desmond, *Concerning Agnes: Thomas Hardy's Good Little Pupil* (Stroud: Alan Sutton, 1982)

Haynes, E. S. P., *The Decline of Liberty* (London: Grant Richards, 1916)

Haynes, E. S. P., 'The Late Earl Russell and Divorce Law Reform' in *Saturday Review*, vol. 151/3933 (14 Mar. 1931), p. 369

Haynes, E. S. P., *The Lawyer: A Conversation Piece* (London: Eyre & Spottiswoode, 1951)

Heffer, Simon, *The Age of Decadence* (London: Windmill, 2017)

Herford, William, *The Student's Froebel: Part 1: Theory of Education* (London: Pitman & Sons, 1916)

Hobson, J. A. & Ginsberg, Morris, *L. T. Hobson: His Life and Work* (London: George Allen & Unwin, 1931)

Holmes, Ann Sumner, '"Don't Frighten the Horses": the Russell Divorce Case' in *Disorder in the Court: Trials and Sexual Conflict at the Turn of the Century*, George Robb & Nancy Erber (eds) (London: Macmillan, 1999)

Holmes, Marion, 'Concerning Countess Russell' in *The Vote*, 30 Apr. 1910, pp. 4–5

Huth Jackson, Annabel, *A Victorian Childhood* (London: Methuen, 1932)

Hynes, Samuel, *The Edwardian Turn of Mind* (London: Pimlico, 1991)

Inman, Billie Andrew, 'Estrangement and Connection: Walter pater, Benjamin Jowett, and William M. Hardinge' in *Pater in the 90s*, L. Brake & I. Small (eds) (Greensboro, NC: ELT Press, 1991)

Jepson, Edgar, *Memories of a Victorian* (London: Victor Gollancz, 1933)

Jepson, Edgar, *Memories of an Edwardian* (London: Victor Gollancz, 1938)

Johnson, Lionel, *Some Winchester Letters of Lionel Johnson*, Russell, John Francis Stanley (ed.) (London: George Allen & Unwin, 1919)

Juxon, John, *Lewis and Lewis: The Life and Times of a Victorian Solicitor* (London: Collins, 1983).

Kaye, Richard, 'Appendices' in *A Marriage Below Zero* (1899), Alan Dale (Ontario: Broadview Press, 2018)

Kempis, Thomas à, *Of the Imitation of Christ* (London, Oxford & Cambridge: Rivingtons, 1875)

Kingston, Charles, *Society Sensations* (New York: E. P. Dutton, 1922)

Kitchin, Shepherd Braithwaite, *A History of Divorce* (London: Chapman & Hall, 1912)

Law Times, *The Law Times Reports of Cases Decided in the House of Lords, The Privy Council, The Court of Appeal*, vol. 73 (London: Horace Cox, 1896)

Lowndes, Mrs Belloc, *The Merry Wives of Westminster* (London: Macmillan, 1946)

Lovell, Colin Rhys, 'The Trial of Peers in Great Britain' in *The American Historical Review*, vol. 55/1 (Oct. 1949), pp. 69–81

MacCarthy, Desmond & Russell, Agatha, *Lady John Russell* (London: Methuen, 1910)

MacQueen, J. F., *A Practical Treatise on Divorce and Matrimonial Jurisdiction under the Act of 1857* (London: Maxwell, Sweet, Stevens & Norton, 1858)

McCormick, John, *George Santayana: A Biography* (New York: Paragon House, 1988)

McGregor, O. R., *Divorce in England* (London: William Heinemann, 1957)

McKenzie, Norman & McKenzie, Jean, *The First Fabians* (London: Quartet Books, 1979)

Mansfield, Robert Blachford, *School-Life at Winchester College* (London: David Butt, 1893)

Marjoribanks, Edward, *The Life of Sir Edward Marshall Hall* (London: Victor Gollancz, 1929)

Mead, F. & Bodkin A. H., *The Criminal Law Amendment Act, 1885* (London: Shaw, 1885)

Mews, John (ed.), *Analytical Digest of Cases Published in the Law Journal Reports*, vol. 66 (London: Law Journal Reports, 1897)

Mitford, Nancy, *The Ladies of Alderley* (London; Chapman & Hall, 1938)

Mitford, Nancy, *The Stanleys of Alderley* (London; Chapman & Hall, 1939)

Monk, Ray, *Bertrand Russell: The Spirit of Solitude* (London: Jonathan Cape, 1996)

Nevill, Ralph, *The Life and Letters of Lady Dorothy Nevill* (New York: E. P. Dutton, 1919)

Newbolt, Sir Henry, *My World As In My Time* (London: Faber & Faber, 1932)

Neil-Tomlinson, Barry, 'The Nyassa Chartered Company: 1891–1929' in *Journal of African History*, vol. xviii/I (1977), pp. 109–128

Oates, J. C. T., 'Charles Edward Sayle' in *Transactions of the Cambridge Biographical Society*, vol. 8 (1982), pp. 236–269

O'Brien, R. Barry, *The Life of Lord Russell of Killowen* (London: Smith, Elder, 1901)

Orme-Bannister, Graham J., *South Harting Hill Climb, 1905–1924* (Alresford: Newlands Press, 2006)

Oulton, Carolyn, *Romantic Friendship in Victorian Literature* (Aldershot: Ashgate, 2007)

Philips, Francis Charles, *My Varied Life* (London: Eveleigh Nash, 1914)

Phillips, Roderick, *Putting Asunder: A History of Divorce in Western Society* (New York: Cambridge University Press, 1988)

Pittock, Murray, *Lionel Johnson: Selected Letters* (Edinburgh: Tragara Press, 1998)

Pugh, Martin, *Speak for Britain! A New History of the Labour Party* (London: Vintage, 2011)

Rabbitts, Paul, *Richmond Park: From Medieval Pasture to Royal Park* (Stroud: Amberley, 2014)

Rappoport, Jill, 'Wives and sons: Coverture, Primogeniture, and Married Women's Property', *BRANCH* (July 2012) <http://www.branchcollective. org/?ps_articles=jill-rappoport-wives-and-sons-coverture-primogeniture-and-married-womens-property> accessed 25 Feb. 2017

Roberts, Charles, *The Radical Countess* (Carlisle: Steel Brothers, 1962)

Römhild, Juliane, *Femininity and Authorship in the Novels of Elizabeth von Arnim* (Plymouth: Fairleigh Dickinson University Press, 2014)

Royal Commission on Divorce & Matrimonial Causes, *Report of the Royal Commission on Divorce and Matrimonial Causes* (London: His Majesty's Stationery Office, 1912) [Cd.6478]

Royal Commission on Divorce & Matrimonial Causes, *Minutes of Evidence Taken Before the Royal Commission on Divorce and Matrimonial Causes* (London: His Majesty's Stationery Office, 1912) [Cd.6479–81]

Russell, Bertrand & Russell, Patricia, *The Amberley Papers* (London: George, Allen & Unwin, 1937)

Russell, Bertrand, *The Autobiography of Bertrand Russell, vol. 1: 1872–1914* (London: George Allen & Unwin, 1967)

Russell, Bertrand, *The Autobiography of Bertrand Russell, vol. 2: 1914–1944* (London: George Allen & Unwin, 1971)

Russell, Bertrand, *The Collected Papers of Bertrand Russell, vol. 1: Cambridge Essays, 1888–99*, Kenneth Blackwell *et al* (eds.) (London: George Allen & Unwin, 1983)

Russell, Bertrand, *The Selected Letters of Bertrand Russell, vol. 1: 1884–1914; vol. 2: 1914–1970*, Nicholas Griffin (ed.) (London: Routledge, 2002)

Russell, Dora, *The Tamarisk Tree: Challenge to the Cold War* (London: Virago, 1985)

Russell, John Francis Stanley, *Lay Sermons* (London: Thomas Burleigh, 1902)

Russell, John Francis Stanley, *Divorce* (London: William Heinemann, 1912)

Russell, John Francis Stanley, *My Life and Adventures* (London: Cassell, 1923)

Russell, Mollie, *Five Woman and a Caravan* (London: Eveleigh Nash, 1911)

Russell, Mollie, *Excellent Mystery* (London: Stephen Swift, 1912)

Santayana, George, *Persons and Places*, critical edn. W. G. Holzberger & H. J. Saatkamp (eds.) (Cambridge, MA: MIT Press, 1896)

Santayana, George, *The Letters of George Santayana*, vols.1–3, W. G. Holzberger & H. J. Saatkamp (eds) (Cambridge, MA: MIT Press, 2001–2006)

Santayana, George, *George Santayana's Marginalia: A Critical Selection*, vol. 2, John McCormick (ed.) (Cambridge, MA: MIT Press, 2011)

Sayle, Charles, *Bertha: A Love Story* (London: Kegan Paul, 1885)

Shaw, George Bernard, *Bernard Shaw: Collected Letters vol. 1: 1874–1897*, Dan Laurence (ed.) (London: Max Reinhardt, 1965)

Shuter, William F., 'The Outing of Walter Pater' in *Nineteenth Century Literature*, vol. 48/4 (1994), pp. 480–506

Smalley, George Washburn & Escott, T. H. S., *Society in London by a Foreign Resident* (London: Chatto & Windus, 1885)

Steinbach, Susie, *Understanding the Victorians: Politics, Culture and Society in Nineteenth-century Britain* (Abingdon: Routledge, 2017)

Stevens, Charles, *Winchester Notions* (London: Althone Press, 1998)

Stone, Lawrence, *Road to Divorce: A History of the Making and Breaking of Marriage in England* (Oxford: Oxford University Press, 1995)

Stopes, Marie Carmichael, *Married Love*, 11th ed. (London: Putnam's, 1923)

Swinnerton, Frank, *Figures in the Foreground: Literary Reminiscences, 1917–1940* (New York: Doubleday, 1964)

Swinnerton, Frank, *Swinnerton: An Autobiography* (London: Hutchinson, 1937)

Symonds, John Addington, *The Letters of John Addington Symonds, vol. 3: 1885–1893*, H. M. Schueller & R. L. Peters (eds) (Detroit, MI: Wayne State University Press, 1969)

Symonds, Richard, *Oxford and Empire: The Last Lost Cause?* (London: Macmillan, 1986)

Thorpe, Andrew, *A History of the Labour Party*, 4th ed. (Basingstoke: Palgrave Macmillan, 2015)

Titterton, W. R., *A Candle to the Stars* (London: Grayson & Grayson, 1932)

Tobin, Agnes, *Letters, Translations, Poems, with some account of her life* (Whitefish, MT: Literary Licensing, 2011)

Turcon, Sheila, 'Russell's Houses: Telegraph House' in *Bertrand Russell Society Bulletin* (Fall 2016), pp. 45–69

Usborne, Karen, *Elizabeth* (London: Bodley Head, 1986)

Vandercom *et al.*, *In the High Court of Justice. Probate Divorce and Admiralty Division. (Divorce). Russell (Countess) v. Russell (Earl). Correspondence. Part 1 [HAR07025] & Part 2 [HAR07026]* (London: Gale Making of Modern Law, 2011)

Wainwright, John Bannerman, *Winchester College, 1839–1906: A Register* (Winchester: P&G Wells, 1907)

Walker, Jennifer, 'After *Ann Veronica*: The Enigma of "Little e": Fact or Fiction?' in *The Wellsian*, no. 34 (2011), p. 54–67

Walker, Jennifer, *Elizabeth of the German Garden: A Literary Journey* (Leicester: Book Guild, 2013)

Walker-Smith, Derek, *The Life of Sir Edward Clarke* (London: Thornton Butterworth, 1939)

Watson, Ian, 'Mollie, Countess Russell' in *Russell*, vol. 23 (Summer 2003), pp. 65–8

Waugh, Arthur, *Tradition and Change: Studies in Contemporary Literature* (London: Chapman & Hall, 1919)

Weber, G., 'Henry Labouchere, "Truth" and the New Journalism of Late Victorian Britain' in *Victorian Periodicals Review*, vol. 26/1, pp. 36–43

Wells, H. G., *H. G. Wells in Love*, G. P. Wells (ed.) (London: Faber & Faber, 1984)

Wood, Alan, *Bertrand Russell: The Passionate Sceptic* (London: George Allen & Unwin, 1957)

Periodicals

London Periodicals
Daily Herald (DH)
Daily Mail (DM)
The Dwarf
The Era
The Globe
Illustrated London News (ILN)
Illustrated Police News (IPN)
Lloyd's Weekly (LW)
London Daily News (LDN)
London Evening Standard (LES)
Morning Post (MP)
National Review
News of the World (NOW)
Observer (OBS)
Pall Mall Gazette (PMG)
Reynolds's Newspaper (RN)
Saturday Review
St James's Gazette (SJG)
St Stephen's Review
South London Chronicle (SLC)
South London Press (SLP)
Sporting Times (ST)
The Star
The Telegraph
The Times
Times Literary Supplement (TLS)
Truth
The Vote
West London Observer (WLO)
Women's Franchise (WF)
Regional Papers
Aberdeen Press & Journal (APJ)
Belfast Newsletter (BNL)
Bolton Evening News (BEN)
Chichester Observer (CO)
Dublin Daily Express (DDE)
Dundee Courier (DC)
Glasgow Herald (GH)
Hampshire Telegraph (HT)
Leeds Mercury (LM)
Liverpool Mercury (LPM)
Manchester Courier (MC)
Manchester Evening News (MEN)
Manchester Guardian (MG)
Nottingham Evening Post (NEP)
Oxford Times (OT)
Reading Mercury (RM)

South Bucks Standard (SBS)
The Scotsman
Shields Daily Gazette (SDG)
Sheffield Daily Telegraph (SDT)
South Wales Echo (SWE)
Western Morning News (WMN)
Western Times (WT)
The Wykehamist
Yorkshire Evening Post (YEP)
Yorkshire Herald (YH)

Reference Works & Online Sources

Alumni Cantabrigienses
Alumni Oxonienses
Ancestry (www.ancestry.com)
Burke's Peerage
Debrett's
Grace's Guide (www.gracesguide.co.uk)
Hansard (www.hansard/parliament.uk)
Oxford Dictionary of National Biography
Perseus Digital Library (www.perseus.tufts.edu)
Proceedings of the Old Bailey (www.oldbaileyonline.org)

Acknowledgements

These few words can only begin to express my gratitude for the unfailing assistance and enthusiasm of so many people throughout the research and writing of this book. In addition to the staff of the various archives in the UK and US who answered questions, gathered documents and made suggestions, I am especially grateful to the following people. Kenneth Blackwell for the inordinate amount of time he spent sharing his vast Russell knowledge with me, for publishing my first article, securing the assistance of John Lenz for Greek translations and introducing me to Nicholas Griffin and John G. Slater. Nick and John have encouraged, enthused, supported and advised me and have critiqued my whole manuscript. They also shared with me Ronald Clark's observations during the writing of *The Life of Bertrand Russell*. The Russell Archives supplied me with a wealth of information and I am particularly grateful to Sheila Turcon. Also, to Bev Bayazat for her many forays into the archives on my behalf. Thanks to Tim Madigan for his help and advice. From the Santayana Society, I could not have done without the assistance and knowledge of Martin Coleman, Herman Saatkamp and Richard Rubin, who have always been on hand to answer questions. Thank you to Jennifer Walker for our email chats about 'Elizabeth'. Suzanne Foster, the archivist at Winchester College, helped me interpret the more obscure *notions* and appreciate what makes Winchester so special and Mrs Dick so unique. Without the help of Richard Williams, LLP, I would have been lost in the circumlocutions of English law. Without the enthusiasm, generosity and scholarship of Sarah Green my appreciation of Lionel Johnson would have been incomplete. My thanks to Suzanne, Richard, Martin, Herman and Sarah for reading relevant sections of my manuscript and making suggestions. Also, to Ros Taylor, Sarah Derham and Pippa Lawrence for their reading and feedback. Thank you to Ian Watson for his genealogical expertise and to Anne Bittleston Somerville for sharing with me her great-grandmother, Countess Mollie Russell, and generously allowing me access to family papers. Angie O'Rourke, the current owner of Telegraph House,

Acknowledgements

welcomed me into her beautiful home. Without the expertise of Connor Stait and the team at Amberley Publishing this book would have all been the poorer. Thank you to Sally Sharpe for her integrity and wisdom and to the following for love, friendship and hours spent listening to me 'talk Frank': Pip, Ros, Teena, Lou, the lovely Lady Jane, my mother, sister and sons, all the marvellous Derhams and my adored husband Ian, whose many contributions have been invaluable and who shared this adventure with me as wholeheartedly as all our others.

Index